THE DESCENT OF MAN

from apes to gods?

BOOK 4 OF THE MACHINE OR MAN APOLOGETICS SERIES

HENRY PATIÑO

Isaiah 44:6
(Gebo Wunjo Othala – Chi Rho Owns Earth)

The Descent of Man
From Apes to Gods?
Book 4 of The Machine or Man Apologetics Series

Copyright © 2021 by Henry Patiño
Published by Areli Media

Unless otherwise indicated, all Scripture quotations are taken from the New American Standard Bible® (NASB), Copyright © 1960, 1962, 1963, 1968, 1971, 1972, 1973, 1975, 1977, 1995 by The Lockman Foundation. Used by permission. www.Lockman.org.

Scripture quotations marked (KJV) are taken from the King James Version (KJV): King James Version, public domain.

Scripture quotations marked (NIV) are taken from the Holy Bible, New International Version®, NIV®. Copyright ©1973, 1978, 1984, 2011 by Biblica, Inc.™ Used by permission of Zondervan. All rights reserved worldwide. www.zondervan.com The "NIV" and "New International Version" are trademarks registered in the United States Patent and Trademark Office by Biblica, Inc.™

All rights reserved. No part of this publication may be reproduced, stored in a retrieval system, or transmitted in any form by any means, electronic, mechanical, photocopy, recording, or otherwise, without the prior permission of the publisher, except as provided for by USA copyright law.

ISBN 978-0-9962441-7-6 (paperback)
ISBN 978-1-7372529-1-7 (ebook)

Special Sales: Most Areli Media titles are available in special quantity discounts. Custom imprinting or excerpting can also be done to fit special needs. Contact Areli Media.

TABLE OF CONTENTS

Foreword	v
Acknowledgments	xi
Chapter 1: The Ascent of Man—Transhumanism	1
Chapter 2: The Elemental Failures of Darwinism	13
Uniformitarianism and the Steady State Theory:	
The Two Primary Pillars of Darwinian Evolution	14
Where Are the Intermediates (the Missing Chain)?	23
The Death of Gradualism—The Punctuated Equilibrium Theory	40
From Reptiles to Birds	51
The Problem of Convergent Evolution	56
Chapter 3: Mechanisms of Evolution (The House of Cards)	61
Microevolution, not Macroevolution	61
The Evolutionary Purpose for Denying Purpose	68
Genetic Variability Is Finite	76
The Quantum Genes	84
Multiple Mutations and Macromutations	91
Mutations in Single-Celled Organisms	95
Mutations in Multicellular Organisms	99
Mutations in Viruses	105
Darwin's Fantasyland Revived	106
Mutations: The Measure of the Decay of the Human Race	110
Artificially Induced Evolution	115
The Tyranny of Paradigms	121

Chapter 4: Dating Methods: The Three Pillars — 129

- What Is the Age of Earth? — 133
- Apollo Asteroids: The Uniformitarian Busters — 166
- The Strata — 174
- The Imagined Evolutionary Order of the Strata — 183
- Gradual or Catastrophic Sedimentary Depositions — 184
- Diagram 10. The Geologic Column — 185
- How Striations Formed in the Geologic Column through the Hydraulics of the Great Flood — 191
- The Destructive Power of a Single Large Meteor Strike — 192
- The Seven Thunders That Ended the First Earth — 206
- The Saving Waters of the Great Flood — 211
- The Source of Water: The Fountains of the Deep — 215
- Mechanisms of Strata Formation — 223
- The Global Near-Extinction Catastrophe — 243
- The Coral Reef Argument — 248
- The Hydroplate Theory — 251
- The Global Volcanic Upheaval — 253
- How Old Are the Dinosaurs? — 259
- Holes in the Cosmic Umbrella — 297
- Earthquake Frequency Rates by Decade — 300

Chapter 5: The Origin of Man — 303

- The Art of Selling Evolution — 330
- Ape-Like Features: Hominid and Hominoid Classifications — 338
- Diagram 11. The Classical Human Evolutionary Lineage — 364
- Diagram 12. Leakey's New Lineage — 383
- Diagram 13. Johanson's New Lineage — 389

References — 435
Index — 443

FOREWORD

The generations of our age are in desperate need of an unmovable, science-based anchor for their faith in the reality of a Creator who is truth, righteousness, justice, and love personified—to paraphrase the late Francis A. Schaeffer, a *God who is there and is not silent*.

Henry Patiño's incomparable series—which begins with *Machine or Man* and is continued in this fourth volume, *The Descent of Man*—is such an anchor. His invaluable series, representing many decades of intense investigational labor, is a must-read for every parent, educator, young person, and adult member of our family in the Judeo-Christian faith. In his works, Henry Patiño has skillfully exposed the fatal deficiencies and gaping foundational cracks in the Evolution Hypothesis, a far from proven hypothesis that for centuries has passed as the approved and sole "scientific" explanation for the existence of life and humanity on our planet. And he irrevocably exposes this fallacy of epic proportions of which our children and our children's children are now the latest casualties.

In this series, evolutionists' underlying agenda is also laid bare: the systematic and permanent erasure of the Creator from our collective awareness. The self-appointed engineers of humanity believe that their success will ultimately endow them with the power to recreate themselves as global deities—that it will direct the evolution of mankind to the next level: a level where machine and man merge to give rise to the long awaited "master race"—the "Heavenly Man" without a Heavenly Father. And it is the Evolution Hypothesis that has served them well as the necessary foundation for a system of propaganda that, in one form or another, ubiquitously poisons the minds of most—from early education to the media, the cinema, academia, advertising, and much of the religious culture.

Once the existence of the Creator has been successfully eradicated from humanity's consciousness so will the image of God—and, with it, the unique and inalienable worth and rights of every human being will be universally denied. Then, evolutionists believe they will have absolute power to determine the global standards of "morality," acceptable beliefs, and permissible behaviors—to determine how each of us is allowed to think and speak.

As Dostoyevsky warned: "If there is no God, nothing is unthinkable."

The Great Lie that deceived the woman in Eden insinuated that God's creation of mankind could and ought to be improved upon. But when we tinker with His creation, the reality has always been that there is one path on which we inevitably tread: toward the descent of man into depravity and darkness—where we will encounter the increasingly grotesque and dangerous creatures of a poisoned imagination.

Henry Patiño has devoted the larger part of his life to defeating this Great Lie. The volumes of his encyclopedic series speak to us with the voice of true Reason and awaken the spirit of every Truth-seeker to the beckoning reality of our Origin.

Integrating the biblical account of the history of the universe and mankind with key discoveries of modern cosmology, physics, medicine, geology, history, and archaeology, Patiño's series reveals the undeniable thread of our Creator's intelligent design within the warp and woof of our universe and all life created therein. He deftly exposes the absurdity of the evolutionary mindset's irrational dismissal of the Transcendent Designer and debunks all alternative explanations for existence and life. And it is the wealth of evidence from true science contained in his volumes that justly convicts the pseudoscientific proponents of the Evolutionary Hypothesis of collusion in perpetrated fraud.

In this latest volume, *The Descent of Man*, Henry Patiño examines the development of the foundational elements of the Evolutionary

Hypothesis from its inception until now. He then proceeds to topple the walls, pillars, and roof of the evolutionary dogma's House of Cards, including the continually morphing hypotheses and versions that have emerged in order to patch up the irreparable cracks in its foundation and compensate for its fatal deficiencies.

In *The Descent of Man*, Patiño effectively challenges the faulty assumptions behind evolutionists' reliance on their dating methods, the glaring contradiction between their geologic timetable and the evidence found in the geologic strata, the inexplicable gaps and absence of transmutational links in the fossil record, the ineptitude of their fabrications purported to support the lineage of mankind, and their discredited reliance on the feckless mechanism of random mutations over vast stretches of time.

In this volume, the author delivers a devastating blow with an exquisitely detailed and panoramic exposition of the growing universal evidence for the Global Deluge. The ineluctable record of this global cataclysmic event, which changed the face of the Earth and the history of mankind, had been lost and buried through a process of distortion, misinformation, reinterpretation, and abandonment that passes for modern "scientific" education. And Patiño clearly demonstrates how the Great Flood, together with all the cosmic events accompanying it, far surpasses the Evolution Hypothesis as the most coherent explanation of our present geologic and fossil record, and it is the best explanation of the mass extinction of notable species that existed on the First Earth.

The final nail in the coffin is thrust permanently in by Patiño's exposition of the genetic research on mitochondrial DNA (which is only passed on from mother to daughter). The irrefutable conclusion is that we are all children of "Mitochondrial Eve," and all humans are in reality one race. The findings were also supported by genetic research on the human Y chromosome (which can only be transmitted from father to son), tracing the human race to one original man. The evidence of a First Mother and First Father to the human race, also demonstrates that the original pair of humans could not have lived more that several thousands of years ago.

By the end of *The Descent of Man*, the evolutionists' House of Cards lies flat on the ground, among the debris of fraudulent and empty mythologies. To quote the author: "We, therefore, can safely conclude that there is such a thing as microevolution, within a species, but there is absolutely no evidence of macroevolution; that is, evolution from one species into another."

For the upcoming fifth and final volume of this series, *The Death of the First Earth*, the author promises to explore overwhelming scientific, anthropological, and historical evidence to support the biblical account of the demise of our planet as it existed before the Great Flood.

Like the ardent archaeologist of Truth that he is, Henry Patiño has unearthed a priceless treasure that belongs to all generations. He gifts us with a universal testimony that trumpets the truth of a *Personal Mover* who purposefully penetrates our universe with His love and His mighty hand, thereby decimating the false constructs of the Evolutionary Hypothesis—a lie that has reigned in the classrooms and halls of science for far too long.

I am confident that, to the sincere and thoughtful reader, the marvelous story in the tapestry woven by the author throughout the pages of his series will eventually emerge with crystal clarity. This is not just another set of books on the defense of the faith; it is the sword of a revelation that cuts to the heart of the truth of our existence. To quote the author again:

> My eyes have not seen the physical face of God, but I have seen the manifold evidence of His intellect by the marvelous design of every aspect of our universe. I have seen the symmetry that permeates our universe at every level, and it is impossible for me to rationally conclude that this was a random accident.

FOREWORD

For me, it has been an inexpressible pleasure to witness the development of this invaluable series from its conception to its present form. From *Machine or Man* to *The Descent of Man*, the reading and editing process has been an enlightening experience, substantially contributing to my own spiritual anchoring and fortification. As I have shared the priceless pearls found in Henry Patiño's apologetic series with my students, I have watched with delight their expressions of wonder, their dawning smiles of understanding, and the light in the eyes of those who have caught a glimpse of a magnificent vision.

It is, therefore, an honor for me to write the foreword to this labor of love and dedication to Truth. And it is my prayer that each and every reader accepts the challenge of this wonderful series with the courage to revisit and proactively reexamine the foundations of those beliefs that they may have acquired like a virus, without the necessary analysis and questioning.

May this book motivate us to take a serious look at the evidence, abandon any irrational leaps of faith—any escape from reason—and embrace the foundations of the True Faith in which there is no shifting or contradiction.

Raul Rodriguez MD,
Doctor of Medicine
Diplomate of the American Board of Psychiatry and Neurology

ACKNOWLEDGMENTS

In the early 1980s, I was privileged to meet Dr. Francis Schaeffer and his son, Franky, at a conference at Coral Ridge Presbyterian Church in Fort Lauderdale, Florida. It was a very important milestone in my life. Schaeffer's words have echoed in my mind countless times as I remember the challenge he gave me. Racked with cancer, in his waning moments, and so weak he could not stand for long, this valiant man of God tirelessly continued in the battle for the minds of our generation.

"I am close to my end now," he said. "I have done what God has given me the grace to accomplish. It is up to you now, the next generation, to stand on my shoulders and continue in the cause."

I have stumbled more than once along the way. I am not worthy to stand on the shoulders of my mentor, and I do not presume in any way to be his successor. But by the grace of our forgiving Father, I am attempting to follow His charge in reaching the minds of those entering into our third millennium after the incarnation.

If there is anything of value in this series that has taken me over two decades to complete, it goes to my Lord and Savior, who has chosen the weak to confound the strong and, by the example of my mentor, has taught me that in God's economy, "there are no little people."

I will be eternally grateful to Dr. Schaeffer who also taught me with love and intelligence that "Christianity is not only the best answer, but the only answer."

And with this quote from Dr. Schaeffer, I now challenge you to continue in the cause:

> The Christian is to resist the spirit of the world. But when we say this, we must understand that the world-spirit does not always take the same form. So the Christian must resist

the spirit of the world *in the form it takes in his own generation*. If he does not do this, he is not resisting the spirit of the world at all. This is especially so for our generation, as the forces at work against us are of such a total nature. It is our generation of Christians more than any other who need to heed these words attributed to Martin Luther:

"If I profess with the loudest voice and clearest exposition every portion of the truth of God except precisely that little point which the world and the devil are at that moment attacking, I am not confessing Christ, however boldly I may be professing Christ. Where the battle rages, there the loyalty of the soldier is proved, and to be steady on all the battlefield besides, is mere flight and disgrace if he flinches at that point" (Schaeffer 1982, 11).

I am also indebted to the Institute for Creation Research (ICR) and its infinitely valuable contributions on behalf of creationism, which provided for me during my formative years an enormous wealth of resources and encouragement. The legendary works of Dr. Henry Morris and Dr. Duane Gish were the point of the spear that brought awareness to the dire need of evangelicals to enter into the public square and provide the scientific evidence that defends the historical narrative of the scriptures. For too long we had retreated behind the motes around our churches, drawn up the drawbridge, and remained content to simply sing hymns to one another while the atheistic Hegelian worldview gained preeminence in academics and thoroughly indoctrinated our children in the Darwinian religion. Since their pioneering work, many have now joined the battle to win the minds of people in our generation. Henry Morris IV continues in his father's footsteps with a host of scientists who are truly making an impact on our evangelical community.

The valuable work of many in the Intelligent Design movement has now added another dimension for the evangelical community to

ACKNOWLEDGMENTS

provide a reason for the hope that is in us for our present generation. There are too many to mention, but most impactful to my thinking is Stephen Myers.

This five-volume apologetics series was inspired by their leadership and encouragement, and I will forever be thankful to them for their courage to stand against the tide when few were in the battle or even aware of its vital necessity. I specifically want to thank Dr. Frank Sherwin of ICR for his personal guidance, advice, and selfless time to help me bring this fourth volume to fruition with his many instructive e-mails and sincere critiques that were of immense consequence to my work.

Most importantly, I wish to thank my Lord and Savior Jesus Christ who loves to use the nobodies of this world to confound the wise, the Davids to defeat the Goliaths. To Him belongs all the glory and praise, for nothing I have written came from my simple mind. He has faithfully moved my pen for more than 25 years, and I am but a simple vessel who, by His grace and mercy, He was somehow able to use for His own glory.

Not by might, nor by power, but by my spirit, saith the LORD of hosts.

—Zech. 4:6 KJV

CHAPTER 1

THE ASCENT OF MAN— TRANSHUMANISM

Long has the Enemy of Man sought to shroud the truth of man's origins. Long has he sought to shroud the minds of the children of Adam to snare them in his wicked web. This is what he says: *Man can ascend the sublime heights of heaven and become a god. Nothing is impossible for him. Man can control his destiny and enter into a new age in which his mental powers and physical abilities are as far removed from our present state as we presently are to the amoebas.*

You may think I am exaggerating. Not so. It is at this juncture in the development of our postmodern society that the consequences of our adoption of the evolutionary paradigm will most radically affect us and our future generations. As a natural continuation of the evolutionary process, modern "thinkers" are now beginning to peddle the next phase of the evolution of man—transhumanism.

Our next rung on the ladder to godhood from single-celled organisms is the merger of man and machine and the creation of a new superhuman species enhanced through genetic manipulation. Through the science of recombinant gene splicing, we can now create a new species of man that is far superior to natural man.

We are now approaching the time of the heavenly man previsioned by Madam Blavatsky in her occult books:

> We have in future the possibility – nay, the assurance of a race, which, like the *V ril-ya* of Bulwer-Lytton's *Coming Race*, will be but one remove from the primitive "Sons of God" (Blavatsky 1877, 296).

The Sons of God she speaks of are the fallen angels that led the first and second insurrections. But it will not be the noble, nearly homogeneous race envisioned by idealistic anthropologists such as Anthony F. C. Wallace. It will be the most heterogeneous and specifically engineered species in all of biology that will lead to fierce competition for the survival of the fittest as never before, and the naturals will suffer greatly due to their physical and mental inferiority.

There will be no movement toward a more refined and noble man with higher moral and intellectual values. There will be a movement toward a being with higher physical, intellectual, and occult powers to rule humankind. It is not the ascent of man as they promise. It is the descent of man into the powers of darkness.

> In his *Contributions to the Theory of Natural Selection*, Mr. Alfred R. Wallace concludes his demonstrations as to the development of human races under that law of selection by saying that, if his conclusions are just, "it must inevitably follow that the higher—the more intellectual and moral—must displace the lower and more degraded races; and the power of 'natural selection,' still acting on his mental organization, must ever lead to the more perfect adaptation of man's higher faculties to the condition of surrounding nature, and to the exigencies of the social state. While his external form will probably ever remain unchanged, except in the development of that perfect beauty . . . refined and ennobled by the highest intellec-

tual faculties and sympathetic emotions, his mental constitution may continue to advance and improve, till the world is again inhabited by a single, nearly homogeneous race, no individual of which will be inferior *to the noblest specimens of existing humanity*." Sober scientific methods and cautiousness in hypothetical possibilities have evidently their share in this expression of the opinions of the great anthropologist. Still, what he says above clashes in no way with our kabalistic assertions. Allow to ever-progressing nature, to the great law of the "survival of the fittest," one step beyond Mr. Wallace's deductions, and we have in the future the possibility—nay, the assurance of a race, which, like the *V ril-ya* of Bulwer-Lytton's *Coming Race*, will be but one removed from the primitive "Sons of God" (Blavatsky 1877, 296).

Wallace was wrong on so many levels. He did not anticipate that humankind could learn to manipulate man's DNA with recombinant gene splicing. His external form will change as radically as his intellectual faculties, but it will not be toward a more refined and beautiful outcome. It will be toward a more sinister and elitist subdivision of humankind that will enslave the rest. You might be saying that these are the writings of occult lunatics, that they do not represent our scientific establishment.

Are you sure about that? Read on.

In accord with this satanic evolutionary process, the transhumanist sees man entering into an era in which man becomes superman. That will be accomplished through two main avenues. The first is the merger of man and machine through the use of nanotechnology. And the second is the hybridization of man with animals through recombinant gene splicing to enhance the human potential.

We are entering the next phase of Satan's plan to rule the planet, and our society is being prepared for the posthuman or transhuman

man who will be enhanced through genetic manipulation and nanotechnology to become superior to natural man.

The merger of computer chips with living cells will one day bring upon us a special breed of humans who are far superior to our natural intelligence. The genetic manipulation of certain animal genes into the human body will make this new breed of man so physically superior that in short order, he will rule the world. But this is no science fiction novel.

> Self-described "transhumanists" advocate that we seize control of human evolution by designing genetic enhancements to "improve" the human race. As an example of this sort of thinking, the Nobel Prize-winning scientist James D. Watson, co-discoverer of the DNA double helix, has claimed that genetically enhanced people will someday "dominate the world." Are these echoes here of the long discredited "master race" idea? (Smith 2004, x).

Man's rebellion toward the creator has spurred him to follow Satan's aberrant dream of godhood, and our very own scientists may be unwittingly bringing that to pass. Princeton University biologist Lee M. Silvers, who is perhaps one of the most ardent advocates of human cloning, has predicted that this genetically engineered species of man will one day be akin to gods.

> A special point has now been reached in the distant future. *And in this era, there exists a special group of mental beings. Although these beings can trace their ancestry back directly to* homo sapiens, *they are as different from humans as humans are from the primitive worms with tiny brains that first crawled along the earth's surface.* . . . It is difficult to find the words to describe the enhanced attributes of this special people. "Intelligence" does not do justice to their cognitive abilities. "Knowledge" does not explain

the depth of both their understanding of the universe and their own consciousness. "Power" is not strong enough to describe the control they have over technologies that can be used to shape the universe in which they live (emphasis added) (Silvers 1997, 249–250).

Few understand the great importance of this fundamental issue that will impact our individual freedoms. It is the element of our Judeo-Christian roots that unequivocally states that all humans are "beings" created in the image of God. That is what determines the intrinsic value of human life. That value is necessarily what legitimizes our individual rights to life, liberty, and the pursuit of happiness. No absolute human rights are possible without it.

It is because we have been created in the image of God that all humankind has infinite value. That is what provides humanity with a solid foundation for human rights. Without it, we are nothing more than an accident in the cosmos, and human rights are no more than illusions in the minds of men. Without it, we are nothing more than the blind product of impersonal matter—energy x chance x time. Personal freedoms and personal rights cannot be granted without first having personhood, and personhood cannot rise from the impersonal.

There can be no intrinsic worth as a human being that is simply the random product of chemical reactions without purpose and prevision. There can be no transcendental value to human life without God as our creator. In a world where the survival of the fittest is the matrix of reality, individual rights do not exist. In such a world, the elite have the legitimate right to enslave, abuse, or obliterate the weak. In such a world, only power rules. Everything else is illogical. Any sentimental notions of mercy, love, brotherhood, and self-sacrifice are irrational and illusory concepts that have no legitimacy in atheistic Darwinism.

If there is no God, then there is no right and wrong. The breaking of a chicken egg is equivalent to the breaking of a human head.

Thoughts in that world without God can be nothing more than merely complicated electrochemical dances without any transcendental significance inside the three pounds of gray matter in our skulls. Man is then nothing more than a biological machine. Our intrinsic desire for freedom and justice becomes only an imaginary hologram of our brains without any legitimate philosophical justification. All moral choices are relative.

That, my brothers and sisters, is the final end plan of the Enemy of Man to justify his global conquest of humankind and establish his rule of tyranny over the children of Adam. He seeks to make man an organic machine that has no intrinsic value other than utilitarian. In a world without a supreme being as the paragon for morals and meaning, the line between machine and man is blurred. You may think I am exaggerating, but I wonder if you know that on October 27, 2017, a robot named Sophia was presented by its maker, Future Investments Initiative, and accepted by Saudi Arabia to be the first robot in the world to become a citizen.

To this end, the Enemy of Man fans the flames of evolution to bring another superhuman to rule the world as he once had with the Neanderthals in the First Earth. Had God not wiped clean that profaned world, we would not be here today. The line of Eve would not have survived to bring forth the Messiah. All of us would have been nothing more than thralls for the Nephilim of old. In fact, it is doubtful that we would have survived at all. The Neanderthals were ritualistic cannibals. The religion of the Serpent has ever been a bloody religion.

So deep is man's deception that even this knowledge has been occluded from his memory of the past. Modern man has been so programmed that the mention of such a thing is foreign and scarcely believable to his materialistic mind. All the ancient cultures knew of it. "And some things that should not have been forgotten were lost. History became legend. Legend became myth," as Tolkien reminds us in *The Lord of the Rings*.

THE ASCENT OF MAN—TRANSHUMANISM

We are now enlightened, or so we think, and no longer believe in angels and demons. But I write these things to warn you that the shadow of the enlightenment hides the truth that you are precious beyond all measure because you are created in the image of God. Some would have you think that you are simply a biological machine that has accidentally evolved from stardust.

The more our Western culture accepts this foundational atheistic worldview, the more it will delegitimize any foundations for personal freedom and individual rights. Our founding fathers wisely declared in the Declaration of Independence that it was our creator who endowed us with these rights. They are not state-given rights; they are God-given rights, and no national government has the authority to take them from us. If we abandon the Judeo-Christian position as a culture, we will be condemning our future generations to dire consequences. It is that atheistic Darwinist worldview of the survival of the fittest that can justify the enslavement of the masses for the benefit of the elite.

All humans long for freedom and despise tyranny. Only tyrants love tyranny. Only slave owners love slavery. Does not every fiber of your being scream against such a notion that would make of us a senseless thrall of the elite?

If there is no God, then human life has no intrinsic value. It is nothing more than an accident in the cosmos. But our hearts tell us differently. Can we crush the head of a baby with the same callousness as we crack an egg? Does not our soul ache at injustice?

If there is no God, nothing can be labeled evil. But we cannot deny that evil exists, no matter how much we try to convince our brains otherwise. It is an intrinsic understanding in each and every one of us that betrays our primordial source, for our spirit came from the breath of God. The knowledge of heaven is within our hearts. It has been hardwired into our souls by our maker. We can run from it, but we cannot hide from it. It is integrated deeply into our conscience. It is the transcendental fingerprint of God. It is an intrinsic part of being a human being. God has set eternity into the human heart.

> He has made everything beautiful in its time. He has also set eternity in the human heart; yet no one can fathom what God has done from beginning to end.
> —Eccles. 3:11 NIV

To deny it is to deny our basic instincts. It can be done, but it must be continuously reinforced in order to suppress the resurfacing of our basic transcendence as a being that cries out for justice and equality. We long for love, joy, and happiness. We long for meaning and purpose. We long to belong. How can that be if we are intrinsically meaningless blobs of proteins that randomly coalesced from dead molecules?

Here is the unvarnished truth, free of the political correctness of the paradigm of our age: Man did not ascend from apes. Man descended from heaven. No, we are not gods, but we came from God. He is our heavenly father. The one true God, the creator of this universe, breathed His spirit (*nshamah*) from heaven into the earthly body of Adam and made him into a living soul (*nephesh*), apart from all other creatures. Humans alone possess the *nshamah* from God. We alone understand the notions of justice and goodness and wickedness and tyranny. We alone value selflessness and humility and mercy as venerable traits. These values descended from heaven. They are not earthly. It is wisdom that comes from above, not made with human hands.

But, like fools, we deny the creator and make ourselves gods, thinking that we are ascending when, in fact, we are descending into a more violent humanity. The evolutionary propaganda that spreads the myth that science will bring us to utopia is utterly false. We have only learned how to kill more effectively, and the dreams of tyrants have been fanned by the technology that was supposed to bring us to utopia.

THE ASCENT OF MAN—TRANSHUMANISM

When we deny our true heavenly heritage, we naïvely declare ourselves gods, the determiners of right and wrong. Sadly, in doing so, we give up our true eternal heritage. We blindly follow the sin of the Enemy of Man who has erred in exactly the same way and has deceived us into following him in his quest to usurp God's throne.

Selfishness is the mother of all sins. The epitome of selfishness is to make ourselves into a god, to bring the self to the throne of godhood. It is the ancient and primordial dragon sin of the usurper in the first insurrection long ago in the Garden of Eden.

The human body is of this earth, but its spirit descended from heaven. It came from our heavenly father and the creator of this universe. None can usurp His throne, but we can share with Him the glories of heaven if we bow in faith to the Messiah.

True truth exists. True science is not in opposition to true truth. But true truth has a cloak that deceives the minds of the selfish and cannot be seen by those who do not seek it. The cloak is the result of the magic of the Enemy of Man, not of God. But those who seek the truth will pierce through that cloak and see its bright rays resplendent. That choice is yours.

The Great Lie of the demonic hierarchy is universal. It knows no cultural or language barrier. It has been with us in every corner of our planet since the Garden of Eden. In each age, it surfaces with a new twist but remains essentially the same. The Great Lie is the Dragon Sin: "You will be like God" (Gen. 3:5 NIV). The theory of evolution is a clever reiteration of that exact doctrine, cloaked with scientific verbiage, that teaches man that he is ascending from apes into godhood.

Evolutionists tell us that the next evolutionary step will be the transhuman stage of man when he will have self-engineered his DNA to make himself into a god. Do not take my word for it. Google the word *transhumanism* and see for yourself.

They may dress their atheistic theological doctrine in scientific terminology, but at the very root is the demonic doctrine of the

Great Lie. It is the Dragon Sin made palatable for the ignorant who wish to make God disappear in order to gain moral independence from Him. This series of books is dedicated to exposing that Great Lie. It will explore the scientific evidence used by the proponents of the Great Lie and show how they are untrue. The purpose of these books is to unmask the Darwinist atheistic religion and lay bare the consequences that will come to our Western culture if we abandon our Judeo-Christian roots.

We are not gods, but we are the children of God. Although we are a stubborn and rebellious people, God's grace has opened a door for us to be reconciled to Him. From the day He framed the stars in the heavens, God left us a path to the truth; a path to redemption from our bondage to sin; a path to the Redeemer who died to set us free; a path to forgiveness and healing; a path we cannot earn through our intellect or human abilities; a path we cannot purchase, bribe, or cheat to attain; a path freely given to those who receive it by faith; a path back to our abode in heaven; a path given to us by God's grace and received only by faith apart from our own merits; a path through the seed of Eve foretold by the very voice of God in the Garden of Eden that will come to strike the lethal blow to the head of the Great Deceiver who brought death to humankind.

True truth never has to be afraid of competing in the free marketplace of ideas. It will always rise to the top. The Darwinian theory of the evolution of the species may be dressed in scientific jargon, but ultimately, it is nothing more than Satan's Great Lie. Those who seek the truth can be assured that real science does not contradict true truth. Truth is unified across all fields of inquiry because it all emanates from our creator. Darwinism is not empirical science. It is a theory that attempts to collate scientific data in an atheistic model for the creation of life.

In the third book of this series, we exposed the myth that life could evolve by random chemical processes from nonliving matter. Dead molecules do not accidentally become living cells. The specified complexity found in even the simplest single-celled organisms could not have developed through random chemical processes. The codes intrinsic to the DNA and the proteins could not have been accumulated through random ordering. It is the evidence of intelligent design and previsioned purpose.

This book will examine the history of the basic elements of the evolutionary theory from its inception until now and show why each of them has been incapable of passing the litmus test of reality. It will provide evidence that Darwinism does not have a valid mechanism to evolve one species from another. And finally, we will examine the fossil evidence for the evolution of man and show it to be nothing more than an elaborate figment of Darwinists' imaginations. Man did not ascend from apes. The spirit of man descended from the heavens. Our true citizenship is in heaven.

CHAPTER 2

THE ELEMENTAL FAILURES OF DARWINISM

What are the basic components that form the foundation of the Darwinian model for the evolution of the species? The theory of evolution has been built on a set of assumptions that, in Darwin's time, successfully created a seemingly complete body of scientific evidence. But the supposedly firm scientific foundation for this so-called evolutionary edifice has since been shown by more recent scientific developments to be nothing more than a flimsy house of cards.

To understand the early success of the Darwinian model, we must first understand the historical development of the theory. In particular, we must understand the foundational principles that science presented during that time as the elemental scientific framework that legitimized the concept of the gradual evolution of the species through natural selective processes. Two scientific theories accepted as factual dogma at that time provided the very foundation for Darwin's idea of natural selection to be plausible.

Uniformitarianism and the Steady State Theory: The Two Primary Pillars of Darwinian Evolution

At the time Charles Darwin was proposing his theory of the evolution of the species, Charles Lyell was proposing his hypothesis of uniformitarianism. That theory postulates that all natural processes in the past have occurred in exactly the same uniform rate and fashion as they transpire in the present.

In other words, science must observe present systems and extrapolate backward, being confident that in the past, things developed at the same rate and fashion. As we previously stated, a component of this theory is rational. We test theories by implementing experiments today, and we assume that all things being equal, the results of those experiments are repeatable and constant universally. However, from this true premise, evolutionists extrapolated incorrectly and dogmatically that all events have taken place in a gradualist form. This basic idea was then used to disqualify catastrophic accounts such the Noahic Flood as unscientific and mythological.

But the true uniformitarian assumption does not automatically preclude the possibility of cataclysms that can cause great changes in short spans of time. Quite often, all things are not equal from a historical perspective. The rejection of catastrophism by those who promoted the gradualist uniformitarian hypothesis was completely unfounded by experimental data. It was simply the subjective wish projection of those who desired to do away with the notion of catastrophism, which smacked of the biblical story of the Great Flood. One idea does not contradict the other. It is a *non sequitur* to state that uniformitarianism automatically leads to an anti-catastrophe position and demands that all processes are exclusively gradual.

In this jaded Darwinist interpretation of the uniformitarian theory at that time, there was no room for cataclysms or sudden large leaps of any kind of change. Fundamental to this truncated view was their intended scientific repudiation of divine catastrophes such as the Great Flood.

This radical and jaded form of uniformitarianism has artificially added a gradualist component in absolute terms, which was and is and will ever remain unfounded on reality. It was simply a biased and subjective philosophical choice predicated on metaphysical reasons.

Gradualism states that things have simply trudged along for eons at the same slow pace as we observe today. Evolutionists falsely assumed that all processes have always moved in almost imperceptible rates, creating minute changes for long periods of time. Those small changes, they claim, eventually aggregate into large changes, only through the passage of immense periods of time.

As a direct result of the acceptance of this jaded perception of the hypothesis in scientific circles, catastrophism was discarded and denigrated as unscientific and superstitious mythology. This gradualist form of uniformitarianism became the bedrock for Darwin's theory of the evolution of the species. It was the understructure from which his idea of gradual evolutionary changes could take root and grow. The resolute adamancy of evolutionists in regard to this subjective assumption was predicated solely on their subjective bias to prop up the evolutionary worldview. Simply stated, without immense time periods, evolution would not be plausible.

It must be noted again that there is an underlying truth to the uniformitarian hypothesis, which is not disputed by the Judeo-Christian worldview. The past is the key to the future, and the present is important in understanding the past. If I boil a given amount of water at a given atmospheric pressure and a given temperature, it will boil at the same time in America as it will in China, all things being equal. In fact, it is the Judeo-Christian worldview that explicitly predicts that our universe is not birthed in chaos and runs in an ordered fashion with universal laws. No such thing can be predicted in a randomly generated universe that has no God.

This is the evidence of the absolute laws of chemistry and physics that infer an ordered and designed universe birthed in the mind of an intelligent architect and omnipotent God. In this sense, uniformitarianism is, in fact, the recognition that absolute laws exist. This can only be framed in a universe in which there are absolutes. It is the direct product of the Judeo-Christian worldview. True science belongs to us.

Too often, Christians speak of uniformitarianism as completely wrong. They are missing the real problem. The problem is Darwinists' exclusively gradualist interpretation of uniformitarianism that automatically disregards any potential catastrophic event as mythological. I call this jaded uniformitarianism as opposed to true uniformitarianism.

When we observe our present state, we can infer that the processes that transpired on Earth in the past were the same. But that does not necessarily exclude the occasional catastrophe that can dramatically change the rates of these processes. The denial of potential catastrophic events is a subjective assumption not based on science or any empirical evidence.

For example, we can deduce by observation over several years that the erosion rate of the beaches in Sri Lanka are fairly stable. A scientist studying the erosion rates could extrapolate backward in years using the mean average within a 10-year span and assume that 100 years ago, the land was 10 times what he measured within that 10-year period. But that does not preclude the possibility of a tsunami, which can radically alter that erosion rate in a very short span of time.

On December 26, 2004, a 9.0 earthquake struck off the shores of Sumatra and triggered a tsunami of catastrophic proportions. The rupture in the Earth's crust was more than 600 miles long and lifted up the ocean floor as much as 10 feet, causing an enormous displacement of ocean water. The multiple waves radiating from the epicenter of the quake affected 11 countries and caused a train of waves that repeatedly assaulted everything in its path for several hours. The aftermath of the earthquake changed the coastline of

Sri Lanka dramatically in a single day. The violent waves were so strong that they traveled more than 3,000 miles and struck Africa, killing people even at that distance from the epicenter. Estimates claim that 227,289 people were killed by this catastrophe in one day. Catastrophes are real. The idea that gradualism is an absolute is absolutely false.

The true driving force behind the overwhelming popularity that this jaded uniformitarianism model enjoyed among evolutionists was not empirical data offered to support this dogmatic, gradualist view. There was a subjective motivation behind its acceptance; that is, their need for the immense ages necessary for the Darwinian process of gradualism to change one species into another to be even remotely plausible. Their subjective antagonism toward the catastrophe of the Noahic flood of the biblical narrative as a judgment of God to a rebellious people was the underpinning metaphysical reason for the wide acceptance of gradualism.

This jaded gradualist uniformitarian concept was thus readily adopted, replacing the previously prevailing theory of catastrophism in scientific circles. Those who held to the space-time historicity of the Global Flood were ostracized from the scientific community, and their beliefs were relegated to the realm of speculative mythology.

For years, the anti-catastrophe component of the uniformitarianism hypothesis was accepted in scientific circles as fact, with no apologies. Coupled with the steady state theory, it made quite a neat little package for naturalists. We have already spoken about the steady state theory in *Supersymmetry or Chaos: A Judeo-Christian Cosmological Model of the Origin of the Universe*, so I will not go into too much detail here.

The steady state theory simply claimed that the universe was eternal in existence, both in time and space. In other words, it had no beginning and was infinite in size. The idea of eons was then quite appealing to the evolutionist who requires enormous spans of time in order for life to have evolved. If evolution has an infinite amount of time and raw material, it makes the improbable plausible through infinitely small increments of change.

But with the advent of the general theory of relativity and the debunking of the steady state theory, evolutionary scientists began to understand that our universe had a beginning. If it had a beginning at a finite point in space-time, then it cannot be infinite. Moreover, with the acceptance of the Big Bang, the jaded form of uniformitarianism was sent into a tailspin, which concurrently sent the evolutionist into a vortex of angst.

Not only was the universe not eternal in existence, but the Big Bang theory, proposed as the origin of our universe and the greatest natural cataclysm imaginable, contradicted the entire anti-catastrophe component of the jaded uniformitarian hypothesis. And yet naturalists refused to open their eyes to other possibilities. As Copernicus, Kepler, and Galileo found out, old dogmas die hard.

Although evolutionists could not avoid the fact that our universe had a beginning and that the available time for evolution to take place had been vastly reduced from infinity to a finite number of years, they simply refused to accept the possibility of catastrophism playing any major role in the formation processes that govern our physical world and especially regarding the geologic strata. For most evolutionary scientists, jaded uniformitarianism had taken a torpedo broadside, but the ship had not sunk.

Then, like a bolt out of the blue, literally, a space rock appeared in our skies that could have brought on us a catastrophe unparalleled in modern history. It just so happened that a few years ago, at the close of our last century, scientists around the world became alarmed at a very close encounter with an asteroid, which was predicted to come so dangerously close to Earth that many were extremely worried. That was the first time in modern history that a close encounter with a massive and potentially catastrophic meteor was observed.

Scientists had known of near-Earth asteroids since 433 Eros was discovered in 1898. In 1937, another asteroid, 69230 Hermes, suddenly appeared in the night sky, going by us only twice the distance to the moon. Much to the alarm of astronomers, the asteroid disappeared from their view, and they had no idea of its accurate trajectory or whether it could possibly strike Earth. Alarm bells began to sound in astronomers' minds. Hermes was actually not seen again until it was rediscovered in 2003.

On June 14, 1968, an asteroid about 1.4 kilometers wide, named 1566 Icarus, was observed when it buzzed by Earth about 16 times the distance to the moon. Students at MIT launched a project (Project Icarus) in an attempt to deviate the course of the asteroid should it be found to be on a collision course with Earth. It was given wide attention by the media, and evolutionists began to understand that a meteor impact with Earth was a very real possibility.

On March 23, 1989, a 300-meter in diameter asteroid called 4581 Asclepius missed Earth by 700,000 kilometers and put the icing on the cake. No one had seen it coming. Many other asteroids had been known to exist, but this one, like Hermes, came like a bolt out of the blue. Scientists began to call them near-Earth orbit (NEO) asteroids, or Apollo asteroids.

Also in March 1989, scientists made early calculations of another asteroid, called (35396) 1997 XF11, that initially scared them to death. They estimated that the asteroid would pass by Earth in 2028 at a distance of only 46,000 kilometers, which means it would be closer to Earth than the moon. The margin of error in such calculations cannot be exaggerated, because often asteroids are perturbed from their course by other space objects and the dynamics of the shape and spin of the asteroid interacting with the solar wind. Later, scientists recalculated the trajectory and determined that it would be approaching at a distance of 960,000 kilometers. But by then, the tide had turned.

I found it amusing to watch the shift in the mentality of these scientists as they became aware of the catastrophic effects this asteroid could have caused had it strayed from its trajectory only a little bit. All of a sudden, theories about the extinction of the dinosaurs were relegated to a catastrophe caused by an asteroid striking the Earth and creating a massive worldwide volcanic upheaval.

A wide variety and quantity of evidence for the existence of cataclysmic events of this magnitude have always been there, staring us in the face. But they were simply ignored because they did not fit into their gradualist jaded uniformitarian paradigm. Today, the scientific community has conceded that major cataclysmic events have shaped our existence as we know it. And they are now becoming a widely accepted and, dare I say, preferred view of the majority of even evolutionary scientists as the cause of several near extinction events in Earth's history.

As a matter of fact, it is now being suggested as the more plausible explanation for what caused the continental drift and the extinction of dinosaurs, a model that the Institute for Creation Research has expounded for many years. The jaded uniformitarian model has been shown to be deficient as a dogma when it automatically precludes the possibility of sudden and major alterations in the rate of natural processes due to cataclysms. After all, cataclysms are natural processes.

It is true that processes do go in a gradualist fashion most of the time. But it is scientifically myopic and purely speculative to assert that cataclysmic events cannot occur from time to time, creating great and rapid changes in a short period of time. The evidence presented in this book will show that much of the Earth's strata were created not by millions of years of slow and gradual deposits but by a catastrophic event that changed our planet completely within a year's time.

At the dawn of the third millennium, scientists are beginning to understand the perilous predicament that the acceptance of this faulty assumption has created for our planet. For the first time since the shift in paradigm caused by the rise of the evolutionary theory, scientists are understanding that sudden drastic and dramatic global climactic changes can occur in the space of a few short years. The warming trend of our planet may potentially lead to the melting of the ice poles and the submersion of much of Earth's coastal regions on all continents.

Because those wanting to socialize our economy have politicized this issue, many conservatives have opposed the potential environmental crisis. Globalists seeking to undermine national sovereignty are attempting to create a situation in which the United Nations would take control of air, water, and space, using environmentalism as a ruse.

The point is that the burning of fossil fuels is not the real reason for this warming trend. It is simply a part of the wider climactic cycle that has been going on since the second ice age. On the other hand, we ought not to insist that global warming is a sham. It is not, but the cause of it is a sham created by socialists. The ice caps will eventually melt as they have in the past.

The United Nations Intergovernmental Panel on Climate Change declared in 2001 that by the end of this century, global temperatures might rise an average of 3–10 degrees Fahrenheit. But I am honestly not quite sure how much I trust anything coming out of the United Nations. If climate change, however, is anywhere close to their prediction, it would create enormous catastrophic changes on our entire planet. The sea levels would rise and inundate low-lying regions, effectively changing the coastlines of all continents and effectively submerging thousands of islands under the sea.

Warming oceans will cause drastic changes in rainfall patterns, and once arable lands will become wastelands as vast areas turn to deserts. Thousands of species of animals that depend on precise weather conditions for a favorable habitat may become extinct. These are distinct catastrophic possibilities that cannot be ruled out.

Just a 10-degree shift in our average global temperature will create such catastrophic droughts that it may cause the death of more than a billion people from resulting famines. That number is a little less than one-sixth of the current human population on Earth. Jews and Christians especially who are familiar with end-time prophecies ought to know that God has long ago predicted these conditions.

Some scientists have suggested that climactic changes can, even within the short space of a few decades, trigger such drastic warming that the ocean conveyor belt (ocean currents) may collapse completely. The conveyor belt is what keeps our planet delicately balanced by evening out the temperatures between the poles and our equator through the heat exchange created by those ocean currents.

If this catastrophe becomes a reality, the number of humans who would die of famine and more would dwarf any other previous catastrophe. Our world would be plunged into another ice age. Almost the entire North American and European continents would be under ice as they were in the last ice age. The limited amount of arable land would cause mass migrations and, no doubt, wars.

This cataclysmic change in weather patterns may take place, not in hundreds of years or even decades but perhaps within years if the ocean currents are completely interrupted. No one knows exactly how quickly that could take place. Evolutionary scientists have now come to understand that dramatic changes can take place in short periods of time. The absolute conformity to the jaded uniformitarian hypothesis during the time of Darwin was simply a wish projection that evolutionists conjured to substantiate their gradualist evolutionary theory.

Both the steady state theory and the strict definition of gradualist uniformitarianism, which discounts catastrophic events, have been shown to be untrue. The two fundamental foundations for the model of evolution of the species during Darwin's time have crumbled under the weight of new empirical evidence. Yet scientists continue to prop up the theory of evolution in a vacuum, building a house of cards upon the rubble of a ruined and nonexistent foundation.

Catastrophism is no longer disputed, but geologists still hang onto the idea that the strata of Earth were created through gradualism and refuse to accept the distinct probability that the Global Flood may have been triggered by a barrage of asteroids hitting Earth and breaking it up into seven continents and seven seas. The fifth book in this series, *The Death of the First Earth*, will deal with this more thoroughly. But I would like to point out that I find it quite ironic that the same evolutionists who continue to insist on interpreting the strata through gradualism are the ones alarming us about the potential catastrophic climactic changes Earth could suffer in a short period of time. In my mind, that is the classical definition of a schizophrenic disorder.

But the problem facing evolutionists goes beyond the foundation of their house of cards. If the evolutionary processes were to go on in this gradual fashion as they propose, with species evolving from one another in an almost imperceptibly gradual way over immense time periods, there should be clear and universally substantiated fossil evidence of these intermediate forms.

The evidence of these intermediate forms would be the critical links that would, without question, substantiate the evolutionary claims that species evolve into other separate and distinct species through selective pressure by gradual and minute but meaningful adaptive steps. When the theory was first espoused, evolutionists were confident that time and research would empirically bear out their evolutionary assumption.

Where Are the Intermediates (the Missing Chain)?

Since Darwin's time, the fossil record has been one of the chief tools of the evolutionists to allegedly substantiate their theory. Darwin postulated that the fossil evidence should depict the gradual, almost imperceptible, transitional process from one species into another. And the evolutionists were confident that time would bear them out. The intermediates of species were predicted to become the third pillar of the foundational evidence for the evolution of the species.

These minute and gradual changes, Darwin theorized, took place as selective pressures gradually modified the existing species by allowing only the fittest to survive and pass on these selective superior capabilities to the next generations. When Darwin proposed his theory of evolution, he was fully convinced that the fossil record in the future would incontrovertibly document these many transitions from one species into another.

After all, this process was supposed to be a gradual and almost imperceptible change requiring a great deal of time. Hence, the fossil record should contain ample evidence of these transitional organisms, linking one species to another with equal distribution throughout the various layers of strata. It is rational to expect that they had ample time and opportunity to leave their trace in the form of fossils throughout this long and gradual process of evolution.

But two centuries later, the glaring lack of transitional fossils serves only to underscore the deficiency of this theory. The facts simply do not uphold that supposition.

There are no pervasive intermediate fossils that shade imperceptibly between the species anywhere in the strata and anywhere on the planet. What we find in fossils is a record of fully developed species without any of these in-betweens.

Here and there, a similar species is artificially propped up between two others to create the illusion of an intermediary fossil. Nevertheless, evolutionists continue to insist that the fossil evidence proves evolution and that intermediates abound.

> Creationists are deeply enamored of the fossil record, because they have been taught (by each other) to repeat, over and over, the mantra that it is full of "gaps": "Show me your 'intermediates'!" They fondly (very fondly) imagine that these "gaps" are an embarrassment to evolutionists. *Actually, wec are lucky to have any fossils at all, let alone the massive numbers that we now do have to document evolutionary history—large numbers of which, by any standards, constitute beautiful "intermediates."* I shall

emphasize in Chapters 9 and 10 that we don't need fossils in order to demonstrate that evolution is a fact. The evidence for evolution would be entirely secure, even if not a single corpse had ever been fossilized. It is a bonus that we actually have rich seams of fossils to mine, and more are discovered every day. *The fossil evidence for evolution in many major animal groups is wonderfully strong. Nevertheless there are, of course, gaps, and creationists love them obsessively* (emphasis added) (Dawkins 2009, 145).

Note again what Dawkins said: "Actually, we are lucky to have any fossils at all, let alone the massive numbers that we now do have" (Dawkins 145). The reason he believes we are lucky to have any fossils is because his underlying jaded uniformitarian presupposition dictates that these fossilized specimens were accidentally encased in mud when they died through gradual natural processes, before their bodies decomposed.

If the only method of obtaining these fossils was due to the normal gradualist processes observed today, then the chances of these bodies being encased in mud prior to decomposition are quite slim. The evolutionist automatically disregards the actions of a global flood as the reason for the "massive numbers" of "rich seams of fossils to mine" (Dawkins 2009, 145).

Perhaps if he would remove his evolutionary-tinted spectacles, he would realize that these massive numbers do not support his gradualist uniformitarian bias but rather the idea that at one time, a global flood wiped out most of Earth's creatures and encased these massive numbers of specimens into turbid waters that eventually fossilized and preserved them for future humankind to know that the biblical narrative is a historical space-time reality and not the myth he proposes.

Ironically, Dawkins freely admits that these gaps do exist: "Nevertheless there are, of course, gaps, and creationists love them obsessively" (Dawkins 2009, 145). But Dawkins does not understand what creationists mean by gaps. Evolutionists think that by placing a similar species between two others, they have created an intermediate and closed a gap. That is not even close to what creationists mean.

If evolution is a gradual and almost imperceptible accumulation of small changes that lead to a different species, then we would find these gradual and incremental steps imbedded in the fossil records and also within the living species extant today. That is not what we find. Each and every fossil is found as a separate species from its supposed evolutionary lineage. There is not one record of any gradual in-between from a single species into another. It is not an intermediate species that is missing; it is the whole chain between species that is missing.

Moreover, Dawkins's bravado regarding his "beautiful" intermediates is built on a hologram. Many of the common intermediate forms used in biology textbooks to substantiate these claims have been scientifically shown to be spurious. For example, the famous chart of the evolution of the horse, which graced all my biology books when I was growing up, has been shown to be absolutely naïve and erroneous. I will speak more on that later.

What we do find in the fossil record of the First Earth is a wonderful variety within the same species. In fact, the varieties were many times more numerous than in our present diminished fauna after the Great Flood. But we do not find a single one between species. Each example evolutionists use to prop up their intermediates is a separate and distinct species.

How is it that we have such massive numbers of fossils, and this gradual and imperceptible chain between species is nowhere to be found? Evolutionists cannot point to a single incident where that has been recorded. And by the way, Mr. Dawkins, many of your fellow evolutionists are also beginning to admit the same.

Not until the late 1970s did some of the evolutionary scientists begin to face the brute and undeniable facts depicted by the fossil evidence. From October 16–18, 1980, a conference called Macroevolution was held in Chicago's Field Museum of Natural History. The so-called watershed conference was organized by J. Cracraft, J. Levinton, N. Eldridge, and D. M. Raup. It called to mind the nature of a previous famous conference in Princeton called Genetics, Paleontology, and Evolution. Thirty-four years later, members of that conference spoke again. They included Sewall Wright, G. Ledyard Stebbins, and Bobb Schaeffer, all committed evolutionists.

The central question of the Macroevolution conference dealt with the major Darwinian hypothesis that microevolution leads to macroevolution. Take a look at this definition from a typical college textbook:

> **macroevolution:** Evolutionary change on a grand scale, encompassing the origin of novel designs, evolutionary trends, adaptive radiation, and mass extinction (Simon, Reece, and Dickey 2012).

Macroevolution is the study of the accumulation of the evolutionary changes through natural selection that leads to the origin of novel designs in organisms—in other words, a new species.

Microevolution, which is a horse of a different color, is the description of the incremental steps within the species that show variations directed by natural selection. The Judeo-Christian model does not dispute that selective pressures can lead to a wide variety within a species. However, there is absolutely no evidence that it leads to another species.

The Darwinian assumption is that microevolution can be extrapolated into macroevolution. Can the mechanisms of microevolution be extrapolated to explain macroevolution? Can the incremental differences that have produced a rich variety within a species eventually, through gradual steps, evolve into a new species? Does paleontology evidence this gradual evolution (modern synthesis)?

The answer by eminent geologists at that Macroevolution conference was a resounding no. Paleontology has not been able to provide the evidence for the proponents of modern synthesis. In fact, evidence shows that all species appear distinct and without intermediates. The paleontological evidence shows stasis, not gradualism.

Francisco Ayala, a major figure in propounding the concept of modern synthesis in the United States, said this:

> We would not have predicted stasis from population genetics, but I am now convinced from what the paleontologists say that small changes do not accumulate (Lewin 1980, 883).

True science is the pursuit of the empirical data wherever it leads. When the data do not fit the presupposition, the presupposition must be amended or abandoned.

> What made the conference such a watershed was that the paleontologists bravely told the biologists what they least wanted to hear: that the fossil record does not, and never will, support the Darwinian scenario of a smooth, continuous progress of life forms, nicely graded from simple to complex. Instead the rocks show a pervasive pattern of gaps: New life appears suddenly, with no transitional forms leading to them, followed by long periods of stability during which they show little or no change at all.
>
> The late Stephen Jay Gould of Harvard dubbed this "the trade secret of paleontology"—revealing, perhaps inadvertently, how powerful the peer pressure can be among scientists by the ruling evolutionary paradigm. (Why did they feel the need to keep it secret?)
>
> Darwin himself acknowledged that the most damaging evidence against his theory was the discontinuous nature of the fossil record—the lack of intermediate forms (Pearcey 2004, 161–62).

The stranglehold held by the Darwinian paradigm in science long kept that "trade secret" out of the public square. But in a March

29, 1982, *Newsweek* article, this mounting realization finally leaked out of scientific circles and made the headlines.

> In 1972 [Stephen J.] Gould [professor of geology at Harvard] and Niles Eldredge—a paleontologist at the American Museum of Natural History—collaborated on a paper intended at the time merely to *resolve a professional embarrassment for paleontologists: their inability to find the fossils of transitional forms between species, the so-called "missing links."* Darwin, and most of those who followed him, believed that the work of evolution was slow, gradual and continuous and that a complete lineage of ancestors, shading imperceptibly one into the next, could in theory be reconstructed for all living animals. *In practice, Darwin conceded, the fossil record was much too spotty to demonstrate those gradual changes, though he was confident that they would eventually turn up.*
>
> *But a century of digging since then has only made their absence more glaring.* Paleontologists have devoted whole careers to looking for examples of gradual transitions over time, and with a few exceptions they have failed. It was Eldredge and Gould's notion to call off the search and accept the evidence of the fossil record on its own terms. Rather than transforming gradually, most of the species in the world appear to have evolved relatively quickly (on the scale of geologic time) and to have persisted, virtually unchanged, for millions of years (emphasis added) (Adler and Carey).

Not only does the stratum not contain this fossil evidence of intermediate life forms, but the idea of gradual imperceptible changes accumulating beneficial adaptations that allow the organism to evolve is just not possible from a biochemical point of view, as we shall later see when we consider their proposed mechanisms to do so.

Perhaps the one enamored obsessively with the fossil record of the supposed beautiful intermediates is Dawkins. Perhaps the true history-deniers are those biologists who deny the space-time historical reality conference on macroevolution in which evolutionary paleontologists plainly stated that the fossil record does not show intermediates. Perhaps Dawkins's history is a figment of his evolutionary magic spectacles. Perhaps he should believe the paleontologists.

Dawkins confidently claims that the gap in the fossil record for Turbellarians "completely destroys the creationist case" (Dawkins 2009, 149). There are no fossils of Turbellarians, which are flatworms, a subphylum in the Platyhelminthes phylum such as parasitic flukes and tapeworms. He mocks those who point to the fact that species appear complete in every fossil record by quoting from some supposed proponent of this view, which he fails to document.

> The Platyhelminthes to a worm, are "already in an advanced state of evolution, the very first time they appear. It is as though they were just planted there, without any evolutionary history." But in this case, "the very first time they appear" is not the Cambrian but today. Do you see what this means, or at least ought to mean for creationists? Creationists believe that flatworms were created in the same week as all other creatures. They have therefore had exactly the same time in which to fossilize as all other animals. During all the centuries when all those bony or shelly animals were depositing their fossils by the thousands, the flatworms must have been living happily alongside them, but without leaving any significant trace of their presence in the rocks. What then is so special about gaps in the record of those animals that *do* fossilize, given that the past history of the flatworms amounts to *one big gap*: even though the flatworms, by the creationists' own account, have been living for the same length of time? If the gap

before the Cambrian Explosion is used as evidence that most animals suddenly sprang into existence in the Cambrian, exactly the same "logic" should be used to prove that the flatworms sprang into existence yesterday. Yet this contradicts the creationist's belief that flatworms were created during the same creative week as everything else. You cannot have it both ways. This argument, at a stroke, completely destroys the creationist case that the Precambrian gap in the fossil record weakens the evidence of evolution (Dawkins 2009, 148–49).

I hope I am not being insensitive when I say this, but the tenor of his writing leads me to believe that Dawkins must have been looking at a mirror and slapping himself on the back when he said, "This argument, at a stroke, completely destroys the creationist case that the Precambrian gap in the fossil record weakens the evidence of evolution." Instead, "this argument, at a stroke, completely" shows that Dawkins is either being deceptive or ignorant of the processes that create fossils.

Fossils are not made of bones or shells. They are impressions of the bone or shell created by minerals leaching into that space while it was encased in mud. The vague outline of the animal may sometimes be seen, but most often, all we find are the impressions of the skeletal system. Fossils do not regularly reveal the soft organs within the body such as heart and arteries. They do, however, readily reveal "all those bony or shelly animals" that "were depositing their fossils by the thousands" because they have bones and shells. Such soft-bodied organisms as Platyhelminthes are very difficult to find in the strata because they decompose too quickly to be preserved by fossilization.

Nevertheless, we do have a few fossilized specimens of such soft-bodied creatures. But these are minute in number compared to the number of hard-shelled animals. Most fossils are, in fact, marine invertebrates, mostly shellfish. They comprise 95 percent of all fossils.

Plants comprise less than 5 percent, and vertebrates comprise less than 1 percent of all fossils. The idea that one soft-bodied worm has not been found fossilized is hardly any surprise. Dawkins's dramatic claim is completely spurious.

Dawkins displays an undercurrent of elitism and intellectual arrogance throughout his writings and a clear disdain for those he deems ignorant, calling them the forty-percenters. He is referring to those who believe in God and the Genesis record. The truth is that Dawkins has a nasty habit of creating straw-man arguments and insinuating that creationists are completely ignorant of science.

> Once again, humans are not descended from monkeys. We share a common ancestor with monkeys. . . . But even though humans evolved from an ancestor that we could sensibly call a monkey, no animal gives birth to an instant new species, or at least not one as different from itself as man is from a monkey, or even from a chimpanzee. That isn't what evolution is about. Evolution not only is a gradual process as a matter of fact; it *has* to be gradual if it is to do any explanatory work. Huge leaps in a single generation—which is what a monkey giving birth to a human would be—are almost as unlikely as divine creation, and are ruled out for that same reason: too statistically improbable. *It would be so nice if those who oppose evolution would take a tiny bit of trouble to learn the merest rudiments of what it is that they are opposing* (second emphasis added) (Dawkins 2009, 155).

Generally speaking, evolutionists claim that we evolved from apes. But technically speaking, apes evolved from ancestral monkeys, which Dawkins readily admits when he says "even though humans evolved from an ancestor that we could sensibly call a monkey." I would love to ask Dawkins from which intelligent design scientist or creationist scientist he heard that a monkey gave birth to a human in a single generation. That is perhaps the most outrageous straw man argument ever recorded in human history.

Dawkins then belittles our intelligence and knowledge by saying, "It would be so nice if those who oppose evolution would take a tiny bit of trouble to learn the merest rudiments of what it is that they are opposing." I need make no comment on this Tartufery other than the shoe is actually on the other foot. As to the statistical probabilities, we have already discussed in *Codes: Random Evolution vs. Divine Design* that it is evolution that is statistically improbable beyond rational consideration. Dead molecules simply do not self-organize and randomly create codes with specified complexity. Codes are the product of a mind.

We can point to the complex gene expression system consisting of a double code—one for the DNA with four nucleotides and another for the proteins with 20 amino acids. And yet the two can communicate and translate the code from one language to the other. But the kicker is that you cannot make DNA without proteins, and you cannot make proteins without DNA. What selective pressure could cause these two to evolve simultaneously?

And then there is the process of glycolysis from which ATP (the fuel of the cell for metabolic processes) is made, which comprises multifaceted integrated systems with many chemical steps that have absolutely no selective advantage until the entire system is completed and could therefore not have evolved in gradual small increments through any selective pressure. They form a closed loop system where each is necessary in order for the other to exist. They are mutually interdependent and could therefore not have been the product of any random evolutionary process.

It would be so nice if those who oppose intelligent design "would take a tiny bit of trouble to learn the merest rudiments of what it is that they are opposing."

It is plain to all who read his works that Dawkins has a deep disdain for those who believe in God, and he goes to great trouble to vilify them as the promoters of ignorance and deniers of history. Dawkins denounces belief in God as the reason for the acceptance of mythical concepts that have plagued true scientists.

> Underlying much of the fallacious demand for "missing links" is a medieval myth, which occupied men's minds right up to the age of Darwin and stubbornly confused them after it. This is the myth of the Great Chain of Being, according to which everything in the universe sat on a ladder, with God at the top, then archangels, then various ranks of angels, then human beings, then animals, then plants, then down to stones and other inanimate creations. Given that this goes way back to a time when racism was second nature, I hardly need add that human beings were not all sitting on the same rung. Oh no. And of course males were a healthy rung above females (Dawkins 2009, 155).

First, this myth is not from medieval times. It actually came from the ancient Greeks through Aristotle and Plato. It was actually promoted by the Neoplatonists during the Medieval period. If you know your history, these Platonists were the same people who gave rise to the Enlightenment as opposed to the Christian Reformation, which I rather call the Christian Reclamation.

Moreover, this hierarchal division of significance is an occult worldview and in direct antipathy to the Judeo-Christian worldview that considers all humanity as created in the image of God, having therefore equal infinite value that cannot be subdivided into any hierarchical segments. I could say again, it would be so nice if those who oppose intelligent design and the Judeo-Christian worldview would take a tiny bit of trouble to learn the merest rudiments of what it is that they are opposing. But I won't.

Ironically, it is, in fact, the evolutionary worldview that created the hierarchal ladder of evolution that gave more recently evolved beings greater value. It was the evolutionists a hundred years ago, as

I shall later expound on explicitly, who said that black human beings were more rudimentary humans and lower on the evolutionary ladder. It was the evolutionary ideology translated into social theory that spawned the eugenics movement and the Nazi ideology that considered humans nothing more than expendable fodder. There is no light in the atheistic "enlightenment."

The indirect insinuation that those who believe in God are racists is not only false but also scandalous. If you study real space-time history, you cannot deny that Christianity was at the forefront of the anti-slavery movement in England, Europe, and America. In fact, it was also at the forefront of the women's emancipation movement. If you are really a student of history, you cannot deny that racism has ever been present on our planet in every age and every nation. It was the Judeo-Christian worldview that promoted the high view of man as created in God's image that led to all the magnificent cultural changes.

Our so-called modern civilization is no exception since it is the Judeo-Christian worldview that champions the human rights of the unborn. If our culture today has any morality reflected in it at all, it is in the memory of the Judeo-Christian worldview that gave rise to our Western culture. A student of history cannot deny that evolution and eugenics are linked at the hips, which has been the major reason for racism in the last 200 years. Millions of Jews have died because of it. I respectfully ask the eminent Dawkins, "Are you a history-denier?"

There is no ladder, evolutionary or otherwise. The supposed divisions in which evolutionists make speculative judgments as to who preceded what are all an imaginary shell game. The idea that one species is more primitive than another is pure bunk. They are chronologically the same age, and they are contemporaries. They may exhibit different qualities, but even the most supposedly evolutionary rudimentary form of life, the single cell, is an absolutely astoundingly complicated organism that could not have arisen by random ordering.

And if you happen to be an evolutionist who puts his eggs in the DNA basket, you will find many examples of allegedly primitive species that have a larger genome component than supposedly more advanced forms. If your measure of advancement in evolutionary terms is the size of the brain, then both Cro-Magnons and Neanderthals are more evolutionarily advanced than modern *Homo sapiens*. Such speculative measures are evolutionary contraptions lacking any substantive scientific reasoning.

The ignorant speculations in Darwin's time that single-celled organisms are simple have been proved false by science. The shark, for example, was thought to be a simple primitive killing machine, but science has debunked that. We will deal with that more exhaustively, but for now, the point is that Dawkins is blaming the wrong people for the evolutionary ladder that has been promoted for the last 200 years. It is the elitist mentality created by those who promote the survival of the fittest that has caused this evolutionary ladder.

Dawkins, either ignorantly or maliciously, blames this Great Chain of Being as the reason, somehow still impacting believers today to ask for the evidence for intermediates. That huge leap is an accusation that is absolutely unfounded and without any empirical evidence to support it.

> But the pernicious legacy of the Great Chain of Being also feeds the challenge "Where are the intermediates between major animal groups?" and, nearly as discreditably, underlies the tendency of evolutionists to answer such a challenge by trotting out particular fossils, such as Archaeopteryx, the celebrated "intermediate between reptiles and birds" (Dawkins 2009, 159).

The truth is that the hierarchal classifications promoted by the Great Chain of Beings would have a greater probability of influencing atheists and agnostics involved in the occult than they would Jews and Christians who do not see angels as being of greater significance than humans. They are fellow servants of the Almighty. We are the clay. He is the potter. We do see God as the higher being of the greatest significance. We see humans as having infinite significance, not because of their intelligence or any other personal faculty but because they were created in the image of God. Our worth is God-endowed.

On the other hand, evolutionists are irrational schizophrenics. On the one hand, they claim that man has ascended from apes (and subsequently, whether Dawkins likes it or not, monkeys). Our human species is widely considered by evolutionists to be the pinnacle of the evolutionary process. On the other hand, they give man no transcendental significance that can account for any special value of human life compared to a slug. Even when Dawkins denies it by his words, he infers it. This is what he says:

> Why should we choose humans as the standard against which we judge other organisms? An indignant leech might point out that earthworms have the great virtue of being more like leeches than humans are. Despite the Great Chain of Being's traditional ranking of humans between animals and angels, there is no evolutionary justification for the common assumption that evolution is somehow "aimed" at humans, or that humans are evolution's "last word." It is remarkable how commonly this vainglorious assumption thrusts itself forward. At its crudest level, you meet it in the ubiquitously querulous, "If chimps evolved into us, how come there are still chimps around?" (Dawkins 2009, 158).

There he goes again with his straw man arguments. Tell me, Mr. Dawkins, what creationist scientist ever asked you that silly question? Dawkins is right, however, to say that evolution is not aimed at humans. It cannot aim at anything. It is a completely purposeless and random process. Jews and Christians do not claim that evolution is aimed at humans. Ill-educated evolutionists do.

Christians and Jews do give infinite value to human life, while evolution denigrates humanity to the level of all other living things, and thus the quip about the leech having just as much right as humans to call themselves the epitome of evolution. To an evolutionist, human life is just another life and has no greater transcendental significance than even nonliving things, which have also evolved alongside living things, all by random ordering in a completely purposeless process. To an evolutionist, all life is just the result of the accidental collocations of atoms in an impersonal chain of chemical reactions.

But I challenge Dawkins to live true to that mantra. He cannot, no matter how many times he repeats it and teaches it. Here is the test. Put a baby and his leech buddy side by side. Then smash the leech with a sledgehammer. Then see if you can smash the skull of a human baby with a sledgehammer. Why does every human soul scream out against such an atrocity? Because we have been created in the image of God, and whether or not our mind admits it, we instinctively know that there is a transcendental value to each human life.

Dawkins is right that human evolution is not the last word. In a process of evolution, there is no last word; it is always evolving. But our technology has now advanced to a place where man can become the god of evolution who can provide a more directed evolution for man.

Transhumanism is the next wave of evolution. The genetic engineering of the superman, which Hitler attempted by the purposefully planned and executed elimination of the so-called inferior genes from the human gene pool, will now be available in the fast track through recombinant gene splicing. For the right price, the rich will be able to modify a new species of human that will far supersede the ability of natural man today. In addition, the merger of man and machine is almost here. All these horrible prospects are the direct consequence of the evolutionary paradigm that is the antithesis of the Judeo-Christian's high view of man.

This whole vainglorious, arrogant, and self-glorifying thing that Dawkins abhors is actually the by-product of the evolutionary naturalistic worldview, not the Judeo-Christian worldview. Moreover, it was the evolutionists who promoted the idea of the ascent of man and created this monster you now blame us for. Evolutionists—not us—are seeking to replace God. Their elitist and "enlightened" views will bring great darkness to our world. What we are witnessing is the descent of man from the initial design and purpose for which God created him.

I am sure this leech Dawkins speaks of is a great evolutionary biologist. I will take him at his word, but I would surely like to meet that leech that talks and thinks like a human. All kidding aside, the vainglorious assumption, my friend, is the direct product of the Darwinian worldview that man is the center of the universe as a direct and logical consequence of denying God.

If evolution is true, then man becomes god. Man chooses what is right and wrong. Each man or woman becomes his or her own personal paragon against which to measure all truth. And since no man has any higher authority over another, each choice is equally valid. All truths are relative. All morals are relative. All choices are sameness. No human can dictate to another human what is good or evil. Slavery cannot be condemned. Rape cannot be condemned. Each pedophile has the right to live as he so chooses. In a universe where the survival of the fittest is the matrix of reality, tyrants rule and equal justice for every human being is an illusion. The concept of liberty and freedom as an intrinsic right of individuals is without justification.

The "deophobes" who peddle such atheistic notions are the real epitome of vainglorious illusions of grandeur. At their crudest level, they are the ones who take every shot they can to frame those who believe in God as the enemies of reason and the stalwarts of closed-minded ignorance. That, my dear Mr. Dawkins, is what is really ubiquitous and rather crude and inhuman with the deophobic peddlers of atheistic Darwinism.

This truth I have learned in life: When facts cannot be disputed, the ignorant turn to mocking and making crude and derogatory characterizations of their opponents. Perhaps I should not respond with such emotion. To be honest, it is really hard for me not to be passionate in my response to deophobes and the cultural consequences they are promoting. I am a hot-blooded Latin refugee from Cuba, and due to my brush with a totalitarian atheistic regime, I hate insensitive bullying of any kind. Sometimes, those who bully with words do not realize they are bullies. But I assure you, my evolutionist friends, I hate the ideology of evolution, but I love evolutionists. I hate sin, but I love the sinner. After all, I am also a sinner, and God still loves me.

The Death of Gradualism—The Punctuated Equilibrium Theory
Dawkins crassly calls religious people ignorant "history-deniers" because they will not believe in the long history of gradual evolution with the many "beautiful intermediates" that "prove" evolution to be a "fact." Contrary to his view, the historical reality is that evolutionists are admitting that the Darwinist extrapolation from microevolution to macroevolution (modern synthesis) is just not supported by the real space-time fossil data in the strata or our modern knowledge of genetics.

> The Modern Synthesis is a remarkable achievement. However, starting in the 1970s, many biologists began questioning its adequacy in explaining evolution. Genetics might be adequate for explaining microevolution, but *microevolutionary changes in gene frequency were not seen as able to turn a reptile into a mammal or to convert a fish into an amphibian.* Microevolution looks at adaptations that concern only the survival of the fittest, not the arrival of the fittest. As Goodwin (1995) points out, *"the origin of species—Darwin's problem—remains unsolved"* (emphasis added) (Gilbert, Opitz, and Raff 1996, 361).

But it is not just that genetics do not offer us a mechanism to go from one species to another. It is that the empirical evidence in the rocks does not support this claim. The obvious lack of fossil evidence has caused some to break ranks, and many evolutionists are now postulating an evolutionary process that is basically a modified form of catastrophism.

This punctuated equilibrium theory is now being championed by biologists such as Stephen Gould and Niles Eldridge. Much to the consternation of the old guard, they have publicly admitted that the fossil record is simply lacking the transitions they had hoped to find. The king is naked, and finally some people are telling the truth about what they are seeing. Dawkins's denial of the foundational importance of intermediate fossils is akin to saying, "Well, the clothes of the naked king matter not."

The steady state theory is dead. Jaded uniformitarianism is dead. And now, gradualism is shown to be a myth, an imaginary fabrication. Furthermore, our advancements in biochemistry have shed new light on the improbability of a gradualist evolutionary origin to these complex metabolic pathways found even in single-celled organisms. The new biochemical evidence shows that there cannot be gradual step-by-step, simple transitions when changes need not linear pathways but rather diverse, multilateral, and interrelated pathways that must function simultaneously in order to accomplish a given metabolic task. When selection cannot take place until the end of a complicated chemical process shows some selective advantage, how can gradualism explain such leaps in complexity without a mechanism or any selective advantage to account for each step? That is a real space-time historical fact that cannot be denied.

The resulting advance in genetics, which has opened our eyes to the incredible complexity of these multifaceted biochemical processes, has now forced some biologists to discard the fundamental evolutionary doctrine of gradualism. Moreover, the evidence in fossil strata shows that species are stable with few physical changes over long periods of time. There is no gradual change into another species. There is only change within the species.

Yet, essential to Darwin's original idea, which previously had been sacred ground, is the fundamental notion of gradualism. This process formed the very historical foundation of the evolutionary paradigm. It was the backbone of the evolutionary process and therefore the motivation to interpret the geological data as the result of millions of years of depositions so evolution could take place.

In the book *The New Evolutionary Timetable* by the renowned Steven M. Stanley, a committed evolutionist, modern science broke through the seemingly impenetrable wall of propaganda created by the gradualist paradigm and spelled out the truth of their dire predicament.

> Today the fossil record—a rich store of information that was long untapped—is forcing us to revise this conventional view of evolution. *As it turns out, myriads of species have inhabited the Earth for millions of years without evolving noticeably*. . . . Even more important is the fact that species of the human family have existed almost unchanged for long stretches of geological times. . . . The fossil record of horses also testifies to an episodic tempo for evolution, and this is particularly notable because for decades the record of ancient horses was heralded as the classic illustration of gradual transformation. *Although this fossil record, like all others, is incomplete, so that it fails to document the full history of the horse family,* one of its striking revelations is great evolutionary stability for tiny dawn horses, which, as the earliest representatives of the horse family, browsed on leaves about forty million years ago. For at least three or four million years, two species of these dawn horses roamed through the woodlands of western North America. In other words, populations of *these small animals replicated themselves through a million generations or so without undergoing*

appreciable change in form. Looking to the upper end of the horse family tree, we find the same kind of evidence (emphasis added) (Stanley 1981, 3-4).

The king is naked, folks! No better example of this can be found than the mammoth. The fossil record shows us that no other mammal roamed with greater distribution throughout the world and faced such a great change in climactic conditions throughout the longest period of time before becoming extinct. And yet there is no appreciable change in the morphology of this magnificent beast during that entire time.

If species are supposed to be so unstable as to be susceptible to mutations and other influences that are supposed to be a catalyst for evolution, then why does this magnificent beast stand as the paragon of stability throughout its entire existence? Even the extinct mastodon is only different from our modern elephants by four or five nucleotides, an almost insignificant variation.

Again, what the fossil record shows is not a missing link but a missing chain. Gould's theory of punctuated equilibrium, modified from Mayer's previous writings, tried to sidestep this overwhelming stumbling block by postulating that evolution must have occurred in sudden and abrupt evolutionary steps.

New species must have appeared randomly from old species by a mechanism yet unknown, in sudden, abrupt, and concise steps. And then they remained stable or unchanged for long periods of time.

Conveniently, the short period of time in which the species underwent this magical conversion or transmutation into another species is so small that there is not enough time to create the fossil evidence to document this extraordinary process of speciation. How special! Talk about a leap of faith into the speculative!

Somehow, we are now supposed to accept that selective pressures in small isolated genetic pools must have created, through a mechanism yet unknown, rapid changes in the genetic components of these creatures, causing them to evolve into another species and then become stable and immutable for long periods of time. How strange that we cannot witness this magical mechanism yet unknown today!

Let us recapitulate what we have discussed thus far. Darwin initially told us that evolution constituted minute, almost imperceptible changes that gradually, through the accumulation of these infinitesimal steps and after immense time periods, changed a specimen from one species into another. Time was no problem, for in his day, the steady state theory had confidently told us that the universe was infinite and had existed since infinity.

Lyell told us that all things went on in a slow uniformitarian manner and that the geologic evidence in the strata could not be explained by catastrophes. The many layers of strata seemed to indicate a slow deposition through immense ages. If you have infinity, then such minute gradual steps are plausible. The obvious inference was that gradualism was necessary to make credible what was fundamentally illogical and unobservable in a short period of time.

Well, Einstein blew the steady state theory out of the water. Now we know that the universe is finite and had a beginning. The comet that struck Jupiter gave us a real space-time view of a catastrophe of immense proportions. The anti-catastrophe component of uniformitarianism is now also dead. Besides that, after two centuries of digging, gradualism has been unobservable in the fossil record of these supposedly long periods of time. Gradualism is also dead, and yet Darwinism is being artificially propped up by magic mirrors and smoke through a mechanism yet unknown. And to make things worse, genetics has not provided us with a viable mechanism that can change one species into another.

Now, we are told that immense and radical changes occurred in very short periods of time, so short that, unfortunately, there just was not enough time for fossils to form and document this fortuitous evolutionary miracle. To date, no one has ever observed this radical change from one species to another. But never you mind that this is an unobservable, unrepeatable, and untestable phenomenon; it is still considered a rational scientific evolutionary theory because it supports evolution.

No biology professors are being drummed out of tenure and classes for believing in the untestable and unobservable mechanism of punctuated equilibrium because it still holds to a materialistic origin whereby moral autonomy is not being challenged. But scientists using reason and empirical facts that hold to the idea that life had to have been intelligently designed are routinely ostracized.

Initially, the improbability of the evolutionary mechanism of transmutation from one species to another was softened by the long ages of their gradualist paradigm. But now, more than 200 years of paleontology have shown that there are no imperceptible changes reflected in the fossil record among all the species. Therefore, they make an about face, and with a Cheshire cat grin on their faces, they simply change the already improbable gradualism into an even less probable system in which evolution goes through an accelerated process, creating a new species in a relatively short period of time. *Voilà!* Another pocket full of fairy dust.

The old-school evolutionists are fuming at these new upstarts who have exposed the nakedness of their cherished king. Yet they are not treated with the same vehemence as those who hold to the scientific position that life shows clear evidence of intelligent design.

The fact is that the evolutionary lineage is not a chain but rather a collection of disjointed links with no intermediates that has been arbitrarily put together to prop up the Darwinian theory. There is no empirical evidence in fossils that can substantiate the idea of evolution from one species to another through natural processes. There is no half-scale/half-feather species in the fossil record. There is no half-leg/half-wing species recorded in the fossil record. Some evolutionists are beginning to admit that the king is naked.

> Feathers are features unique to birds, and there are no known intermediate structures between reptilian scales and feathers. Notwithstanding speculations on the nature of the elongated scales found on such forms as Longisquama... as being featherlike structures, there is simply no demonstrable evidence that they in fact are. They are very interesting, highly modified and elongated reptilian scales, and are not incipient feathers (Feduccia 1985, 76).

Moreover, if a reptile leg had evolved into a wing, it would have gradually become a useless leg long before it could have become a useful wing. What selective pressure would cause the leg to deteriorate in order to later become a wing when it would make the creature less capable of surviving in a competitive environment through this long process? Such a process would, in fact, contradict the heart of their proposition that selective pressures favor the fittest. Hence, punctuated equilibrium tells us that it happened suddenly. And we are supposed to believe that through what testable and reproducible data?

Dawkins claims that the fossil record has been, is, and will be intact because it is a fact. He writes:

> All the fossils that we have, and there are very very many indeed, occur, without a single authenticated exception, in the right temporal sequence. Yes, there are gaps, where there are no fossils at all, and that is only to be expected. But not a single solitary fossil has ever been found *before* it could have evolved. That is a very telling fact (and there is no reason why we should expect it on the creationist theory). As I briefly mentioned in Chapter 4, a good theory, a scientific theory, is one that is vulnerable to disproof, yet is not disproved. Evolution could so easily be disproved if just a single fossil turned up in the wrong date order. Evolution has passed this test with flying colours (Dawkins 2009, 147).

All right, let us examine this bombastic claim. Evolutionists have compiled a family tree that places separate species that have certain similarities in form into imagined lineages. In the past, when Darwin imagined this continuous lineage, it was based solely on morphology, a concept that is today recognized as completely spurious from a scientific perspective. Today, this is perhaps more often done through similarities in DNA, which also cannot be used as absolute evidence of evolutionary lineage other than to say that certain species share more genes than others.

Evolutionists insist that the common components and functions of organisms are evidence of evolution. In contrast, the intelligent design model predicts that the biological functions created by a single intelligence would show similarities in design. It follows that a single architect of life would use the same code and language of life in all His creation. It has nothing to do with lineages.

Dawkins claims that this evolutionary lineage is impeccable and proof of evolution and that no fossil has been found before it could have evolved. In other words, the previous ancestor must evolve before the next one comes on the scene. Each of them would then be found in different temporal sequences.

However, in practice, this is a myth. Time and time again, these supposed ancestors are found living in the very same strata in which their supposed evolutionary descendants are also living. Apparently, their ancestors forgot to evolve. But no worries, the evolutionary theory simply throws out the old lineage and draws up a new one, without even batting an eye. Such relativistic underpinnings cannot be used to establish any absolutes. A scientific theory that is so elastic is useless.

> As Medawar observed, if a theory is so flexible that the same explanation can be used to account for two entirely contrary tendencies, then the theory is meaningless. Once it was held that man's enlarging brain caused his

emergence as Homo sapiens, the great tool-user, so that smaller brained creatures were lower in the scale. Now that small-brained creatures have turned up as tool users, it is being argued that the very use of tools is what enlarged the brain to man size. Evolutionary theory is highly "adjustable" (Custance 1975, 24).

This fallacious and audacious claim of the existence of an absolute bedrock of fossils that form a clear lineage of our ancestry, as we will see, is as solid as a hologram. Moreover, the evolutionary ladder of lineage from all other organisms is just as much a product of their evolutionary magic spectacles.

Let us hear what an evolutionist says about this "not a single solitary fossil" claim that Dawkins makes. Speaking of the superb fossil data collected in the Big Horn Basin in Wyoming, which clearly illustrates this evolutionary dilemma, Steven M. Stanley writes:

> *It used to be assumed that certain populations of the Basin could be linked together in such a way as to illustrate continuous evolution. Careful collecting has now shown otherwise. Species that were once thought to have turned into others have been found to overlap in time with these alleged descendants. In fact, the fossil record does not convincingly document a single transition from one species to another.*
>
> Furthermore, species lasted for astoundingly long periods of time. David M. Schankler has recently gathered data for about eighty mammal species that are known from more than two stratigraphic levels in the Big Horn Basin. Very few of these species existed for less than half a million years, and this average duration was greater than a million years . . .
>
> It is ironic that among the sluggish changing species of the Big Horn Basin were members of the "dawn horse" genus *Hyracotherium,* (formerly called Eohippus) the

animal generally believed to be the distant ancestor of the modern horse. The fossil species *Hyracotherium* show little evidence of evolutionary modification. One species lasted for at least three million years, and another for perhaps five million! For many years, while gradualistic thinking dominated evolutionary science, it was widely assumed that *Hyracotherium* had slowly but persistently turned into a more fully equine animal (emphasis added) (Stanley 1981, 95–96).

It is ironic because this supposed evolution of the horse was touted as another of the most magnificent proofs of evolution during Darwin's day. The problem is compounded by the fact that evolutionists cannot cop out as in the past and exclaim that the fossil record is not yet quite complete and that future excavations will support their hypothesis. Even Dawkins admits that the fossil evidence is massive. Evolutionists have been digging for more than 200 years. That future has come and gone, and they have nothing in the strata that can substantiate their early claims. In fact, the only thing that has truly evolved is their theory.

The gap between single-celled forms of life, plants, invertebrates, insects, vertebrates, fish, amphibians, reptiles, birds, mammals, primates, apes, and man still yawn, uncrossed by the many intermediates that should have been amply recorded in the fossil record if evolution had transpired. But even more devastating is the fact that no evolutionary mechanism has yet been proffered that can be scientifically substantiated to cause one species to evolve into another. In fact, our extant species have been in existence within their supposedly ancient strata all along.

> Something like 86 percent of the species of mammals now living in Europe have been found fossilized in Pleistocene sediments. According to the Finnish paleontologist Bjorn Kurte'n, who has undertaken a comprehensive review of

European Pleistocene mammal species, the few living species lacking Pleistocene records are species that one might expect not to find as fossils because they are either small, fragile forms or recent immigrants to the region (Stanley 1981, 97–98).

Some species not currently found in Europe have become extinct through the cataclysm of the Great Flood. But most species in Europe today already existed in the Pleistocene, according to the evidence of their evolutionary strata, which we will later examine. Nevertheless, the point is that these species have apparently forgotten to evolve since the Pleistocene.

Although I do not agree with evolutionists' long evolutionary timetables (I will deal with that matter later), I certainly applaud their scientific honesty, which has caused them to declare that the fossil record clearly shows that current species have been extant and unchanged for very long periods of time. I find this honesty refreshing. The king is naked, folks!

And furthermore, these species all appear suddenly and abruptly, fully formed in the strata with no gradation of predecessors. But the difficulty in explaining the sudden appearance of all creatures in the fossil record as complete and abrupt is not a new problem for evolutionists.

As far back as Darwin and Huxley (known for his defense of the evolutionary paradigm as the Bull Dog of Darwin), this obvious problem created in them a considerable amount of angst and led them to suggest some imaginative and speculative proposals, which, for obvious reasons, have been kept hush-hush by most evolutionists. It seems that evolutionists have many trade secrets.

> Huxley, lacking the broader knowledge at our disposal today, sought refuge, where Darwin himself had hidden. *Huxley postulated fantasylands in which long, unrecorded*

evolutionary histories might have unfolded . . . he now sought to preserve gradualism by granting it more time. He stated that "if there is any truth in the doctrine of evolution, every class must be vastly older than the first record of its appearance upon the surface of the globe." *He then envisioned a lost continent of Late Paleozoic and Mesozoic Age, upon which the many advanced mammal groups of the Early Cenozoic, might have evolved in a gradual fashion before making their way to Eurasia and America.* We can now rule out this fanciful scheme (emphasis added) (Stanley 1981, 97-98).

From Reptiles to Birds

My friends, the time for speculation is over. It is time to consider the true empirical data. The king is naked. Period. End of story. But lest you think that fantasy, fabrication, falsification, and dishonesty no longer play a part in the contrived schemes of some modern scientists, let me point out a very curious claim recorded in *National Geographic* in 1999 regarding supposed transitional fossils between reptiles and birds.

The transition between reptiles and birds, for obvious reasons, has been a sore spot for evolutionists from the very beginning. Efforts to mend this glaring gap in their chain of evolution have failed miserably. But in 1999, evolutionists with great enthusiasm heralded the discovery of a fossil that finally substantiated their proposed evolutionary process. With the discovery of Archaeoraptor, Darwinian evolutionists were allegedly proudly vindicated:

> Lewis M. Simons from *National Geographic* magazine tells an embarrassing story of how, a year earlier, the magazine ran a story about an alleged dinosaur fossil bird called "Archaeoraptor." After the story had been printed and shipped, *National Geographic* learned that the fossil was

faked. Archaeoraptor originated and was assembled in China before it was sold for $80,000 in the United States. Simons describes this fascinating story:

> It's a tale of misguided secrecy and misplaced confidence, of rampant ego clashing, self aggrandizement, wishful thinking, naïve assumptions, human error, stubbornness, manipulation, backbiting, lying, corruption, and most of all abysmal communication.
>
> *National Geographic* published its mistake in the October, 2000 issue and accepted its share of responsibility. However, as illustrated in this story, in any endeavor where time, glory, careers and money is [*sic*] at stake, objective thinking can be obscured (Bendewald 2004, 23, 25).

Now, it must be made clear that not every archaeologist or Darwinian evolutionist is attempting to consciously hoodwink the world. But it can be said that not a single supposed transitional fossil has been found to document their theory. And as a result of this embarrassment, there is great pressure on them to come up with something that could substantiate their failed claims.

Evolutionists, determined to provide proof of their evolutionary dogma, are predisposed to interpret so-called facts in a way that favors their evolutionary presupposition. Evolution means change; hence, the fossil record must demonstrate these subtle changes that gradually bring one species into another.

Sometimes, those changes are simply variations of the character complex of a single kind. Because of evolutionists' consuming faith in evolution, it is necessary to find substance that can be demonstrated. By overemphasizing the evidence to the extent of distorting it out of all proportion to its true significance, they create a new species out of the normal variation of a single kind within the character complex of that animal.

But this process is not always skewed only through subjective bias. Sometimes it is simply downright forgery. As the reader follows my narrative of the fossil record, a definite pattern will emerge.

The problem, which the fabricated Archaeoraptor tried to remedy, is that there is an even bigger gulf between birds and their supposed reptile ancestors than between any other groups due to the vastly different structures of birds and the lack of any intermediates between these two groups. That places an immense gulf in the supposed gradual and imperceptible evolution of these animals, which completely contradicts evolutionists' claims.

The birds are so radically different in so many ways that there is no credible way that reptiles could have developed these adaptations in one fell swoop as suggested by the punctuated equilibrium theory. Here is their conundrum: If evolution is the mechanism for the development of birds, some gradual process must have occurred, which should be amply evidenced in the fossil record. But none exists anywhere in the planet. If it is not gradual, then what mechanism could possibly create such massive changes in short order?

Let's look at some examples.

1. Reptiles have solid, massive bones, while most birds have hollow, flexible bones filled with air. Some have air sacs in their bones to make them light, and upon inspiration, these magnificent flying creatures not only fill their lungs with air, but air is transmitted to the very marrow of their bones to allow them flight, as these air sacs are directly connected to their lungs.
2. Birds do not have the typical heavy jaws, teeth, and heads of reptiles. Their heads are much smaller and lighter. The weight of the typical reptile head would be too high and forward to allow the bird to fly.

3. Birds have a gizzard, which is lower and further back in the body, allowing the fulcrum to be where the wings are. This gizzard (not found in reptiles) helps digest their food, whereas reptiles have teeth to aid digestion.
4. Birds are warm-blooded, while reptiles are cold-blooded. That is quite a significant leap in the differences in their metabolic rates. For warm-blooded birds, a high metabolism is absolutely necessary and indispensable for prolonged winged flight. The slow metabolism of a cold-blooded animal would not have the sufficient energy level to power the wings necessary for flight.
5. Most outstanding of all the features that set apart birds are their feathers. Feathers are remarkably engineered instruments of flight that are designed to be light and yet strong and are magnificently adapted for fanning the air to achieve propulsion while providing insulation against inclement weather and even, for some, the ability to remain insulated while they float on water.

But the very design of bird wings is remarkable, for certain feathers are used to power their lift, while others, such as the alula feathers (also known as bastard wings), are used for stabilization or anti-stalling devices in flight.

For a reptile, which depends on its brute force, massive bones, and head to overpower its prey, it would be a decided disadvantage to develop lighter, more fragile bones in order to later become a bird. In order for reptiles to evolve into birds, an enormous number of significant changes would have to occur simultaneously without any selective advantages. What selective pressure could have engineered such a feat? And again, the proposed punctuated equilibrium theory falls flat on its face. With a simple wave of a magic wand, poof! A bird developed from a reptile?

The Archaeopteryx, often used as the only possible example of an intermediate between birds and reptiles, is woefully inadequate.

The fact that Archaeopteryx exhibited some aberrant features is not argued. But these atypical aberrations are found today in some living birds and can, therefore, be barely used as a transitional model. For example, the claws in its wings are found today in the hoatzin (*Opisthocomus hoatzin*), a bird that inhabits South America. This peculiar shape is also found in the tauraco (*Tauraco corythaix*) of Africa.

The fact is that the fossil record simply does not depict a gradual change from species to species. Species are found abruptly in the record and fully formed. What the fossils do show is that most of these animals had been rapidly buried as in the sedimentation process following a flood that had agitated large amounts of material in suspension. Huge currents of cold water must have been at play in the fossilization of soft-bodied animals such as jellyfish. Had the waters been warm, the animals would have decomposed long before fossilizing. It would not be possible to explain these except through a cataclysmic flood.

Many fossilized jellyfish, for example, show that the sedimentation was quite quick, and fossilization took place before their soft fleshy portions had time to decompose. That could have only happened if there were a drastic temperature difference (much colder water) from their natural environment that forestalled decomposition. Only the hydraulics of a global flood can explain this cataclysmic temperature change in such a short time frame that would allow a species that survives only in temperate climates to become fossilized before decomposing.

The hydraulics of a catastrophic global flood does explain the fossil record with more accuracy and efficiency than gradualism. Mass graves of animals that are twisted and contorted lend evidence to the fact that these were run-offs such as those typically created in floods that encased animals of every size and description before they also had a chance to decompose.

Many fossils also crosscut through different layers of sediment that could not have been separated by large periods of time during their development. (We will deal with the fossil evidence and the geological and meteorological data as we more thoroughly explore the possible mechanisms of the Great Flood in the last book of this series, *The Death of the First Earth*.)

The Earth's sedimentary layers are typically parallel to adjacent layers throughout the planet. We can view this grand spectacle in the magnificent walls of the Grand Canyon, evidence that the sedimentation process took place in a short period of time. Had these layers been deposited over millions of years, we would not see them as parallel, for the tectonic forces would have thrust them in many undulating directions, and natural erosion would not have allowed such parallel striations. We find these on occasion today, but if our history is measured in millions of years, it would be the norm and not the exception.

If the deposition was gradual throughout long ages, the erosion rates would have differed from one region to another, creating greatly undulating layers of deposit that corresponded to the varying rates of erosion. That, too, would have resulted in unparallel layers.

Today, we can see this process in a limited form. But if all these layers had been deposited over long periods of time, as the gradualist evolutionary model demands, then it would have been the rule and not the exception in the fossil strata.

But even beyond the fossil evidence, evolution faces an uncrossable abyss called the problem of convergent evolution. Even die-hard evolutionists such as Francis Crick recognize the statistical improbability and the lack of evidence in the fossil record to substantiate the evolution of life on Earth.

The Problem of Convergent Evolution

Proponents of the space trash theory (evolutionists such as Crick) also cite the immense improbability of convergent evolution as proof that the evolutionary record on Earth is not complete.

Convergent evolution is the independent development through random evolutionary processes of specific traits in unrelated lineages.

In other words, certain evolutionary traits developed in one lineage would also have to be independently developed in another unrelated lineage.

For example, if the development of the eye is quite improbable in one species, the odds of it having evolved must be infinitely multiplied in order for this trait to arise in other species that are not related in lineage. Each species not directly related to another must independently develop the eye in order to genetically pass it down to its descendants.

This convergence enigma must also be calculated for all other metabolic processes such as the gene expression system, glycolysis, the immune system, the chemistry of photosynthesis, and many other irreducibly complex chemical processes that cannot be explained in gradual steps and that have no selective advantages until fully complete.

In other words, the problem for the evolutionist is that the development of these highly sophisticated organisms and metabolic processes must not only evolve once but must evolve many times over in every species that is not interrelated in order for them to also possess these common and extremely complex organs and metabolic processes throughout all species.

Evolutionists will say that all species are interrelated. By this, they mean that somewhere in their past they have a common ancestor. But there are forks in the road to the phylogenetic tree. The separate branches no longer share genetic information that supposedly evolves after the fork. Hence, any developing traits in each of the separate branches must emerge independently of the other.

The staggering improbability of this occurring simultaneously in all unrelated species is absolutely astronomical. This is the great irrational abyss created by the problem of convergent evolution for those who insist that the fossil record proves evolution. What are the statistical probabilities of simultaneously evolving this convergence throughout every phylum?

Proponents of the directed panspermia theory, of course, claim that this evolution took place on alien planets. What we see here, they claim, is the result of their evolutionary progress in a land far, far away beyond the pale blur into the black—our real mother planet from afar. And she might have been colonized by yet another planet—we will call her the granny planet. But who knows if she was the first?

If we just keep adding planets into the equation, the odds then become less improbable. And to boot, they have the added bonus that the fossil record of this convergence is neatly hidden away in those other mommy or granny or even great-granny planets, and therefore, our fossil strata are spared from the humiliation of not having any record of it. How very nice! Now that is some fantastic piece of empirical science.

The problem of convergent evolution is no small matter. Each trait requires parallel evolutionary processes in order to be developing the various components that, when put together, make that specific trait function as a dynamic whole. All of this takes place without any known selective advantage to create a need for each branch of the multifaceted process to reach its final climactic point when it all comes together and it works within each genetically unrelated species.

In other words, it is difficult to conceive of the incredible odds of developing such specialized functions as stereoscopic vision, cognition, or the ability to hear just one time in the history of the universe. But if evolution is true, then these traits would have to evolve not once, but many times over in parallel since they would not have been genetically passed on to unrelated species in different lineages.

Each species, which is no longer directly related in the phylogenetic tree, would have to independently evolve these mechanisms within each of their own lineages in order to end up with the world that we observe today.

The statistical hurdles that evolutionists must jump over to imagine that evolution can account for life as we know it on planet

Earth are so immense that any objective scientist would have to admit that it is simply a ridiculous impossibility. It is nothing less than a swan dive into a rabbit hole that would make Alice seem ordinary.

Evolutionists are correct to admit the improbability of evolution, no matter how much time is given in a single planet, due to the problem of convergent evolution. But they take a blind leap of faith into the irrational in asserting that it could have happened in conjunction with the cumulative odds of the development of life on other planets.

Now, the reader must understand very clearly that these objections to the idea that life could have evolved on planet Earth are not being made by the proponents of intelligent design but by bonified, tried-and-true evolutionists such as Crick, with all the bells and whistles, shoulder patches, coffee mugs, and rubber ducks from their esteemed academic institutions.

On the other hand, evolutionists such as the proponents of the anthropic cosmological theory readily admit that "the evolution of intelligent life, comparable in information-processing ability to that of *Homo sapiens*, is so improbable that it is unlikely to have occurred on any other planet in the entire visible universe" (Barrow and Tipler 1996, 133). They believe that this staggering improbability is evidence of their need of an anthropic cause. Apparently, they cannot quite swallow the directed panspermia solution.

> For the above reasons, and many others which we omit for reasons of space, *there has developed a general consensus among evolutionists that the evolution of intelligent life, comparable in information–processing ability to that of* Homo sapiens, *is so improbable that it is unlikely to have occurred on any other planet in the entire visible universe. The consensus view has been defended by many of the leading evolutionists such as Dobzhansky, Simpson, Francois, Ayala et al. and Mayer.* The only evolutionist

of any standing who has disagreed with the consensus is Stephen Jay Gould, and *even Gould claims conscious intelligence is sufficiently unlikely to evolve that, should Mankind blow itself to bits, "Conscious intelligence . . . has no real prospect for repetition [on the Earth]"* (emphasis added) (Barrow and Tipler 1996, 133).

"Conscious intelligence . . . has no real prospect for repetition [on the Earth]." In other words, the specified complexity in the gene expression system displays integrated, specified complexity at such an improbable level that it would be impossible to ever happen again. Equally, the specified complexity of the brain is so complex and interconnected that we do not yet know how it even works. They do not know how it happened the first time; all they can say is that it must have happened because we are here. It's somehow here. However, it could never happen again.

Well, they are getting there!

CHAPTER 3

MECHANISMS OF EVOLUTION (THE HOUSE OF CARDS)

Microevolution, not Macroevolution

There are some who have attempted to reconcile evolutionary theory with the biblical narrative, but a careful analysis of the respective components rules that out completely. The friction between the evolutionary model and the biblical model is mainly in three points.

The primary clash is the existence of the divine. The naturalist claims our universe is closed and there is no divine presence beyond it that brought things into existence. All things run in a cause-and-effect linear motion ruled by dysteleological (randomly generated) causes void of prevision and design. Our Judeo-Christian cosmological model claims that we are in an open universe and that there is a directed energy that is responsible for the creation of matter and all life (God, the primal cause). Moreover, all things consist because of His ongoing relationship with the universe He created. He is not an absentee landlord.

The universe did not come from nothing. It came from the energy of God. The universe had a beginning. God also actively sustains it throughout its development. He is neither an absentee landlord nor a tyrant. He has created us with a free will, and yet, in the final reckoning, His will shall be fulfilled. Hence, all of creation has been created with previsioned design and purpose. It provides for us a consistent framework from which we can understand that the specified complexity intrinsic to life came from the mind of the creator. For the documentation of this evidence, see the second book of this series, *Supersymmetry or Chaos*.

Second, the historicity of the fall of Adam and Eve is inextricably tied to the redemption promise of the second Adam, who provided for humankind through His grace the remission of sins and forgiveness that binds us back or reconciles us to the creator. This is the fundamental doctrine of the Judeo-Christian worldview, and if it is torn from its historical roots, then our theology becomes nothing more than a religious sentiment. It becomes an over-boiled spaghetti without sauce.

It is that historical space-time fall that allows us to understand how evil has marred our universe. It gives us a realistic view of humans as infinitely valuable because they are created in God's image and yet explains that they are flawed because of the fall. Hence, the only redress is the reconciliation freely offered by the redemption promise through faith in the Redeemer of Israel by His grace alone and apart from our human efforts.

That offers a uniquely balanced view of humans that is realistic. It is neither overly optimistic, like the positivistic humanistic worldview that is built on the firm foundation of a hologram, nor nihilistic or pessimistic fatalism that states that humans have no transcendental significance whatsoever. It gives us an understanding of the source of evil based on the selfish drive for autonomy universal to all humankind and provides the solution through the selfless sacrifice of the Son of God upon the cross.

Third, the biblical model specifically states that the organisms God created would each reproduce after its kind. That rules out the process of one kind evolving into another. To merge the evolutionary hypothesis with Christianity is to denude the Christian message in its entirety and to dress an atheistic religion with a Christian veneer. It is antithetical to all the Judeo-Christian worldview holds as fundamentally true. Such a choice is made not from scientific data but from the lack of knowledge or willful and subjective denial of that scientific data.

According to the Judeo-Christian scriptures, at the point of creation, ancestral species were given a wide variety of potential expressions within their genes, which forms what scientists call a character complex of a kind. That is to say, the genes of the primordial archetype of all creatures contained the wide potential for the spectra of phenotypes that have subsequently developed from that single kind.

I would like to emphasize here that the biblical category referred to by the word *kind* is not 100 percent in accordance with the man-made category of species developed by evolutionists. At times, evolutionists make artificial differentiations of particular species between creatures that are of the same kind. In doing so, evolutionists attempt to create an illusion of evolution where none exists. The term *genre* may be closer to the biblical concept of *kind*.

These man-made classifications are instrumental in helping us study the many living creatures in our world, but evolutionists, in forming an imaginary lineage of descendants from one species to another, sometimes manipulate them. But no matter how hard they try to gerrymander the distinction of species, some animals refuse to fall under their devised categories.

The duck-billed platypus found only in Tasmania and Australia, for example, is an egg-laying, warm-blooded mammal sporting a prominent duck's bill, the web feet of an otter, and the tail of a beaver. The males of this kind possess extremely poisonous claws that can inject venom like a pit viper. It has a single ventral opening for elimination, mating, and birthing.

It has a shoulder girdle and claws, as most reptiles do, and yet it is not a reptile. It is able to detect electric currents (alternating current as well as direct current) as some fish such as the shark are able to do, and yet it is not a fish. Only birds, some fish, and reptiles lay eggs, but the platypus is not a bird, a fish, or a reptile. We know of no birds that possess poisonous defense mechanisms.

We know of no mammals that lay eggs. Is it a bird or a reptile since it lays eggs? Or is it a mammal because it suckles its young? The duck-billed platypus simply does not fit into the evolutionary taxonomic scheme created by man. It is completely unrelated to its alleged evolutionary precursors. Scientists have had to invent a new classification for the platypus. It is now called Ornithorhynchidae. It is the only animal in this category in the entire world. But where are the intermediates?

Although our artificially contrived taxonomic groupings are useful in studying animals, they are incapable of providing any proof of evolutionary dogma. These artificial divisions that man has made in order to study animals in an orderly fashion are thus not absolute in nature.

Often, the character complex of a kind is not considered by evolutionists, and certain morphological dissimilarities may be used to artificially create the appearance of a new species when the creature simply belongs to a single kind. Evolutionary-minded biologists eager to establish familial evolutionary ties between organisms often overlook the extent that morphological variations occur in a single kind, especially as existed during the overwhelming abundance of creatures that were far more numerous in their character complex in the ideal habitat that existed prior to the Great Flood during the First Earth.

This tendency becomes even more problematic when the fossil evidence is slight and noncontinuous geologically. Previously, unknown variations of a given kind may be spuriously labeled as a new kind. That has been the case for the majority of fossil specimens touted as evolutionary ancestors of man, as we will see later.

These dramatic claims are made due to their unproved and fallacious assumption that the genetic components that make for a

MECHANISMS OF EVOLUTION (THE HOUSE OF CARDS)

given kind can be changed through natural selection into a new kind. Man has never observed or artificially prompted the genes of one species to evolve into another. Outside of direct human intervention through recombinant gene experiments in which man physically takes the genetic components of one kind and physically translates it into the genetics of another kind, no animal has ever evolved into another through natural processes. Not one documented case has ever been recorded in the annals of science.

The scriptures declare the God created the animals and grouped them into kinds. "Then God said, 'Let the earth bring forth living creatures after their kind'; and it was so. God made the beasts of the earth after their kind, and the cattle after their kind, and everything that creeps on the ground after its kind; and God saw that it was good" (Gen. 1:24–25).

There is a great variety of potential phenotypes (physical appearance or variation) within a given kind. The mixing of different genes, which brings out one characteristic over another, creates the many variations within each kind. The proponents of intelligent design are well aware that selective pressures can bring about the predominance of one specific phenotype over another.

Nevertheless, the change is never outside the kind. It is horizontal microevolution rather than vertical macroevolution from one kind into another. The change may isolate certain characteristics within the kind, but it does not change one kind into another.

At the moment of creation, each archetypical primordial organism contained within its genes, designed and pre-engineered, all the varieties possible of that specific kind. But that variety does not shade indefinitely into another kind. And the variations contained in the design of their genes are finite in possibility.

In other words, there are specific limits to those varieties. That is, the variety has a predetermined limit within each kind—a finite genetic, numerical value, coded within the genes—as we will explore more fully in the next section.

Different combinations of genes cause the differences in the varieties of each kind. That is not caused by the evolution or appearance of a new gene. The idea that a mutation causes a new gene is misleading, to say the least. It may deform or alter a given gene, but it never creates a new gene. The gene was there to begin with. The mutation simply corrupted it, a process that, for the vast majority of cases, is lethal. Therefore, to be scientifically correct, it is describing devolution and not evolution.

Simply stated, it is an empirical fact that mutations do not create new genes. They simply deform or alter already existing genes. That consequently results in a corruption or loss of genetic information and not the addition of new genes. In that sense, natural selection and mutations are, in fact, nothing more than devolution. Mutations do alter the information by deleting information, not adding new, richer complexity to the organism.

As we will now examine, neither the process of natural selection nor the mechanism of largely deleterious mutations has ever resulted in a documented evolution of one kind into another. It must be stated again that there is no new information added to the genes through the process of natural selection. On the contrary, natural selection most often limits the parameters of the genetic variability left by favoring one phenotype over another and eliminating the less viable within that microcosm, which may or may not be a favorable trait within the larger macrocosm.

No known mutation has ever been shown to produce a living organism that displays greater complexity and viability than its ancestors. The only examples that evolutionists claim might produce greater viability are in single-cell forms where a genetic pool shifts when drug-resistant cells survive over another or where a more specialized ability to use nutrients in a limited environment develop. But there is, again, no new genetic information, only the environmental pressure to select one genetic trait over another, as we shall see later.

MECHANISMS OF EVOLUTION (THE HOUSE OF CARDS)

The few isolated examples of species creating offspring with other species, which evolutionists use to support their claim that a species can turn into another species, are spurious. These isolated examples inevitably involve *species* that are within a kind such as the horse and the burro or donkey. Isolating genetic components through geographical barriers can often produce genetic incompatibility. We can observe that in some breeds of dogs such as poodles and wolves. The offspring of the horse and burro is the mule, which are most of the time unable to reproduce. That would, in any case, disprove the feasibility of what they propose, that even if they were another kind (which they are not), it would not create a survival advantage.

There are instances in the past, although quite infrequent, where mules have been known to reproduce. Some of the more recent cases are documented in the University of Idaho's *Project Idaho* news release on May 29, 2003.

> Near Champion Nebraska, the owners of a mule named Krause saw things differently when she produced a foal, Blue Moon, in 1984. . . . In 1987 Krause produced another foal, White Lightning.
>
> Two mule foals were documented in China. In October 1985, the Journal of the Royal Society of Medicine reported one of them produced a foal that was named Dragon Foal (*The Utah Statesman* 2003).

But the mule, the zebra, and the burro all belong to the same kind as the horse. Their ability to mate with one another is documented, even though they have been classified as separate species. The horse is classified as *Equus caballus*. It belongs to the genus Equus and the species caballus. The donkey is classified as *Equus asinus*.

The zebra is divided into three species: *Equus burchelli* (plain zebra), *Equus grevyi* (Grevyi's zebra), and *Equus zebra* (mountain zebra). Horses have been bred with zebras, creating the zorse. Zebras have also been bred with donkeys, creating the zeedonk. There is no evolution here into another kind.

The Evolutionary Purpose for Denying Purpose

Third, the incompatibility of evolutionary dogma and the Genesis record is their doctrinal position that all processes are dysteleological in nature. In antithesis to their dysteleological doctrine, which is a subjective doctrine of faith, the biblical model stipulates that the world and the organisms found within it are created with purpose and design. The evolutionary model directly contradicts this, stipulating that change occurs only through the stimulus of natural selection in a random undirected fashion; that is, without any directed purpose. There is no way to harmonize the evolutionary process with scripture. Scripture is teleological, and evolution is dysteleological (purposeless).

For this reason, any teleological approach to biology or any other science, for that matter, is denigrated and ridiculed by most evolutionary scientists as unscientific. In reality, it is simply unevolutionary, not unscientific. There is an evolutionary purpose for denying that the universe was purposefully created because that implies a designer God. It is evolutionists' purpose to claim that all things have been accidentally created by blind, random, and purposeless chemical forces in order to substantiate their atheistic deophobia.

But the paradox for the evolutionary biologist is that he or she cannot step away from the teleological approach when describing any organism since all organisms display purpose and design to achieve their functions in their particular bodies. As we previously stated, how do you describe an organ without describing its function and purpose and then, by implication, its design for that purpose?

The eminent French biologist Jacques Monod clearly realized that inconsistency in biology. He thus ridiculed the use of teleological terms by other biologists in an effort to be more consistent with the evolutionary doctrine of dysteleology; that is, with his fundamental faith in chance and purposeless, undirected evolution.

MECHANISMS OF EVOLUTION (THE HOUSE OF CARDS)

Mayr attempted to come up with a solution by coining a new term: *teleonomics*. Through the use of the word *teleonomic* rather than *teleology*, he hoped to escape the design implications in trying to describe purposeful action. But that is simply a semantic delusion. The conundrum is inescapable. And the hurdles, which they must jump, become increasingly higher.

Design is an inescapable reality of the entire universe, beginning with the simplest particles. And without exception, it is intrinsic throughout all reality, even in the stellar realm. It is the undeniable fingerprint of the creator.

Somehow, it escapes Mayr that a rose by any other name is still a rose. Even the much celebrated vestigial organs used to legitimize the claims of evolutionists that life is not designed have been found wanting. As we learn more about our metabolism and the chemical processes involved, we find that these vestigial organs are not as useless as we once ignorantly supposed. Evolutionists' assumptions have been found false.

The evolutionist is trapped in a naturalistic presupposition that right off the bat does not recognize design as the matrix of the universe. It automatically disqualifies any notion that an intelligent mind could have engineered the complex organs and metabolic pathways that allow for life to exist. Instead, the naturalist subjectively chooses to believe that all things have evolved by blind, undirected chemical processes. Yet he is forced to admit, contrary to his underlying dysteleological presupposition, that the end product is purposeful. Hmm!

He continues to dogmatically insist that randomness has created order spontaneously. But I am a skeptic at heart. And consequently, I have great difficulty stretching the limits of credulity to accept the preposterous assertion that blind chance, left to itself, has created order, design, and purpose accidentally.

In conclusion, the very foundation of the theory of evolution is that a gradual change in an undirected, uniformitarian fashion has resulted in the evolution of species, from a less complex to a more complex biological form. We have seen that the skewed interpretation of the uniformitarian presupposition is incompatible with reality. Cataclysms do come periodically, and evolution no longer has an infinity of time to accomplish the impossible.

We have seen that there are no intermediates to record the evolutionary gradualist process when they should be equally plentiful throughout the fossil record. We have seen that the notion of simplicity in biological terms is an illusion predicated on ignorance and that the development of these complex forms by random processes is, practically speaking, impossible and therefore unreasonable and irrational. We have seen that many of these processes are irreducible and therefore could not have evolved their many chemical transpositions by any selective external pressures since there can be no selective advantage until the process is completed.

We have seen that specified complexity does not come from natural processes but from intelligence. We have seen that such codes as the four base language of DNA and the 20 amino acid protein language could not have been the product of random ordering. Codes are the product of intelligence. There are no natural processes that can develop codes, and not a single example can be cited outside of living organisms, especially when the specified complexity is integrated into several interrelated systems that cannot be functional in the organism without that specified integration coming to its final state.

We have seen that the evolution of such metabolic processes must have evolved in parallel in all unrelated species, making the odds even more untenable for the convergence of these traits. We have been witness to man's so-called leap of faith in his escape from reason in order to force-fit facts into his atheistic presupposition and, through convoluted reasoning, posit that we are but the product of space trash.

Undeterred by their lack of foundation, evolutionists build on their illusion the walls of the house of evolution. The unsuspecting and uncritical populace is not able to distinguish the truth of the matter,

MECHANISMS OF EVOLUTION (THE HOUSE OF CARDS)

relying on the "credentials" of evolutionists as the rationalization to blindly accept what they adamantly espouse, lock, stock, and barrel. Our culture has been conditioned to believe that science is free from presuppositional bias. The divided field of knowledge that dominates Western culture has created the illusion that naturalistic science deals only with objective facts. The public has failed to understand that naturalism is a metaphysical worldview that provides a filter or grid through which "facts" are interpreted.

Let us now take an objective look at these "facts" that construct the evolutionary house of cards.

1. Selective Pressures and Natural Selection (the First Wall)

Darwin and Wallace's pronouncement of natural selection as the mechanism for the evolution of the species was heralded as the death blow to teleology and specifically relegated the scriptural narrative to the irrelevant backwaters of mythological bunk. Naturalists such as Huxley, adverse to the concept of a deity, saw this new concept as the all-pervasive, underlying force that created life and all the subsequent species.

Deophobes naïvely rejoiced in the newfound mechanism that freed evolutionists from the shackles of accountability to a creator. But contrary to their claims, even under perfectly controlled laboratory conditions, the natural selection process has not yet been able to create a new species. Even under carefully engineered and controlled breeding experiments that could greatly enhance the speed of the genetic combination artificially, they have failed to show the evolution of one species into another. The very process has been found to be bogus as a realistic means to create new species.

Selective pressures may cause one variant to be more successful than another due to a specific attribute. But this variation will always remain locked within the kind.

Consider the peppered moth, *Biston betularia*, for example, which has been lauded by evolutionists as one of the most dramatic examples of the process of selective pressure creating significant changes in genetic pools.

In pre-industrial England, the peppered moth was most commonly white with dark spots and stripes. The tree trunks of pre-industrial England were also light gray or white, making it an ideal camouflage environment for the moths.

There was another variety of this same species of moths, the carbonaria. The genes (genotype) of this peppered moth dictated that its wings would be colored differently than the peppered ones. These were melanic or dark colored (phenotype) and stood out against the light background of the trees in pre-industrial England. According to the story evolutionists told, the dark moths created a stark outline on the white background of these clean, pre-industrial age tree trunks, making them an easy target for predators.

As the industrial revolution progressed, tons of toxic chemicals and gases spewed onto the English countryside. The soot began to collect around the white tree trunks, darkening them considerably. As the story goes, the result was that the dark-colored moths became better adapted to hide on the dark trunks. That, of course, resulted in a dramatic population change.

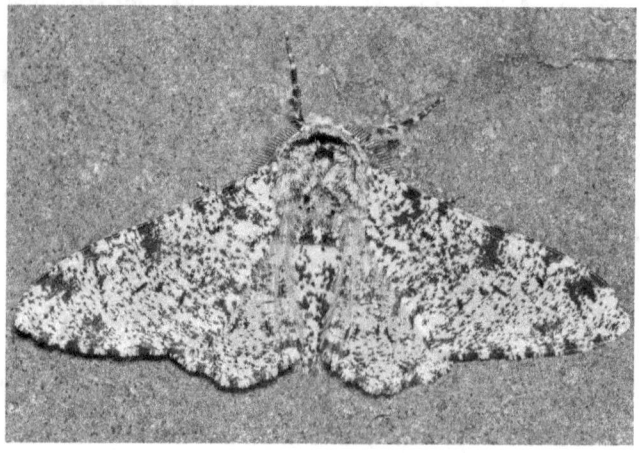

The peppered moth, Biston betularia, perching on tree trunks

Preying birds could now spot the lighter moths on the dark trunks. And consequently, their population numbers plummeted in post-industrial England. There developed within that genetic pool of moths a greater preponderance of dark moths compared to the light moths that had previously been more numerous. Evolutionists hailed that as direct evidence of the evolutionary theory. But was it? Did it show that the moths became another species?

There was an obvious adaptive change in the genetic makeup of the population of the moths due to a specific selective pressure. If their data are correct, then we can say that there was a shift within the community (genetic pool) but not in the genes of the species. What the proponents of intelligent design reject is the speculative extrapolation that these changes will lead organisms beyond their species into a new species.

If their data are correct, what occurred here is very simply that one genetic genotype represented a phenotype (a distinct physical appearance of a given genotype) that was better suited to a particular change in environment. Thus, the overall genetic pool reflected a preponderance of the better adapted member of that species through natural selection. The moth better suited to survive the given environment became the predominant genotype within that specific gene pool.

But it must be duly noted that from the beginning, the moths had the genes for the two varieties. There was no change in the genes, only the selection of a variant that already existed. That variant, as a result of its phenotype, fared better in the particular environmental shift. There was nothing new added to the genetic code of the moth.

There are still white peppered moths in England, although in much fewer numbers than before. There is only an illusion of evolution since there is effectively no change in the genes, only in the collective gene pool.

The collective genes of any given population (gene pool) are the summation of each individual genotype. Selective pressures were removed from the gene pool of the majority of those genotypes, which resulted in the phenotype of white wings. Then the gene pool changed and reflected a higher percentage of darker moths.

But there was no change in the individual genes. The genes of both colors were already present from the moment of creation. From the very first primordial moth, there was within its genes the entire variety that manifests itself today in all the interrelated moths. Were conditions to change, making the white moths more camouflaged, the situation would return to the previous balance.

Nancy Pearcey sheds more light on this peppered moth, which had become an iconic poster child, a key evidentiary propaganda of Darwinists to allegedly show evolution working before our very eyes.

> The case for naturalistic evolution has been seriously damaged in recent years by reversals in key evidence. Take the peppered moths in England, which most of us remember from photos in our high school science textbook. The moths appear in two variants—a light gray and darker gray—and the standard textbook story goes like this: During the Industrial Revolutions, the new factories poured out smoke and soot, which darkened the tree trunks where the moths perched and made it easier for birds to see the lighter variety and eat them. Over time the process led to a larger proportion of the darker moths. This has long been touted as *the* showcase example of natural selection.
>
> *In recent years, however, a small problem has come to light: Peppered moths don't actually perch on tree trunks in the wild.* (They are thought to perch in the upper canopy of trees.) *How then do we explain the photographs we see in the textbooks? It turns out that they were staged*: To create the photos, scientists glued dead moths onto the tree trunks. One scientist who helped make a television documentary

MECHANISMS OF EVOLUTION (THE HOUSE OF CARDS)

acknowledged that he glued dead moths on the trees in producing the film. . . .

Why was such a shoddy piece of scientific research accepted in the first place? And how did it attain to iconic status in evolutionary biology? Because scientists wanted desperately to believe it, says journalist Judith Hooper in a recent exposé. The problem with Darwin's theory is that evolutionary change requires thousands or millions of years, so we never actually see it happening. In the case of the peppered moth, however, for the first time evolutionary change seemed fast enough to be actually observed. It was just what Darwinists had been waiting for, and before long it had become "an irrefutable article of faith."

The scandal has now been thoroughly aired in the scientific literature, to the great embarrassment of evolutionists. The peppered moth was a "prize horse in our stable of examples," lamented one well-known evolutionary biologist. Learning the truth, he said, was like learning "that it was my father and not Santa Claus who brought the presents on Christmas Eve."

Yet amazingly, the moths continue to appear in science textbooks. One enterprising reporter interviewed a textbook writer who admitted he knew the photos were faked—but used them anyway. "The advantage of this example," the writer said, "is that it is extremely visual." "Later on," he added, students "can look at the work critically." Apparently, even falsified evidence is acceptable, if it reinforces Darwinian orthodoxy (emphasis added) (Pearcey 2004, 161–62).

"Later on?" When? When will Darwinists tell the deceived students that this peppered moth "proof" of evolution was falsified by their scientists? When will they be told that even after the falsification was revealed, it was still kept in science textbooks? This is not education; it is not even indoctrination. It is intentional and premeditated brainwashing with lies. They know the king is naked, and they draw him with clothes in their science textbooks to fool the students.

Indoctrination is not education. It is the teaching of a single viewpoint by excluding all others. But at least it does not stoop to the falsification of evidence. The typical elitist mentality of modern educators is evidence of their relativistic worldview that insists that the ends justify the means. They snobbishly stand on pedestals, looking down their noses at the public, and think they know what is best for us. Hence, even if they fudge a little here and there, deceiving us, it is justified as being done for our best interest so the ignorant masses will accept their Darwinian model of reality.

Genetic Variability Is Finite

Ironically, even if the moths had perched on the tree trunks, the population shift does not prove evolution. It only shows the ability of a species to use the variants within their character complex dictated by their genes to allow the species to survive.

But, there is a finite limit within this variability found in the genetic components of all species. The Darwinian extrapolation that claims these changes can go on indefinitely, thus gradually changing the species, is proved wrong by both experiences in breeding and modern genetics. This finite capability has been documented by artificial crossbreeding. When scientists crossbreed, they isolate particular genes, which results in a different phenotype they might desire. But there is a finite limit to the extraction of these characteristics that is directly proportional to the genetic capacity intrinsic to that genome.

One cannot extract from the gene what was not there from the beginning. We can mix and match, thus isolating particular characteristics desired to create a new breed within a particular organism. But through natural breeding, we cannot go beyond this finite numerical capacity indefinitely in order to create a different kind of organism. Even specific characteristics have a limit to their expressions, which is bound and predetermined within the genes from the very beginning. It was bound in Genesis 1—"after their kind" (Gen. 1:24).

Another form of change which is often cited by evolutionists as evidence for evolution is the origin of domesticated plants and animals by artificial selection and breeding. Evidence of this nature is again irrelevant to our discussion, since nothing new or more complex arises and the change accomplished is always extremely limited.

What artificial selection and breeding actually accomplishes is to rapidly establish the limit beyond which no further change is possible. We wish to cite just two examples. In 1800, experiments were begun in France to increase the sugar content in table beets, which at that time amounted to 6 percent. By 1878, the sugar content had been increased to 17 percent. Further selection failed to increase the sugar content above that figure.

One worker tried to reduce the number of bristles on the thorax of fruit flies by artificial selection and breeding. In each generation the average bristles became fewer until the twentieth generation. After that, the average remained the same, although he selected as before. Selection was no longer effective; the limit had been reached.

Similar experimental approaches have been used to develop chickens that lay more eggs, cows that give more milk, and corn with increased protein content. *In each case limits were reached beyond which further change has not been possible. Furthermore the breeders ended up with the same species of chickens, cows and corn with which they began. No real change had taken place.*

> It must be strongly emphasized, also, that in all cases these specialized breeds possess reduced viability; that is, their basic ability to survive has been weakened. Domesticated plants and animals do not compete well with the original, or wild type (emphasis added) (Gish 1979, 41).

Even when artificially induced so the results are more acute and the time required for change is greatly reduced, selective pressures can only bring out the maximum variability of the character complex within a kind, which was already there to begin with.

That is, they more quickly bring the limits that are contained within the genes, which were preprogrammed by God in each original archetype of every kind from the very onset of creation. This process has created no new kinds. There is only a process of isolating a particular set of genes, which brings about a particular characteristic within that kind.

Therefore, the process of selective pressure can bring about an illusion of evolution within a given kind (microevolution), but it cannot bring about evolution from one kind into another (macroevolution). Darwin correctly observed that selective breeding made the English racehorses faster than their parent Arab stock, thus implying an evolutionary process that could produce an infinite number of changes. But in reality, there is an upper limit to that speed. There is a finite limit to the changes that can be made.

> By a similar process of selection, and by careful training, the whole body of English racehorses have come to surpass in fleetness and size the parent Arab stock, so that the latter, by the regulations for the Goodwood Races, are favoured in the weights they carry (Darwin 1979, 93–94).

Throughout the hundreds of years of intentional breeding, no animal has ever matched the speed of cheetahs. My grandfather bred horses in Argentina where I was born. I know from experience

MECHANISMS OF EVOLUTION (THE HOUSE OF CARDS)

that selective breeding can bring out genetic factors that may be advantageous. My uncle did that with the cattle on our farm in Cuba.

Some breeders may breed for size and strength. The Clydesdale is a magnificently large and strong horse. You may have seen these marvelously majestic horses pulling the iconic Budweiser coach. Their strength was so great that loggers used them to pull huge tree trunks from the forest. But a horse will never be as large as an elephant. The elephant has a different set of genetic blueprints; it is a different kind.

Some may breed horses for speed, but there is a limit to a horse's speed no matter how long the breeding program. The species has a finite boundary, a finite amount of genetic variability. The boundary is created by the intrinsic genetic properties of the horse. We cannot breed beyond what genetic traits existed within them to begin with. In fact, if you isolate certain genes and interbreed them too long, the animals become weaker and prone to disease. Moreover, they eventually become sterile. Any horse breeder can tell you that.

Any dog breeder can also tell you that. It is hard to find German Shepherds today that do not suffer from hip problems due to excessive selective breeding. By the way, the German Shepherd is a wolfdog, a breed produced by mating a domestic dog with a wolf. The dog is classified a *Canis familiaris*, and the wolf is classified a *Canis lupus*. They are two different species but of the same kind.

Imagine every dog, from the Great Dane to the Chihuahua, as a descendent of the one proto-archetype dog, which also includes the many varieties of wolves, wild dogs, jackals, coyotes, and foxes. Within that proto-genotype existed the potential phenotypes of the immense variety of sizes, shapes, colors, temperaments, and defining features of all the dogs we see today. Bird dogs, hunting dogs, rescue dogs, cattle dogs, and even purse dogs came from the incredible variety within the genetic blueprint in dogs that formed its character complex. But no dog was ever bred into any other kind.

In fact, even some classified under a different genus are still of the same kind. The fox is of the genus *Vulpes*, which is in contrast to the dog genus *Canis*. Some may think that animals as different as foxes and dogs could not have come from the same ancestral kind. The interesting experiment of Russian geneticist Dmitry Belayev may shed some light on this. Belayev worked at a Russian fox farm that specialized in the pelts of silver foxes, a variant of the red fox (*Vulpes vulpes*), highly valued for their beautiful silver fur.

Belayev set out to breed tameness into the foxes. He classified cubs' responses to trainers and chose to breed only those who had allowed trainers to handle them while they fed them. After six generations, the ones classified as the tamest were categorized as the domesticated elite. After breeding the elite foxes for 35 generations, 70 to 80 percent of their offspring were classified as domesticated elite. But a curious thing happened; the foxes began to look and behave like dogs. They lost their foxy pelage and became piebald black and white in color.

Their morphology looked not like foxes but like Welsh collies. Instead of the prick ears of foxes, they developed floppy ears like dogs. Their tails turned up like some dogs rather than down like foxes. The females came into heat every six months, just like dogs, rather than once a year like foxes. The end result was a dog that looked, acted, and sounded like a dog.

Now evolutionary scientists may arbitrarily assign a member of the same kind the status of a different species or even genus. But that proves nothing. Those arbitrary assignations do not in any way show the evolution of one kind into another. We could breed those foxes for all eternity and still not produce any offspring that did not belong to that kind.

Neither has any horse breeder bred a different kind from a horse, no matter how intense the artificial selective pressure was engineered. If intentional selection cannot produce macroevolution, how can accidental/natural selection produce macroevolution?

MECHANISMS OF EVOLUTION (THE HOUSE OF CARDS)

Another iconic example of the efficacy of natural selection that has been used since the earliest days of the Darwinian revolution and has graced our biology textbooks is Darwin's finches from the Galapagos Islands. The term *Darwin's finches* was first used by Percy Lowe in 1936 when he wrote a book by that name. The great variation in the size of their beaks was seen as evidence of evolution in progress.

In his second edition of *The Voyage of the Beagle* (1845), Darwin wrote:

> Seeing this gradation and diversity of structure in one small, intimately related group of birds, one might really fancy that from an original paucity of birds in this archipelago, one species had been taken and modified for different ends (Darwin 1845, 185).

Darwin noticed that in this almost desert-like environment on this isolated archipelago, segments of these related finches had chosen to eat different parts of the cactus as well as a variety of seeds and flowers. The variations in their beaks allowed them special access to these differing parts of the existing food chain. He therefore concluded that the paucity of food created selective pressures that allowed the finches to grow different kinds of beaks.

1. Geospiza magnirostris. 2. Geospiza fortis.
3. Geospiza parvula. 4. Certhidea olivasea.

The four major variations in beak sizes and shapes for Darwin's finches

These small measures, he believed, could be extrapolated into the future, and it thus provided him with the grounds to think they could, in this gradual way, eventually accumulate enough changes to become a different species. But in fact, the observations he made only showed that there is great variation within the genetic pool of finches that creates their character complex. No finches were observed to evolve into another kind of bird.

The selective pressures simply help a certain phenotype survive in a given environment. The wide variation simply evidences the preexisting genetic variability that finches inherited from the proto-archetypical finch. In her excellent book *Total Truth,* Nancy Pearcey cites a modern study that brings this into focus:

> One of the most widely cited pieces of evidence for evolution is the variation among finches on the Galapagos Islands off the coast of South America. The finches are small, rather dull-looking birds, whose main claim on our interests is that their beak size differs according to the habitats where they live—suggesting that they have adapted to different conditions. Virtually every biology textbook repeats the story of Darwin's voyage to the Galapagos as a young naturalist, and contemporary biologists have gone back there to confirm his theory.
>
> Sure enough, one study found that during a period of drought, the average beak size among the finches actually increased slightly. Apparently the only food available in the dry period were larger, tougher seeds, so that the birds with slightly larger beaks survived better. Now, we're talking about a change measured in tenths of a millimeter—about the thickness of a thumbnail. Yet, it was hailed enthusiastically as confirmation of Darwin's theory. As one science writer exulted, this is evolution happening "before [our] very eyes."

MECHANISMS OF EVOLUTION (THE HOUSE OF CARDS)

But that was not the end of the story. Eventually, the rains returned, restoring the original range of seeds. And what happened then? The average beak size returned to normal. In other words, the change that Darwinists were so excited about turned out to be nothing more than a cyclical fluctuation. It did not put the finches on the road to evolving into a new kind of bird; it was simply a minor adaptation that allowed the species to survive in dry weather.

Which is to say, the change was a minor adjustment that allowed the finches to stay *finches* under adverse conditions. It did not demonstrate that they originally evolved from another kind of organism, nor that they are evolving into anything new.

When the National Academy of Sciences (NAS) put out a booklet on evolution for teachers, it decided the story really needed a more positive spin. And so, the booklet *did not mention* that the average beak size returned to normal. Instead, it speculated what might happen if the change were to continue indefinitely for some two hundred years—whether the process would even produce a "new kind of finch."

This was clearly a misleading treatment of the facts, suggesting that the change was directional rather than reversible. The *Wall Street Journal* responded with an apt rejoinder by Phillip Johnson: "When our leading scientists have to resort to the sort of distortion that would land a stock promoter in jail," he said, "you know they are in trouble."

Nor is the problem limited to finch beaks. Examples of minor, reversible diversification are the stock-in-trade of textbooks on biological evolution (Pearcey 2004, 158–59).

The fact that the genetic pool of a specific creature in a given habitat may vary the percentages of the phenotypes (outward physical appearance) expressed during specific selective pressures does not prove the evolutionary directional speculation that would lead inexorably to a different kind. Instead, what we see in nature is an oscillating and reversible expression of phenotypes defined by the selective pressure at that moment and restricted within the genetic limits of the character complex of each kind.

The Quantum Genes

It was previously thought, before Mendelian genetic science was understood, that the mixing of a male and female organism produces an offspring that is a hybridization of the two parents—similar to the mixing of blue paint and red paint to make purple paint. But this is not what happens with genes. A gene is a discreet packet of genetic information that remains intact, a quantum packet of hereditary information, if you will.

When two parents produce an offspring, the offspring contains a different combination of genes, some of which are either from the father or from the mother. Each particular gene of that offspring is in whole inherited from one and only one of the four grandparents of that offspring. Each set of grandparents had previously provided both the father and the mother with a reshuffling of their genes, like the reshuffling of cards. And now those parents provided a reshuffling of their genes to the offspring.

There is also a potential for reshuffling that allows for the differences between siblings. Plain observation should have shown us from the beginning that the paint-mixing idea could not be true. For example, when a male and a female mate and produce an offspring, they expect to get either a male or a female, not a hermaphrodite.

That reshuffling of the genes allows for great variability but not for an infinite number of variabilities. There is a finite number to the variants within the character complex of the parents that they can produce. And all variants remain within that kind.

MECHANISMS OF EVOLUTION (THE HOUSE OF CARDS)

The false idea in Darwin's day that inherited characteristics could be mixed like paints gave evolutionists the impression that an infinite amount of variability could eventually produce an organism that was far removed from the great-great-great-grandparents. Such is not the case. There are no new genes created through breeding. There is only the reshuffling of the genes that have been there from the beginning, which directly determines that particular kind with a fixed number of variabilities, even when that number is very great, indeed. That reshuffling capability is still a given finite number.

Natural selection simply allows one genetic variation to survive under adverse conditions over another. No new information is added to the genetic code. Contrary to Dawkins's boast, it is not evolution that is a fact; the fact is that no random process has ever been shown to create the gene expression system or change the genetic components of one kind into another. That is a fact that is undeniable. That is a fact that Dawkins cannot refute. That is a fact that history cannot deny. And yet it is a historical fact that the naturalist naysayers, motivated by their deophobia, continue to evade and obscure.

The examples used by biology teachers everywhere of organisms that have become resistant to poisons or medicines are very misleading. There is no new gene that offers the organism a new ability to resist the poison or the medicine. The gene was already there in the particular organism, which was resistant. The genetic traits were therefore selected favorably while the others were temporarily eliminated from the genetic pool. If conditions were to change, then the previous phenotype still present within the genotype that composes the character complex of that particular organism would rebound.

If natural selection cannot drive the evolutionary change from one species to another, then what can?

2. The Inheritance of Acquired Characteristics (the Second Wall)

Another mechanism originally proposed by evolutionists for the gradual development of one species into another was the inheritance of acquired characteristics. Most in the Baby Boomer generation have seen illustrations in the biology books of giraffes straining to reach the only leaves left on the treetop. Each successive picture showed an elongation of the neck as the result of a natural evolutionary process. Modern genetic science has shown conclusively that this is an utter genetic impossibility. No evolutionist today believes in this debunked mechanism, but it was heralded as true empirical data when Darwinism swept through academia. The academics are not always right.

One cannot pass on to offspring any characteristics acquired during their lifetime. Not a single trait can be passed to offspring unless it is already encoded in the genes from the moment of conception. At that precise moment, the combination of parental genes presets the genetic composition within the offspring of all creatures. Only what the organism received at conception—the combination of the two parental genes—can be passed on, bringing forth a uniquely encoded offspring.

That is to say, the children of Arnold Schwarzenegger will not automatically be born with a sculpted physique. The genes may determine whether his offspring will be tall, depending on the precise combination acquired between the two parents, but his sculpted muscular physique must be acquired through the same rigorous training during their lifetime. They must go through the same training to achieve the desired results that he obtained during his lifetime. Those learned behaviors or learned physical abilities are not magically transferred to the genes and then passed on to the offspring as Lamarck and Darwin had expected and dogmatically insisted on not so long ago.

One could say that selective pressure in a drought condition allowed those giraffes with longer necks to survive, which may therefore be reflected in an overall change in the genetic pool. The selective pressure then favored the phenotype of the longer neck, and this led to a change in predominance of this type of giraffe over another with a shorter neck, but the variability for the longer neck had to exist genetically from the beginning.

MECHANISMS OF EVOLUTION (THE HOUSE OF CARDS)

The genes of the long neck had been there all along. The environment did not cause the gene to appear. All the straining in the world would not cause the length to increase. And there is a limit to the length of the neck that was predetermined by the genes, which we can trace all the way back to the first proto-archetype giraffe.

Once again, it is important to point out that at the time of Darwin, very little was known about genetics. It was roughly about the same time that Mendel published his celebrated study of peas. Mendel, a devout Catholic monk, is now referred to as the father of genetics. Therefore, Darwin had very little knowledge of the science of genetics at that time, and neither did Lamarck.

Our technology has allowed us to travel light years from that time. And the once black box of genetics has become increasingly clearer as our technological advancements have allowed us to peer more deeply into the realm of molecules. The clearer our understanding of genetics becomes, the more evidence there is that evolution is not possible as it was imagined by Darwin. In fact, the only real evolution is the evolution of the theory of evolution that has had to reinvent itself continuously as each of its once fundamental building blocks has been proved false by new technology.

Modern genetecists today understand that our DNA determines the various characteristics of all human beings. However, the separate variations within the character complex of a species or kind have nothing to do with the radical genetic changes required to make a completely new kind. Richard C. Lewontin a prominent genetecist at Harvard University confesses that evolutionists do not really know how these radical changes happen. He says, *"We know virtually nothing about the genetic changes that occur in species formation"* (Lewontin 1974, 159; emphasis added).

In contrast to Lewontin's candid admission, evolutionists in Darwin's time insisted that we could pass on acquired characteristics through a medium they called gemmules. Do you suppose they imagined tiny mules were carrying gems? These gemmules were imagined to somehow pass on to germ cells an individual's acquired characteristics. Of course, this has been utterly discredited. There are no such things as gemmules.

Although all modern evolutionists have long ago conceded through the awareness brought upon us by genetics that the notion of acquired characteristics has been disproved, there are several reasons I have chosen to mention it:

1. So the reader can get a historical perspective of the speculative claims that were fundamental in Darwin's model and provided the wind behind the sails of his theory in academic circles.
2. So the reader might grasp the technological limitations that flawed Darwin's understanding of biological processes in the molecular level.
3. So the reader can recognize that all mechanisms (from Darwin's day until now) proposed for the evolution of one species into another have been systematically proved to be, in fact, spurious.

Plainly put, history has documented that there has been a progressive debunking of all evolutionary myths, which built the straw man of Darwin's theory. Although modern evolutionists no longer believe in Lamarckian evolution, they sometimes misleadingly give the impression that learned behavior could drive evolution forward. Let's look at one example:

> The idea of sculpture calls to mind the over-muscled physiques of human body-builders, and non-human equivalents such as the Belgian Blue breed of cattle. This walking beef factory has been contrived via a particular genetic alteration called "double muscling." There is a substance called myostatin, which limits muscle growth. If the gene that makes myostatin is disabled, muscles grow larger than usual. . . . Another example is the breed of pig called the Black

Exotic, and there are individual dogs of various breeds that show the same exaggerated musculature for the same reason. Human body-builders achieve a similar physique by an extreme regime of exercise, and often by the use of anabolic steroids: both environmental manipulations that mimic the genes of the Belgian Blue and the Black Exotic. *The end result is the same, and that is a lesson in itself. Genetic and environmental changes can produce identical outcomes* (emphasis added) (Dawkins 2009, 37–38).

While it is true that environmental changes can mimic the results of genetic alterations in the lifespan of an individual organism, these environmentally induced changes cannot be inherited; hence, they cannot add one iota to the evolution of the species. Therefore, they do not have identical outcomes from an evolutionary perspective. Dawkins's claim is spurious and misleading.

In light of a glaring absence of any selective mechanism that could drive forward the evolution of the species as scientists became more aware of genetics, most evolutionists placed their hopes in mutations. They reasoned that the alteration of the genes through chance mutations could accomplish the task of changing one species into another. This new interpretation of Darwinism was consequently labeled neo-Darwinism.

3. Mutations: Neo-Darwinism (the Third Wall)

Do you realize, reader, that you are an error of heredity, a biological error? . . . And not only *an* error, but an error on an enormous scale. At least, Darwinians say you are (Stove 1995, 307).

As the science of genetics "enlightened" Darwinists of the impossibility of explaining the origin of species through the mechanisms of either natural selection or the inheritance of acquired characteristics by their gradual evolutionary model, a new mechanism was sorely needed. Genetics brought forth a new possibility: the process of a mutation. Thus the theory of evolution evolved yet another step further away from Darwin's original speculations on the mechanisms that could change one species into another. Neo-Darwinism received a tremendous push in the middle of the nineteenth century by combining Mendelian inheritance and the science of population changes.

Since then, neo-Darwinism—with mutations as its principle collaborator for change in the species—has dominated evolutionary circles, with few exceptions. Neo-Darwinists hoped they could find a transmutation that could, in a single step, change one species into another. These were labeled macromutations. Others were a bit more reserved in their hopes and thought that a series of fortunate mutations could combine to create a new species. Only recently have scientists dared to diverge from the status quo and begin to shed some doubt on the new principal mechanism.

Multiple Mutations and Macromutations (the Hopeful Monsters Theory)

Two schools of thought developed regarding mutations. Classical neo-Darwinism depends on many chance mutations to produce significant changes in a population's genetic pool over a long period of time. It proposes that the mutations will cause a favorable capability or adaptation in the plant or animal that, through the process of natural selection of the fittest, would be favored and then passed down to offspring through genes. In this way, it was reasoned that these superiorly adapted specimens would eventually accumulate enough changes through the process of mutations to change into another species.

In other words, evolutionists theorized that eventually the process would result in a gradual change in phenotype that would ultimately culminate in a new genotype species after long periods of time.

MECHANISMS OF EVOLUTION (THE HOUSE OF CARDS)

The terms *genotype* and *phenotype* may be confusing. The genotype describes the genetic components that result in a particular physical appearance or phenotype.

Others believed that genetic change could take place in short periods through the process of macromutations. They hoped that large genetic changes could create a new species abruptly, but most believed in a more gradual evolutionary process.

A macromutation is a mutation that creates a large phenotypic change from the original form. For example, in fruit flies (Drosophilidae), a homeotic mutation transposes the legs to grow out of the antenna sockets forming an antennapedia. The idea that macromutations could in one fell swoop create a new species began to be known as the "hopeful monsters theory."

While it is true that a mutation may seem to bring a new expression of the genetic components by corrupting the genes, no new genetic information is created. Most of the time, mutations create a loss of information. When the information is changed and not altogether lost (corrupted), the results are almost invariably deleterious or lethal.

Nevertheless, there are some mutations that are survivable. However, there is a vast difference between survivability and beneficial that is notoriously overlooked by evolutionists who want to spin genetics as the new mechanism to change one species into another. The process is simply incapable of becoming the very underpinning of evolutionary change into another species.

The primary assumption of neo-Darwinism is that the mutations could give an organism a superior adaptive edge over their normal kin. But in reality, if anything, mutations add up to trouble and not hope for the species.

Regarding the hopeful monster macromutation, after many years of research, scientists have found that of the millions observed by scientists, no mutation has ever resulted in abruptly changing one species into another. Let me say that again. No macromutations have ever been observed to magically change one species into another. Those who claim otherwise are the history-deniers.

Evolutionists love to exclaim how many mutations are going on continually in order to create the appearance that under such large numbers there remains a chance for one good mutation to create a beneficial capacity to survive. But it must be noted that no mutations in somatic cells can be inherited. For a mutation to be inheritable, it must occur only in the sex germ cells.

Nevertheless, mutations are real, and they also impact our human family. Scientists tell us that mutations can occur from cosmic radiation or poisons that damage our genes. If the biblical model is correct, then we would expect that our early ancestors would have had a less polluted set of genes (fewer genetic mistakes). If so, then they would have been able to marry within closer familial lines without the potentially disastrous effects we face today since our genes have increased the accumulated number of genetic errors over time.

Our Judeo-Christian cosmological model stipulates that prior to the Great Flood, our planet was an almost perfect habitat for life. There were no frozen poles, and the temperature throughout the entire planet was very moderate. For this reason, we believe the First Earth had a small water vapor canopy that created a greenhouse effect and kept temperatures fairly even throughout the entire planet. We also believe the First Earth had a larger ozone layer than we have today. We surmise that was due to the 37 percent concentration of oxygen in the atmosphere compared to our present 21 percent. Both the water vapor canopy and the increased ozone layer would have afforded humans much greater protection from cosmic rays.

In addition, the most important protection we have against cosmic rays is our magnetosphere. There is good evidence that it is declining in strength and would have been greater before the Flood. Some scientists have declared that the strength of our magnetosphere has declined as much as 15 percent in the last 200 years. Some think it may be getting ready to flip poles. No one knows exactly how quickly that process could take place, but what is known is that during that transition, vast amounts of cosmic radiation would impact the Earth, causing havoc with our electrical grids and battering human beings with dangerous radiation. Such a calamity would markedly increase cancer-related deaths and mutations.

The truth is that our Second Earth is a much more hostile environment for humans than the First Earth. Certainly, the pollutants that industrialization has brought to our modern environment were not there prior to the Great Flood. The First Earth was covered in grasslands and forests that pumped greater amounts of oxygen into the atmosphere. All in all, the data seem to point to an increase in mutations in the future and a much-reduced rate of mutations in our ancient past.

Such is the evidence we have recorded of the history of humankind in the scriptures. We see that early humans were able to live much longer than today in spite of the fact that they were marrying within a much smaller genetic pool (we will address that more thoroughly in *The Death of the First Earth*). The age of death has steadily diminished since that time, and at some points in our history, we see that dramatically. In fact, this diminishing lifespan trend was not reversed until modern times through the miracle of antibiotics and the rise of modern agricultural yields that provided better nutrition for the masses.

So we can see that mutations have not helped humanity; on the contrary, they have negatively impacted our health and longevity. Mutations are the genetic evidence of the second law of thermodynamics. It is the measure of the increase in entropy in the gene expression system and could not have accounted for the formation of new species when, in fact, the gene expression system was at its optimum at the beginning of life. And it can be argued with almost certainty that the rate of mutations would have been much lower during the time of the First Earth and thus could not have impacted speciation in any way whatsoever.

The attempt to use mutations as the mechanism for the evolution of the species is evidence of evolutionists' deep desperation. It is not unlike their attempt to use black holes as the creators of galaxies when they are, in effect, the death of galaxies and the natural consequence of the increase in entropy predicted by the second law of thermodynamics.

The problem is not only that paleontologists have admitted that the fossil record does not bear witness to this gradual change from one species into another, but also that the very mechanism of mutation is now known to be inadequate as a credible mechanism for macroevolution.

A mutation occurs when, during the reproductive process, the DNA of the cell makes a copying mistake. These mistakes are almost always lethal, and when they are not, they are almost always harmful.

Scientists use a variety of methods to accelerate the rate of mutations in order to study their effects on organisms, including repeated radiation exposure. But under normal circumstances, the present normal rate of mutations is so tiny as to be almost negligible. It is estimated that a mutation occurs only one in 10 million times during cell division. That degree of error is so small that no man-made computer can even begin to approach it.

Moreover, the living cell is an amazingly complex system that is self-repairing. Our bodies were designed to repair the genes our environment might have damaged. Within the cell, there are 50 enzymes whose task is to locate any mutations, extract them, and then replace them with the correct nucleotide. That is another incredible example of specified complexity in our reproductive systems, which could not have been created through dysteleological chance reactions. It is evidence of a master design to maintain accuracy in the system.

The fact is that the major pillar of the entire neo-Darwinist theory depends on a very infrequent random chance mistake, which, if it occurs, (1) will hopefully not be lethal; (2) will hopefully not be harmful if, by chance, it was not lethal; and (3) if not lethal or harmful, will hopefully produce a characteristic that will enable the organism

MECHANISMS OF EVOLUTION (THE HOUSE OF CARDS)

to better survive in its environment. The key phrase in evolution is *better survive*, not just survivability. To be a valid mechanism for natural selection, it must produce an advantage over the previous genetic makeup of the creature.

There are, therefore, six major problems that mutations face as a mechanism for speciation in evolution:

1. It is doubtful that the sheer number of mutations is sufficient to account for macroevolution.
2. The evolutionist is hard-pressed to produce examples of beneficial mutations. No natural selective advantages have been documented from mutations.
3. No mutation has ever resulted in a new kind. It may alter the kind in some capacity, but the kind remains the same.
4. For this mutation to be passed on to the next generation, it must occur only in the sex cells; all other mutations are not inherited.
5. There is no record in the fossils of a gradual change from one kind into another.
6. Mutations never add new genes. They either corrupt or delete previous genetic information. The corruption of a gene does create new information in the changed gene but not necessarily a selective advantage. Therefore, to expect a mutated gene to create a new species is irrationally absurd.

Mutations in Single-Celled Organisms

In single-celled organisms where mutations have a more pronounced effect on the overall organism, the rapidly regenerating bacteria may show effects in a much shorter period of time. That would consequently provide, if you will, a fast-forward view of evolution, if it exists. Yet in all observed data, there has never been a mutation from bacterium to something else. There are adaptations within the particular kind but no change from one kind into another.

Evolutionists, hard put for any positive evidence that can substantiate their claim that mutations are a viable mechanism for macroevolution, have worked to simulate the effects that organisms would have, were they granted the long years they claim life has been evolving on Earth.

Dawkins brings special attention to an experiment undertaken by bacteriologist Richard Lenski of Michigan State University. He imagines that the results of this experiment are quite distressing to creationists. I wonder which creationist he spoke to who was distressed by this experiment?

> As we shall see, the Lenski experiments are distressing to creationists, for very good reason. They are a beautiful demonstration of evolution in action, something it is hard to laugh off even when your motivation to do so is very strong. And the motivation for dyed-in-the-wool creationists is very strong indeed (Dawkins 2009, 117).

The experiment was done with the *E. coli* bacterium. In 1988, Lenski began the experiment by taking 12 identical flasks with the same nutrient broth and infusing the flasks with identically cloned bacteria.

> These twelve flasks founded twelve lines of evolution that were destined to be kept separate from one another for two decades and counting.... The twelve tribes of bacteria were not kept in the same twelve flasks for all that time. On the contrary, each tribe had a new flask every day. Imagine twelve *lines* of flasks, stretching away into the distance, each line more than 7,000 flasks long! Every day, for each of the twelve tribes, a new virgin flask was infected with liquid from the previous day's flask. A small sample, exactly one-hundredth of the volume of the old flask, was drawn out and squirted into the new flask, which contained a

MECHANISMS OF EVOLUTION (THE HOUSE OF CARDS)

fresh supply of glucose-rich broth. The population of the bacteria in the flask then started to skyrocket; but it always levelled off by the next day as the supply of food gave out and starvation set in. In other words, the population in every flask multiplied itself hugely, then reached a plateau, at which point a new infective sample was drawn out and the cycle renewed the next day. Thousands of times through their high-speed equivalent of geological time, therefore, these bacteria went through the same daily repeated cycles of bonanza expansion, followed by starvation, from which a lucky hundredth were rescued and carried, in a glass Noah's Ark, to a fresh—but again temporary—glucose bonanza: perfect perfect perfect conditions for evolution, and, what is more, the experiment was done in twelve separate lines in parallel.

Lenski and his team have continued this daily routine for more than twenty years so far. This means about 7,000 "flask generations" and 45,000 bacterial generations—averaging between six and seven bacterial generations per day. To put that into perspective, if we were to go back 45,000 human generations, that would be about a million years, back to the time of *Homo erectus* (Dawkins 2009, 118–19).

What were the supposedly distressing results for creationists? What was this supposed proof of evolution that had creationists laughing nervously?

In these conditions, the Darwinian expectation was that if any mutation arose that assisted an individual bacterium to exploit glucose more efficiently, natural selection would favour it, and it would spread through the flask as mutant individuals out-produced non-mutant individuals.... Well, this is exactly what happened in all twelve tribes (Dawkins 2009, 121).

Let me see. A million years of generations in "perfect perfect perfect conditions for evolution," and they still ended up with *E. coli* bacterium? Can you imagine that? Mr. Dawkins, just how do you imagine that to be distressing to us? All the experiment accomplished is to show the dyed-in-the-wool evolutionists that microevolution within a species exists.

Not one proponent of intelligent design or any creationist scientist I know refutes the fact that variations within a kind exist that form a character complex. Some variations may be more advantageous than others in a particular environment. Mutations can occur that may corrupt and alter the genetic code, but no macromutations exist that change one kind into another.

Even after these many generations, the *E. coli* bacterium does not evolve into anything other than an *E. coli* bacterium. A million years of evolution and yet a single-celled bacterium did not even change into either a different kind of bacterium or a multicellular organism. Hmm! Who is laughing nervously?

First, Dawkins did not produce any evidence that the adaptation was due to a mutation and not a genetic variant that was there from the very beginning. At the very best, all he can say is that mutations in single-celled organism are not as deleterious as in multicellular organisms, which is not quite as distressing to us as Dawkins imagines.

It is Dawkins who should be distressed by the failure of the bacterium to evolve into something else throughout a million years of evolution. If evolution were true, then one would expect that after a million years of evolution, the *E. coli* bacterium would have at least become a colonial organism, even if not a multicellular organism.

In fact, Mr. Dawkins, I predict that after a billion years of evolution, this experiment would not produce anything other than an *E coli* bacterium. And I challenge you to reconsider your presupposition when that day comes and my prediction is fulfilled. Even though your motivation to be autonomous from God is very strong, indeed, perhaps you might open your eyes to truth. Evolution is only in your mind. It seems to me that you, Mr. Dawkins, ought to heed Aristotle's advice regarding the theory of evolution:

> We must not accept a general principle from logic only, but must prove its application to each fact. For it is in facts that we must seek general principles, and these must always accord with facts. Experience furnishes the particular facts from which induction is the pathway to general laws (Aristotle).

If the facts do not substantiate the principle, no matter how logical it might seem to the theorist, it must be discarded from consideration.

Mutations in Multicellular Organisms

Most of the examples proposed by evolutionists as beneficial mutations, such as flies with multiple sets of wings or mountain goats with short legs, are inadequately categorized. In an environment of selective pressures, these mutants would be the least likely to survive. A mutation in a multicellular organism is almost invariably a handicap instead of an improvement in the survivability of the organism.

Typically, scientists experimenting with mutations will use either single-celled organisms or creatures such as flies, which have a very short life span and can therefore generate the expressions quite frequently. For more than half a century, scientists have been radiating these insects with the hope of finding a way to prove their evolutionary hypothesis. What have they accomplished?

First, they have mutated flies that are wingless. These poor little guys have to run all day long. They don't stand a chance of getting away from a frog or a lizard. They have also made flies with wrinkled tiny wings. They simply cannot fly. They also have to run, but they look better doing so with those cute wrinkled wings.

Then they have the flies with no eyes. These cannot fly or run because they cannot see where they are going. Apparently, flies have not yet evolved to the Braille method of flying. Then they have flies with vestigial wings. They have a mutation in the "vestigial gene" on the second chromosome.

I strongly suspect that evolutionists very much like calling things "vestigial organs." But these vestigial wings are not some throwback to an example of an evolving wing. The wings are so tiny that they are utterly useless. What selective advantage would this small wing have that it could be passed on to their offspring and eventually evolve into a full-fledged wing? Unfortunately, these flies also have to run all day. I hope they have a good pair of sneakers. Naming these tiny wings vestigial wings is purely deceptive. It is not evolution that they represent, but rather genetic devolution.

Then we have the flies with curled wings. Instead of the flat wings resting over their bodies facing toward their backs, they are curled wings stretched out sideways like airplane wings. This mutation is on the "curly wing gene" on the second chromosome. I have to admit, they look cool. They look like they have small jet engines on their wings. I suppose that could give them a survival advantage by intimidation. But it's all bluster; they do not have a bomber bay. Oh, and then there is this other tiny problem to consider. The problem with this mutation is that it is a dominant mutation. That means that if only one parent has the mutated gene, the curled wings will appear on the offspring. But if both parents have the gene, the offspring will die. Oops! This may not be a good survival strategy. Just saying!

Have you ever stuck your finger in your eye? Imagine a leg. That leads me to my favorite fly mutant, the leg-headed fly. You read correctly. Each head has two legs sticking out of it. Well, I have to hand it to the evolutionists; they finally came up with a beneficial mutation. This fly can work for the circus.

Imagine being able to kick everything you see. That must be a wonderful benefit, except it would be hard on the budget to buy that many sneakers. These flies have a mutation in their antenna gene that causes it to grow a leg, and the mutated gene becomes an "antennapedia gene." The mutated gene instructs the cells that normally become antenna to become legs. I can relate to that gene; I am a "leg man" myself.

Then they have the "show-off fly" with four wings. They have double recessive mutated bx-c genes. That is, there is a recessive mutation in the bithorax gene (bx) and also a recessive mutation in the postbithorax gene (pbx), which causes the fly to have two pairs of wings. But unfortunately, the rear ones are just to show off; they don't have an "on" and "off" switch, and they don't work. But a little gel on the back wings, and man, can they strut! They have a tendency to be a bit narcissistic, but I must admit, they do look good doing it.

Perhaps it is the Darwinists that must be distressed over their failure to create, discover, or invent a viable mechanism for macroevolution, even though their deophobic motivation is very strong, indeed.

Well, I think by now the reader is getting the message. All the intense radiation experiments have yet to produce a different organism through mutations. Those they do produce are weaker and dysfunctional members of the same kind; that is, if the mutation does not kill them.

Some evolutionists point to single mutations in dogs that allow breeders to produce unique expressions of this kind as evidence that mutations can create large changes. Wow! Evolution right before our eyes! For example, the genetic mutation called *achondroplasia* is a single-step mutation that causes a drastic phenotype change in dogs. It causes them to have very short legs like basset hounds or dachshunds.

The dogs may look cute, but in a natural environment, it would not be a beneficial mutation, and they would likely not survive in the wild. A similar mutation causes the most common kind of human dwarfism. They have a body with a trunk that is nearly the normal size, while their legs and arms are very short. But in each of these cases, the mutation does not change the organism from one kind into another. It simply alters the phenotype and creates a handicap rather than an advantageous adaptation.

In short, experiments with single-celled or multicellular organisms have not yielded any proof of evolution. No mutation experiments in single-celled organisms have ever produced multicellular organisms or even a different kind of the unicellular organism.

Nevertheless, evolutionists have used the mutation argument to posit that certain selective advantages could be garnered by these mutations that would enhance an organism's survivability in a particular environment. An example of such an advantage is the difference in human skin pigments. It is claimed that people with dark skin pigmentation living in equatorial regions have a marked selective advantage over people with light skin, which would be more susceptible to skin cancer and severe sunburn.

They thus posit that people who have a mutation in their genes that would inhibit the production of melanin would most likely be more prone to get skin cancer and die before reproducing. That would naturally create a selective advantage to darker-skinned people in equatorial regions.

Conversely, those with darker skin living in more northern climates would be less apt to receive the necessary amount of ultraviolet light necessary for their bodies to synthesize vitamin D due to the melanin that causes the darker skin pigmentation, making these darker-skinned people more at risk to contract rickets in low-light latitudes.

A common consequence of childhood rickets is the narrowing of the pelvis, causing women who have suffered from rickets to have a much higher mortality risk during childbirth. That, of course, would consequently result in a selective disadvantage for them in regions with less light.

In other words, the increased amount of light in equatorial regions would sufficiently penetrate darker pigmented skin, allowing those individuals to synthesize vitamin D. But in more moderate regions with less light, darker skin would inhibit the proper amount of ultraviolet light necessary to synthesize vitamin D.

But there are two problems with this argument for the evolutionist. The first is that it is quite doubtful that the production of melanin, or the opposite inhibition of the production of melanin, was caused by a genetic mutation. It is more probable that the primordial genetic human stock had both genes within the genetic pool of our ancient ancestors.

The second problem is that although we concede that certain selective pressures can change the predominant genotype within a genetic pool, this particular example is a rather weak selective pressure. It is doubtful that this particular characteristic alone could have resulted in the complete eradication of humans with dark pigmentation from low-light climates.

If this were so, then we would be able to notice the high mortality rate within our own generation for individuals with darker skin living in northern climates. It is possible that the selective advantage simply created a more favorable condition that would predispose humans with a given skin pigmentation to want to reside where they were best suited to survive, or even yet, where they were more comfortable in a given environment. But it is more likely that the result of that division was simply that the ancestors who colonized that region simply had this trait when they arrived there.

The proof that mutations did not cause this selective propensity is found in Tasmania. The aboriginal natives of Tasmania, before they were completely exterminated by European settlers, had very dark skin, yet the latitude of the Island of Tasmania in the Southern Hemisphere is comparable to the latitude of the state of Massachusetts in the New England area of the United States. In other words, Massachusetts is the counterpart of the Island of Tasmania in the Northern Hemisphere, not quite what one would call an equatorial region.

Even if we were to grant the more exaggerated dates of evolutionary designation to the time they inhabited the Island of Tasmania, which is reported by evolutionists as some 8,000 years, no mutations of that kind occurred in the entire 8,000 years. Throughout their entire history, the inhabitants remained quite dark.

But this evidence is not exclusive to Tasmania. North American Indians with moderately dark skin pigmentation also existed for thousands of years in the Pacific Northwest, with no such mutations creating a shift in the genetic pool to a lighter-skinned people. As a matter of fact, when mutations do occur in such individuals as albinos, whether in northern latitudes or equatorial latitudes, there is no selective advantage in either place.

It is not surprising that renowned scientist Ernest Chain, a Nobel Prize winner for his research in penicillin, said this:

> *To postulate that the development and survival of the fittest is entirely a consequence of chance mutations seems to me a hypothesis based on no evidence and irreconcilable with the facts.* These classical evolutionary theories are a gross oversimplification of an immensely complex and intricate mass of facts, and it amazes me that they are swallowed so uncritically and readily, and for such a long time, by so many scientists without a murmur of protest (emphasis added) (Chain 1982, 34).

The fact that mutations can bring about changes within a species is an accepted fact that in no way contradicts the Judeo-Christian worldview. However, the assumption that these mutations lead to a change from one kind into another is an unverifiable speculation. It is nothing more than a wish projection propagated as science by the religion of scientism to augment their subjective metaphysical choice of a materialistic origin to life.

Mechanisms of Evolution (The House of Cards)

Mutations in Viruses

Examples of viruses mutating are spurious since a virus is simply an RNA molecule and, according to most scientists, not even considered a living entity. Again, there are no examples of single-cell bacteria becoming multicellular through mutations. If a bacterium mutates and, by luck, the new organism is resistant to an antibiotic, there is a noted change in the overall genetic pool that results in one genotype becoming more predominant than the other. But that change does not result in another kind of organism; it is still a bacterium.

No serious scientist, whether in the creationist camp or the intelligent design camp, denies that the genetic pool of a species provides for a wide variety of phenotypes. As selective pressures allow for one gene characteristic to become more successful in a given environment, it is only logical that those characteristics give the organism a favorable opportunity to thrive over those that do not.

In that same way, one could theoretically speculate that mutations can, on very rare occasions, produce changes within the species that may add a selective advantage, but it never changes the species into another. And the positive advantages gained by such mutations are so extremely rare compared to the overwhelming number that are either lethal or debilitating that they could never have been the large-scale mechanism for the evolution of the species of all organisms.

Most geneticists today, even when remaining in the evolutionary camp, have conceded that macromutations have never been shown to change any organism into another species:

> Mutation, of course found a home in the new evolutionary genetics, but in a scaled down fashion—*not as the macromutations that had been believed capable of instantly creating a new species*, but as a process continually generating variability randomly and by small degrees. Geneticists came to stress the detrimental nature of most mutations (emphasis added) (Stanley 1981, 67).

But the gradual change of one species into another is not borne out by the evidence recorded in the fossil record, and it is not borne out in the evidence brought forth in laboratory conditions. No mutation, whether accumulated micromutations over long periods of time or macromutations, even when artificially produced in laboratory conditions, has ever produced a new species.

Darwin's Fantasyland Revived

The scientist who accepts macroevolution does so with a blind leap of faith in a scientifically unverifiable postulate. But many biologists are still doggedly insisting that the king has clothes. Since the physical evidence contradicts their hypothesis, they conjure speculative scenarios on which they can hang their hats. Francis Crick proposes alien sources to explain how dead molecules could have evolved into life and left no record of it on Earth. Darwin did similarly:

> *For many years, the fossil record of advanced life seemed to appear suddenly,* in rocks more than half a billion years old, more or less at what we recognize as the base of the Cambrian, but it was not clear that this resulted from sudden evolution. What was clear early on was that this most obvious biotic discontinuity of the entire geologic column deserved special recognition. . . . *How could Darwin's gradualistic evolution be squared with the sudden appearance in the fossil record of varied forms of higher life? His only recourse was to conjure up a long, hidden interval during which higher forms evolved* (emphasis added) (Stanley 1981, 67).

This "hidden interval" Stanley is referring to is the fantasyland interval conjured up by Darwin and Huxley to explain the lack of transitional fossils necessary to explain the evolution of higher life not found in the geologic column. Both Darwin and Huxley had envisioned a lost continent of the Late Paleozoic and Mesozoic

MECHANISMS OF EVOLUTION (THE HOUSE OF CARDS)

Ages, upon which the many advanced mammal groups of the Early Cenozoic might have evolved in a gradual fashion before making their way to Eurasia and America. The in-betweens (intermediate forms) must have evolved in another place, a hidden place.

Conjuring seems to be a popular evolutionary habit. It is the hidden interval that Crick proposes exists in other planets that long ago seeded ours with life when space trash was left here. Of course, this is not really speculation. It is "pure" and "bona fide" science because it helps the evolutionary paradigm. How convenient!

Their thinking goes something like this. Since we know evolution is a fact, any evidence against it must be explained away through highly improbable, miraculous, unprovable, unobservable, untestable, conjectures—but *not* divine intervention. Oh, I see!

This obstinate adherence to the evolutionary concept, in spite of the facts, is fundamentally a direct result of their dogmatic philosophical presupposition. If one begins from a premise that there can be no God in this material universe, then one must resort to an inevitable leap of faith in order to explain our existence.

We have seen this in the alternative universes dreamed up to prop up the chances for chemical evolution to bring forth our universe and the life that inhabits the Earth. We have seen it in the space trash theory that imagines that life must have come from an alien planet to explain its inordinately and unexpected specified complexity in the most fundamental level. And we see it also in this fantasyland imagined by Darwin and Huxley that would contain the fossil evidence in the strata that would document the in-betweens not visible in our strata.

We have seen it in the Anthropic Principle, which stipulates that man is the cause that began the evolutionary process. We have seen it using the Kantian notion that only what man observes is reality. Since man observes the universe, it must have been man who caused the universe to exist. Be it a fantasyland, an alternative universe, an alien planet, or the absurd idea that man in the present is the cause of reality in the past, the leap of faith into the irrational is their only escape. We have seen it in all the proposed mechanisms for the evolution of species as each has shown itself deficient to show how one species can turn into another.

Our Earth simply does not harbor the evidence of evolution. Hence, evolutionists must again turn to their magic wand and fairy dust to produce an imaginary continent where the evidence supposedly abounds. Unfortunately, this is out of reach for those of us who live in the real world without magic wands.

Some evolutionists may balk at this, and in all fairness, no evolutionist today believes in this fantasyland, for our satellites have scoured every inch of this planet. But that is only because time has shown this premise to be untrue.

At one time, many evolutionary scientists accepted this as scientifically credible. Even Hollywood took note of it, and movies of lost continents inhabited by dinosaurs became popular. And although the particulars may be different, the same tunnel vision created by their underlying atheistic bias still reigns supreme in evolutionary circles. That is evidenced by their dogged insistence that mutations can create new species when science has amply shown otherwise.

The only examples evolutionists can produce of greater survivability due to mutations are bacteria or viruses, which are much simpler organisms and can hardly give credence to their claims since the mutations always produce either a virus or bacteria accordingly. The virus never mutates into a bacterium, and the bacterium never mutates into something other than a bacterium.

To assert that gradual change due to mutations can cumulatively reach the point of evolving into another kind is at best wishful thinking on their part. There has never been a documented, naturally occurring transmutation or macromutation (a mutation that created a different kind) in the annals of science, a fact that cannot be denied even by prominent evolutionists. "[N]o human has ever seen a new species form in nature" (Stanley 1981, 71).

In conclusion, the real fact is that mutations do not actually add any new genetic information to an organism. Instead, they reduce the amount of genetic information originally there. They corrupt the genetic information. The corruption is new, but it is not functionally more proficient. It could therefore never hope to be the source of providing the added functional genetic information necessary that could lead to a more complex new species.

Lee Spetner, who holds a Ph.D. in physics from Massachusetts Institute of Technology, has studied the issue of new information extensively. In his book *Not By Chance*, Spetner wrote,

"But in all the reading I've done in the life-science literature, I've never found a mutation that added information. The NDT (neo-Darwinian Theory) says, not only that such mutations must occur, they must also be probable enough for a long sequence of them to lead to macroevolution. . . . All point mutations that have been studied on the molecular level turn out to reduce the genetic information and not to increase it."

Spetner says that mutations *reduce* genetic information. In extremely rare circumstances mutations turn out to be an advantage to the creature in a particular environment; even so, it is from a loss of information (Bendewald and Sherwin 2004, 33–34).

We can say that a mutation can cause a new genetic makeup by the alteration of the particular gene affected, but there is no evidence that this leads to an increase in genetic information or a more complex and beneficial form. There is new information that shows a preprogrammed scrambling ability in some genes such as the HLA gene that is so important for our immune system. That, however, does not point to an accidental process but rather a preprogrammed process engineered to increase our immune system's capacity to protect us against new pathogen foes. Furthermore, they cannot rationally be called mutations since they are preprogrammed modules not caused by deleterious cosmic rays or ultraviolet bombardment.

Mutations: The Measure of the Decay of the Human Race

It is important to correct a common misimpression created by the misinformation propaganda of evolutionary apologists. Contrary to those apologists' misguided claims, creationists and intelligent design advocates do not teach that mutations do not exist. Quite the contrary, they believe that mutations are, in fact, rising in frequency.

Actually, what is amazing is that even today, the entire human population has a very low genetic diversity. Evolutionists therefore claim that humankind went through a near extinction bottleneck that reduced the overall original diversity. They are right, of course; they just don't realize that it is the consequence of the Great Flood and Noah's ark.

What creationists claim is that mutations do not provide the mechanism for an upward evolutionary ascent into a more perfect species, as evolutionists claim. Quite the contrary, mutations are the measurement of our decay from the original and more perfect specimens of Adam and Eve, and those mutations are building in speed as time moves forward.

We do not deny that mutations can be survivable, but there is a dramatic difference between survivability and the evolutionary claim that they can be beneficial. Mutations most often delete and sometimes corrupt and scramble information, and in doing so, they alter the original design of our human species and can produce changes within our kind in a horizontal fashion, which is cumulatively the literal measure of our decay from our original intended state.

Not all mutations, however, are lethal. Some are survivable but carry negative consequences as the number of mutations accumulate.

MECHANISMS OF EVOLUTION (THE HOUSE OF CARDS)

We can call these slightly deleterious. It is quite curious how slightly deleterious mutations seem to be invisible to the natural selection process that ought to move us in an upward direction by choosing the good and discarding the bad.

Strikingly important to the unmasking of the evolutionary illusion is that the increase in the negative mutations in our species proves without question that natural selection has failed to remove them and create a more perfect human being. It is the empirical evidence of the descent of man instead of the evolutionary imagination that we ascended from apes through beneficial mutations. We are not evolving; we are, in fact, devolving, no matter how much we advance in technology.

It is an empirical fact that mutations are increasing as we see the effect in the variations created in subpopulation groups that developed after the dispersion of the Tower of Babel, which, as a consequence, isolated our human family into distinct geographical areas. That increase in mutations is what makes the union of siblings so dangerous, which could result in offspring with severe handicaps. It is the reason that inbreeding today can cause many medical deficiencies in offspring.

It is again important to reiterate that only germline mutations are inheritable. Somatic cell mutations cannot be inherited. However, the fact that mutations are occurring in somatic cells at an ever-increasing rate may quite likely be the reason for the rise in cancer and many other diseases that seem to be on the rise in our modern culture. Those somatic cell mutations now number in the trillions during a normal human life span.

I find it quite ludicrous that evolutionists try to use the number of mutations as an accurate and reliable chronograph that could allow us to date the age of humanity. It is essential to understand that the rate of mutations is directly tied to the rate of cosmic ray bombardments our bodies receive. That cosmic radiation rate is subsequently dependent on two things:

1. *The energy output of our sun.* It is the intensity of our sun that determines the cosmic ray output it provides. The amount of energy that reaches Earth's surface atmosphere at any given point is called the total solar irradiance. The measure of the total incoming solar electromagnetic radiation is called the solar constant.

    The problem is that the sun is, in fact, heating up as it ages. The solar constant is increasing, and so is the total solar irradiance. But what is most alarming is that the amount of radiation hitting us is escalating at an even steeper rate due to our diminishing protective systems.

    So delicate is that balance to the habitability of Earth that if the solar constant increases only 6 percent, Earth would hurl headlong into a runaway greenhouse effect, and our oceans would boil away into space as they did on Mars.

Life as we know it on Earth is linked to our star, the sun, which provides our planet with just the right amount of heat and energy for liquid water to be stable in our lakes, rivers and oceans. However, as the Sun ages, it is steadily growing brighter and brighter. Eventually, the sunlight that supports life will become too great, and it will bring an end to habitability on our planet (Gronstal 2014).

Earth's sun seems to operate on an 11-year cycle when the solar constant is impacted by an increase in solar electromagnetic storms. We see those electromagnetic twisting storms as darkened sunspots. As these twisting currents are shot arching outward into space from the Sun's corona, they often break and shoot outward into the solar system as coronal mass ejections. The solar wind created by these cosmic rays is what causes comet tails to light up. But that cosmic radiation is variable over many time scales, and that variability is a parameter that cannot be known absolutely.

For the past three decades NASA scientists have investigated the unique relationship between the sun and Earth. Using space-based tools, like the Solar Radiation and Climate Experiment (SORCE), they have studied how much solar energy illuminates Earth, and explored what happens to that energy once it penetrates the atmosphere. The amount of energy that reaches Earth's outer atmosphere is called the total solar irradiance. Total solar irradiance is variable over many different timescales, ranging from seconds to centuries due to changes in solar activity (Gran 2008).

2. The second determinant of the cosmic ray interaction with humans that causes inheritable germ cell mutations, as well as the non-inheritable somatic cell mutations, is the degree of protection Earth provides against the incoming cosmic rays to shield humankind.
   a. Primarily, our protection against mutations is a function of the strength of our magnetosphere, which acts like an electromagnetic umbrella to repel those cosmic rays. The evidence shows that our magnetosphere has not been constant and is, in fact, now diminishing at an alarming rate. We will speak further on that in the section on radiometric dating.
   b. Second, the thickness and size of our ozone layer is also critical in forming a buffer for us against these deadly rays. The evidence that the First Earth contained 37 percent oxygen (compared to 21 percent today) would have provided for its inhabitants a much more robust protection from cosmic rays. Evidence shows that our ionosphere also has not

been constant and is, in fact, thinning at an alarming rate. Our ozone layer now contains major holes over large areas of Earth's poles. Evolutionists do not dispute this, but environmentalists herald it with deep concerns for our future.

c. If, in fact, the First Earth contained a thin water vapor canopy that allowed the entire Earth to have a temperate climate, that would have provided another layer of protection against harmful cosmic rays, which we no longer have.

Therefore, the evolutionary tendency to use mutation rates as a reliable chronometer naïvely assumes five unprovable assumptions:

1. The cosmic radiation coming from the sun has been a constant throughout human history.
2. There have been no changes to the thickness of our ozone layer, a region in our stratosphere that absorbs most of the ultraviolet radiation from the sun.
3. There have been no changes in the thickness of our ionosphere, a region above the mesosphere composed of ionized gases (with free electrons) that extends from 50 to 600 miles above Earth's surface.
4. Our magnetosphere has been constant in strength throughout all human history.
5. The First Earth did not have a thin water vapor canopy to protect our early descendants more perfectly from cosmic radiation.

It is either naïvely absurd or intentionally deceptive to claim these five assumptions as empirical data that can provide us with a reliable chronometer. If anything, what the empirical data show is that mutations are increasing at an alarming rate, which goes directly against the evolutionary ideology that natural selection is improving our human species.

Artificially Induced Evolution

We must now consider the possibility that man, playing god, is now able to artificially induce evolution by manipulating the genes externally. With modern technological advancements in genetic splicing, man has entered into a new era. He has crossed into a territory heretofore not trod by man. We are delving into an area that will bring upon humankind dire societal consequences.

Do not misunderstand me. I am not speaking about correcting genetic problems through recombinant gene splicing. I am speaking about synthesizing several species into another completely different species. Man, through recombinant gene splicing, is now able to create genetic hybrid monsters. And these experiments are not some science fiction scenario in the distant future; they are a very real reality today. H. G. Wells's *The Island of Dr. Moreau* is no longer in the future, and it is no longer science fiction. But that will by no means prove evolution since it could never happen in the natural.

You might say that these are hypothetical futuristic scenarios and will never happen in the United States. Think again! On October 5, 2000, as we entered into our third millennium after Christ, our world crossed over into a dark moment of history that few know about. In a biotech consortium, a research breakthrough was announced that sends shivers up my spine every time I think of it. Joseph Bottum, the books and arts editor of *The Weekly Standard*, wrote this in his article, "The Pig-Man Cometh":

> On Thursday, October 5, it was revealed that biotechnology researchers had successfully created a hybrid of a human being and a pig. A man-pig. A pig-man. The reality is so unspeakable, the words themselves don't want to go together (Bottum 2000).

The Australian company Stem Cell Sciences, in conjunction with American company Biotransplant, successfully created a pig-human, a chimera hybrid, by inserting a human somatic fetal cell into the egg of a pig. Theoretically, the embryo that resulted could have been implanted either in a human or a pig. Make no mistake, we are well on the way to the future posthuman or transhuman race and the creation of a hybrid slave caste that will serve to maintain the genetic elite.

Our modern advancements in science have allowed us to transplant organs with increasing success. However, it is estimated that some 16 people in Europe and some 22 people in the United States die every day while waiting to receive an organ that does not become available. A few years ago, scientists believed that by using an artificial scaffold, they might be able to create organs with stem cells called progenitor cells, which have the innate ability to form into different kinds of tissue. But as it turns out, creating an actual functioning organ was much more difficult then anticipated.

Sixteen years after Botum wrote "The Pig-Man Cometh," the focus has turned to creating chimera that can host the organ's development within them, which scientists would then harvest at the end of the gestational period. What is chimera? It is a half-human, half-animal hybrid created by man through genetic manipulations.

In 2016, *Scientific American* published an article by Juan Carlos Izpisúa Belmonte called "Human Organs from Animal Bodies." Apparently, the bioethics of the industry has moved further along their evolutionary path into accepting that as normal. Belmonte, who is involved with the Salk Institute, received a bachelor's degree in pharmacy and science from the University of Valencia, Spain; a PhD from the Universities of Bologna, Italy, and Valencia, Spain; and postdoctoral fellows at the University of Marburg, European Molecular Biology Laboratories at Heidelberg, Germany, and the University of California, Los Angeles.

The research for this experiment is being carried out in California and Spain. The procedure begins with a genetic tool that acts as scissors to cut out a wanted gene from the pig embryo. The gene is called CRISPR/Cas9, and it targets the Pdx1 gene in the embryo, which is responsible for triggering the growth of the pancreas. The pancreas is, of course, where the beta cells in the Islets of Langerhans create the insulin molecule that allows us to use glucose in our metabolism. People with diabetes have malfunctioning beta cells, so the harvesting of the pancreas could provide a very profitable market niche.

Once the CRISPR tool removes the pig's Pdx1 gene, the fertilized egg is allowed to grow into the blastocyst. The pig's cells divide over and over again until they reach the blastocyst stage, which is when the differentiative process begins that turns certain cells into their predesigned organs. At that point, the scientists inject into the blastocyst human stem cells containing the missing Pdx1 gene, which then replaces the pig's gene. The blastocyst is now a chimeric animal composed of pig and human genes. The goal is to grow a human pancreas or any other desired organ inside the half-human, half-pig body.

They then implant the chimeric blastocyst into a surrogate sow and allow it to develop to term. Pigs gestate for four months, but humans take nine months to mature, so scientists hope to develop ways to trick the organ into growing faster.

> My colleagues and I believe that it may be possible to grow organs—made entirely, or almost entirely, of human cells—in an animal such as a pig or cow. The resulting animal would be a chimera—a creature that combines the parts of two different species, much like the mythical griffin, which sports the head and wings of an eagle and the body of a lion. Our dream is to create a chimera by injecting human stem cells into carefully prepared animal embryos so that when they become fully grown, they contain some organs made up of human cells. After sacrificing the animal we would then harvest the single heart, liver, or kidney made up of human cells and give it to a person in need of the transplant (Belmonte 2016, 34).

Experiments in mice to grow rat organs have proved quite successful. But the difference between a rat and a mouse is not the same as the difference between a human and a pig or a human and a cow. In the diagram illustrating the six-step process in the above *Scientific American* article, there is a small box in the center of the diagram written in a very light shade that is almost unreadable —unlike all the other comments, which are in dark ink. It states, "During development, some of the human cells may infiltrate other areas besides the pancreas, which could sometimes be undesirable" (Belmonte 2016, 34).

Now that is the understatement of the year. The truth is that these human stem cells may migrate into either sperm cells or eggs, which could cause the chimera to reproduce a half-human, half-pig chimera. There is also a danger of that happening with the surrogate sow. Another danger is a human cell migrating into the nerve cells and creating a hybrid creature with a human brain and a human conscience. If you think I am sensationalizing, then hear it from the words of the article:

> There are additional concerns, however, that are specific to this technology. Truly naïve stem cells, as I have said, can give rise to any kind of tissue. But we must pay special attention to three types—nerves, sperm and eggs—because humanizing these tissues in animals could give rise to creatures that no one wants to create.
>
> Imagine the human nightmare, for example, if enough human nerves populated a pig's brain that it became capable of higher-level reasoning.... Although it is a long shot, there is always the chance that some of the human stem cells we implant could migrate to the niche that gives rise to the reproductive system instead of staying in the desired niche that yields the desired organ. The result would be animals that produced sperm or eggs that are virtually iden-

tical to those found in people. Allowing these animals to breed would lead to the ethically disastrous case in which a fully human fetus (the result of a humanized sperm from one pig fertilizing a humanized egg from another) starts growing inside a farm animal (Belmonte 2016, 37).

While growing a fully human being in a farm animal is, in my mind, quite undesirable, it is not just because the child will be without parents but also because it can have unknown influences that are unintended. The role of proteins specific to other animals can cause significant changes to the human being created in this fashion. But even more disastrous would be the creation of a half-human, half-pig animal. Under the present "ethical standards" these scientists have adopted, they are limited to allowing this chimera to live only up to the fourth month. Then both the surrogate mother and the chimera are killed.

However, the idea of socially engineering society to accept a half-human, half-pig chimera to exist at all is just another step in the direction of the powerful to eventually breed a class of beings that could be harvested for their organs. Once man has accepted the notion that man is but an evolved animal of no more intrinsic worth than any other evolved animal, where do you draw the line? What is to stop the elite in a godless system from farming cloned humans for their organs?

Our new century will witness a new arms race. We are living in the very dawn of the genetics arms race. Just as in the last century, when the fear of falling behind and becoming vulnerable to another nation's nuclear technological advantage spurred the nuclear proliferation between the super-powers, genetics will become the new arms race of this century.

> [B]ioengineering may be able to physically [and intellectually] improve man across the entire spectrum of our functions—yielding extraordinary economic as well as

strategic advantages. (Neanderthal man was a magnificently successful early man. But when he met the more intelligent CroMagnon man, he quickly went extinct.)

Of course, mistakes will be made. Island of Dr. Moreau-like monsters may well be formed. God may punish a people who presume to tinker with his handiwork. But, as the Chinese push forward, hell-bent for industrial levels of genetic manipulation and cloning, supported by the massive bioengineering research they are now beginning to fund, American voters and congressmen will have to balance their strong ethical and religious revulsion of cloning against the danger of being surpassed by a gene-manipulated super-race (Blankley 2003).

The time will quickly come that the rich will be able to translate their economic prowess into a clear genetic advantage in their progeny. And the new class of genetically rich humans will be so far superior to the naturals that they will not be able to compete intellectually or physically on an even level. If this is allowed, it does not take a rocket scientist to see that eventually the naturals will become extinct as the genetically programmed chimera (human-animal hybrids) especially designed for manual labor will replace them as the slave caste of the coming New Age.

There is here a great danger in meddling where we were not meant to meddle. But that is another story that I will deal with in my book *Smokescreens: The Hoodwinking of America*.

The fact remains that without our artificial genetic manipulation, evolution simply does not take place in the normal course of nature. The concept of transitioning into another kind has not ever been documented in natural conditions, either by gradual steps or by sudden jumps. The idea that minute changes could accumulate in time to create a new kind is simply untenable. But old dogmas die hard.

MECHANISMS OF EVOLUTION (THE HOUSE OF CARDS)

The Tyranny of Paradigms

Unfortunately, once a paradigm is fixed in the sciences, it is quite difficult to overturn its premise, even in the face of daunting evidence. Stanley, referring to the gradualist presupposition held by most evolutionists prior to the 1970s, admits to this political resistance to change found in evolutionary academic circles.

> What is unfortunate is that, in a political sense, there was little room for dissent. This is not to say that there were no nay-sayers. Throughout the 1940's for example, the plant biogeographer J. C. Willis and the geneticist Richard Goldschmidt argued for the sudden appearance of species by macromutation. Because of his preeminence as an experimentalist, Goldschmidt was too conspicuous to be ignored *and he, in particular, was ostracized by the evolutionary community* (emphasis added) (Stanley 1981, 71).

Goldschmidt correctly understood that the process of natural selection that created microevolution within the species was insufficient to account for the enormous changes that led to a new species. Nevertheless, he was an avowed evolutionist. He therefore insisted that only through macromutations could these major changes take place. Here is what he said:

> The change from species to species is not a change involving more and more additional atomistic changes, but a complete change of the primary pattern or reaction system into a new one, which afterwards may again produce intraspecific variation by micromutation....
>
> They [Biologists] seem inclined to think that because they have not themselves seen a "large" mutation, such thing cannot be possible. But such a mutation need only be an event of the most extraordinary rarity to provide the world with all the species that it has ever contained....

The facts of microevolution do not suffice for an understanding of macroevolution (Goldschmidt 1940, 211).

He therefore contended that macromutations had to be the mechanism to create new species in one fell swoop. Criticizing the gradualist dogma of those who preferred the micromutation accumulation of small changes as inefficient to create a completely new species won him the wrath of the defenders of the paradigm. Thus, although no man had ever seen one, he placed his hopes on the "hopeful monster" created by a macromutation.

For this, he was ostracized by the scientific community of his day. Later on, when genetics proved that microevolution does not extrapolate into the future to become a new species, Stanley tried to find another alternative that would better match the paleontological record. But adding to his problem, we also now know after decades of research and experimental attempts to prove otherwise, that macromutations simply do not exist. That is, as I previously stated, there are no mutations that have ever been shown to change one kind into another. Hence came Stanley's evolutionary idea that change from one species to another happens in quantum leaps of short durations with long periods of equilibrium in between through an "unknown mechanism."

Never mind that this "unknown mechanism" is just another evolutionary conjure that lies outside our ability to test, like the space trash theory and the missing continents that harbor the fossil evidence for the intermediates of the evolving species. But the point I am making is that the gradualist paradigm would not even allow Goldschmidt's evolutionary consideration, even in the face of the mounting geologic evidence that pointed to abrupt appearances of fully formed species in the fossil record and the inability of micromutations to change the genetics of one species into another.

Stanley, a committed evolutionist, plainly states this glaring inconsistency with the gradualist paradigm that still holds the controls in the arena of academia. He documents the almost tyrannical pressure levied over scientists to conform to their gradualist paradigm of the day.

The known fossil record is not, and never has been in accord with gradualism. What is remarkable is that, through a variety of historical circumstances, even the history of opposition has been obscured. Few modern paleontologists seem to have recognized that in the past century, as the biological historian William Coleman has recently written, *"The majority of paleontologists felt their evidence simply contradicted Darwin's stress on minute, slow, and cumulative changes leading to species transformation"* (emphasis added) (Stanley 1981, 71).

The voices of these brave paleontologists were obscured from public ears. But Stanley's position is no less obtuse. He continues to insist that evolution is still true. But in light of the physical evidence that shows all kinds abruptly appearing in the fossil record, he concludes that nature must have created these jumps from one kind to another in sudden bursts, through a mechanism "yet unknown."

Like Goldschmidt before him, Stanley admits that the gradualist paradigm is just not reflected in the fossil evidence and concludes, because evolution must be true, that it must have happened in very dramatic and large changes within a very short period of time so short that it would not appear in the strata.

Goldschmidt thought the mechanism must have been macromutations dubbed the hopeful monster theory and hoped that time would prove him out. Stanley, however, astutely realized that since 1940, no macromutations have ever been witnessed by any evolutionary biologists or geneticists and wisely chose to vaguely call the mechanism a "yet unknown" mechanism. According to him, large changes occur in a punctuated and short period of time followed by a large period of equilibrium with little variation for the species.

In other words, the theory of Darwinian evolution has simply run out of valid biological mechanisms in the real world and have consequently opted for a virtual reality "unknown mechanism" called punctuated equilibrium. How nice! Of course, in the minds of these evolutionists, it is not speculation. The theory of punctuated equilibrium is considered hard science. Hmm! In reality, it is simply just more magic wands and pixie dust.

4. The Survival of the Fittest (the Fourth Wall)

There is an overlap between the concept of natural selection and the survival of the fittest. Some may think I am being repetitive, but I think it is important to isolate the two distinctions in order to show you that the fittest are not always the true survivors. Reality is not always as straightforward as the evolutionists contend.

It is true that in the wild, generally speaking, the fittest have the edge on survival, but it is not always so. And even then, it only allows the respective genetic components the animal initially possessed and not any acquired behavior patterns to be passed on. And yet it is often the case that a more robust organism competing in a more treacherous environment may not survive, while a less robust organism competing in an opportune environment may survive. Sometimes, just plain luck determines the survival of one genotype over another.

For example, a monkey living close to civilization may learn to steal food from humans. Others in more remote areas may not have that option. The more remote monkeys may die when food is scarce, while a possibly weaker and less able or intelligent monkey may survive, only due to serendipity.

His ability to survive did not depend on a superior intelligence or brawn but simply on his fortune in being close to an alternative food supply. The condition of a particular environment may have a greater food supply than another and may allow the survival of less robust specimens through simple serendipity. But I must once again stress that in either case, the genes passed on were predetermined from the birth of the animal, and nothing learned during the creature's life can be passed on genetically.

It is true that learned behaviors can be taught to offspring by the parents. But these learned behavior adaptations couldn't produce a different kind, no matter how significant the adaptive behavior, because it cannot be translated to the genes. Hence, the concept of the survival of the fittest is not as black and white as evolutionists often claim with such resolve.

There is also the problem of humans. According to the evolutionary concept, the most successful, intelligent, and capable individuals within the gene pool should be the ones whose genetic components become prominent in the following generations. But this assumption is fallacious in regard to humans.

Certainly, the rule in human society seems to be that the lower-income populations are the ones with the most offspring. That is an undeniable verity worldwide. The more supposedly evolutionarily advanced humans, the more educated and economically progressive, have less offspring universally. It is argued that the most prosperous nations are the most nutritionally rich and that malnutrition can influence the potential mental development of individuals. Nevertheless, as a species, it is a fact that the more technically advanced nations are the ones with the lowest birth per capita in the world. How, then, does evolution explain this?

There are great contradictions in this concept, and the thinking person must question the implications of such a presupposition. Human intelligence is stated as the grand culmination of this evolutionary quest toward superior forms. Thus, the process of encephalization, the crowning achievement of which is man's cognitive powers, is touted as the inevitable result of natural selection and the survival of the fittest.

But in a selective environment, it is not really clear that intelligence offers a better survival capability. That is to say, the very process of developing intelligence offers no absolute selective advantage initially. Once intelligence is obtained, then one can say that it has a limited advantage in this regard.

In other words, if, in fact, the evolutionary presupposition of natural selection is the guiding element in the evolution of life, then it must be noted that intelligence is not always the most successful quality in the survival of the fittest. It is not intelligence alone that creates a selective advantage in that kind of a system. A much more appropriate term would be *cunning*, the ability to overpower and kill without remorse or guilt. That, and not intelligence, would rank highest in the selective advantage grid.

There are great disadvantages in the process of the development of greater intelligence, which, in a selective environment, would be a real danger to their survivability. First, the gestation period for organisms with a highly developed nervous system is longer. Second, their young take considerably longer to train and become self-subsisting. Third, the energy level that is required by the brain is such that it requires about 20 percent of the energy consumed by the body, even when resting. That is clearly a disadvantage in surviving during periods of scarce food supplies.

Finally, the theory of evolution must conclude that man is not the most fit for survival simply because of his greater intelligence. On the other hand, the shark, a much less intelligent but sleek and efficient killing machine, would, in evolutionary terms, be more progressive than man. If, in fact, the criterion of the evolutionary presupposition is the survival of the fittest, then the concept of morality, which is according to their evolutionary dogma a natural development of intelligence in man, becomes quite a handicap.

It would follow that evolution would move toward its most successful and simpler design and not to the more complicated and tenuous. The optimum human being from an evolutionary standpoint would not be the most intelligent but rather the most fearsome, calloused, and cold-hearted predator.

A cruel and heartless killer with no conscience would most adequately take the top of the food chain. Ironically, this behavioral pattern is what we would call a psychopath in our human society. What selective advantage would create in man a sense of morals and self-sacrifice toward his neighbors and the rest of humanity? The concept of the survival of the fittest goes contrary to the intrinsic psyche of most humans as they go out of their way to help the handicapped and less fortunate.

This high moral view in man would be a real detriment to the weeding out of genetic undesirables from future generations. Natural selection could not produce such a moral worldview in man. Quite the contrary, those elements of the human race that throughout history have ruthlessly victimized others and benefited from pillaging and destroying all in their path for booty would logically be the most highly developed humans under this ideology. These cold-hearted brigands are the zenith of the evolutionary ladder if the matrix of reality is the survival of the fittest.

So we see that not only does the survival of the fittest not provide any new genetic information to pass on to offspring, but it is also quite contrary to the basic nature of man. It elevates pragmatic ruthlessness over altruism. It justifies cruelty and selfishness. In fact, it logically leads to anarchy and chaos, which may not be a very good or viable survival strategy for a species in the long run.

In short, there are no real or documented mechanisms for the evolution of one species into another. Furthermore, the axiom of the evolutionary mantra (the survival of the fittest) cannot explain the reality of the way man thinks.

Yet evolutionists continue to tenaciously insist that the evidence for the evolution of the species is overwhelming. We have seen that the foundation of the so-called house of evolution is nothing but smoke and mirrors. And the illusion created by the pseudo-structure of its walls is simply more of the same. It is preposterous that evolutionists attack intelligent design and creationism as junk science when all of their mechanisms have proved to be the real junk science.

CHAPTER 4

DATING METHODS: THE THREE PILLARS

Undeterred by the utter failure of their cherished foundational premises and the crumbling structure of its walls, evolutionists try to prop up those walls with three pillars. Those pillars attempt to establish an immense time frame for the process of evolution in order to give evolution at least a plausible chance. For gradualism to be even plausible, it requires enormous spans of time so the mechanism of small incremental changes can eventually lead to a new species.

It must be made clear, however, that establishing long ages for Earth does not prove evolution. The evolution of life must be proved only by crossing several monumental gulfs.

1. The first gulf evolutionists must cross is proving that accidental chemical reactions could create a protein molecule made exclusively of left-handed amino acids. Although right-handed amino acids and left-handed amino acids occur equally in nature, proteins in living things are exclusively made of left-handed amino acids. Since there is no chemical reason for choosing one antipode over another, how does random ordering manage to choose exclusively one form?

2. The second gulf they must cross is explaining how random chemical reactions could create the complex macromolecule of the protein with its unique and specified sequential order. Thus far, they have not proved this. Only protenoid-like substances have been created under laboratory conditions that require constant interference by the experimenter in order to succeed.
3. The third gulf evolutionists must cross is proving that random chemical reactions could create codes. Codes require a mind to conceive. They carry rich information in asymmetrical forms described as specified complexity. Nature can only achieve simple complexity such as repetitive forms in crystals or ripples in the sand or vortexes in air and water. They are repetitive and symmetrical systems that are incapable of carrying rich information. This was also covered in Book 3 of this series.
4. The fourth gulf they must cross is proving how random chemical reactions could create an irreducibly complex system that requires multiple sequential and simultaneous evolutionary steps that offer no selective advantage to the organism until all the steps are completed. That, too, was covered in Book 3 of this series.
5. The fifth gulf for evolutionists is providing a credible mechanism that can change one species into another through random chemical reactions. Thus far, no credible mechanism has been proposed or shown to change one kind into another.

In the third book of this series, *Codes: Random Evolution vs. Divine Design*, we showed the failure of natural selection to cross the first four monumental gulfs. We also showed the failure of any proposed evolutionary mechanism to turn one species into another and concluded that the fifth gulf is an impassable gulf to cross through a naturalistic explanation. And although dealing with the age of the Earth and our universe is unnecessary to discredit the

DATING METHODS: THE THREE PILLARS

evolutionary myth, we will nevertheless show that the huge time scales necessary for such gradualist hopes are based on more smoke and mirrors.

Evolutionists must begin with a fundamental assumption that is absolutely indispensable to their theory—for gradualism to have a chance, there must be huge periods of time in order for these incremental changes to add up to significant biological changes. And this is not just in the biological realm. In all realms where order is created from disorder, there must be enormous spans of time. In other words, for evolution to take place, there must necessarily be vast eons of time in order to gain the credibility of random processes accomplishing the highly improbable through sheer countless repetition. In the minds of evolutionists, the more years for an improbable random choice to occur, the greater the chance becomes for the impossible to masquerade as credible.

But the statistical problem they encounter is that, contrary to what Darwin and Wallace had counted on during their time, they no longer have an infinity of time or an infinite amount of material to accomplish their evolutionary feat. We have since discovered that the universe had a beginning and is therefore finite in both space and time.

The mere 15 billion years now believed to be the age of the universe is simply not enough time for disorder to accidentally become ordered through random chemical reactions to the extent that our universe exhibits such universal symmetry. Chaos cannot randomly produce symmetry and especially not the highly sequential symmetry expressed by the specified complexity found in the DNA and proteins in living things.

Even if evolutionists were to have triple the eons of time they propose, the enormous improbability of random processes achieving chemical abiogenesis is so high that their proposed time frames are completely insignificant numbers in terms of the statistical improbability involved.

We have already documented in *Codes: Random Evolution vs. Divine Design* that the universe does not contain either the material resources or the length of time for the statistical hurdles they must surpass to create one living cell through random and undirected evolutionary processes.

Granting the evolutionists every possible assumption they require in their speculations and the 15 billion years they declare to be the age of the universe, the chances of pure random, chemical processes creating the number of proteins necessary to form the simplest theoretical living cell is absolutely staggering.

> The odds against one minimum set of proteins happening in the entire history of the earth are $10^{119,775}$ to 1 (Coppedge 1973, 111).

Most of us have no real way of appreciating how huge that number is, so let me compare it to other things so we can get a perspective on its enormity. If we were to count how many seconds have transpired in the entire 15 billion years that evolutionists believe our universe has existed, it would be 10^{17}. If we were to count how many elementary particles would exist in the entire universe, or every star, planet, moon, asteroid, nebulae, and intergalactic gas together, that number would be 10^{80}.

The number $10^{119,775}$ is so extremely remote that it is, for all practical purposes, irrational for a thinking person to believe it could be possible, even in 15 billion years. But that protein must be created on Earth in order for life to arise. It would not do us any good for that protein to be made in the Andromeda Constellation. And yet, the age of Earth, according to their figures, is one-third of the age of the universe. That is somewhere between 4 billion and 5 billion years. What is the amount of material available on Earth compared to the entire universe?

To put a finer point on it, how much of all the material on Earth is actually on the surface and capable of participating in this process? If we were to rework the computations to just 5 billion years by granting them the largest estimate of the age of Earth's history and the much-reduced material contained within the surface of the planet, compared to all the material in the entire universe, it would be even more unrealistic and utterly irrational to consider a randomly generated living cell as a viable possibility when the chances of establishing one set of minimum proteins necessary for a single theoretical cell to exist, using all the time and material in our entire universe, is $1 \times 10^{119,775}$. Therefore, regardless of the age of Earth, evolution has no realistic chance of developing through random ordering within the timetable evolutionists accept as correct.

What Is the Age of Earth?

The age of the universe is not the age of Earth, even from an evolutionary perspective. Evolutionists believe that Earth is between 4 million and 4½ million years old. Our Judeo-Christian cosmological model proposes that the age of Earth is measured in thousands of years, not millions. Nevertheless, just how old is Earth? For a long time, scientists have attempted to find a way to date the age of Earth. Initially, Newton predicted in his *Principia* that a red-hot globe made of iron and the size of Earth would take 50,000 years to cool off and be able to support life.

Later on, the great French scientist Buffon attempted to confirm Newton's prediction of the age of Earth by conducting experiments that measured the cooling time of metal balls heated to a glowing temperature. He then extrapolated and computed a similar time in proportion to the estimated mass of Earth. His calculations estimated that it would take 39,000 years for Earth to cool off enough for life to exist.

The problem with these calculations is that scientists conducted these experiments in an ambient temperature that is not consistent with the temperatures of extreme cold in space. The obvious cooling time of a red hot metal ball will be much less if exposed to an environment of extreme cold, as in deep space, especially if Earth was without an initial atmosphere.

There is much we do not know about the formation of planets. How is it that the revolving matter around the sun could coalesce into planets of such remarkably different compositions? How is it that even the moons of some of the giant planets are so diverse from one another in their basic compositions? Some of them are even revolving retrograde to the others and are more likely to have been captured objects. However, the planets are revolving around the sun in relatively the same plane, showing that there is some interconnection between them in regard to their genesis.

How is it that even the galaxies are spinning? All things in the universe seem to be rotating. Nothing is static. All things are intertwined in a dynamic cosmic dance. Even the very basic elements of all reality, the tiny strings or membranes predicted by the M-theory, are said to be dynamically vibrating at a given resonance. The very dynamics of the specified pitch in their resonance determines the nature of the thing composed.

The universe is literally dancing in harmony, with each subatomic component vibrating at a unique and complementary pitch to all the other dancing subatomic entities. Their joint efforts determine their particular quality to create the reality about us; that is, the seen as well as the unseen reality. Is this not evidence of design? If all things were truly guided by random ordering, we would expect some things to be static. But in our universe, even the spatial dimensions are dynamic. Nothing is truly static.

The question at hand is this: How long has it been dancing in this marvelous symphony? And here is the greater question: Who wrote the symphony? It is hard to swallow that this symphony could have just popped up from nothing and written itself.

We have already explored the implications of time dilation and the possible differences in the age of the universe according to the precise area being investigated. In the second book of this series, *Supersymmetry or Chaos*, we discussed how Albert Einstein taught us that time is not a universal constant. In other words, two people in two different places can experience a rate of time that is different during the very same interval. The density of space affects the rate of time. For example, a clock on a GPS satellite 150 miles out in space runs faster than the same clock on the surface of Earth. Because gravity is stronger on the surface of Earth, space is crunched; it is denser and causes time to run more slowly. But space, 150 miles from the surface of Earth, is less dense. It is stretched, and thus time runs faster.

We discussed the extreme dilation of space-time due to enormous gravitational fields such as in the critical circumference of black holes. If the universe exploded from the Big Bang (an unimaginably immense singularity that would have contained all space-time, matter, and energy in the universe), the gravitational force exerted would have created an immense effect on matter and on space-time exiting the critical circumference of that white hole (a white hole is the opposite of a black hole; things are ejected rather than consumed).

Calculations made by astrophysicists tell us that the gravitational force in the critical circumference can be so powerful that it can bend space-time into infinity. To an outside observer, that means a rocket traveling into a black hole would seem to slow down as it approaches the critical circumference (space becomes denser due to extreme gravity). The spaceship would seem to freeze in time—for eternity—as it arrives at the very edge of the critical circumference. That is called extreme time dilation. Because space-time is literally crunched and contorted by the enormous gravitational force of spinning black holes, it impacts the rate of time, dramatically bringing it to a crawl and eventually to a dead stop.

Imagine the gravitational curvature experienced by space-time and matter as it exited the primordial critical circumference of the Genesis Big Bang containing all the gravity in the entire universe concentrated into one massively powerful singularity. Since time is not a fixed constant but is relative to the position of the observer, it is the density of space that determines the speed of the rate of time at every coordinate in our universe.

Because the material leaving the Big Bang first had to overcome the greatest amount of gravity when all the matter in the universe was still contained within the initial or primordial critical circumference, this area of space (toward the edge of our universe) had to be moving outward at an extremely fast speed in order to overcome gravity, and therefore space was stretched the farthest. It had to be traveling at a precise and enormous acceleration rate in order to escape the grip of gravity when the primordial critical circumference was the strongest ever possible in our universe. Because space is stretched the most in the farthest regions of the edge of our universe, the rate of time there is also moving the fastest.

The power of gravity exerted by the Genesis singularity of the Big Bang as matter exited the primordial critical circumference was reduced as it diminished in size. That subsequently caused the distance from the singularity to the critical circumference to be reduced accordingly. Matter ejecting through it then needed less speed to achieve escape velocity that was proportional to the magnitude of its gravitational intensity.

That means that the matter that first exited had to overcome the greatest amount of gravity. Space-time in that region, which is now the outskirts of our universe, would have stretched the most. It would have had to travel faster than any other area to overcome the maximum critical circumference at its strongest magnitude of power.

We also know now that the density of matter and energy in that initial Genesis singularity was infinite in power. What finite force could overcome infinite density? The answer is none. Nothing inside our finite material universe could have overcome the infinite density of the Genesis singularity. Only a being with infinite power can overcome infinite density. There can be no natural explanation in a finite universe that could overcome the infinite density of the Genesis singularity.

Naturalists' insistence that we live in a closed universe is at an impasse. If there were no outside forces that could affect our universe, there would never have been a Big Bang. Our universe would have remained a giant black hole forever. The problem for the naturalist is not only to explain how nothing became something but how the most powerful singularity ever possible in our universe could expand against the enormous force of gravity it contained.

Those of the Judeo-Christian cosmological model believe we live in an open universe. They believe that God exists outside our universe and can act upon it as He wishes. Not only do they believe He created the Genesis singularity and all the spatial dimensions out of His infinite energy, but they also believe that He carefully planned every aspect of the universe He wanted to create in order for life to exist. The evidence of the universal symmetry found in the entire universe is therefore a previsioned and carefully engineered process that demands an infinitely intelligent creator not bound within our finite universe.

Evolutionists, pointing out that the stars at the edge of our universe are 15 billion light years away, then conclude that the entire universe has existed for 15 billion light years. They speculate that it would have taken billions of light years for suns and galaxies and planets to form through their gradualist gravity model and be able to coalesce matter into these various structures.

The Judeo-Christian cosmological model suggests that gravity was not the major force used to create celestial objects. All matter in our proto universe was in plasma form, in which electrons were stripped from the nucleus of atoms, causing them to have negatively charged particles (electrons) as well as positively charged particles (the nucleus). That peculiarity makes it highly susceptible to the electromagnetic force, which we believe played the prominent role in the formation of celestial bodies through powerful and giant Birkeland Currents that are able to create solid matter almost instantaneously. The electromagnetic force is 10^{39} times more powerful than gravity. Millions of years were not necessarily needed in order for gravity to coalesce matter (see *Supersymmetry or Chaos* for an expanded explanation of this process).

But what force could counter the gravity of the Genesis singularity to send that churning ball of plasma across the primordial critical circumference? We propose that God set the Genesis singularity spinning at just the right acceleration to develop the centrifugal force necessary to overcome the gravitational force of that Genesis singularity. The initial Genesis spin acceleration constant is the factor responsible for all things in this universe to be spinning and for our universe to be accelerating outwardly in speeds that are in proportion to their distance from us.

If you imagine a spinning merry-go-round with seven bands of colors, beginning with a red bull's-eye in the middle, each band moving outward from the middle is moving at an increased rate because any coordinate in that band has to travel a further distance in order to complete the circuit. Each circuit farther from the axis is then moving faster in direct proportion to its distance from the center. That increase in speed also creates an increase in an outward centrifugal force, which pushes away from the axis or center.

If we stand in the middle of a merry-go-round near the axis, the spin is slower and the centrifugal force is also subsequently lower. But if we stand at the edge on the seventh band of color, the speed of rotation has increased relative to the distance from the center, and the centrifugal force causes us to lose our footing as we are thrown outward from the spinning merry-go-round. As a child, I had great fun trying to make the merry-go-round spin fast enough to catapult my friends.

But our universe is not a rigid metal surface like the spinning merry-go-round. It is made of an elastic matrix we call space that stretches as it is thinned out by the centrifugal force exerted on it. The further we move out to the edge of our universe, the thinner space becomes. That means that time is also speeding up in proportion to the rate of the stretching of space in each particular coordinate from the Alpha Point to the edge of the universe.

As matter and energy steadily ejected through the critical circumference, the Genesis singularity diminished in size and intensity. The gravitational effect also diminished the curvature of space-time in the critical circumference proportionally, requiring less escape velocity. Hence, space-time was not as stretched, and time was running more slowly as each consecutive region crossed the critical circumference until all space-time and matter of the singularity was ejected and the singularity ceased to exist.

Since space and time are a continuum that cannot be separated, we find that what we do to one affects the other. When space is less dense, space-time is stretched out, and time runs faster. When space is denser, space-time is crunched, and time moves more slowly. That explains how humans at the center of the universe experienced perhaps several thousand years of history from the Alpha Point, while during the same interval, the outer rim stars would have experienced 15 billion years of history since the same moment of the Big Bang.

As the universe expanded, the light waves within it also expanded, causing them to stretch and red-shift, the red Doppler shift effect, which we recognize as we study stars that are moving away from us. Hence, evolutionists are both right and wrong. The outer universe has experienced 15 billion years, but that does not mean that the interior part of the universe has experienced 15 billion years of history during the same interval. Time in the interior of the universe, which has a much denser space, moves at a drastically different rate—a much slower rate—and would not have aged as quickly (for a more detailed explanation, see *Supersymmetry or Chaos*).

Evolutionists insist that the edge of our universe depicts our early universe. While it is true that there are 15 billion light years between our coordinates in the center and the stars at the edge, they are actually looking at time in fast-forward. That area of the universe does not depict the early universe but a more mature and older specimen that has been ravaged by the increase in entropy through the second law of thermodynamics. They are looking at the future depiction of what our area of the universe will be like should we reach that age. For that reason, the farthest areas of the universe are where we find the greatest predominance of quasars, supermassive black holes eating up their galaxies. The edge of our universe is not a nursery for baby galaxies but rather a cemetery. It shows the cannibalism of the galaxies through gargantuan black holes that may have even merged together several times to become the so-called eaters of worlds.

Let us now explore the dating methods used by evolutionists to support their gradualist doctrine.

The Phylogenetic Tree (the First Pillar)

What, then, is the age of the Earth? Evolutionists use several tools to date the Earth, including the phylogenetic tree, the fossil strata (geologic column), and radiometric methods of dating. In the last part of the twentieth century, evolutionists asserted with great confidence that the age of the Earth is in the billions of years.

Their proof is contained within three main arguments that are deployed to undergird the long ages needed for evolution. As previously stated, the basic evolutionary presumption is that living things evolved from simple to more complex forms.

They assume that simple unicellular organisms developed into colonial organisms, which in turn developed into multicellular organisms. The multicellular organisms then developed into the more differentiated societal organisms. Tracing back the ancestry of all living things, evolutionists have developed a theoretical family tree based on the similarity of organisms to one another and their relative complexity.

They automatically assume, based on their evolutionary presupposition, that the more simple looking organisms are more ancient. It is a case of classical circular reasoning based on the premise that the evolution of the species is an actual fact. Looking at the phylogenetic tree, they can then date strata according to their initial evolutionary assumption through certain index fossils that stipulate the exact place in the phylogenetic tree and what age they presume them to have according to the evolutionary assumption that the more complex organisms evolved after the more simple organisms.

DATING METHODS: THE THREE PILLARS

In other words, evolutionary scientists some 200 years ago established an evolutionary tree that began with single-celled organisms at the very base of the tree and culminated with humans and all the extant fauna at the tippy top of the branches. From the beginning, associations of ancestry were made purely upon speculations based on physiological similarities.

Today, that speculative process is not as certain and absolute as it was once deemed. DNA has thrown a wrinkle in this once-believed concrete structure. Outward physical similarities are found across many species where there is no straightforward interconnection possible since their DNA has been found to be too dissimilar.

When a fossil is found, these three considerations are applied to determine its age:

1. By the observed complexity of the organism, it is located on the supposed evolutionary slot that has been assigned to it in the phylogenetic tree. Never mind that this is an arbitrary designation based entirely on their presupposition that simpler organisms are more archaic and complex organisms are more recent, since evolution in their minds is an absolute fact (the first pillar: the phylogenetic tree).
2. The stratum in which it is found is declared to be within the presupposed position that correlates to the geologic column by the observed complexity of the organism. That is also an arbitrary designation based on the circular reason created by their presupposition that the more complex the forms found in it, the more recent the strata; and the simpler the life forms, the more ancient the strata (the second pillar: geologic strata).
3. A date for the specimen is attempted by radiometric dating methods, which are compared to the timetable suggested by the phylogenetic tree and the strata in which it has been

THE DESCENT OF MAN

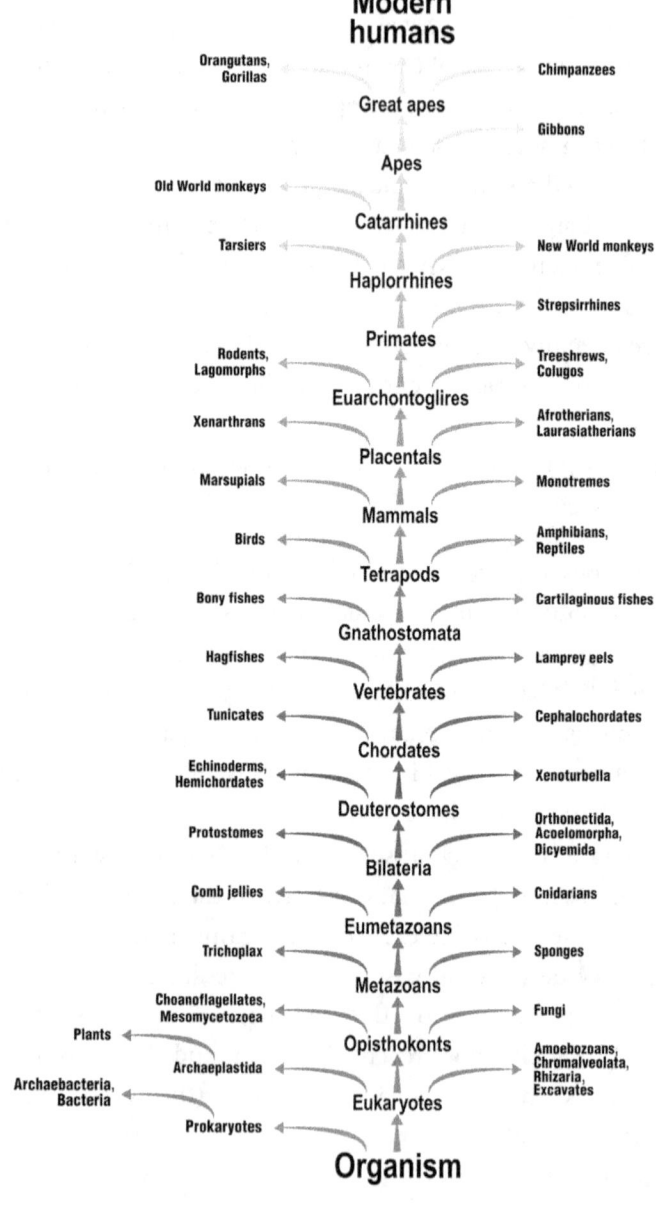

The Phylogenetic Tree

found for verification. Any divergent dates not compatible with the first two pillars are unceremoniously thrown out. But radiometric dating is not always possible, and even when it is possible, reliability is based on several dubious assumptions, as we shall see (the third pillar: radiometric dating).

The first two pillars are completely arbitrary designations devised entirely from evolutionists' presupposition that animals have evolved from simple to complex forms. The third has serious limitations, as we will see later. But the point is that circular reasoning is utilized to feign absolute proof where none exists.

Since no change from one species to another has ever been witnessed or proved, the entire lineage in the phylogenetic tree is the product of Darwinian speculation. The original phylogenetic tree, then, was artificially produced with a mixture of science and wishful thinking. Based on the phenotypes, or physical characteristics of the organisms, Darwinists assembled them in lineages that made the simpler organisms the ancestors of the more complex organisms.

If we were to listen to evolutionists, they would lead you to think that there is an uninterrupted sequence of creatures blending one into the other as they evolve. When we see these elaborate phylogenetic trees with all the branches leading ever upward to more complex organisms, we are led to believe that this is absolute proof that evolution is a fact.

In reality, the phylogenetic tree is nothing like that at all. It is a sporadically assembled lineage that is absolutely arbitrary and follows only their imagined evolutionary process. Each organism in this phylogenetic tree is related to the other through hairpin turns in the tree. The specific animals that produce this hairpin linkage may not even be known to actually exist. But because evolutioinists begin with the assumption that evolution is true, they assume that these creatures must have existed. So the entire lineage is the product of an evolutionary assumption of hyper dimensions.

Dawkins explains rather candidly the evolutionary interconnection they assume:

> On the evolutionary view, there is a series of intermediate animals connecting a rabbit to a leopard, every one of whom lived and breathed, every one of whom would have been placed exactly in the same species as its immediate neighbours on either side in the long, sliding continuum. Indeed, every one of the series was the child of its neighbour on one side and the parent of its neighbour on the other. Yet the whole series constitutes a continuous bridge from rabbit to leopard. . . . Take a rabbit, any female. . . . Place her mother next to her. Now place the grandmother next to the mother and so on back in time, back, back, back through the megayears, a seemingly endless line of female rabbits, each one sandwiched between her daughter and her mother. We walk along the line of rabbits, backwards in time, examining them carefully like an inspecting general. As we pace the line, we'll eventually notice that the ancient rabbits we are passing are just a little bit different from the modern rabbits we are used to. But the rate of change will be so slow that we shan't notice the trend from generation to generation, just as we can't see the motion of the hour hand on our watches—and just as we can't see a child growing, we can only see later that she has become a teenager, and later still an adult. . . . Nevertheless, steadily and imperceptibly, as we retreat through time, we shall reach ancestors that look less and less like a rabbit and more and more like a shrew (and not very like either). One of these creatures I'll call the hairpin bend, for reasons that will become apparent. This animal is the most recent common ancestor . . . that rabbits share with leopards. *We don't know exactly what it looked like,*

but it follows from the evolutionary view that it definitely had to exist. . . . We now continue our walk, except that we have turned the bend in the hairpin and are walking forwards in time, aiming towards the leopards. . . . Each shrew-like animal along our forward walk is now followed by her daughter. Slowly, by imperceptible degrees, the shrew-like animals will change, through intermediates that might not resemble any modern animal much but strongly resemble each other, perhaps passing through vaguely stoat-like intermediates, until eventually, without ever noticing an abrupt change of any kind, we arrive at a leopard (emphasis added) (Dawkins 2009, 24–25).

What does he mean by "aiming towards the leopards"? Is not evolution supposed to be an undirected and completely random process? The true fact is that we can walk down that line through all the ancestors of the rabbit until we come to the first rabbit. From beginning to end, we have rabbits. The true fact is also that we can walk down that line through all the ancestors of the shrews until we come to the first shrew. From beginning to end, all we have are shrews. With the imperceptible changes that supposedly turned into the intermediate forms of the shrew-rabbit (let us call it the shrewbit), one would assume it would be just as long as the lineage from the first rabbit to the last, and yet there are no fossils to corroborate that unprovable assumption. It is mere conjecture based on the evolutionists' underlying evolutionary bias.

However long the line of rabbits and their variations are should also be the length of the lineage of the shrewbit. After more than 200 years of digging with all the resolve imaginable to corroborate their evolutionary theory, not one paleontologist has ever dug up a fossil of a shrewbit.

When we compare the differences between that ancestral rabbit to the rabbit living today, we find that the differences are not more than the differences between the character complex variation in the current population ambling about the valleys and fields today.

We can also do the same for a shrew. However, we cannot find any of those countless intermediates that "look less and less like a rabbit and more and more like a shrew (and not very like either)" that Dawkins is so convinced "definitely had to exist" (Dawkins 2009, 24–25).

Dawkins's faith in evolution is strong, indeed, when he says, "We don't know exactly what it looked like, but it follows from the evolutionary view that it definitely had to exist" (Dawkins 2009, 24–25). Unfortunately for him, we have no fossils from this long and enormously large lineage of shrewbits. There is not even one single fossilized shrewbit. How odd that there is no record of it in the entire geological column! It exists only in the minds of the inventors of the phylogenetic tree. The magical shrewbit must be like the invisible unicorn. But the evolutionary magic does not stop with our celebrated shrewbit.

According to evolutionists, the shrewbit is also the common ancestor of leopards. We will call this new intermediate form the shrewbitpard. Dawkins confidently declares as empirical fact: "One of these creatures I'll call the hairpin bend, for reasons that will become apparent. This animal is the most recent common ancestor . . . that rabbits share with leopards. We don't know exactly what it looked like, but it follows from the evolutionary view that it definitely had to exist" (Dawkins 2009, 24–25).

So we can look in the strata and find an enormous number of fossils documenting the lineage of ancestral leopards to our current leopards, and we see that they were all leopards. But how odd that we cannot find in the geological strata anywhere in the world one single fossil specimen of the shrewbitpard. Not only can we not find the long lineage of shrewbits, but we also cannot find the equally long lineage of shrewbitpards—not even one little fossil of this most important hairpin animal.

DATING METHODS: THE THREE PILLARS

Now multiply that scenario by each and every animal found in the phylogenetic tree, and you will begin to understand that the trunk of the phylogenetic tree is made of pixie dust. In other words, there is absolutely no physical, empirical evidence that these creatures ever breathed on this Earth, "but it follows from the evolutionary view that it definitely had to exist" (Dawkins 2009, 24–25). That is the circular reasoning that Dawkins considers the "fact" of evolution. He confidently and arrogantly calls creationists history-deniers. But who is the one denying the empirical geologic data that evidence true history?

How strange that we can find numerous examples of the entire lineage of rabbits and leopards, but for some unexplained, miraculous reason, we cannot find any of the in-betweens. If we multiply this stark disparity of theory and reality by all the creatures that exist in our world, you can begin to appreciate that the number of intermediates that are missing ought to be larger than the number of species that now exist. And yet the geological empirical data do not contain any of them.

*

"It must be a fundamentalist Christian plot," said Rocksy as he kicked the strata before him.

"What do you mean?" asked Bullshingle.

"I can't find any of the intermediates," said Rocksy as he paced back and forth with his hands on his hips.

"What kind of plot?" asked Bullshingle, shrugging his shoulders.

"I don't know, but I tell you it's their fault."

"How could it be their fault?" asked Bullshingle, shaking his head.

"They must all be going out at night and digging up and hiding all the intermediates," answered Rocksy as he kicked a stone in anger.

*

Dawkins claims the changes that merge one species into another are proceeding at such a gradual pace as to be imperceptible:

> The rate of change will be so slow that we shan't notice the change from generation to generation, just as we can't see the motion of the hour hand on our watches—and just as we can't see a child growing, we can only see later that she has become a teenager, and later still an adult.... Nevertheless, steadily and imperceptibly, as we retreat through time, we shall reach ancestors. (Dawkins 2009, 24–25)

Then how can it be that this myriad of intermediates stretched out through eons are completely absent from the fossil record? The chain is missing, folks. The king is naked. There are no links between species that fade unperceptibly into another. That is the real fact, Mr. Dawkins. You can dispute it with your witty sarcasm all you want, but you have no facts to prove evolution.

Moreover, the naïve idea that Darwin proposed, which categorized simple organisms as primitive, is no longer in accord with our knowledge of biology. The naïve imagination that these supposedly simple organisms could be handily organized by random physical processes has been shown to be absolutely false. The molecular complexity in even the smallest single-celled organism is astounding. The "ultrastructural and biochemical complexity" of the least complex single-celled organisms is far removed from "the laboratory simulation of chemical events" created by Darwinists to explain the evolution of life. The gap is so great that in his later years, Dean Kenyon, the inventor of the theory of biochemical predestination, has come to doubt that this deep chasm could ever be crossed.

To start with, a cell membrane must be created, which can contain the metabolic machinery, protect it from the environment, and yet be selectively semipermeable so that chemicals, which are needed, can go through the membrane, while unwanted ones are kept out. In addition, the needed chemicals and compounds inside must be kept from leaking out and at the same time be able to remove waste products. This is no small order.

The oxygen molecule (O_2) is for instance, essential to life; but only a life form that can efficiently wrap and transport the devil O_2 exactly to a place where it can be used as an energy source would benefit from its angel side. Otherwise, O_2 becomes life's greatest enemy.

Rupture the membrane of a living cell, exposing it to the air, and you will see the great damage O_2 and a myriad of other chemical invaders can do to a perforated cell. Death would be swift and sure. From an engineering standpoint, then, it was essential that a way be found to protect the cell, life's most basic unit. The solution was clever: The cell was surrounded by a strong chemical shield, from the very beginning.

It is often said that a solution always brings with it two additional problems, and a chemical cellular shield is no exception. A simple shield could indeed protect the cell interior from deadly invaders, but such a barrier would also prevent cell nutrients from reaching the inside of the cell, and it would trap cellular waste within. Small neutral molecules could pass through the membrane, but not larger and normally electrically charged biomolecules. A simple shield would be a recipe for swift sure death. For early cells to survive and reproduce, something more sophisticated was needed. Selective channels through these early cell membranes had to be in place right from the start.

Cells today come with such doorways, specialized protein channels used in transporting many key biomolecules and ions. How was this selective transport of both neutral molecules and charged ions engineered? Evolutionary theory appeals to a gradual step-by-step evolutionary process of small mutations sifted by natural selection, what is colloquially referred to as *survival of the fittest*. But a gradual step-by-step evolutionary process over many generations seems to have no chance of building such wonders, since there apparently can't be many generations of a cell, or even one generation, until these channels are up and running. No channels, no cellular life.

So then the question is: How could the first cells acquire proper membranes and co-evolve the protein channels needed to overcome the permeability problem?

Even some committed evolutionists have confessed the great difficulty here. As Sheref Mansy and his colleagues put it in the journal *Nature*, "The strong barrier function of membranes has made it difficult to understand the origin of cellular life."

And that's putting it delicately. Somehow, a double layer membrane—flexible, stable, and resistant—needed to be engineered, one that would promptly and efficiently protect the cell from the devastating O_2 permeation, remain stable in aqueous acid media, and ably handle fluctuations in temperature and pH. To do all these tasks the cell's molecular shield also would need a mechanism to sense changes in temperature and pH[2] and react accordingly, adjusting the membrane chemical composition to handle these physical and chemical challenges (Eberlin 2019, 122).

A membrane that just accomplishes a few of these things is useless. It must accomplish all these things even in the simplest unicellular life form. The simplest cell membrane is a protein and phospholipid "sandwich" called a bi-lipid membrane, which is an extremely complicated and elaborate design.

Although all membrane proteins are located at the membrane, they have a wide range of structures and functions. Some are bound to the surface. Others have one region buried within the membrane and domains on one or both sides of the membrane.

Protein domains found on the outside of the membrane surface are, for the most part, involved with such processes as cell-to-cell signaling or interactions. Domains within the membrane, especially those that form channels and pores, are transporters that move only selected molecules across the membrane.

*

Moreover, a modern earthworm is no more primitive than a modern chimpanzee. They are chronological contemporaries living at the same time, having the same ancestral age behind them. Even Dawkins admits this:

> So glibly do the phrases "higher animals" and "lower animals" trip off our tongues that it comes as a shock to realize that, far from effortless slotting into evolutionary thinking as one might suppose, they were—and are—deeply antithetical to it. We think we know that chimpanzees are higher animals and earthworms are lower, we think we've always known what that means, and we think evolution makes it even clearer. But it doesn't. It is by no means clear that it means anything at all. Or if it means anything, it means so many different things as to be misleading, even pernicious (Dawkins 2009, 156).

Nevertheless, the evolutionist's presupposition still maintains that there is an evolution from a more primitive state to a more complex state. But we do not find that in nature. Some animals may have aspects that may be labeled primitive, while another aspect may be (from their evolutionary perspective) more advanced, and Dawkins readily admits that.

> An animal might be primitive from the waist down but highly evolved from the waist up. Less facetiously, one of them might be more primitive in its nervous system, the other more primitive in its skeleton. Notice especially

that "primitive" in the sense of "resembling ancestors" does not have to go with "simple" (meaning less complex) (Dawkins 2009, 157).

In other words, the evolutionary assumption that species evolved from other ancestral species is the scientific proof that qualifies what is supposed to be primitive and what is supposed to be advanced. Yet the animal that is primitive from the waist down has had the same amount of time to evolve his lower half as his upper half, which is highly evolved from the waist up. It seems clear that a rational mind would conclude that labeling an extant organism primitive, whether in halves or in whole, is an oxymoron.

If anything, it evidences the fact that a designer chose many variations to express life. The false assumption created by their circular reasoning that presupposes evolution to be a fact renders their common sense null and void. Dawkins admits that what he labels primitive is not necessarily less complex.

Let me show you some examples of this fallacious assumption in the drawing of the original phylogenetic tree. The first phylogenetic tree linked earthworms and nematodes as primitive organisms and considered humans to be much more advanced, having evolved much later in the evolutionary ladder. Nematodes and earthworms are both worms, as are the flatworms that Dawkins said were absent from the fossil record.

Flatworms are in the phylum Platyhelminthes, which include free-living worms like the planarian. Nematodes were originally labeled in the phylum Nemathelminthes but have now been renamed Nematoda. They are roundworms and not flat like the Platyhelminthes. They include hookworms, trichinella (causes trichinosis from eating uncooked pork), and heartworms (the nemesis of dog lovers). Earthworms, which are segmented worms, are in the phylum Annelida.

Their divisions, among other things, came mainly from the types of body cavities they exhibit. Flatworms are called acoelomates. They have three germ layers but no coelum. Roundworms (nematodes) are pseudocoelomates. They have a cavity that forms between the mesoderm and the endoderm. The segmented worms (earthworms) are coelomates. They have a true coelom, which is formed inside the mesoderm. Obviously, setting aside their internal anatomical differences, these worms surely must be considered more closely related to one another than to humans. From an evolutionary standpoint, worms existed long before humans ever came on the scene.

This linkage was first created in the phylogenetic tree due to considerations of the organisms' developmental and anatomical features (their physical appearance). In other words, it was an arbitrary system based on the assumption that animals evolved from simple life forms to more complex or advanced life forms and subsequently that those with greater physical resemblance were more closely related. Thus, similarities in their anatomical structures were used to categorize them. This view has been found deficient. It turns out that physical similarities are common even among species with widely divergent DNA.

Today, with the advent of genetic technology, an attempt is being made to organize this phylogenetic tree through genetics. As our technology has increased in the area of genetics, evolutionists have begun to group animals that are more genetically similar with one another. If animals really do evolve, then the trail can be ascertained by the genetic components and relative similarities between evolving and intermediate organisms.

Hence, the original phylogenetic tree that, since the time of Darwin, was supposed to be the concrete proof of evolution has been found not to be so solid after all. Again, it is the theory of evolution that is really evolving as each of their major assumptions is found to be at odds with reality and empirical data.

Nevertheless, the new genetic phylogenetic tree is not concrete, either. In reality, genetics only allows us to link animals that are of the same kind. All other links in the new phylogenetic tree are, in fact, still based on the evolutionary assumption that life has evolved. All that genetics can provide for us is a measure of how much genetic components some species have in common with others. It does not in any way prove lineage. What it insinuates is that the creator simply chose to use some similar genetic components among animals that in their scheme are called primitive and others that in their scheme are called advanced.

Once more, circular reasoning takes center stage. Darwinists call this expression of common genes between species evolutionary conservation. Since they "know" evolution is true, then the similarities in the genes must mean that they have a common lineage, which has been conserved in the genome of each species.

> Evolutionary conservation is echoed at the genetic level. Of the 8129 unique ESTs previously isolated from the earthworm *Lumbricus rubellius* (Sturzenbaum et al. 2003; Owen et al. 2008), a cohort of 1728 gene objects (i.e., over 21%) display significant homologies to counterparts identified in the genomes of the fruitfly (*Drosophila melanogaster*), the nematode (*C. elegans*) and humans (*Homo sapiens*). This underlies the notion that key biological and metabolic pathways are conserved within the majority of eukaryotic organisms. *Perhaps more interesting are the cohorts that display homology only between the earthworm and the fruitfly (68 genes), earthworm and nematode (49 genes), or earthworm and humans (220 genes). That more earthworm genes are conserved between earthworms and humans provides anecdotal support of the original Punch cartoon strap line: "man is but a worm." . . . The recent availability of substantive genetic datasets has been essential for the execution of far-reaching phylogenetic analysis and the attempt to answer questions relating to fundamental evolutionary relationships between the various animal*

phyla (Philippe et al. 2005). This fresh approach has challenged some evolutionary classifications, dogmas based on developmental and anatomical features described some 150yr ago (Jones & Blaxter 2005) (emphasis added) (Stürzenbaum, et al. 2009, 789-797).

Hence, evolutionists now seek to group animals by the similarities in their genetic makeup, just like they used to group animals with similar physical characteristics, assuming that they are therefore related. But that is again faulty and circular reasoning. The link is imposed because evolution is assumed.

But here is the real evidence (for any reasonable person) of the level of the Tartufery of their assumption: How strange that there are only 49 genes in common between segmented earthworms and the roundworms we know as nematodes! And yet there are 220 genes in common between earthworms and humans. Perhaps the new phylogenetic tree should place man closer to the earthworm and nematodes higher up the evolutionary ladder. Certainly, this genetic information makes the old and new phylogenetic tree completely obsolete and evidences that it is the product of mere speculation—nothing more than pixie dust and magic wands.

The irrational absurdity of claiming that humans, who are supposedly so far up the evolutionary ladder from earthworms, share 220 genes and roundworms share only 49 genes is self-evident to the rational mind. The whole scheme is nothing more than wish projection, unverifiable by any empirical data.

The fact that common components such as genes are used in all living systems does not force upon us the conclusion that all things evolved. It more accurately evidences the fact that a designer chose to use the same functional components in many organisms. That is all.

An impassable obstacle for creating this phylogenetic tree strictly through genetics is created by the fact that most of the animals that have ever lived are now extinct (estimates are about 95 percent), and we have little recourse in gaining their genetic information. In addition, genetics cannot be extracted from most fossils. This assignation can thus only be truly used within extant species or the relatively few species from whose fossils we have been able to extract DNA. If genetics is the proof of evolution, then the assignation of extinct fossil animals to any specific branch of the family tree is even more imprecise because it can only link their physical attributes and not their genetic components.

The phylogenetic tree is thus an artificial grouping based on two unprovable presuppositions. First is the presupposition that the more complex the organism, the more recent its advent, and that the simpler the organism, the more archaic its origin. And second, more recently, the belief that similarity in genetic composition necessitates a familial tie.

From this general comparison, evolutionists then develop an age-sensitive grouping that they claim is recorded in the rock strata. This grouping has been divided to reflect the phylogenetic tree in five main age divisions that comprise the evolutionary geologic column.

We have already exposed in the third volume of this series the myth of simplicity in organisms and have shown that the specific complexity in even the simplest life form is impossible to attain by random chance processes. The foundational fallacy in this presupposition established by the phylogenetic tree is that organisms that seem to have simpler structures are less complex.

For example, most evolutionists would agree that a dog is superior to an ant in the evolutionary scale and therefore more advanced on the trunk of the phylogenetic tree. The dog is a chordate mammal, like humans, and is on a high branch of the tree, while the ant is an arthropod insect whose branch of the tree is lower on the trunk.

But the ant is no simpleton. In studying the ant, scientists have found that there are some 10,000 varieties. The interesting thing is that around 400 of those varieties are now known to be farmers. Yes, you read correctly—farmers. They actually farm certain molds and fertilize them, use pesticides, and even select certain other molds that would compete with the mold that they are trying to grow. In other words, they also weed their gardens.

Some ants cultivate bacteria on the outside of their bodies that produce an antibiotic that specifically suppresses the growth of the weed fungi. Were you under the false impression that modern man was the first to use antibiotics? Have you ever seen a dog farm or weed a garden?

Scout ants are sent to forage for food. They leave a trail with pheromones to mark the spots where food was found, like Hansel and Gretel left breadcrumbs in the forest. Some, like army ants, create rigid bridges with their bodies to mark a path when their colony is on the move. They interlock themselves into a nearly tubular structure that reminds me of the subway system in London. The queen ant in some species has bodyguards that attack and kill all females that may be vying for her crown. The political campaigning in these colonies is no less complicated or ruthless than in ours. In an ant colony, however, there is no such thing as individual rights. Each ant has been specially designed to serve its own particular purpose for the colony at large. It appears that these ants are the very first communists.

The shark, long considered by evolutionists a rudimentary animal of great antiquity, is anything but a rudimentary and simple organism. While it is true that the skeleton of a shark is made of cartilage, a characteristic assumed by evolutionists in the past to depict their evolutionary simplicity, the shark possesses an incredibly complex nervous system with electrical receptors that allow it to sense the presence of animals that emit electrical fields.

Inside their heads are special jelly-filled canals called ampullae of Lorenzini that can detect the weak electrical stimuli from the muscle contraction of animals in their surroundings. As a matter of fact, they may be more sensitive to electrical fields than any other animal in the world. It is also thought that this organ helps them detect the Earth's magnetic fields, which they use for navigation.

They also possess pressure receptors that allow them to sense any motion in the water. Running along the length of their sides is a network of neuromasts called the lateral line. These fluid-filled vessels are just under the skin. Small pores on the skin open up as they detect the intensity and direction of vibrations in the water. That allows them to zero in on their prey, even when they cannot see it.

Their ability to "smell" blood as far as a quarter mile from the source is an incredible feat. They can detect one drop of blood in a million drops of water. The shark has nostrils, which have nothing to do with their breathing and are not even connected to their mouth. We need to inhale in order to smell. We cannot smell as we exhale, but not so for sharks. Water continuously flows through their nostrils and gives them uninterrupted olfactory information that performs like radar on airplanes flying through the clouds so they can see where their prey is.

Their hearing is also superb. Sharks are extremely sensitive to low-frequency sounds. The endolymphatic pores on the top of their heads are the only external evidence of their ears, but inside these pores are endolymphatic ducts that lead to a series of semicircular canals called the macula neglecta, which give them superb directional hearing.

Sharks' incredibly sophisticated sensing apparatuses allow them to rule the sea in the darkness of night. But that is not all. Like lions and other predatory cats, they have a mirror-like layer at the back of their eyes, the tapetum lucidum, another example of convergent evolution. How did two completely unrelated species evolve the tapetum lucidum?

This mirror-like film uniquely allows them to double the intensity of incoming light. What is more, unlike other fish, they have the capability of dilating and contracting their pupils to adjust to ambient light. Their retinas have a greater proportion of rods than cones. Rods are light-sensitive, and cones are color-sensitive, which means they are uniquely capable of seeing in very dim light. Yet the cones allow sharks to also have color vision.

DATING METHODS: THE THREE PILLARS

The fact that they travel immense distances, appearing at certain precise times in designated regions to feed and copulate, all without wristwatches, computers, gyroscopes, or GPS, is due to the marvel of the sophistication of the shark's design.

The more we learn about sharks, the better we understand what incredibly complex creatures they are and the more we begin to understand that they are quite intelligent predators, able to learn from mistakes. They are not the simple brute killing machines that early evolutionists presupposed. Sharks are anything but a primitive, ancient predator. They are sophisticated predators armed with a wide array of incredible features that allow them to be the undisputed kings of the oceans, except for orcas.

Orcas have figured out that if they turn sharks upside down, they go into a catatonic state and become basically unconscious. Whales have been known to kill great white sharks with this amazing predatory tactic.

The first evolutionary assumption that automatically classifies simple life forms as a more ancient form of life is completely unfounded. There is no such thing as a simple life form. The idea that we could establish a hereditary line through the grouping of living things from a more simple structure to a more complex structure is based on the ignorance of early evolutionists who did not yet have the technology to truly understand the marvelous biological sophistication of all living things.

There is nothing intrinsically wrong with grouping living things in a taxonomic pattern. The noted Swedish scientist Carol Linnaeus proposed our modern system of taxonomy. It provides for an orderly way of studying all organisms, which would otherwise be too unwielding and cumbersome. It is no different than our alphabetical order of names on our cell phones. It is an arbitrary convention that allows more efficiency. These groupings are useful for many reasons, but they hardly constitute proof, absolute or otherwise, that these organisms evolved from a common ancestry.

It could equally be argued that a common creator used forms (common designs) that He thought successful in creating the wonderful variety of living organisms that have existed on our planet. It no more proves evolution than if I were to place a Volkswagen next to a Mustang next to a Cadillac next to a Rolls Royce and then conclude that the Rolls Royce evolved from the Cadillac and the Cadillac evolved from the Mustang, which evolved from the primordial Volkswagen.

True, the Volkswagen is a simpler design, the Mustang is a little more advanced, and the Cadillac possesses even more gadgets. And no doubt, the Rolls Royce superficially exhibits the most sophisticated engineering qualities.

But their similarity in function and appearance is not due to a natural evolutionary process through which a Volkswagen has turned into a Rolls Royce. Their similarity is due to the fact that the engineers held in common the view that certain aspects of their design were adequate for their purpose, and so there was a repetition of these aspects by purposeful choice in each separate model, and that by design, they chose to add more technically superior elements in one over another.

Using the example of the car and an imagined developmental strategy (evolution) according to the complexity of their anatomical structures, we could file the Cadillac in a vehicular phylogenetic tree under the imaginary phylum *Automobilus cadillacus* (*cadillacus* being the particular species). Looking at the branches below it in the phylum *Motorcyclus*, we would see a simpler vehicle with only two wheels. The most popular species in America is *harlicus davesonia*, known for its distinct sound. But the most popular globally is the simpler *mopedius*, especially in the East. Below that branch, we find an even more popular phylum, *Bicyclus*, which fills the streets of India and China and is the species most universally found.

Looking further down the trunk of the phylogenetic tree, we come to a unique phylum that may have originated in the United States, *Skate Boardicus*. They descended from their more rudimentary ancestors *Rollericus Skatesia*.

DATING METHODS: THE THREE PILLARS

All kidding aside, it is the mind of the engineer that chooses to use certain patterns such as the shapes of wheels for his or her specific purpose. Design commonalities do not necessarily require or imply familial lineage. We could analyze the molecular structure of the steel used in each car, motorcycle, bicycle, and skateboard and then attempt to order them in the ratio of how closely matched their alloys are. We could analyze the steel of the VW and then place whatever car is closest in alloy to it. But all that would really prove is that the engineer or inventor chose similar materials in the designs. That parallels the argument of the familial connection through similarities in DNA.

I realize that this analogy is rather simplistic, but it serves to bring home the point that similarities in design or components do not, in and of themselves, constitute absolute evidence of evolution. It would be preposterous for us to think that an engineer who is creating cars should, every time he makes a new car, begin from scratch and totally change the entire design of gasoline engines, tires, transmissions, or the components that make steel and such.

Why then, should the creator scrap all successful designs in the creation of organisms and create organisms that are completely different in the components that would be used in the same fashion? That is preposterous, and no thinking person would demand that of an engineer in private business.

The evolutionary illusion created by their phylogenetic tree just does not hold up under scrutiny. In fact, if animals had really evolved, the tree would be infinitely larger, containing all the intermediates between the species such as the shrewbitpard. We have already addressed the glaring inconsistencies in the intermediate forms that should have been equally plentiful to substantiate the interrelationships of all living things on our planet. But the intermediates simply do not exist.

The naïve assumption that these so-called simple forms of life could have evolved into more complicated forms of life is completely unsubstantiated by empirical data. Their grouping, whether through genetic similarities or physical similarities, is an arbitrary choice that does not prove evolution.

The phylogenetic tree is not, therefore, proof of evolution. It is only a reflection of evolutionists' theories. It is merely a speculative, artificial grouping of life, which, by direct intent, mirrors their preconceived evolutionary bias. But the similarities they use to legitimize their assumption can be more accurately explained by a conscious intellectual choice to repeat successful designs in living things by the creator. When all is said and done, the phylogenetic tree cannot be used as scientific evidence for the evolution of the species. It is only evidence of evolutionists' evolutionary bias.

From a purely scientific viewpoint and because there is no known mechanism to change from one species to another since every proposed mechanism since the time of Darwin has been found wanting (as documented earlier in this book), the option of intelligent design is the only rational choice that can explain the continuity of patterns created for specific purposes because they reflect teleology.

The Geologic Column (the Second Pillar)

Perhaps the two most influential historical figures that influenced the Darwinian model of gradual evolution in the area of geology were Charles Lyell and William Smith. In 1819, Lyell received his bachelor of arts degree second class in classics from Exeter College in Oxford. Two years later, he received his master of arts degree and took up law as a profession.

Unlike Smith's family, Lyell's family was wealthy. Although Lyell practiced law for a short while, he was more interested in the field of geology. His financial situation gave him the liberty to pursue that field. In 1830, he published his first book on geology called *Principles of Geology*. The central argument set forth in his book is a reiteration and synthesis of James Hutton's earlier work. In 1788, Hutton wrote, "From what has actually been, we have data for concluding with regard to that which is to happen hereafter" (Hutton 2004).

Lyell's barely different proposition was that the present is key to the past. One faced forward in time, and the other faced backward in time. Lyell meant that geologic events in our present time are the key to interpreting all geologic events in the past. Hutton's explanation connected them from the past to the present and future, while Lyell connected them from the present to the past. That became known as the uniformitarian theory. The philosophic background to this perspective may have been inspired from the earlier Scottish Enlightenment writer David Hume, who said that "all inferences from experience suppose . . . that the future will resemble the past" (Hume 1772).

Hume rejected any theological traditions such as the Great Flood as mere mythology. His naturalistic, Enlightenment presupposition was then bolstered by the scientific credibility afforded by Lyell's and Smith's work in geology. Uniformitarianism took on a jaded form in which global cataclysms such as the Great Flood were absolutely ruled out as mythological.

The major misapplication of this proposition is the dogma that geologic processes have always progressed in the past at the same gradual rate that they are progressing today in our fairly stable environment. Hence, naturalists erroneously concluded that any major changes are strictly the result of long spans of time that accumulate the many minute changes into gradual great changes. According to this view, the Earth is shaped entirely by very slow moving forces that can be observed in the present.

At the root of this philosophical position is a deep antagonism toward the idea that the geologic strata could be explained by sudden catastrophic events such as the biblical flood. Prior to that time, many scientists held to the idea that a global flood was responsible for the major part of the geologic evidence in the strata. That geologic proposition was known as catastrophism.

That most things normally go in this uniformitarian manner is not disputed by the Judeo-Christian worldview. But the denial of the potential impact that cataclysms have brought to our world is unsupported by the empirical evidence and any rational basis. It is mere speculation fueled largely by evolutionists' enormous need to have long spans of time in order for evolution to appear to have a plausible chance of succeeding.

This new direction in naturalistic science spurred by the Enlightenment's intrinsic atheistic presupposition began to gain popularity and sway the minds of many, including a young man named Charles Darwin. Lyell had asked Robert FitzRoy, the captain of the *HMS Beagle*, to search for erratic boulders during the surveys conducted on their voyage. Before setting out, FitzRoy gave Darwin a copy of the first volume of Lyell's *Principles of Geology*. The impact of Lyell's book on Darwin was significant. When he arrived in South America, he received Volume 2 of the book, which outlined many of the ideas of Jean-Baptiste Lamarck, who erroneously believed that animals could pass on acquired characteristics to their offspring.

This Lamarckian feature proposed that the species had gradually changed over time by the acquisition of new characteristics passed on from their progenitors. Of course, as we have already discussed, modern genetics has completely discredited the Lamarckian idea that acquired characteristics could be passed on genetically.

Nevertheless, at the time, that was not yet known. The combination of the skewed or jaded gradualist geologic theories and the false and genetically ignorant Lamarckian proposition proposed by these three men gave Darwin the hologram of a foundation from which he developed the revolutionary idea of the evolution of species. His naturalistic contribution added the natural selection process produced by the mechanism of the survival of the fittest as the mechanism to change one species into another.

Upon returning from the voyage, Darwin and Lyell became close friends. However, it was not until the latter part of Lyell's life that he finally capitulated to the idea of organic evolution. He had originally favored a concept he called centers of creation, in which he envisioned the development of the diversity of species.

DATING METHODS: THE THREE PILLARS

Lyell died in February 1875. Unfortunately, he did not live to see the comet that struck Jupiter at the end of the next century. He may well have retracted his anti-catastrophic component to the jaded uniformitarian dogma after viewing such a cataclysmic strike. But for close to 200 years, uniformitarian scientists have historically turned a blind eye to such possibilities due to their subjective evolutionary bias.

For years, the scientific establishment ignored the very real potential for such catastrophic events. Lyell's idea that the present is the key to the past led to the dogmatic and myopic assumption that automatically disregarded any catastrophic events as real. Fantastical miracles such as the Great Flood or the parting of the Red Sea declared in scripture were automatically labeled mythological or embellished superstitious fables. The naturalistic and materialistic dogma of evolutionists insisted that only what is sensible to our senses and repeatable can be accepted as factual or scientific.

But modern science has come to understand that the Enlightenment scientific dogma, which stipulated that nothing can be accepted as factual that cannot be experimentally repeated, is not an absolute. While it may hold true for most things, it cannot be subjectively and dogmatically required of all things. Can evolutionists test another universe? Can they see or test dark matter or dark energy? Can we repeat the Big Bang? Can we sense a singularity with our senses?

Do not misunderstand me. I am a believer in the scientific process. But I do not believe the scientific process can be extrapolated to negate the possibility of the supernatural. The supernatural is only the natural that we have yet to understand. To limit reality only to that which can be perceived by our finite natural senses is simply an ignorant speculation.

We cannot physically see the asteroid that killed off the dinosaurs, but we can see the impact crater it created. We may not have seen the exact six-mile-wide asteroid that struck the Yucatan Peninsula, but we can simulate proportional experiments and extrapolate from them to see the true impact of its catastrophic force. To deny the physical evidence of the crater and the geophysical evidence left in its wake would be absurd. In much the same way, the evidence left behind from creation is testable, and we contend that a reasonable analysis of it can point us to the truth. Cataclysms are real, not mythological.

But sometimes, our metaphysical presuppositions create scientific dogma that gets in the way of reason. The uniformitarian hypothesis automatically excluded catastrophes such as the Global Flood to explain the strata. The Judeo-Christian worldview considers catastrophism, not in the exclusion of gradualism but in conjunction with it. That is the proper balance that allows us to study the real history of Earth. In other words, things usually go on in a gradualist manner, but here and there, catastrophes do take place that radically shape our environment in a very short period of time.

So strong was this fundamental Enlightenment bias against catastrophism that even though we had witnessed the immense destructive power of smaller asteroids striking our planet in modern history, most naturalistic scientists were lulled into a false sense of security through their biased and jaded uniformitarian presupposition. For more than two centuries, the idea of a catastrophic global event was simply ridiculed because it smacked of the biblical narrative and was therefore simply considered mythological. Since the time of Lyell, Darwin, and Smith, we have had more than a few warnings that such events were not only possible but actually a very real recurrent reality in Earth's history.

Apollo Asteroids (Earth-Crossers): The Uniformitarian Busters

At the beginning of the twentieth century, we had a warning, but it did not immediately register any alarms with naturalistic scientists. On the morning of June 30, 1908, a small 30-meter asteroid sliced through the air above the basin of the Stony Tunguska River in central Siberia. The blast was so intense and the hot winds created by the impact were so powerful that they completely flattened 2,100 square kilometers of forest. That is an area about half the size of the state of Rhode Island.

The energy released was equivalent to 1,000 nuclear bombs the size of the one dropped on Hiroshima. Had the meteor entered our atmosphere several hours later, it would have landed in Europe rather than the remote, unpopulated region in Russia. Millions could have lost their lives.

In Germany, weather stations reported a pressure wave from the impact of this small asteroid that circled the Earth twice before it exploded. The soot, which was carried into the atmosphere by the ejecta of the asteroid, affected the entire planet, and the skies as far away as California were darkened for weeks. One would think that supposedly objective scientists would have looked at this event and extrapolated the possibility of large meteor strikes in our past. But such was not the case, so entrenched was the uniformitarian bias.

It wasn't until 1994 that scientists began to admit the possibility of such an enormous catastrophe when, like the proverbial ostrich, they could no longer hide their heads in the hole in the ground. Right before their very eyes and before a watching world, they witnessed the effect of a devastating impact of a comet on a planet. And we had the added bonus of documenting and photographing the impact from both the *Hubble Space Telescope* and the spacecraft *Galileo*.

From July 16–22, 1994, the fragmented comet Shoemaker-Levy 9 struck Jupiter with such catastrophic power that scientists were finally forced to reconsider the anti-catastrophe component of their underlying jaded uniformitarian presupposition. The force of the gravity on Jupiter was so intense that it literally spaghettified the comet into a string of fragments.

The fragmented comet crashed into Jupiter's atmosphere at a speed of more than 200,000 kilometers per hour, creating an impact estimated to be about the equivalent of 25,000 megatons of TNT for each fragment. The fragments were catalogued by letters of the alphabet in the order of their impact on Jupiter.

Fragment A hit Jupiter's upper atmosphere just before 4 P.M. EDT on July 16. As the fragment blew up in a giant fireball, a plume of ejecta rose to more than 3,000 kilometers above the point of impact. As the debris came crashing down, it left a dark spot roughly a third of Earth's size. And that was just the first collision. . . . *Fragment G, one of the largest, left a bruise roughly the size of Earth. . . . We did not conjecture this event, or reconstruct its consequences from gathered evidence: we saw it! What are we to do?* (emphasis added) (Gleiser 2001, 124).

Can you imagine if this catastrophic strike had hit our planet Earth? Would geologic processes change dramatically in a very short period of time? What would it do to the rock strata? What intellectual arrogance could deny that such catastrophes have happened in the past and insist that all geologic processes must always happen in a slow and almost imperceptible rate?

Scientists, at the request of the United States Congress, began to investigate the potential for a meteor strike on Earth. At that time, they found that there were 859 near-Earth-orbit (NEO) objects that intersect with our vicinity and could cause high consequence events. At any given time, there are more than a dozen NEOs that cannot yet be ruled out for an impact with Earth. Some are comets, and some are asteroids.

Comets differ from asteroids in that they are composed of mostly frozen water and gases instead of rock. This difference in their composition is what causes comets to display their spectacular luminous tails during their trajectory as they come close to the sun. As they approach the sun, solar winds cause them to disintegrate. The ice is vaporized, and the dust and gases released are left in the wake of the trajectory, and thus, we see their spectacular glowing tails millions of miles in length refracting the sunlight.

Astronomers have catalogued three major asteroid clouds that may contain trillions of these orbiting ice chunks (comets) and space rocks (asteroids). The closest to us is the asteroid belt near the orbit of Mars. The middle one is the Kuiper cloud or belt named after Gerard Kuiper who earlier suggested that this asteroid belt existed beyond the orbit of Neptune. The furthest from us is the Oort cloud, which takes light a year to reach it from the sun.

A few of those icy chunks are almost as large as our moon. So far, astronomers have catalogued more than 60 of these icy worlds in the Kuiper cloud, which circle our solar system around its outer edge. The once-called "planet" Pluto is one of the largest of these ice chunks. There is some debate among astronomers about the cataloguing of Pluto. Some still want to call it a planet, others a dwarf planet, and still others a large asteroid.

I believe there are only seven planets, and Pluto is not one of them. Its orbit is not in alignment with the plane of the other planets.

For the most part, these bodies, as well as the asteroids and comets, are in a trajectory that is fairly consistent. But sometimes, near misses or collisions with other objects can derail them from their initial, stable course. Occasionally, that may cause them to enter a trajectory that could intercept a planet such as Earth. What would the impact of even a small asteroid strike be for our civilization?

In the middle of January 2000, an asteroid estimated to weigh some 200 tons (the weight of four typical stone blocks from the Great Pyramid) sliced through the atmosphere above the small town of Atlan in northern Canada. Around 8:30 in the morning, the residents of Atlan saw a bright flash of light followed by an enormous sonic boom.

Witnesses who heard the large explosion say a flash of brilliant white light and a second enormous explosion immediately followed the first one. The first boom was heard when the asteroid entered Earth's atmosphere. The second boom came when it exploded. Fortunately, the asteroid exploded midair. But the explosion still had the destructive force of a nuclear bomb, leaving a luminescent cloud in the sky that could be seen for miles.

In 2001, another meteor exploded over the Pacific Ocean, with the comparable force of 10 nuclear bombs, each about the size of the bomb dropped on Hiroshima. In 2002, yet another meteor exploded over the Mediterranean Sea, but most of us are not aware of these events since news of such things might understandably create panic.

The truth is that there is an enormous number of asteroids that have crossed our planet's trajectory and that continue to do so. Astronauts in space see a small meteor entering Earth's atmosphere approximately every two minutes. On any day, several tons of space dust showers our Earth. Each day, hundreds if not thousands of new asteroids are being discovered by astronomers trying desperately to catalog them in order to determine whether they are potential Earth-strikers.

Fortunately for us, most meteor strikes on Earth burn up in our atmosphere because they are rather small. Moreover, the vast areas of oceans that cover the surface of our planet absorb the larger ones that manage to strike. A good-sized meteor strike in the ocean, however, would offer us little protection from catastrophe. Huge tsunamis would devastate everything in their circumferences.

Occasionally, however, a meteor strikes land. And some are large enough to destroy a major city. In the past, most of them landed harmlessly away from population centers. But on our modern crowded Earth, meteor strikes are a greater threat. The reason our planet is not visibly scarred by these meteor strikes is because the forces of erosion have hidden many of them that struck landmass in the past.

Ironically, today most evolutionists believe that the dinosaur extinction was caused by the asteroid that hit the Yucatan Peninsula. They are right, except that it did not happen 65 million years ago. It happened about 6,000 years ago when the First Earth was ended by the Great Flood (we will address this later in the fourth book of this series, *The Death of the First Earth*).

Some of the asteroids in the belts may have been debris shot out of our planet from the impact of the asteroid that caused the Great Flood. Most of the immediately returning ejecta from the initial

DATING METHODS: THE THREE PILLARS

A typical meteor crater in Arizona, similar yet smaller than the giant crater 110 miles across off the Yucatan Peninsula in the Gulf of Mexico and the even bigger 300-mile wide crater in Antarctica. This crater is only ¾ of a mile in diameter and more than 1,000 feet high on the borders. A building of 100 stories could just reach the rim from the floor below.

impacts would have been covered by the sedimentation of the Great Flood or eroded by the enormous hydraulics involved. However, those catapulted into space orbits may now be coming home to roost.

A simple observation of the surface of the moon or the planet Mercury is enough to assure us that asteroids have abounded in our particular area of the solar system. In any case, the long and the short of it is that the potential for a catastrophic strike is now being considered with more seriousness than ever before.

As a result of observing the impact of the Shoemaker-Levy 9 comet on Jupiter, scientists, in response to presidential and congressional pressure, have attempted to undertake the awesome task of cataloguing all potential Earth-crossers or Apollo asteroids, as they are called. They are in the initial stages of preparing contingency plans, should the need arise.

The potential Earth-crossers are named Apollo asteroids after the first asteroid that was approximately 8 kilometers in width, which in 1932 and again in 1980 came within 9 million kilometers of Earth. That is quite close in astronomical terms, only about 30 times the distance to the moon.

But some of these Apollo asteroids or comets are much larger. For example, the Swift-Tuttle comet, responsible for the well-known annual Perseid meteor shower, is about 25 kilometers in diameter. That is roughly 2½ times the size of the one that struck Mexico and, according to evolutionists, almost caused the extinction of all life on Earth. That awesome comet soars through space at a speed of 61 kilometers per second. The impact it would create, should it strike the Earth, would be equivalent to 1 billion Hiroshima bombs. Its next approach to Earth is scheduled for August 14, 2126, at an estimated distance of 24 million kilometers.

But the real kicker comes in the next millennium if it is not jarred from its present course by a near miss or by coming near the path of another planet. It is estimated that in 3044, it will pass only 1.5 million kilometers from Earth. That is quite alarming since that is roughly the distance to the moon. Any slight deviation or miscalculation on our part may spell complete catastrophe for our Second Earth.

If it strikes the moon instead of the Earth, there will be an even more destructive force. The sky would rain down fire from above, destroying our planet completely. God would have to create a new earth. The book of Revelation speaks of a day very similar to that at the end of the Davidic Kingdom.

In 2004, a new asteroid about 600 yards across was discovered and named Apophis. The asteroid (2004 MN4) is estimated to pass between the Earth and the moon on Friday, April 13, 2029. It will be 18,895 miles from the surface of the Earth, which is closer than some of our communication satellites. The same asteroid will approach the Earth again seven years later in 2036.

If the pass between the Earth and the moon changes the trajectory due to the gravitational pull of the Earth (passing through a small window called the gravitational keyhole), it is quite possible that it could strike the Earth or the moon on the second approach. An asteroid that size, although significantly smaller than the one that caused the Great Flood, would create a cataclysmic impact that would affect the entire planet. If it strikes the Earth, the path is predicted to be over Siberia and down the Western Pacific coast of the United States, crossing into the Atlantic over Central America and heading toward Africa. This path is called the line of probability. It could land anywhere along that line.

It is estimated that around 1 million asteroids are larger than 1 kilometer. Of those, some 10,000 asteroids are larger than 10 kilometers, the size of the one that caused the Chicxulub crater in Mexico. In 2001, 2,000 asteroids were classified as potential Earth-crossers.

> Earlier I said that estimates put the number of asteroids larger than 10 kilometers at over ten thousand and those larger than one kilometer at almost one million. Of these, Gene Shoemaker and collaborators estimated that at least two thousand are Earth-crossers, that is, potential hitters (Gleiser 2001, 128).

By 2012, scientists had catalogued some 10,000 potential Earth-crossers. That figure, of course, relates to the objects we have seen and catalogued. There may be many more we have not yet discovered.

The problem is that we have not yet been able to catalog all the asteroids. Every week that goes by, more and more asteroids are being discovered and catalogued. Their trajectories are being computed and their relative danger noted. Today, no astronomer doubts the fact that one day a meteor will strike the Earth. Here are the only questions left unanswered: When will it hit? How large will it be?

The potential of an asteroid strike is a very real danger that is no longer taken lightly by the scientific community. But there is another catastrophe that looms ever closer on our horizon. Our climate is no longer stable.

The scientific consensus has now changed. Many are afraid that an accelerated warming of our planet could lead us into a catastrophic ice age in less than 100 years. If perhaps their jaded uniformitarian horse-blinds had been removed earlier, they would have seen this coming.

The long and short of it is that the jaded form of uniformitarianism is dead. The justification for long periods of time and vast geological ages is now debunked. Catastrophes of global consequence have been scientifically vindicated by empirical data and eye witnessed events recorded with cameras and other modern devices.

The phylogenetic tree cannot provide us with absolute proof, and the uniformitarian hypothesis, which claimed dogmatically that our strata were formed through long ages of slow accumulation, has been shown to be unrealistic. Thus, as scientists, we must be open to the possibility that at least some of these striations could have been created by catastrophic measures that impacted our planet in the past. To refuse such a conclusion is nothing less than self-deception of the first magnitude.

The Strata

Now we come to the strata and the evolutionary timetable they supposedly prove. We must begin with William "Strata" Smith. He was born on May 23, 1769, in the village of Churchill, Oxfordshire, England. He was the son of a blacksmith who died when William was only eight years old.

Raised by his uncle, Smith soon found work as a surveyor. The nature of his work allowed him to travel throughout England as he surveyed the land. He had a keen eye for the topography he was surveying. In his travels, he became interested in the rock layers unearthed by train tracks and roads cutting through hills as well as exposures in canals, escarpments, quarries, and coal pits. He noticed the striations in cliffs and began to collect fossils.

He began to notice that there were patterns of fossils found in the layers. He also noticed an easterly dip of the bedrock, smaller near the surface and more pronounced in the deeper layers. He concluded from his findings that there was a principle of faunal succession that could

DATING METHODS: THE THREE PILLARS

be testable through the fossils found in the strata. During his many travels, he managed to gather a rather sizable collection of fossils. But his work was ignored by academia of his day. I find it quite ironic that because Smith did not possess the academic credentials that have artificially become the requirement in our modern era for any contribution to science, his work was overlooked by the same scientific community that now heralds his work as evidence for the evolutionary process. In 1815, he published the first geologic map of England, but it was soon plagiarized, and he was not able to recoup financially. It brought him to financial ruin.

He was released from King's Bench Prison, a debtor's prison, on August 31, 1819. Upon returning home, he found a bailiff waiting for him. His home and property of 14 years were seized. It was not until later in his life while employed by Sir John Johnston that his work was duly recognized. In 1835, he received an honorary doctorate of laws from Trinity College in recognition of his work in promoting the science of geology. He died four years later on August 28, 1839.

Darwin formulated his Darwinian evolutionary hypothesis about the time that Smith died. The work of Lyell and Smith as well as that of Lamarck provided Darwin with the fundamental information that allowed him to postulate his theory of the evolution of the species.

Smith's nephew John Phillips, who lived with Smith during his youth, was his apprentice. In 1841, it was Phillips who was first credited with specifying most of the table of the broad geologic eras, which is still used today.

This table of the geologic column has become the second leg in the evolutionist's makeshift tripod to prop up the evolutionary timetable. According to evolutioinists' stratigraphic column, the simpler life forms are found in the more archaic, deeper strata, and the more complex and advanced life forms are found in the more recently deposited layers.

The assumption in the geologic column is that as we search the strata for fossils, we should be able to find in the deepest and oldest strata the simplest life forms. They would gradually increase in complexity as we travel up the column to the more recent strata. Therefore, based on their preliminary assumption that living things evolve in the escalating fashion represented in the phylogenetic tree, geologists officially classify layers and date them by the type of organisms found within them.

This, again, is circular reasoning doubled. That is, they depend on a system (the phylogenetic tree) that has been arrived at through circular reason to establish another system (geologic column) that has also been established with circular reasoning. In other words, the previous assumption proves the following assumption, all of which is predicated on their fundamental assumption that species can evolve into other species. That is what I call the Triple Lindy of circular logic.

Lyell's uniformitarian assumption formed the necessary basis for legitimizing huge periods of time in slow, gradual, small steps. But evolutionists claim that the groupings of the fossils in the strata form the lynchpin of the physical evidence left behind by this gradual evolutionary process because it is physical in nature. The fossils can be seen and touched; hence, they deem it empirical evidence for their theory.

However, it is not the physical nature of the fossils that we question. Yes, fossils do exist, and they can be seen and touched. But they do not exist in their imagined evolutionary geologic column as represented in textbooks. Furthermore, the eons in their imaginations that passed to deposit those layers are based on their jaded uniformitarian bias that insists these deposits were not made by catastrophic events, an assumption that is quite speculative and not provable.

Their geologic column is divided into five major sections or eras. The first and supposedly most ancient is the Archeozoic Era, which, they claim, is about 1.8 billion years ago. According to evolutionists, that era spanned some 800 million years.

The second era was the Proterozoic Era some 1 billion years ago, supposedly lasting about 400 million years. That brings us to the third era, the Paleozoic Era, which is said to have also lasted some 400 million years. The fourth era is the Mesozoic Era some 200 million years ago. That era supposedly lasted approximately 130 million years. And the fifth and most recent era is the Cenozoic Era, which, according to evolutioinists' timetable, began about 70 million years ago. Each of these eras is then further divided into various component periods.

By looking at the fossil (where it fits in the phylogenetic tree), they can infer the date by the number of years they assume it took to evolve. Thus, the geologic column, like the phylogenetic tree, is nothing more than a reflection of both their jaded uniformitarian bias that catapulted the acceptance of enormous spans of time for the geologic column and their gradualist model that presupposes that species change through small selective adaptations over extremely long periods of time.

The most essential element necessary for gradualism to explain the leaps from one species to another is *long periods of time*. Hence, the enormous spans of time given to these geologic ages are indispensible to the evolutionary model. Without these vast ages, the small incremental changes they envisioned in Darwin's model could not have happened.

We have shown that the simplest life forms are filled with multiple systems of irreducible complexity that could not have evolved in small, discreet, gradual steps. We have shown that even with these enormous ages, which by necessity evolutionists propose, the statistical impossibility of creating a single-celled organism is so great as to be an irrational proposition.

We have shown that the specified complexity found in many systems of life, such as the gene expression system, has never been duplicated by random natural processes. It is indicative of intelligent design. We have shown that integrated specified complexity is even more complicated since the systems are interrelated, and each system must work independently before the total system can be functional.

Such integrated specified complexity cannot be rationally explained except as the design of a higher intelligence.

We have already discussed that there are no credible mechanisms to change one species into another. Microevolution cannot be extrapolated into macroevolution. Changes take shape within a species to a finite point according to the genetic variability programmed from the beginning in the particular genome of the organism.

We have shown that mutations cannot account for the evolution of species. We have shown that the Lamarckian illusion, which evolutionists had previously so dogmatically insisted on as empirical data (i.e., that environmentally acquired characteristics could propel evolution from one species to another) was nothing more than wishful thinking.

We have shown that the anti-catastrophe component of uniformitarianism does not match with the real universe we observe. Large-scale catastrophes that can cause drastic geological impacts have been physically observed and documented.

We have shown that the universe is not infinite in size and that the age of the universe is finite. The steady state theory was also dead wrong. Our universe had a beginning. Life has not had an eternity of time or an infinite amount of resources with which to evolve. In fact, we have shown the statistics that prove random processes do not have the time or the resources in our entire universe to accidentally create life.

All the gradualist mechanisms have proved to be deficient. But what of this magnificent correlation of fossils in the strata that go from simple organisms to more complex organisms? Is there a clearly defined consistent and sequential grouping that is universally found?

Contrary to the illusion evolutionists have so cleverly managed to promote, the fact is that nowhere in the world has this geologic column been found in the complete order in which they presume it all evolved. There is no complete geological column anywhere in the world.

> [T]he complete geologic record is hardly ever, if at all, found in any one place on the surface of the Earth. Usually several

or many of the strata systems are missing compared to the overall geologic record. . . . However, quite commonly there is little or no physical or physiographic evidence of the intervening period of erosion or non-deposition of the missing strata systems, suggesting that at such localities neither erosion nor deposition ever occurred there (Snelling 2009, 728).

Logic dictates that if the geologic record were the result of millions of years of gradual sedimentation, as the jaded uniformitarian evolutionary assumption insists, the entire world would contain a fairly monolithic stratum without any interruptions of large time periods. After all, the normal geologic processes could not just magically be suspended for many millions of years in these sporadic areas all around the Earth to cause these particular strata to magically disappear.

If, in fact, these layers were made slowly over millions of years, then all the sedimentary deposit layers would show typical erosion patterns, and the layers would hardly ever be found even as bands. Yet that is not what we find in the geologic record.

Furthermore, the fossil evidence would be consistent everywhere. It would show the fossilization of particular creatures according to their specific biodomes. For example, we would not expect to find in the same strata of a given area fossils of marine animals mixed up with terrestrial animals and flying creatures that live in completely separate biodomes. Yet that is exactly what we find in the geologic record filled with mass graveyards of creatures from every kind of habitat imaginable and in every stage of life.

On the other hand, it is exactly what we would expect if the sedimentation were the result of a global cataclysmic flood that is subject to numerous localized cataclysmic processes, which include any variety of such mechanisms as volcanism, tsunamis created by the shifting continents, and massive earthquakes triggered by crashing meteors that caused the cracking and separation of the continents.

In fact, the process of fossilization is quite rare in our present stable system. Sediments must bury the creature rather quickly before the body decomposes and scavengers eat them. The sheer number of fossils that exist and are, quite importantly, undisturbed clearly points to a series of sudden and catastrophic sedimentation events that were repeated in rapid succession and buried the animals even before they could decompose or be scavenged by other creatures.

The sheer volume of suspended sediments necessary to create these massive fossil graveyards that trapped all living things in every stage of life and from such different biodomes cannot be explained by gradualism. But that is exactly what we would expect from the hydraulic mechanisms that ruled during the cataclysmic Great Flood. It is especially so for the corrosive hydraulic power of the breaking fountains of the deep as the Genesis record indicates.

> *In the six hundredth year of Noah's life, in the second month, on the seventeenth day of the month, on the same day all the fountains of the great deep burst open, and the floodgates of the sky were opened.*
> —Gen. 7:11

Notice that the Genesis record says "the fountains of the great deep burst open," implying first that it was not one fountain but a series of them and that the opening was a violent event. Imagine a curtain of jetting hot water and steam gushing upward at supersonic speeds, thrusting up from the base of the continents perhaps 10 to 16 miles below the surface through the cracked fissures of the fractured continents. That curtain of gushing water would extend as far as the eye could see to the horizon either way. In fact, that curtain of water would run along the mid-ocean ridges over the entire face of the world where the continents had been cracked by a series of meteor strikes. I will deal with this mechanism and the evidence of the seven meteors that caused it more exhaustively in the fifth volume of this series, *The Death of the First Earth*. In this volume, I will only provide a condensed narrative in order to address the origin of the strata deposits.

But it is not just water that exploded from below. There were also large quantities of limestone and other dissolved minerals and gases, which prior to the meteor strikes, were enormously pressurized by the weight of the 10 to 16 miles of granitic rock above them within their underground chambers. They were thrust to the surface at supersonic speeds, eroding the sides as they shot up into the atmosphere.

It was the impact of the seven meteors that not only opened the cracks of the surface of Earth's crust but also, through the successive pressure waves caused by the force of their impacts, dramatically disturbed the dissolved gases and minerals in the subterranean waters and caused the explosive outgassing to fuel the fury of the geysers worldwide. To imagine the power of this explosive outgassing, take a soda pop bottle, shake it violently, and then quickly open the top. These geysers were so strong that they actually reached the ionosphere and beyond.

The powerful forces of the jetting geysers created by the breaking of the fountains of the deep then eroded the sides of the continents, sending boulders flying and creating tremendous turbidity in the new oceans it was creating. It is the reason that our continental shelves are all shaped like a V.

It also injected enormous volumes of water, some in the form of steam, some in thick jets of dirty water filled with emulsified minerals. After reaching their maximum height, they came down on both sides like waterfalls on steroids. Tiny droplets of water from the spraying waterfalls further saturated the atmosphere, causing it to destroy the delicately balanced small water vapor canopy that had not only protected humans from cosmic radiation but also provided a greenhouse effect on the planet and kept it from having frozen poles.

The relentless infusion of water droplets into our upper atmosphere created the storm clouds that allowed the Earth to be pounded by torrential rains for 40 days and 40 nights. It was the first time humans saw rain and lightning bolts or heard the frightening sounds of thunder claps. It must have been a terrifying experience for anyone to witness.

Up to that point, humans had not experienced the dread created by earthquakes, volcanoes, tsunamis, hurricanes, and tornadoes. The First Earth was a virtual paradise with a completely stable meteorological system that watered the plants every morning by the dew that collected from the latent atmosphere as it cooled.

> *[F]or the Lord God had not sent rain upon the earth, and there was no man to cultivate the ground. But a mist used to rise from the earth and water the whole surface of the ground.*
> —Gen. 2:5–6

A morning mist watered the whole Earth evenly. The water vapor canopy that enveloped our First Earth no doubt caused this phenomenon during the cooling of the night. Between the abundant moisture latent in the atmosphere and the larger concentration of oxygen, all creatures thrived in rich habitats as never after. It was the age of gigantism.

I suspect that the added weight of the small water vapor canopy also caused a greater saturation of oxygen in creatures' blood, and they thrived on our First Earth with greater and more robust variations than any of the remnants of the diminutive species that exist today. The Second Earth is but a shadow of the First Earth.

But the reader must understand that when God said it rained upon the entire Earth for 40 days and 40 nights, it was not a typical summer thunderstorm as many have erroneously imagined. The intense heat generated by the striking asteroids coupled with the catastrophic volcanism it unleashed caused the temperature in our atmosphere to spike radically. The hot waters and steam emanating from below added fuel to the fire. The jetting streams of water created ferocious winds through the Venturi effect as it sucked up the air from the sides and shot it upward. The combination of high winds and heat provided the perfect recipe for mega-hurricanes.

Never before had humans seen super tornadoes or super hurricanes. And never again shall they witness such unbridled fury as these mega-hurricanes grew to immense size and power. Now they ruled the watery world that was. And once the land was covered by floodwater, they were subsequently unopposed by any land structures such as mountains to disrupt them. Large-scale sheet flooding also covered the landmasses with a catastrophic effect, dragging material across enormous spans of the continents in successive waves.

As these global chaotic forces affected each local habitat, they created the sudden catastrophic sedimentation we observe in several distinct episodes that brought different material from coastal regions, sometimes from one side of a continent all the way to the other, and deposited layer after layer throughout the 150 days of the total event when the fountains of the deep finally ceased and the waters of the Great Flood peaked.

It is the Judeo-Christian position that these massive layers of sedimentation were not deposited over millions of years but over the span of a single global cataclysmic event. Furthermore, we believe the empirical evidence clearly supports the historicity of the flood of Noah's day, and we will now provide some of that evidence.

The Imagined Evolutionary Order of the Strata

The ideal evolutionary division of the strata that evolutionists have invented simply does not exist in this complete, neat, and sequential order anywhere on Earth. As a matter of fact, there are never more than four of their strata in the order they presume. Most of the time, the orders are reversed or mixed in different ways so that if it were not for the underlying phylogenetic presupposition, there would be no objective way of classifying the strata. Again, evolutionists resort to more circular reasoning.

Sometimes, intrusions from the upper layers can occur. They are often formed by the natural erosion of strata in a given location. In other words, the erosion of certain layers can bring a lower layer to the surface, and then deposits of living material on that layer can seem to indicate an older age than truly warranted. But a careful study of the strata in a wider circumference of that area can usually show the areas of erosion. That is, of course, what we would naturally expect globally throughout the entire geologic column if the deposits were formed gradually through billions of years, as the evolutionists maintain.

As a matter of fact, one would expect to see the effects of erosion in practically every layer if they were actually deposited gradually over billions of years. Instead, what we find most of the time are uniform layers of strata that seem to extend for huge distances almost undisturbed. They may buckle and contort, but the layers are not only almost uniform in depth for enormous spans, but also, even more perplexing for evolutionists, the folds created by lateral stresses of continental shifting show that the sediments were still pliable when folding.

That pattern is difficult to reconcile with the idea that sediments were deposited over billions of years and that the continents slowly separated through very small incremental steps, as we observe today. If that were true, the folds of the long hardened rock would show extensive cracking, having hardened long before the slow lateral stresses imagined by gradualism could impact the layers into folds.

The uneven patterns of natural erosion, which ought to be more common everywhere, are just not there. Such long spans of multiple, evenly distributed layers are instead the telltale evidence of successive catastrophic sedimentary deposits under water during closely grouped incidents in a single catastrophic event.

Gradual or Catastrophic Sedimentary Depositions

How can we differentiate between slow and gradual uniformitarian deposition and sudden cataclysmic deposition? There are five elements in the geologic evidence that need to be considered in order to determine whether they are gradual depositions or catastrophic depositions.

Diagram 10. The Geologic Column

THE GEOLOGIC COLUMN		
ERA	PERIODS	YEARS AGO
CENOZOIC	Quartinary: Recent Epoch Pleistocene Epoch	25,000 3,000,000
	Tertiary: Pliocene Epoch Miocene Epoch Oligocene Epoch Eocene Epoch Paleocene Epoch	12,000,000 25,000,000 35,000,000 60,000,000 70,000,000
MESOZOIC	Cretaceous Jurassic Triassic	70,000,000 to 200,000,000
PALEOZOIC	Permian Pennsylvanian Mississippian Devonian Silurian Ordovician Cambrian	200,000,000 to 600,000,000
PROTEROZOIC		600,000,000 to 1,000,000,000
ARCHEOZOIC		1,000,000,000 to 1,800,000,000

The first two telltale signs of catastrophic sedimentary depositions are the wide breadth of scope and the homogeneous continuity of the individual layers. It must be noted that often these layers are so large that they are literally continental in breadth. Gradual, uniformitarian depositions, according to evolutionists, are created by the passage of millions of years of slow deposition. But if that is correct, those layers could not possibly exhibit homogeneous characteristics in thickness and composition for such enormous spans of geographical areas because of the variability of local erosion patterns that would have applied unequal forces to such large areas.

Gradualism would predict uneven erosion patterns that would prohibit such large and regular deposition layers. The layers would be subject to localized erosion forces that vary greatly from one area to another. It would also predict a more heterogeneous composition of the sedimentary layers due to the natural variation of different forces that large spans of time would have necessarily impacted by the nature of changing local conditions.

The third telltale sign is the enormous distance that the source of the deposits traveled before sedimentation, which evidences the immense global hydraulic forces that were involved in the transport of the foreign material to that area rather than a localized event.

The fourth telltale sign is the pristine nature of the sedimentation without showing widespread signs of perturbation by burrowing creatures, as would be expected by the slow gradual evolutionary process. If these multiple layers formed millions of years apart, as evolutionists insist, they would contain widespread signs of perturbation. What this lack of perturbation signifies is a large-scale catastrophic annihilation of these burrowing creatures during the cataclysmic sedimentation process.

The fifth telltale sign is the incontrovertible evidence that massive volumes of rapid sedimentation occurred globally and was responsible for killing marine creatures, fresh water creatures, and terrestrial and even flying creatures in massive fossil gravesites. The enormous compilations of such varied and naturally separated habitats particular to these fossilized creatures can only be explained by catastrophic large-sheet flooding scenarios that impacted all ecosystems simultaneously.

The fact that such massive gravesites, which include creatures from many ecosystems killed together, are found so frequently all around the world that it is simply more rationally explained by the mechanism of a global catastrophic flood than repeated and independent large-sheet flooding scenarios over millions of years. The gradualist would have to explain each of the multiple independent mechanisms that caused these large-scale flooding scenarios that created the many fossil graveyards around our entire planet and affected such diverse biodomes simultaneously.

Taking into consideration the five points we just discussed, let us now consider some of the empirical evidence in the geologic data that substantiates a catastrophic origin of the strata.

The detailed discussion of the Grand Canyon strata demonstrates in a conclusive manner that the evidence associated with these limestone, sandstone, and shale strata strongly favors their catastrophic deposition by water on a grand scale over a widespread area, contrary to the oft repeated claims that these strata were deposited over long ages of slow-and-gradual deposition. Indeed, for such rapid sedimentation to have occurred on a widespread scale, the evidence points to the ocean having been over the continent, the sediments being transported very long distances after erosion in great quantities from far away source areas. The sum total of evidence in the strata is thus compelling for their flood deposition.

However, it also needs to be recognized that many of these same features found in this strata that are consistent with catastrophic flood deposition are also found in similar and other types of strata in many other parts of the world (Snelling 2009, 519).

Andrew Snelling is a geologist and research scientist who earned his PhD from the University of Sydney, Australia, in 1982. Unfortunately, the technical nature of his two-volume series is not appreciated by the majority of readers in our present culture who have difficulty maintaining more than five minutes of concentration and prefer to communicate through tweeting sentences of 140 characters or less.

Let us look at some of the giant deposition zones around the world. In Utah, we find the Shinarump Conglomerate that has an average thickness of 15 meters, or almost 49 feet, of a single sedimentation layer that spans more than 260,000 square kilometers in Utah and several of its neighboring states.

The composition of this layer is sand and rounded pebbles, typical in streambeds or river deposits, but the area is so vast and continuous and so uniform that it is quite impossible that it could have been created by any meandering stream or river. Its uniform consistency implies a single event of massive hydraulic force such as sheet flooding in a relatively short period of time and not a slow and gradual process created by meandering rivers over millions of years.

> However, the Shinarump Conglomerate does not match any modern depositional environment, and especially does not compare to the modern analog of a braided stream system. Specifically, where is there any place in the world today where streams are depositing sand and conglomerate of such massive uniform thickness like this over such a vast area of 260,000 square kilometers, or even close to that? There is simply not one known. Streams make deposits that meander through a valley, but they don't create uniform deposits over tens of thousands of square kilometers. Thus it is far more realistic to explain this conglomerate formation as deposited by a massive sheet of rapidly flowing water *en masse*, in what therefore had to be a catastrophic event over such an area in a very short time. Such conditions are totally consistent with flood deposition (Snelling 2009, 519–20).

The phenomenon we observe in North America is not a local phenomenon. Going all the way to the other side of our planet in central Australia, we find two massive conglomerates, the Uluru Arkose and the Mount Currie Conglomerate, that also evidence catastrophic depositions by massive hydraulic forces in conjunction with repeated earthquakes in a single catastrophic event.

DATING METHODS: THE THREE PILLARS

Technically known as an inselberg, Uluru is an isolated rock-mass or monolith that rises sharply on all sides to a height of about 340 meters above the surrounding desert plain of Central Australia. It is in effect, an enormous outcrop of beds of arkose, a coarse sandstone consisting of poorly sorted, jagged grains of other rock types and feldspar. The arkose occurs in multiple layers that together form a cohesive massive rock unit, and these beds dip at 80-85°. The cumulative thickness of the arkose through the entire length of Uluru is at least 2.5 kilometers, but from drilling below the surrounding desert sands, the total thickness of this arkose has been determined at almost 6,000 meters. Its full lateral extent is poorly known due to paucity of other outcrops, but the Uluru Arkose is very conservatively estimated at covering an area of at least 30 square kilometers.

Thirty kilometers west of Uluru is Kata Tjuta, a series of huge, rounded, rocky domes, the highest being Mt. Olga about 600 meters above the desert floor. These spectacular domed rock masses cover an area of about 40 square kilometers (8km x 5 km), and consist of layers of conglomerate dipping 10-18° to the southwest, with a total cumulative thickness of 6,000 meters. This massive conglomerate unit, known as the Mt. Currie Conglomerate, extends under the desert sands to other outcrops over an area of more than 600 square kilometers. The conglomerate is poorly sorted and contains boulders up to 1.5 meters in diameter, as well as cobbles and pebbles, held together by a mixture of finer fragments and cemented sand, silt, and/or mud. The pebbles, cobbles and boulders are generally rounded and consist mainly of granite and basalt, but also some sandstone, rhyolite and several kinds of metamorphic rocks.

Though the outcrops of the Uluru Arkose and the Mt. Currie Conglomerate are isolated from one another, the available evidence clearly suggests that both rock units were formed at the same time and in the same way....

While large alluvial fans are known on the Earth's surface today, none are forming over such vast areas with such massive thicknesses, or with the scale of intensity of the sheet flooding that would have been required to transport such enormous quantities of conglomerate and sand such long distances with a ferocity capable of carrying boulders up to 1.5 meters across. Furthermore, if deposition had been episodic over millions of years, there ought to be evidence of erosion (such as channels) and weathering surfaces between the layers within both the conglomerate and the arkose, while some compositional and fabric variations would be expected between successive layers. However, in the exposure at Uluru and Kata Tjuta, the arkose and conglomerate compositions, respectively, and their fabrics, are uniformly similar throughout the 2.5 kilometer thickness at Uluru and the 1.8 kilometer thickness exposed at Kata Tjuta and the layering is extremely regular and parallel....

Furthermore, the ubiquitous fresh feldspar crystals in the Uluru Arkose would never have survived the claimed millions of years of deposition, as feldspar deposited in sheets of sand only centimeters thick spread over many tens of square kilometers and exposed to the sun's heat, water, and air over countless years would decompose relatively quickly to clays....

The implication of all this evidence is that the deposition of the arkose and conglomerate concurrently as lateral equivalents required an amount and force of water sufficient to erode, transport, and deposit at least

DATING METHODS: THE THREE PILLARS

Uluru or Ayer's Rock in central Australia

4,000 cubic kilometers of boulders, pebbles, cobbles and sand distances of at least tens of kilometers in successive continuous pulses, so as to stack the resultant layers to a thickness of 6,000 meters over at least 600 square kilometers all probably in a matter of hours or days at the very most. This description is consistent with what we know of turbidity currents and submarine debris flows. However the scale and intensity and rapid repetition would not only have required cataclysmic flooding, but repetitive fault movements and earthquakes to trigger the currents and flows responsible for the rapid successive pulses of erosion transport and deposition (Snelling 2009, 520–22).

What is abundantly clear in the strata is that a global cataclysm of unprecedented and almost unimaginable power affected our planet and left for us the evidence that cannot be explained by the gradualist evolutionary model.

How Striations Formed in the Geologic Column through the Hydraulics of the Great Flood

The evidence seems to favor that most of the layers were deposited in the strata in one event such as the Global Flood, which caused very specific patterns in the layering of these sediments. What possible mechanism could trigger such catastrophic geological upheavals? The answer is multiple meteor strikes.

If the Chicxulub meteor was so earth-shattering that evolutionists claim it caused the extinction of dinosaurs, imagine the impact of seven equal or even larger meteors. We propose this was the multifaceted trigger that broke apart our tectonic plates and caused the Great Flood.

Most of the animals we find fossilized would have perished in the global cataclysm that followed, which effectively ended 95 percent of the variety of fauna that existed on the First Earth. The effect of this catastrophic event severely diminished the variability of the genotypes of the surviving creatures and subsequently the phenotypes expressed out of the marvelous array God had originally created.

Our severely diminished fauna is but a shadow of the mighty world that was. We propose that there were seven meteor strikes that broke the crust of the First Earth and ripped our once single and stable super-continent into seven smaller continents and seven oceans. I will deal with the specifics of this claim in the book detailing the Great Flood. But for the purpose of this book, it should be noted that aspects of the etymology of the flood are the key to understanding the strata.

It explains the intense volcanism that followed and provides the clue to the enormous power necessary to cause the physical separation of the continents within a rather short period of time and unleash the underground aquifers that brought upon our planet the immense hydraulic forces and catastrophic sedimentation that affected the entire globe. In order for us to appreciate the enormous power necessary for the cracking of the crust of the Earth, we must first appreciate the enormous power of a single large meteor strike.

The Destructive Power of a Single Large Meteor Strike

The destructive and globally catastrophic power of a single large meteor strike is almost unimaginable to us. The power of seven striking within a relatively short period of time is monumental and literally earth-shattering. Let us consider the single impact of the meteor that caused the Chicxulub crater that evolutionists claim killed off the dinosaurs. The reader must also understand that most of the meteorological scenario I am about to relate (except the idea that this is what caused the ripping of the continents) is agreed upon and promoted by evolutionists in describing the Chicxulub meteor strike in the Yucatan Peninsula of Mexico that they now propose was the culprit that killed off the dinosaurs and caused the mass extinction of 95 percent of the animals and plants on our First Earth.

Prior to the discovery of the Chicxulub crater, evolutionists were puzzled by the sudden disappearance of such a wide variety of creatures that were obviously superbly successful in a selective capacity to survive. Some suggested that some sort of disease could have been the culprit that caused their extinction. But it is hard to imagine that any disease could affect all the organisms, which were quite diverse in their metabolism. We observe no such virus today that could affect all animals and plants.

And if that had been the case, then in a gradualist scenario, we would expect that most of the fossils found today would have been scavenged by predators, leaving the telltale signs of teeth and claw marks on the bones of their prey. While it is true that in some cases, such as in the La Brea tar pits, these telltale signs of scavenging are present, the vast majority of fossils are mysteriously intact and undisturbed by predators. That is very difficult to reconcile with the gradualist theory. Moreover, if the extinction of these animals were a gradual process taking millions of years, we would not expect mass burials of undisturbed fossils.

Nevertheless, let us consider the enormous power of the Chicxulub meteor impact in the Yucatan Peninsula of Mexico. It is estimated that the force of the blow of the meteor was so extreme that it penetrated Earth's crust more than 45 miles, bypassing the granitic substructure of the continents (10 to 16 miles deep) and the basaltic layer of rock below into the lithosphere just above the molten magma. According to evolutionists, all the matter in the immediately surrounding area where the 6-mile-long meteor struck would have instantly vaporized.

But the destruction would have begun even before it struck the ground. The impact of the meteor striking the edge of our atmosphere would have created a literal inferno surrounding it, causing the atmosphere to become hotter than a modern furnace. The meteor is estimated to have been traveling at 44,640 miles per hour, which is about 20 times faster than a rifle bullet. The colossal energy released into our atmosphere at the impact of this massive rock would have radiated out in shock waves through the air, causing a sonic boom that would have been heard throughout the entire world.

Once it struck the ground, a second boom even louder than the first would also have been heard around the world. As the very tip of the meteor touched the surface of our planet, its rear end was higher than our modern jet airliners are able to fly. The force of the impact of such an enormous rock, larger even than Mount Everest, would have triggered immense earthquakes radiating outward that would have toppled any structure within thousands of miles from the impact zone.

A plume of rock, debris, and dust estimated by evolutionists at about 950 cubic miles in volume would have shot upward—some say a quarter of the way to the moon. The ejecta from this single strike would have entirely filled Earth's atmosphere with dust and debris. The darkened skies would have severely restricted sunlight from reaching the surface of Earth. Plants' ability to survive, which is dependent on photosynthesis, would have been severely compromised. The entire food chain would have collapsed in short order.

The powerful impact left behind a crater more than 100 miles wide. Adding insult to injury, the pressure waves created by the massive strike would have penetrated the interior of our planet, passing through the core and coming out the opposite side. This powerful pressure wave would bounce back and forth from one side

DATING METHODS: THE THREE PILLARS

of the Earth to the other, much like ripples in a pool when a rock is thrown into it. That would have undoubtedly triggered a cataclysmic increase in volcanic activity throughout the world that would have exacerbated the atmospheric conditions with their own plumes of tephra and toxic gases.

In the evolutionary extinction scenario, evolutionists claim that the lack of sunlight would have radically affected herbivorous animals and subsequently the carnivorous animals that fed on them. They would have died of starvation and disease as they were weakened by the famine. If their model is correct, we would expect sporadic finds of fossils strewn throughout the entire surface of the Earth. Those who were alive would have scavenged the first to die and left the telltale signs of predation etched on their bones.

In our model, the impact of the seven meteors would have caused a global catastrophe that would have killed most animals long before famine and disease could kill them. Our flood model would predict that these animals would be buried together as large sheet flooding inundated the continents, thus preserving many diverse biodomes in giant fossil burial grounds free of the telltale signs of predation.

In the evolutionary model of the single meteor strike, evolutionists claim that the darkened skies created by the massive ejecta plume would have blocked the sunlight, significantly affecting the global climate. Temperatures throughout the world would have been severely impacted as they plummeted into a so-called nuclear winter scenario, causing many species that could not quickly adapt to become extinct. That is the global effect of the impact of just one large asteroid strike. But what if there were seven asteroids, some even bigger than the one that evolutionists claim killed the dinosaurs?

In Antarctica, scientists have found a meteor crater three times larger than the one in Mexico. The crater measures more than 300 miles in diameter. The space rock that would have created this crater is estimated at around 30 miles in diameter. If the one in Mexico that was 6 miles in diameter could have made the dinosaurs extinct, what destruction potential could the one in Antarctica that was five times larger have posed to all the species on the planet?

Evolutionists do believe that this meteor strike in Antarctica was also an extinction event, but they date it back 350 million years when the supposed evolution of life was just beginning. If, as we have documented before, the evolution of life was so miraculous a step from dead molecules becoming living cells, how much more implausible is the idea that this would have to happen again? The problem is further complicated by the fact that this strike in Antarctica was not the only one.

Believe it or not, there was an even bigger meteor that struck in Greenland. The Big Seven, as I call these giant meteors, have craters that range from 90 to 600 kilometers in diameter. If we accept the long and gradual evolutionary timetable for all these meteor strikes, that means that life would have become extinct seven times and yet rebounded through random chemical reactions. The faith necessary to believe that life could have begun seven times in a row is an astronomically enormous improbability.

The largest of these seven enormous meteor strikes is in the northernmost crater located in Maniitsoq, Greenland. The second-largest is the southernmost crater in Wilkes Land, Antarctica, that I just referred to.

Let us describe the big one in Western Greenland. Just recently, this giant crater was discovered quite accidentally. Geologists looking for nickel and other ores stumbled on the evidence of a giant meteor strike. Evidence of broken-up, contorted, melted, and hydrothermally altered rocks could be explained only one way: a high-energy impact followed by an influx of seawater immediately after. No other terrestrial geologic process can explain the enormous size of the affected zone in Maniitsoq, Greenland, which presently shows a crater more than 100 kilometers rim to rim. But there is more to this story than immediately meets the eye.

DATING METHODS: THE THREE PILLARS

Both Greenland and Iceland have been driven upward from the floor of the Atlantic Ocean as the Mid-Atlantic Ridge has literally come up out of the water from its previous depth during the tectonic processes that fractured Earth's crust. But when the Mid-Atlantic Ridge was first formed, the present surface layer of the strata in Greenland and Iceland was actually some 10 to 16 miles below the surface of the Earth.

The force of this impact was so great that an enormous amount of rock was instantly evaporated. Rushing waters then solidified undulating waves of molten rock, showing the massive shock waves radiating outward, and the rest of the 16 miles of granitic rock that was not immediately vaporized was violently shot into space as a gigantic plume of ejecta.

When it was first made, the crater is estimated to have been 500 to 600 kilometers wide. As far as we currently know, it is the largest meteor to have ever struck the Earth—six times more devastating than the one evolutionists claim killed the dinosaurs. Some of that giant crater has eroded during the years, but most of the material around it was shot out into space as a massive plume of dust and rocks. I believe that the ejecta actually struck the moon and caused one side of it to be 35 miles denser than the other from the meteor shower it absorbed.

If we place our seven present continents into the jigsaw puzzle that once was our single continental landmass and track the positions of the seven meteor strikes, it is easy to trace the rip created in our crust that broke the single landmass into seven continents. The ejecta plumes created by these seven giant meteors may have been powerful enough to strike the moon and actually affect its rotation pattern.

There is evidence that the far side of the moon may have been hit by a swarm of asteroids in a relatively short period of time, making the crust on the far side 35 miles thicker than the side that faces us. Obviously, that far side was facing us when the meteors struck the Earth, and now, the extra weight on the opposite side of the moon is what slowed its rotation to once a month so we can never see that far side again from the point of view of the Earth.

The fact that almost 80 percent of the meteor strikes are on the far side of the moon tells us that this was no gradual process over millions of years; otherwise, it would have surely affected equally the entire surface of the moon as it rotated. The chance that nearly 80 percent of these strikes hit one side of the moon is extremely remote in a gradualist scenario.

I believe this is evidence of our multiple meteor strikes that broke the crust of Earth and sent an enormous amount of debris toward the moon and beyond. That swarm of rocks that catapulted from the impacts on Earth was so massive that I believe it changed the rotation speed of the moon by making one side heavier, which, through the normal action of centrifugal force, has kept the heavy side to the far end of its orbit around our planet.

Much of that ejected material, however, probably returned to Earth as ejecta of varying sizes, passing through the atmosphere once again and reheating even further the already heated atmosphere before striking the freshly fractured continents around the spinning Earth. To any who were alive, it would have been akin to a very spectacular shower of atom bombs all around the planet. Each of the returning rocks would have created sonic booms as they reentered our atmosphere again and then struck the Earth.

The immediate and drastic atmospheric change in temperature caused by the seven initial impacts would have thus been compounded afterward around the entire planet by reentering ejecta falling back through the atmosphere and causing unchecked conflagrations of forest fires wherever they landed. But our problems were just beginning.

I believe that the combined force of the seven impacts is what broke the crust of our planet into seven continents. The cracking of the crust of the Earth would also have unleashed enormous earthquakes of magnitudes humans have not since experienced. The

Mid-Oceanic Ridge is the physical evidence of the unzipping crust of the First Earth as the rip traveled all the way around our globe.

As the 10 to 16 miles of granitic rock of the single continent of our First Earth was removed by the seven impacts that cracked our continent into seven pieces, the fountains of the deep were uncorked. The gushing geysers that removed the enormous weight of 16 miles of rock opened the door for the basalt layer to surge upward. The basalt rock that was below the continents began to rise from the internal pressures inside the planet. Once the enormous weight of the granitic rock above was removed, the basalt rock below bounded upward and created the Mid-Atlantic Ridge in a very short period of time. That no doubt was also aided by the seven pressure waves of each of the meteor strikes bouncing back and forth from one side of the Earth to the other through its interior and impacting volcanic upheavals on the surface of the dying First Earth.

The gradualist scenario that rising molten rock in the Mid-Atlantic Ridge could move continents is, in my mind, an irrational scenario. There just is not enough physical power for molten rock to move a continent. It would simply extrude and seek any opening of least resistance as we see today when we photograph the much reduced process still going on in the Mid-Atlantic Ridge some 4 miles below the surface of the Atlantic Ocean.

This rising of basaltic rock below caused the seven broken granitic continents to slide away from it and created in short order the motion that moved the continents in the varying direction we see them moving today. Massive super volcanic eruptions of unprecedented magnitude would have added even more heat and tephra into the atmosphere. Much of the tropical forests that abounded in the First Earth would have been burning wildly from the magma erupting from the volcanoes and the fires caused by the reentering ejecta. Our First Earth became a burning inferno. In our model, the first phase of the global catastrophe was not a nuclear winter but a hellish torrent of fire and lava that heated the atmosphere of the Earth to unprecedented levels. Had it not been for the rain and the flood, our First Earth would have been reduced to a burned out cinder.

Now, evolutionists claim that our crust has always been cracked. They assume that the continents have moved back and forth throughout the many millions of years they propose our Earth existed, coming together into a loosely connected single landmass and then separating by the forces of the magma flows below the crust. They propose that the movement of the tectonic plates is slow and gradual and not related to a global cataclysm.

Our model states that the crust of the First Earth was solid as it is for Mercury, and in complete homeostasis. Evidence that the cracking of our continents was, in fact, a cataclysmic event is found in the rocks of the adjoining continents. For example, if we travel to the northern border of Argentina in South America, between Brazil and Uruguay, we find a wondrous marvel of nature, known to us as the world-famous Iguazu Falls. That is surely one of the grandest spectacles of nature and the largest of all waterfalls in the world. This breathtaking waterfall is known for its spectacular beauty and grandeur, but most are not aware of an even more spectacular secret it holds.

The Iguazu Falls cascade over an enormous bed of lava that is more than a mile thick. But what is even more astounding is that

The Iguazu Falls of South America

this lava bed covers an area twice the size of the state of Texas. The magnitude of the volcanic upheaval necessary to cover 250,000 square miles one mile deep in lava is astronomical. But even more astounding is the fact that the lava flow of this very same incident continued across the Atlantic and into Africa.

Samples of the basalt rock under the Iguazu Falls in South America were chipped from this bedrock and compared to the bedrock of Namibia in southwest Africa. They were found to have the exact same composition, which proved two things:

1. The continents of South America and Africa were once joined.
2. The cataclysmic volcanic eruption that created the gigantic basalt bedrock found on the surface of both continents was contemporary to or prior to the splitting of the continents.

The presence of so much lava at this breaking point between the continents speaks volumes against the gradualists' eternally oscillating scenario of wandering plates envisioned by the evolutionists. Instead, it points to a single massive cataclysm that violently broke up our crust. It was not at all a peaceful and gradual divorce.

It is around this area in the southern hemisphere where the Mid-Atlantic Ridge bifurcates that the continents of Antarctica and Australia were severed from South America and Africa and shoved toward their present locations. And we can see the Mid-Oceanic Ridge making a 90-degree turn under the horn of Africa and heading toward the Indian Ocean, where it cracked the Indian continent from the eastern side of Africa and sent it crashing north into Asia. It was in this relative area that the initial impact of the Wilkes Land meteor struck and fractured the four continents of the southern hemisphere.

The cracks created under the immediate area of the impacts would have weakened the granitic plate, allowing the pressurized salt water beneath it to break forth and escape as the fountains of the deep. The rebound pressure waves returning from the opposite side of the world through its interior would have further agitated and aided in this expulsion process of the underground aquifers.

We can see, when fitting the continents of South America, Antarctica, and Africa together with the base of the Mid-Atlantic Ridge, that the areas of most erosion by the jetting streams are in this region where the larger southern meteor struck. But there is yet another Big Seven meteor that struck near that region, aiding the already catastrophic process.

That area is in the northwest province of South Africa at the southern tip of the continent. The Vredefort crater is southwest of Johannesburg and measures from rim to rim some 160 kilometers. It is estimated that when first formed, it may have been 300 kilometers wide. No doubt, this massive impact contributed to the fracture of Africa from Antarctica and South America and also fractured India and Madagascar from the eastern coast of Africa.

If we piece the continents back together using the Mid-Atlantic Ridge as the starting point for the movements of the seven continents, we can see that the trajectory of the Greenland meteor through the interior of the Earth probably intersected with the Siberian Traps in Russia. The impact was so great that as the pressure wave passed through the interior of the Earth that it bulged out the crust in the opposite end, causing the massive lava flows known as the Siberian Traps. The area covered by this massive flood basaltic lava is today some 770,000 square miles. Some scientists believe that the original extent of the coverage was around 2.7 million square miles with a corresponding volume of approximately 960,000 cubic miles of flood basalt. We can see this same phenomenon on the landscape of the near side of the moon. The pressure waves from the impacts on the far side of the moon caused massive lava outbursts that now cover the near side of the moon.

We can also see that the trajectory of the meteor that formed the Vredefort crater in South Africa could have also intersected on the opposite end with the massive Deccan Traps found in west-central India, which was still attached to the eastern coast of Africa prior to the strike. The force bulging outward from the pressure waves that traveled through the Earth to impinge on the opposite side was so great that it literally tore India away from Africa and sent it northward on a collision course with Asia.

The Deccan Traps, like the Siberian Traps, is a volcanic eruption feature in the form of a massive outflow of flood basalt. Traps are massive area eruptions of melted basalt that span great distances, unlike the typical volcano that forms from a single location, creating cones and calderas.

In China's Sichuan province, we find the Emeishan Trap with its typical multiple layers resulting from the bouncing pressure waves created by striking meteors. The Emeishan Trap covers an area of 250,000 kilometers squared. The thickness ranges from several hundred meters to 5.5 kilometers. It is estimated to contain a volume of 300,000 km^3 of flood basalt.

These traps, or basalt provinces, as they are sometimes called due to their large territorial spread, have been found in many other places in the world, including the large Ontong Java Plateau, the Chilcotin Group, and the Columbia River Basalt Group in North America.

The Ontong Java Plateau is a huge oceanic plateau in the southwest Pacific Ocean just north of the Solomon Islands. There are two smaller oceanic basalt provinces known as Manihiki and Hikurangi. Together, these three basaltic provinces have a volume of 80 million km^3 of basaltic magma.

The Chilcotin Plateau Basalts form a large basaltic province that extends about 50,000 km^2, with a volume estimated at about 3,300 km^3, running parallel to south central British Columbia in Canada.

The Columbia River Basalt Group forms another large basaltic province in the northwestern United States. It covers an area that engulfs parts of the states of Washington, Oregon, Idaho, Nevada, and California. It covers an area of about 163,700 km^2 with an estimated volume of about 174,300 km^3.

Many explanations have been offered to explain this phenomenon, but I think they fall short of the mark. It seems to me that these enormous area eruptions are better explained by the bulging and cracking of the crust where the pressure waves of these large meteor strikes traveling through the interior of our planet impinged on the distal crust of the planet and can be linked to the very trajectory of the meteors that caused them.

The pressure waves would bounce back and forth from one side of the Earth to the other until the energy dissipated in the same way that throwing a rock in a pool can cause waves to bounce back and forth from the edges. The distinctive steps in these traps are, in my view, the physical evidence of those pressure waves bouncing back and forth through the interior of the Earth, each time thrusting out enormous amounts of lava that seeped out of the cracks created by the initial bulging of the crust.

In midwest India is an enormous area of solidified flood basalt that covers an enormous area of 200,000 square miles at a depth of 6,600 feet (more than 1 mile thick) and has an estimated volume of 200,000 cubic miles. Time has eroded much of it, but when it was first formed, scientists believe it would have covered three times as much territory as it now contains.

The combination of the South Africa meteor impact and the Antarctic impact relatively close to one another is, in my view, the cause of the enormous flood basalts that also covered both the area of the Iguazu Falls in South America and Namibia, Africa, with a layer of magma almost 2 miles thick. The rebound pressure waves returning from the opposite end of the Earth's crust would have then pushed the flood basalt back out through the much larger continental cracks created by the combined meteor strikes.

The force of the impacts was so powerful that Antarctica and Australia were separated, and Australia was sent eastward. Antarctica was sent southward as the Mid-Atlantic Ridge rose from the rebounding basalt rock that used to lie below the unbroken single continental block of the First Earth. As the weight of more than 10 miles of granitic rock above the basalt rock below was dissolved and eroded by the jetting streams, these basaltic ridges formed all along the cracks that fractured the continents. Prior to the meteor strikes, the basaltic layers were some 10 to 16 miles below the surface of the Earth.

Once the weight of the granitic rock had been removed by the blasts and the hydraulic forces of the geysers, these deeper basaltic rocks lifted upward from the internal pressures inside our planet, forming the Mid-Atlantic Ridge we see today below the Atlantic Ocean. In Greenland, where the largest meteor struck, blasting and vaporizing an enormous volume of the granitic rock of the continents, the basaltic rock was allowed to rise the highest. That basaltic layer can be seen above the ocean level today.

As the ridges rose higher, the continents literally slid down their sides, moving away from the basaltic ridges and gliding over the underground aquifers underneath the continental granitic blocks. These aquifers, now uncorked, were gradually drained by the erupting fountains of the deep that brought their waters to the surface of the planet. Once the aquifers were sufficiently drained, the granitic substructure of the newly broken seven continents began to grind to a halt.

That, of course, caused the grinding continents to buckle at the leading edge and form mountain ranges. Hence, we see that the mountain ranges are greatest at the end of the continents that are on the leading edge of the direction they were sliding away from the ridges.

Our model stipulates that the combined energy of the Seven Big Ones would have been enough to crack the surface of our First Earth. They ripped the crust between the impact zones and then circumambulated the entire globe like a giant zipper that busted loose, creating our seven separate continents. If we study the ancient records of the civilizations that evolved after the Great Flood, we find that their record of the event matches perfectly with our account.

The Babylonians described the Global Flood with similar terms. In the following verses of Tablet XI of the *Epic of Gilgamesh*, it is clear that the land had been broken like a pot and become completely darkened. All men were covered with clay. The whole world was embroiled in mud. The raging fountains reached unto heaven. The flowing geysers reached the stratosphere.

> vs.105 – The raging of Adad reached to heaven
> vs.106 – And turned into darkness all that was light.
> vs.107 – The land He broke like a pot.
> vs.111 – No man could see his fellow.
> vs.112 – The people could not be recognized from heaven.
> vs.118 – In truth, the olden time has turned to clay,
> vs.133 – And all mankind had turned to clay (Heidel 1949, 85–86).

Surely, anyone who has experienced a tsunami, a sheet-flooding event, or a flash flood can tell you that in the aftermath, everything is covered in mud. It is that clay that encased the many fossils that now give us a glimpse of the wide variety of living things that once roamed the First Earth. It is the evidence written in the rocks that substantiates the historicity of the Genesis account.

But it is also written in the memory of our human ancestors. In every part of our planet, we can find branded onto the memory of its survivors the same telltale signs of this cataclysmic event that ended our First Earth. The commonalities of these elements in all the ancient cultures show us that they are realistic depictions of a historical space-time catastrophic event. For those interested, I document many of those ancient stories from every corner of the world in the last book in this series, *The Death of the First Earth*.

The Seven Thunders That Ended the First Earth

If you have been through a terrible thunderstorm, you know that those thunderclaps can be quite intimidating. The sound of thunder is a pressure wave in our atmosphere created by the sudden heating of the air by a lightning bolt. Every dog I have ever had was afraid of thunder. I always wondered how animals are able to sense the coming of a storm or even a tsunami long before humans ever see them on the horizon. I read an account of a young girl riding on a baby elephant. She was saved from the tsunami that struck Sri Lanka because the elephant refused to obey her and ran uphill far enough to avoid the coming disaster. It is almost as if animals have a collective memory of the catastrophe that ended our First Earth.

The scriptures tell us that this catastrophe was a judgment of God because of the unbridled wickedness and violence that gripped the First Earth.

Then the Lord saw that the wickedness of man was great on the earth, and that every intent of the thoughts of his heart was only evil continually.
—Gen. 6:5

Today, we are beginning to understand the wickedness of terrorism in our Second Earth. Violence is once again spreading through every continent. When that violence reaches a certain point, God will once again step in to end it. It is not until humankind experiences the horror of unbridled violence that they can begin to understand why a holy God could take such drastic measures.

In the six hundredth year of Noah's life, in the second month, on the seventeenth day of the month, on the same day all the fountains of the great deep burst open, and the floodgates of the sky were opened.
—Gen. 7:11

I suspect that the bursting of all the fountains of the great deep was caused by seven huge meteor strikes. There are seven meteor craters on Earth that are in a class by themselves due to their enormous size. All the others are distinctly smaller. I will speak further on this in the last book of this series, *The Death of the First Earth*. But for our present purpose, I will give a brief introduction to this cataclysm. It is necessary to understand the enormous nature of this catastrophe in order to recognize the mechanism that formed both the fossils and the strata that evolutionists use to prop up their theory.

That fateful day, on the seventeenth of the Hebrew month of Heshvan, seven thunders sounded the trumpet of God's judgment on the First Earth. As each of the seven Big Ones entered the atmosphere, the pressure waves were so intense that the booms they created were heard around the world. They were the loudest sounds ever heard by humankind.

Sadly, the book of Revelation tells us that at the end of the Second Earth, when the indignation of violence has reached its full measure on our present Earth, God will sound His seven trumpets and declare judgment upon the Second Earth. Right before the seventh trumpet sounds, in the middle of the seven-year tribulation period when the Antichrist attacks Jerusalem and conquers the whole world, seven thunders shall sound again, turning what Satan thought was victory into defeat.

> *I saw another strong angel coming down out of heaven, clothed with a cloud; and the rainbow was upon his head, and his face was like the sun, and his feet like pillars of fire; and he had in his hand a little book which was open. He placed his right foot on the sea and his left on the land; and he cried out with a loud voice, as when a lion roars; and when he had cried out, the seven peals of thunder uttered their voices. When the seven peals of thunder had spoken, I was about to write; and I heard a voice from heaven saying, "Seal up the things which the seven peals of thunder have spoken and do not write them." Then the angel whom I saw standing on the sea and on the land lifted up his right hand to heaven, and swore by Him who lives forever and ever,* WHO CREATED HEAVEN AND THE THINGS IN IT, AND

DATING METHODS: THE THREE PILLARS

> THE EARTH AND THE THINGS IN IT, AND THE SEA AND THE THINGS IN IT, *that there will be delay no longer, but in the days of the voice of the seventh angel, when he is about to sound, then the mystery of God is finished, as He preached to His servants the prophets.*
>
> —Rev. 10:1–7

I do not know for sure what those seven thunders are, but I suspect they may be seven asteroids that will bring the kingdom of the Antichrist to its knees within three and a half years. But that is a story for another book in another series, *The Coming of the Prince of Peace*.

Evolutionists insist that all seven of these giant asteroids came at different moments in their imagined eons of evolutionary history, causing mayhem and havoc with large numbers of species becoming extinct at different ages. I find it quite difficult to believe that anything could have survived even one of these asteroids without the countereffect of the Genesis Flood. Our world would have been sterilized seven times had it not been for the floodwaters that saved our planet from total extinction and once again brought order out of chaos.

That these asteroids could have struck at the same time is not as far-fetched as some may think. In fact, it may be more probable than most people imagine. Astronomers have been surprised to find that many asteroids fly in tandem with another asteroid. Sometimes, they are found in small clusters; that is, two or more asteroids may fly in tandem, each with a moon or even several moons. In fact, even stars more often than not come in pairs, circling one another and even in clusters of more than two.

Evolutionists claim that the telltale evidence of the vast expanse of the destructive power of the meteor strike that killed the dinosaurs is preserved for us today in what geologists call the KT boundary. This 6-mile-long space rock hit with such force that it cracked Earth's crust with such power that it penetrated 45 miles deep and created a crater 110 miles wide.

Above the KT boundary, geologists claim to find no fossils of dinosaurs. It seems to mark the extinction of the vast majority of the flora and fauna and species that existed before the Great Flood. They claim that the KT boundary was caused by the meteor that hit the Yucatan Peninsula in Mexico due to the concentration of iridium found in that layer of deposit. Iridium is an extremely rare element in the surface of our planet, yet it is found in much higher concentrations in space rocks. The KT boundary has in its layer 1,000 times the amount of iridium normally found in the surface of our planet. Yet that layer spans the entire globe.

Now, here is the curious thing, according to evolutionists: One of the smallest of these seven giant impacts created a global KT layer that is not found in any other layer of our geological strata. Yet evolutionary geologists insist that these seven meteors struck on very different dates.

Let us examine a few of these giant meteors, the ones I call the Big Seven. The enormous 30-kilometer-wide space rock that struck the Wilkes Land area of Antarctica was almost five times larger than the Chicxulub meteor that struck the Yucatan Peninsula. Evolutionists claim it struck during the Permian Triassic boundary, but there is no observable iridium layer of the ejecta that would have come from such a gigantic impact anywhere in the strata.

No such iridium layer is found for the even larger meteor that struck Greenland. In fact, none of the other meteors that were much larger than Chicxulub can be traced by the kind of broadband evidence on a global scale marked by the KT boundary.

That suggests that the impacts were a single catastrophic event. Evolutionists' dating is more wishful thinking than fact. It is reflective of their underlying bias to create vast spans of time for evolution to have a chance at all. Thus, they go to great lengths to imagine multiple extinction scenarios that plagued our Earth in their imagined evolutionary history. To this I ask: Show me the KT boundaries for all these other six enormous meteor strikes.

The naturalistic argument that there is no mechanism large enough to bring forth a global catastrophe such as Noah's Flood can no longer be considered a credible argument. When considering the large number of Apollo asteroids and comets that threaten Earth, it is no longer possible for humanity to ignore the catastrophic account of the Global Flood that may have been triggered by such a catastrophic scenario.

The raging volcanic activity that would have been precipitated by these seven meteors combined with the energy of the impacts and the voluminous returning ejecta could have burned our First Earth to a cinder and sterilized it completely. But God had another plan. It was the Great Flood that saved the Earth from total destruction and at once washed the wickedness away that had brought the abhorrent violence of cannibalism and sorcery to the children of Adam.

The Saving Waters of the Great Flood

While it is true that the flood was a judgment on humankind for the great wickedness and violence that marred our world, it was also the mechanism that saved us from total incineration. I find it rather doubtful that any life could have survived the impact of just one of these giant meteors without the Great Flood to counter the volcanism and conflagrations that would have been visited on our planet in the aftermath.

At the very sites of the seven impacts where the granitic continental rock was cracked open all the way through, enormous quantities of water vapor from the waters of the deep below our once singular granitic continent would have been shot heavenward, filling our atmosphere with even more moisture and debris. The bursting open of all the fountains of the deep may very well have been the uncorking of subterranean waters that were underneath the previously stable and unified granitic continental crust. These would have been under the immense pressure of the weight of miles of granitic rock above them. This is no fairy tale. It is a historical account.

Perhaps you will be surprised to find out that we now know for a fact that today there is still even more salt water below the crust than exists in our oceans today. Evolutionary scientists knew nothing of these subterranean waters until just recently. On June 12, 2014, a scientific study by Steven Jacobsen of Northwestern University in Illinois and Brandon Schmandt, a seismologist at the University of New Mexico, was published in the journal *Science*. They claimed to have found a giant subterranean ocean in the transition layer between the upper and lower mantle.

Certain high-pressure minerals in Earth's mantle are likely to contain oceans' worth of water dissolved into their crystal structures. Exactly how water dissolves into ringwoodite, an important mineral in the mantle transition zone, influences our ability to detect mantle water using geophysical tools. . . . They found that hydrogen substitutes for any of the major cations, dramatically lowering the speed of seismic waves in the mineral (Grocholski 2014, 311–12).

The water is contained in a rare mineral called ringwoodite, which is formed under extremely high pressures deep in Earth from another mineral called olivine. Some reports estimate that this underground ocean may contain as much as three times the water in our present oceans.

This transition zone is found between 250 and 410 miles below the surface of the Earth and proves conclusively that large volumes of water could have been ejected as the biblical "fountains of the great deep" (Gen. 7:11) that created the global inundation chronicled by all ancient civilizations.

The sudden initial pressurization created by several large meteor impacts were followed by the subsequent depressurization created by the ejecting matter from these strike zones that cracked the granitic continent, allowing it to escape. The sudden removal of the granitic rock by the action of the meteor impacts would have allowed the opening of these underground aquifers to escape as they ripped like a zipper all around the globe, breaking the once solid landmass into our present seven continents.

Jets of water like a giant curtain spanning across the Mid-Atlantic Ridge and circling around the globe through the Ring of Fire around the Pacific Ocean would have cascaded upward at supersonic speeds by the immense pressure unleashed. These jetting cascades would have severely eroded the side of the continents as they shot upward. Some of the eroded debris may have hit the moon, and some of it may have been sent into orbit around the sun.

In other words, some rocks, if they did not slam into the moon as they were violently thrust upward, could have continued further into outer space as smaller asteroids or comets. Any water escaping Earth's gravity would have turned to ice in deep space and created comets. It is entirely possible that at least some of the comets and asteroids flying around our sun were created by the massive impact of the Seven Big Ones. If our proposition is correct, we can expect to find some comets and meteors rich in olivine and containing water that is more akin to Earth's chemistry than has been yet found in space.

At first, the whole planet burned as enormous forest fires raged in hellish conflagrations, fed by the winds created by the Venturi effect from geysers. Had it not been for the rain, our Earth would have burned to a lifeless black cinder. As the single continental landmass of the First Earth fractured into seven smaller continents, it no doubt set off super-volcanoes as well as swarms of mega earthquakes and tsunamis traveling from 500 to 600 miles per hour through the ocean.

All coastal regions would have become completely decimated by repeated waves traveling inland for many miles as the continents slid apart. Once the waters receded from the flood into the frozen poles instead of one large ocean, the Second Earth now had seven oceans.

The superheating of the air saturated with moisture would have spawned massive category 5 and category 6 hurricanes, along with destructive swarms of type 5 tornadoes as the atmosphere struggled to find equilibrium. Lightning storms of unprecedented fury would have lit the sky with the anger of God for all people to see. I suspect that it is this memory that humans carried into the Second Earth that depicted God in most ancient cultures as the lightning bearer. It is also the reason that all ancient cultures saw comets and asteroids as symbols of doom and catastrophe.

Massive earthquake swarms would have been triggered in rapid sequence around the entire globe as the seams of the ripping continents unzipped. The fury of these earthquakes would have been unimaginable to us today. Even the speed of the rotation of the Earth was changed and its original nearly circular path around the sun elongated on one end of its trajectory by the force of these seven impacts. Perhaps even the tilt of the Earth and the wobble of the precession of the equinoxes was affected and altered by the massive impacts.

I suspect that prior to the Great Flood, the sun (as seen from Earth) traveled along its ecliptic and moved across the background constellations of the Zodiac during the Precession of the Equinoxes at a much faster pace. In other words, the wobble in Earth's rotation may have moved at a faster rate, causing a tilt of 23 degrees. That would have allowed the constellations that rule the Spring or Vernal Equinox (the ruling constellation of that epoch) to shift from Virgo to Leo, to Cancer and Gemini in a much shorter period of time than they do today.

I suspect that it was during the time of Gemini that the Nephilim (Gen. 6:4) of the First Earth brought sorcery, war, and cannibalism to the sons and daughters of Adam and Eve. I suspect that the ruling houses went from Virgo to Taurus within the time frame of the 10 patriarchs. The Gemini constellation speaks of the two lineages of man, one legitimate and also known as Cro-Magnon man, and the other not legitimate and known as Neanderthals. For their wickedness, God destroyed the First Earth as Taurus rose on the Vernal Equinox (Gen. 6:4–13).

I further suspect that the Great Flood came when the sun was moving from the ruling constellation of Gemini to that of Taurus. Since that impact, the Earth now travels 5 million miles further from the sun during the northern winter months, changing from its almost circular orbit (like Venus) to a more elliptical orbit on one end of its circuit as a result of the extra push given by the seven asteroid strikes.

It just so happens that the Genesis Flood account documents the beginning of the breaking of the fountains of the deep in the Hebrew month of Heshvan on the 17th day (Gen. 7:1), which is comparable to our October/November calendar in autumn. Thus, the total force of the impact of these seven meteors may have caused Earth's rotation around our sun to be extended a distance of 5 million miles further and from then on took on a more elliptical orbit during that side of its circuit around the sun. That is physical evidence that the Genesis account is, in fact, a historical account.

The Source of Water: The Fountains of the Deep

The question skeptics ask most often is this: Where did the water to create the Great Flood come from? We have already mentioned the enormous stores of water found under the crust of the Earth, but we also have the testimony of the ancients and the findings of deep wells bored in our modern times. We can find a clue hidden within the ancient writings of our ancestors. Throughout ancient cultures, there are references to the fountains of the deep. What are these fountains of the deep? We are familiar with natural springs that percolate water from below the ground. In Florida, there is an underground river that originates all the way from northern Georgia, bubbling up in many areas and filling the Everglades until it empties into the Gulf of Mexico at the tip of southern Florida. Most of us associate natural springs with placid bubbling springs of water in lakes and rivers, a generally gentle, bubbling flow. But the record of the ancients regarding the Great Flood had no such gentle flow in mind. The Greek poet Hesiod described it this way:

> Harshly then he thundered, and heavily, and terribly the earth re-echoed around; and the broad heaven above, and the sea, and streams of ocean, and the abysses of earth. But beneath his immortal feet vast Olympus trembled, as the king uprose, and earth groaned beneath. And the heat from both caught the dark-coloured sea, both of the thunder and lightning, and fire from the monster, the heat arising from the thunder-storms, winds, and burning lightning. And all earth and heaven and sea were boiling (Thatcher 1915, 22).

In a tablet found at Nippur, the Sumerian account also speaks of the fountains of the deep stopping after the rain had stopped. It is understood in this tablet that the source of the waters from the Great Flood is not primarily the rain but also the fountains of the deep.

> Above, Adad made scarce his rain,
> Below (the fountain of the deep) was stopped, that the flood rose not at the source (Clay 1922).

The Holy Scriptures say that all the fountains of the great deep were broken open and that afterward the floodgates of the sky were opened. Notice that all the accounts agree that it was not a single fountain but multiple fountains that were broken open simultaneously from the great depth of the Earth.

> *[I]n the second month, on the seventeenth day of the month, on the same day* all the fountains of the great deep burst open, and the floodgates of the sky were opened. *The rain fell upon the earth for forty days and forty nights....*

The water prevailed upon the earth one hundred and fifty days. But God remembered Noah and all the beasts and all the cattle that were with him in the ark; *and God caused a wind to pass over the earth, and the water subsided. Also the fountains of the deep and the floodgates of the sky were closed, and the rain from the sky was restrained (emphasis added).*

—Gen. 7:11-12, 24; 8:1-2

In every case, we find it was not a single fountain but rather numerous and simultaneous fountains. In fact, it was a curtain of fountains gushing from the great deep all along the ruptured cleavage between the continents. That phrase is indicative of the depths of the oceans and not some local bubbling spring in a lake or on the Earth's surface.

The ancients were skilled in canal building, and the phrase "the floodgates of the sky were opened" is a reflection of that knowledge in hydraulics. The imagery depicts not a light shower, not even a heavy downpour, but something like a cascading waterfall when floodgates are opened in canals.

Anyone who has lived in South Florida can attest that sometimes it really seems like it is raining in buckets. But these giant curtains of jetting water would have arched over and come back to the earth as if Niagara Falls extended along the entire breadth of what we now recognize as the Mid-Atlantic Ridge and the Circle of Fire in the Pacific where the continents were once joined.

So powerful were these geysers that they reached all the way into the stratosphere and beyond. This spectacle would have dwarfed the thunderous sound of the Niagara Falls. Anyone who has witnessed a high or large waterfall can attest that they generate an enormous amount of mist with tiny droplets of water floating in the wind.

The Venturi effect, caused by the upward jetting column of water, literally sucked up the wind around it and sent it skyward into the stratosphere. That would have also caused much of the mist to hyper-saturate the upper and lower atmosphere with moisture. Because of the much colder temperatures in the upper atmosphere, that would have created a torrent of hail raining down along the curtain of water that stretched around the Earth.

But in the lower and warmer atmosphere, the injection of so much moisture would have resulted in many super-storms covering the entire face of our planet as never experienced by humans. Rain, hail, thunder, and lightning battered the entire planet for 40 days and 40 nights.

That heavy downpour was like no other that has ever happened since. The super-heated atmosphere created by the seven meteor strikes and subsequent vulcanism would have been laden with not only more moisture than normal, but the energy in the temperature of the air and ocean waters would have created fierce super-hurricanes and super-tornadoes that ravaged the planet.

Several times in my life, I have seen the ravage that a category 5 hurricane can create. Every increase of 5 miles per hour in a hurricane's wind doubles the destructive power. I saw Hurricane Andrew crack two-foot-thick concrete poles like matchsticks. I cannot even imagine what power the hurricanes during Noah's time would have unleashed.

When those meteors struck and cracked the crust of the Earth, they uncorked enormous subterranean aquifers that gushed upward, eroding rock and soil as the continents unzipped. It was that emulsified soil that caused the black rains (attested by the Mayans as well as the Sumerians) to fall upon all creatures on the First Earth. And it was that erosive action that carved the V-shaped continental shelves and provided the voluminous content of sediment that formed the enormous sedimentary beds existing in every sector of our planet. Those geysers running the length of the rips in the continents flowed outward and cascaded to earth as a continuous waterfall. It was literally as if the floodgates of heaven were opened. This was no hyperbole.

DATING METHODS: THE THREE PILLARS

Some of you may doubt that these huge underground aquifers could have existed and erupted with such force. We have already documented that even today we have great oceans of water underground trapped deep below the granitic level of the continents. Nearer the surface of our planet's crust, the aquifers are sweet water. But deep below are saltwater aquifers that span the entire globe and contain more water than all our oceans put together.

The deepest well man has accomplished is more than 7 miles deep. The granitic substructure of the continents of the First Earth was probably uniformly more than 10 miles deep. Today, because of the continental shifts, some areas have buckled and others have thinned out so the granitic depths of our seven continents vary from 5 miles deep to 16 miles deep.

At the depth of our deepest drill of 7 miles, salt water was found at pressures so intense that water seeping from above could not ever reach that depth. The pressures are so great after 5 miles below the surface, that water cannot creep between the rock particles. That salt water has been there from the beginning of the creation of the Earth, which is exactly the testimony of Genesis, which states that God created a water-world before the dry ground emerged.

In the beginning God created the heavens and the earth. The earth was formless and void, and darkness was over the surface of the deep, and the Spirit of God was moving over the surface of the waters.
—Gen. 1:1–2

It is an absolute certainty that the cracking of the surface of the Earth could have uncorked these underground reservoirs that, under the great pressure of the granitic substructure of the continents weighing above them, caused it to gush upward at supersonic speed and unimaginable force. At those tremendous pressures and high temperatures deep under the continents, the salt water contains gases that are emulsified in the water as well as in the magma.

Volcanologists understand the tremendous power exerted by the sudden change in pressure causing explosive outgassing in the massive eruptions of super-volcanoes when the rock pressure above the magma chambers give way. It is that sudden change in pressure that causes such violent eruptions that dwarf the power of normal volcanoes in much the same way as these pressure waves.

The impact of several meteors in rapid succession would have not only superheated the atmosphere but also caused immense pressure waves into the ground and through the core that bounced back and forth to one side of the Earth and back. Each time the wave bounced off the crust, it triggered many volcanic eruptions of the entire spectrum of intensities. In some cases, the crust just cracked open as it bubbled up magma by the force from below and created huge areas of seeping lava, which we now call traps. They generally mark the distal end of the trajectory of the initial meteor strike on the opposite side of Earth.

The sound of the meteors hitting our atmosphere would have seemed to the ancients as the loudest thunders ever heard by humankind from the pressure waves created in the atmosphere. Once they struck Earth, the sound of the impacts would have been even louder. Thus the Greek account correctly says, "Harshly then he thundered, and heavily, and terribly the earth re-echoed around; and the broad heaven above, and the sea, and streams of ocean, in the abysses of earth" (Thatcher 1915, 23). That also is no hyperbole.

That cacophony would have been followed by the sound of exploding geysers, whose noise would have made the roar of the Iguazu Falls or the Niagara Falls sound like whispers. Every living thing on the First Earth would have heard these horrific thunders in rapid succession. Curtains of gushing water along the continental rips would have reached the heavens, causing high winds through the Venturi effect as it sucked the air around it and pushed it upward into the stratosphere. Aside from the cascading waterfall in the immediate vicinity, moisture in fine spray would have supersaturated the atmosphere on the entire planet.

The gushing torrents of water flowing upward from the deep would have eroded the sides of the continents, sending an enormous amount of rocks, large boulders, and particulate matter emulsified in water to the surface of the planet. Those muddy curtains of water are responsible for most of the strata layers that, when analyzed today, show the evidence of sudden and catastrophic sedimentation and not slow deposition as the gradualists wish.

But had the geysers not burst forth to cool the Earth, the planet would have burned to a cinder, and the superheated air would have cooked all living things. The heated air became the perfect temperature to absorb the latent humidity created by the geysers. It became the perfect recipe for continuous thunderstorms and multiple hurricanes of unimaginable intensity, hurricanes of a destructive force that humankind has not experienced since.

Between the gases released by volcanic activity and the curtain of geysers, the Earth's oxygen concentration was reduced drastically from 37 percent in volume to the measly 21 percent we have today. In an instant, the ideal habitat of the First Earth was changed forever.

Perhaps now we can understand that Hesiod's description may be quite literal. The harsh initial thunder would have been the sonic boom of the entering meteors, and the re-echo may have either been the distant booms of the other six meteors or the secondary booms made by the actual impacts. The entire planet trembled from the numerous earthquakes created by the impacts and the sliding continents. Read the description once again:

> Harshly then he thundered, and heavily, and terribly the earth re-echoed around; and the broad heaven above, and the sea, and streams of ocean, in the abyss of earth. But

beneath his immortal feet vast Olympus trembled, as the king uprose, and earth groaned beneath. And the heat from both caught the dark coloured sea, both of the thunder and lightning, and fire from the monster, the heat arising from the thunder-storms, winds, and burning lightning. And all earth and heaven and sea were boiling (Thatcher 1915, 23).

Hence, the descriptions left for us by the ancients speak of multiple thunders and streams coming from the abyss of the Earth. They speak of the Earth groaning and an enormous release of heat and fire. They speak of thunderstorms and hot winds and burning and lightning. They speak of black waters and black rain. They are the literal descriptions of what would have naturally developed after catastrophic meteor strikes. But the Greeks are not the only ones who attested to this.

The Mayans spoke of this Global Flood of black rain and describe it as a punishment on humankind for forgetting their Creator, and because of their wickedness, they were judged.

And instantly the figures were made of wood. They looked like men, talked like men, and populated the surface of the earth. They existed and multiplied; they had daughters, they had sons, these wooden figures; but they did not have souls, nor minds, *they did not remember their Creator, their Maker. ... They no longer remembered the Heart of Heaven and therefore they fell out of favor. ... Therefore they no longer thought of their Creator nor their Maker. ... These were the first men who existed in great numbers on the face of the earth. ...*

Immediately the wooden figures were annihilated, destroyed, broken up, and killed.

A flood was brought about by the Heart of Heaven; a great flood was formed which fell on the heads of the wooden creatures. ... But those that they had made, that they had created, did not think, did not speak with their Creator, their Maker. And for this reason they were killed, they were deluged. *A heavy rain fell from the sky. . . . This was to punish them because they had not thought of their mother, nor their father, the Heart of Heaven, called Huracán. And for this reason the face of the earth was darkened and a black rain began to fall, by day and by night* (emphasis added) (*Popol Vuh*).

God judged humankind with a global flood. The ancients all declare the same story. Evolutionists don the elitist mantle of arrogance and completely disavow any reality to this universal story acclaimed by every ancient culture. The historical and physical evidence is there for any who have eyes to see and ears to hear. Evolutionists refuse to consider this mechanism, not because there is no evidence or science to support this reality but because of their a priori inclination to deophobia.

While it is true that the ancient stories from around the world have been embellished through time, the kernel of truth cannot be denied without the bias of self-deception. Hardly can it be assumed that this uniformity in the ancient record is merely accidental. These who disclaim the record of our ancestors are the history-deniers.

I suspect that the Mayan reference to the wooden people who had no soul is a reference to the Nephilim or Neanderthals who lived in the giant forests in the First Earth and deceived most of humankind into their occult worship of the Mother Goddess. Cannibalism and ritual sacrifices abounded in their bloody occult religion.

Mechanisms of Strata Formation

Consider the drastic meteorological consequences of such a cataclysm. Mega-storms, fueled by the almost immediate increase in global temperature from the initial and subsequent impacts of space rocks, ravaged our planet. Forests everywhere raged in firestorms. Continuing volcanic eruptions and massive lava traps further added to that temperature spike in our atmosphere as well as in the ocean water.

The increase in heat fueled the most intense hurricanes and tornados that have ever existed in our planet's history. As they moved over land and water, they stirred up silt and buried many marine animals alive. The first to be buried would have been the bottom-dwellers and those densest in body such as the crustaceans. They would naturally be in the lowest layer of the strata. And that is precisely what we find in the layer that evolutionists call the Cambrian strata.

The super volcanoes created by such cataclysmic forces spewed tephra into the atmosphere and caused the rain to come down as black rain. This tephra then became part of the massive sedimentation catastrophe, and so we find that many of the layers contain volcanic material mixed with limestone and sandstone ground by the ejecting geysers that shaped our continental shelves.

Giant tsunamis from the sliding continental plates and the falling ejecta hitting the oceans would have raged around the entire planet, causing the massive transport of sediment across great distances, which we observe in the strata today. Repeated waves of mega-hurricanes would have also agitated the ocean waters in repeated fashion and caused much of the striation we presently observe as each succeeding storm passed through.

The striations we see in the strata were formed through several key aforementioned natural factors during the massive cataclysmic sedimentation process, which tended, in most instances, to quite naturally group animals of particular densities in common levels of the strata.

Decomposition and Body Density

When an animal's body begins to decompose, it creates gases, which causes it to bloat and then float on the surface of the water. After a while, the gases escape, and the body sinks again. It is expected that the larger animals would float the longest and therefore would be the last ones to be caught in the sedimentation process that took place with each passing storm. The denser, smaller crustaceans would undoubtedly sink to the bottom first, thus creating the illusion that the smaller crustaceans were more primitive than the larger animals because they are found in the lower layers.

In other words, the gases emitted during the process of decay, causing the larger animals to float the longest, would effectively cause the smaller animals to sink first into the muddy silt of the Great Flood, thus creating the appearance that the animals died at different intervals. For this reason, 94 percent of the animals encased were mostly seashells of higher body density. Less than 5 percent were plants, and less than 1 percent were vertebrates of all kinds.

Remember that to form a fossil, a creature must be encased in mud. Prior to the Great Flood, most of the animals that would have been fossilized would have been smaller and more easily covered in mud by normal conditions. The fossilization of larger animals would have been extremely rare in normal gradual conditions, as the bodies would have decomposed long before the normal sedimentation process could have encased them completely. The fact that we find such high numbers of large animals fossilized speaks of a catastrophic inundation with massive and rapid sedimentation that encased them before decomposition took place, instead of the gradual deposition proposed by the evolutionists.

Thus, before the Great Flood, the deepest layers of fossils would be expected to contain only the smallest creatures that naturally dwell or fall to the bottom of the ocean or lake beds and became buried in the normal silt conditions.

Runoffs

In some cases, the floodwaters created runoffs between hills and mountains that trapped animals of all sizes and varying ecosystems together. The huge fossil graveyards of all types of animals, including land-dwelling vertebrates and marine and freshwater species, are clear and conclusive evidence that they were encased together in a single cataclysmic global event. This is especially evidenced by the contorted positions in which they were found. In a normal ecological system, animals would tend to be found in a flat position after dying and then being buried under the silt.

Normal runoffs such as flash floods, common in our present geologic conditions, do not contain flying creatures, marine animals, and terrestrial animals all buried together. The presence of such varied ecosystems all jumbled together means that the flooding originated from rising ocean waters and a global catastrophe and were not the product of sedimentation deposits we observe today created by gradual normal precipitation, as evolutionists claim.

Moreover, we find in all the highest mountains evidence of marine animals, which shows that these areas were once covered by ocean waters. It is highly possible that these areas did not become high mountain ranges until the sliding continents began to bulge at the distal ends and their separation movements ground to a halt. There is also further evidence that these sedimentations were of a catastrophic nature and not gradual in process since they do not contain bioturbation, the evidence of burrowing by worms and other marine animals, which is common in slow sedimentation scenarios. This clearly evidences a complete kill-off of all ecosystems simultaneously.

In numerous cases, the animals in a vast area were so quickly buried that they did not have time to decompose. In other cases, we see that the animals were dragged across great distances, breaking them up into fragments before they were buried. That evidences large sheet flooding scenarios and not local and gradual deposition. In addition, the sheer sizes of the fossil graveyards are such that it cannot be attributed to a gradual local phenomenon but rather to a catastrophic scenario over very large-scale areas. Moreover, these areas are found in all parts of the world, evidencing a global catastrophe.

Included are fossil graveyards containing conifers (e.g., pine trees) that are terrestrial, along with insects such as cockroaches, many in nymphal forms, indicating a total and catastrophic destruction of the entire habitat and not a natural gradual dying scenario as posed by evolutionists. They are buried together with marine organisms such as fish and mollusks. That indicates a flood scenario where trees and insects were mixed with terrestrial and marine animals. A slow and gradualist process cannot explain that, as evolutionists insist.

In some cases, the weight of the sedimentation above them and the depth of the water column from the rising waters of the Great Flood caused these animals to be flattened into a two dimensional shape while their bodies were still pliable. In other words, this process was a singular catastrophic event that caused this flattening of all the specimens shortly after their death. This quite clearly indicates an extreme and sudden catastrophic flooding scenario and not a gradual process of millions of years.

Here are several examples of such deposits from around the world, which clearly evidence a catastrophic global flood as described by Andrew Snelling in the following sections:

1. ***The Cambrian Burgess Shale, British Columbia, Canada***
   More than 120 species of marine invertebrates have been preserved at various closely spaced stratigraphic levels within the shale in the Canadian Rockies. Most of these were soft-bodied animals, but they have been preserved with soft parts intact, often with food still in their guts. Arthropods make up nearly 40% of the fossil species, including trilobites, while worms of various types make up more than 25%. Other animals preserved in the shale include four species of coelentarates, at least four species of echinoderms, three species of mollusks, and eighteen species of sponges, plus five species of chordates and hemichordates, and species from ten or more unknown phyla. Many thousands of specimens have been collected from quarries in the shale since their discovery in 1909.

Usually found squashed flat into thin films, these animals were not fossilized in their normal life position, and though difficult to interpret, it is believed that more than 40% were mobile bottom dwellers, the remaining 30% representing free swimmers and burrowers. . . . Indeed the turbulent flow is evidenced by the disposition of the fossils in the rock, the animals being dumped at a variety of angles to the bedding. The Burgess Shale is therefore, an enormous fossil graveyard, produced by countless animals living on the sea floor being catastrophically swept away in landslide generated turbidity currents, and then buried almost instantly in the resulting massive turbidity layers, to be exquisitely preserved and fossilized (emphasis added) (Snelling 2009, 537–38).

2. **The Ordovician Soom Shale, South Africa**

The Soom Shale member of the Cedarberg Formation in the Table Mountain Group outcrops in the Cedarberg Mountains of the Cape Province of South Africa. *The Soom Shale is only 10 meters thick and thinly laminated, the mud and silt laminae being less than 1 mm thick (rarely up to 10 mm) and laterally persistent and undisturbed by any penetrative bioturbation. This is consistent with rapid deposition and lithification, before burrowing organisms could obliterate the laminae.* Thousands of exceptionally preserved animals have been found throughout this shale unit at several locations hundreds of kilometers apart, which suggests that this shale unit is an incredibly large and widespread fossil graveyard. Among the identified fossils are brachiopods, straight shelled nautiloids, various anthropods, worms, conodonts, chitinozoan chains and a number of enigmatic organisms, including one represented only by scattered spines.

The most spectacular fossil specimens are those of arthropods called eurypterids. They not only display complete cuticular skeletons, but also show the sensory chelicerae and walking appendages that are normally lost to early decay after death (emphasis added) (Snelling 2009, 538).

3. **The Devonian Thunder Bay Limestone, Michigan**
Outcropping along the western shore of Lake Huron south of Alpena, Michigan, the Thunder Bay Limestone is at least 4 meters thick and stretches laterally for many hundreds of kilometers. It dips westward into the Michigan Basin, which covers many hundreds of square kilometers right across Michigan.... Most of the fossil remains in this limestone are fragments and broken pieces of the body parts of the original organisms, such as the discs or columnals of crinoids' stems or stalks, which were connected and stacked on top of one another in the living crinoids. After death, crinoids fall apart very quickly, so it is common to find fossilized columnals from broken stalks scattered and jumbled indiscriminately through limestones such as Thunder Bay Limestone. *The Limestone, like so many other limestones in the geologic record, is largely composed of the debris and broken remains of all these marine organisms. They were destroyed then transported by fast moving water before being dumped and buried in what is an enormous fossil graveyard. Thus the Thunder Bay Limestone contains countless billions of fossils that have been catastrophically buried over many hundreds of square kilometers across Michigan* (emphasis added) (Snelling 2009, 539).

4. **The Carboniferous Montceau Shale, Central France**
This shale, in the Montceau Basin of central France, is associated with coal seams, and so far has yielded the fossilized remains of nearly 300 species of plants and pollen, and 16 classes of animals representing about 30 genera. These animals and plants are found flattened within the shale between layers of silt, or in nodules believed to have formed as a result of finer sediments accumulating around the organisms as they were buried and fossilized. Among the fossilized plants are giant

seed ferns and conifers, the former represented by specimens that must have grown as tall as trees, judging by the trunks found fossilized. Fossilized leaves and thorns are plentiful. *Arthropods are by far the most numerous and well preserved animals in this fossil graveyard, crustaceans alone representing about 33% of the fossil fauna.* These include the shrimp-like syncairids, and ostracods and estherians, both minute crustaceans with bivalve shelves. Other aquatic arthropods included the euthycarcinoids (resembling millipeds with tails), and xixiphosurans, believed to be related to the horshoe crabs. *Among the terrestrial arthropod fossils are millipedes, spiders, and scorpions, the latter in many cases being beautifully preserved, complete with their venomous vesicle and sting. Representatives of eight orders of insects, including cockroaches, are present, many of the insects being found as nymphal forms.* . . . The vertebrates found belong to at least for classes—bony fishes, cartilaginous fishes, amphibians, and reptiles. Fish are the most numerous including small sharks. . . . As this fossil graveyard contains a mixture of freshwater, marine, and terrestrial animals and terrestrial plants, some rapid transport of organisms had to take place, along with the rapid sedimentation and burial. *Such a mixture of organisms from vastly different habitats buried catastrophically together is consistent with conditions during the Genesis Flood* (emphasis added) (Snelling 2009, 539–40).

5. **The Triassic Mont Giorgio Basin, Italy, Switzerland**
The shales of Mont San Giorgio are in a basin that is estimated to have been from 6 to 10 kilometers in diameter and only approximately 100 meters deep. Yet thousands of well-preserved fossils in a diverse assemblage of fish and reptiles have been found in these bituminous shales. Once buried in the fine-grained muds, compression flattened the animal skeletons as they petrified. In some instances the force of compression crushed the skeleton

so severely that interpretation of the anatomical detail is difficult, if not impossible (emphasis added) (Snelling 2009, 541).

6. **The Triassic Cow Branch Formation, Cascade, Virginia**
The fossileferous shales of the Cow Branch Formation in the Virginia-North Carolina border area contain an abundance of complete insects, and preserve even the soft part anatomy of some vertebrates, along with an unusual diversity of flora.... *However it is in the microlaminated, organic rich shales that the great diversity of fossilized insects has been found, together with the articulated remains of the tanystrophed reptile, Tanytrochelos, complete with impressions of soft tissue, and the best preserved plant remains.* The matrix is an exceptionally fine-grained black shale that shows no evidence of bioturbation, and the insects are preserved as two-dimensional silvery images... The most abundant fossilized insects are aquatic sucking bugs, two families being represented by numerous nymphal and adult specimens.... Ferns, cycadeoids, and conifers predominate, but also present are lycopods, scouring rushes, gingko, and cyad-like seed plants, as well as a number of seed. Many articulated specimens of the aquatic reptile *Tanytrachelos* have been described from these black shales.... Fragmentary remains of two as-yet undescribed tetrapods have also been found. Also numerous specimens of bony fishes, both ray-finned and lobed-finned, have been recovered from these black shales, along with an isolated shark tooth. *It is the mixture of organisms (terrestrial, freshwater, and marine) buried together, fossilized and so well preserved, that again is consistent with very rapid deposition and burial* (emphasis added) (Snelling 2009, 543, 545).

7. **The Cretaceous Santana Formation, Brazil**
The Santana Formation of Brazil possibly represents the finest fossil locality in the world, due to the incredible preservation of fishes and other animals.... *The fossil assemblage is dominated by fishes, including numerous species of armored*

fishes and ray-finned bony fishes, with rare sharks, a skate, and two species of coalecanth. Associated with the fishes are rare crocodiles, frogs, turtles, dinosaurs and pterosaurs, particularly pterodactyls with wing spans of over three meters. The invertebrate fauna includes shrimps, crustaceans, ostracodes, bivalves, gastropods, echinoderms, rare foraminifera, insects, and spiders. Fossil plants are also present.

The most spectacular of the fossil fishes are the three-dimensional specimens that are found in the calcium carbonate nodules. . . . Preservation has been so rapid and so perfect that structures such as muscle fibers with banding present, some displaying ultrastructure, fibrilis, and even cell nuclei arranged in neat rows, have been fossilized. Underneath the scales, small pieces of skin are preserved and show thin sheets of muscle and connective tissue. In a female specimen the ovaries have been preserved with developing egg inside, and one egg had phophatized yolk. Many specimens display the stomach wall with all its reticulations, and often with the last meal still in the stomach. One specimen had no fewer than 13 small fish in the alimentary track, with a number of shrimps, that even had their compound eyes preserved with the lenses in place. But the most spectacular tissues found are the gills preserved with the secondary lamellae intact.

These tissues are very useful for estimating the speed of the phosphatization process. After the death of a fish, blood pressure is reduced and the secondary lamellae collapse within one to three hours. In the Santana fossil fish, the secondary lamellae are intact, with very little sign of collapse, cells are inflated, but the ultrastructure is not preserved. It is clear, therefore that the fossilization process took place moments after the fish had died, and was completed within only a few (probably less than five) hours. . . . However the fishes are not the only animals whose remains have been phosphatized.

For example ostracodes are found phosphatized, with the tiny animal still inside with its hairy legs preserved. *However even more spectacular are the fossilized wings of pterosaurs, which somewhat unusual are the most abundant reptiles in the Santana Formation.* Preserved in an uncrushed condition, the bones can be extracted from the matrix and related to each other to work out how they functioned., including the aerodynamics of pterosaur flight. Even better still, The Santana Formation has yielded pterosaurs with phosphatized wing membrane, which has been cross-sectioned to reveal a highly complex organ consisting of a variety of tissue types, including skin, a vascular layer, and muscle tissue.

It is abundantly clear from examination of the incredible preservation of so many fossils in the Santana Formation that this fossil graveyard represents a spectacular catastrophic event, given that flying reptiles and terrestrial dinosaurs, plants, insects, and spiders are found buried together and exquisitely preserved as fossils with fish of many types, crocodiles, turtles, and various marine invertebrates. Burial has to be very rapid, because scavenging and water current activity did not disturb the carcasses, which had to be phosphatized rapidly between death and their very rapid burial (emphasis added) (Snelling 2009, 544–45).

8. **The Cretaceous Tepexi Limestone, Mexico**
Fissile red limestone near the town of Tepexi southwest of, and close to, Mexico City contains a fossil graveyard with an assemblage of organisms not too dissimilar to the Santana fossil graveyard in Brazil. Fishes are again the most prominently represented, with more than 30 new species. This fact coupled with the exceptional preservation of the specimens, makes Tepexi a spectacular fossil fish site. For some species the site has yielded a complete developmental series from hatchling to adult. . . . Some fishes have been preserved with their last meal still in their guts, and these often include other fishes. The generally

perfect preservation of the fish shows that no scavenging took place as the fish died.... Fish are not the only vertebrates found in the fossil graveyard, as there are also extinct reptiles, including lizards, a turtle, a new type of crocodile. A leurosaur, and a pterosaur (some isolated bones are attributed to pterodactyls, although no complete specimens have been found).... *It is quite obvious that a catastrophic process was involved in transporting and depositing a diverse mixture of organisms, from flying and terrestrial reptiles, to fish and marine organisms. Turbidity currents carrying fine lime mud were interspersed with falls of volcanic ash, so that organisms were killed, squashed together, and rapidly buried so as to be well preserved in the fossil graveyard* (emphasis added) (Snelling 2009, 546–47).

9. **The Cretaceous Djadokhta Formation, Nemget Basin, Ukhaa Tolgod Area, Mongolia**
In the Ukhaa Tolgod area of the Gobi Desert of Mongolia, an unmatched abundance of well-preserved vertebrate fossils is found in the Djadokhta Formation, including the highest concentration of mammalian skulls and skeletons from any Mesozoic site. From an area of about four square kilometers, the recovered and uncollected articulated skeletons of theropods, ankylosaurian, and protoceratopian dinosaurs represent over 100 individuals. Specimens collected also include skulls, many with associated skeletons, of over 400 mammals and lizards, and include the first known skull of the bird *Mononykus*. Certain sites have been interpreted as nests, because fossilized eggs at these sites contain what are believed to be theropod embryos. A distinctive feature of this Ukhaa Tolgod fossil graveyard is the marked diversity and abundance of small vertebrates. Also striking is the preservational quality of these delicate specimens. Many skulls are still complete with lower jaws still in articulation, and tympanic rings and ear ossicles well preserved. . . . *The excellent preservation of*

DATING METHODS: THE THREE PILLARS

these vertebrate fossils at Ukhaa Tolgod prompts questions concerning the mode of their death, burial and preservation. Given that the well-preserved fossils are all found in a distinctive sandstone layer, it is obvious that this fossil assemblage resulted from rapid post-mortem in situ burial in sand. Evidence for this is the abundant articulated skeletons, which suggest minimal post-mortem surface weathering and transport, positions of skeletons that suggest "death struggles," and monospecific death assemblages for certain dinosaurs such as Protoceratops and Pinacosaurus. Many of the small mammals may simply have been buried in their burrows. Above the fossiliferous sandstone layer is a moderately coarse conglomerate bed, which is indicative of high-energy water deposition. Furthermore, the structurelsss (non-cross-bedded) sandstone in which all the vertebrate fossils are found contains pebbles and abundant coarse sand. . . . Thus to virtually bury alive such large animals as dinosaurs implies rapid water flow and catastrophic deposition of the sand (emphasis added) (Snelling 2009, 547–48).

The evolutionary insistence that these enormous fossil beds were created gradually through millions of years does not match the geologic data. Coal beds, for example, are commonly associated above and below with strata that have obviously been formed by transported sedimentary material. This indicates that they were formed during a single catastrophic event that had multiple mechanisms in rapid succession, as the biblical flood indicates.

The presence of marine fossils in those sedimentary layers shows that flooding ocean water caused rapid sedimentation over layers of floating vegetation that were ripped by the hydraulics and deposited between repeated storms or tsunamis, which effectively encased and crushed the vegetation layers over enormous spans across the entire face of the United States.

It is the enormous lateral extent of these fossil beds that cannot rationally be attributed to gradual local mechanisms in local swamps but indicate a global catastrophic scenario.

We can point to our own coal seams in North America:

> For example, detailed statigraphic research has found that the Broken Arrow coal seam of Oklahoma can be correlated with the Crowburgh Seam (Missouri), the Whitebreast Seam (Iowa), the Colchester No. 2 Seam (Illinois), the Coal IIIa Seam (Indiana), the Schultztown Seam (west Kentucky) and the Lower Kittaning Seam (Ohio and Pennsylvania). Thus these seams together form a single vast bed of coal exceeding 260,000 square kilometers in area in the central and Eastern United States. No modern swamp has an area even remotely similar to that of these carboniferous coal seams (Snelling 2009, 551).

The uppermost layers of the strata formed as the turbulence subsided. The churned up waters of the flood settled, and tons of suspended soil began to form layers of sediment over the carcasses. The smaller animals would have become the first to be covered, creating the present illusion that is sometimes observed in some of the strata. But it should not be assumed that all of this happened in one single moment. Repeated tsunamis and hurricanes of magnitudes never since experienced would have repeatedly caused multiple sedimentation events for the entire length of 150 days.

Since the larger organisms provide a much larger surface area, it would have taken longer for their bodies to sink and then become imbedded in the sediment. Repeated hurricanes could have easily pushed them along the colder waters at the bottom, thus retarding their sedimentation and decomposition further and creating a span of sedimentation between the smaller creatures and the larger creatures.

The strata do generally show that there is a unique gradation in the strata according to the size of the creatures. But this gradation is not always facing the same direction. We find in some cases larger animals further down and in other cases the opposite. It is possible that animals from different habitats were transported over large distances by individual hydraulic events, and for this reason, they may be found in different layers of the strata.

It must be noted that there are many examples where the layers contain supposedly more evolved animals mixed in the deeper layers. Often, evolutionists attempt to dodge this bullet by claiming that overthrusting can change the order of the strata. But when so-called overthrusting takes place, the friction of the two layers, as one slips over the other, will cause a layer of gravel to form between them, which is easily discernible. That essential telltale evidence of overthrusting is not always seen in these topsy-turvy strata found out of sequence.

These anomalies are simply ignored and completely disavowed, for they do not fit with evolutionists' gradualist paradigm. In much the same fashion, they turned a blind eye in the past to evidence that opposed the jaded uniformitarian paradigm. In their minds, the geologic column is a fact. All strata labeling then follows from that imagined fact, no matter which way the layers are found. Because of their evolutionary/gradualist predilection, they fail to recognize the global nature of this sedimentation process.

> In southern England the chalk beds are estimated to be about 405 meters thick, and from there they extend inland across England to the Atrim area of Northern Ireland, southwest Ireland, and to extensive areas of the sea floor in south of Ireland. In the opposite direction they extend from northern France across northern Germany and southern Scandinavia to Poland, Bulgaria, and eventually Georgia in the south of the Commonwealth of Independent States. However, identical chalk beds are also found in Egypt, and

Israel. On the other side of the Atlantic Ocean the same chalk beds are found in Texas, through Alabama, Arkansas, Mississippi, and Tennessee, In Nebraska and adjoining States, and in Kansas. Incredibly identical chalk beds, complete with the same black flint nodules and the same fossils are found in the Perth basin of Western Australia. As well as the countless microfossils, this fossil graveyard of global distribution contains many macroscopic fossils including barnacles, crustaceans, brachiopods, oysters, gastropods, pelecypods, cephalopods, ammonites, bryozoans, echinoids, corals, crinoids, and even fish, as well as abundant trace fossils, particularly burrows. That catastrophic deposition rates were involved in forming these thick chalk beds is evident from the size of some of the ammonite fossils (which may be up to one meter in diameter), and the large *Mosasauros* skull found near Maastrich (Netherlands), as well as by the recognition of storm-deposited tempestite layers within the chalk (Snelling 2009, 570-71).

The fact is that the geologic record is more consistent with the biblical record than with evolution. It more accurately depicts a cataclysmic inundation of our planet that brought most living things to an end in a watery chaos through violent and repeated hydraulic events.

The many thick and relatively parallel layers of sedimentation observed all over the world is the empirical evidence that they were deposited in a relatively short period of time such as is the global deluge referred to in the Bible.

Waves

Large waves would have added to the layering of the fossils in the sediments below them. The wave peaks would have compressed sediments slightly due to the extra column of water above them. But when the trough of the wave passed over the sediments, water trapped around the sediment particles would have moved upward (rebound), causing the denser sediments to sink and the lighter sediments to rise. Anyone who stands on the seashore experiences this as their feet sink into the sand by the motion of repeated waves. The negative pressure created by the passing wave lifts the sand and separates it from other particles, causing the denser particles to fall deeper and faster than the more finely suspended particles into the loosely packed recent sediment. This repeated action over time would have effectively striated the sediments and the fossils according to the density of their bodies.

Length of Water Column
The weight and shape of falling sediment will also cause layering. That is especially so if the column of water is very high so that the density differences are magnified by the long period of time it takes to reach the bottom. Slight differences in the shape or density of sediment particles will cause them to descend to the depths of the sea at varying rates. That effectively sorts material into layers, causing the typical striations we see in sedimentary rocks.

Liquefaction
Liquefaction, a settling process, is created by seismic waves from earthquakes. If the process of sedimentation is accompanied by enormous and repeated earthquakes, as the creationist model indicates, then the process of liquefaction evidenced in sedimentary earth would have also caused interred objects of greater density to sink in proportion to their density. The high-energy shock waves in earthquakes cause sedimentary particles to vibrate and become less compact. That allows objects that are of greater density to sink lower due to the action of gravity.

Seismic waves created by striking ejecta and the ripping of the continents would have swarmed over the globe for months on end until the continents came to grind to rest near their present destinations. As these numerous seismic waves traveled across the landscape, denser animals sank lower into the liquefied ground, while less dense animals tended to sink less or even rise.

Most of us have seen pictures of buildings on sedimentary foundations literally sink into the earth during earthquakes. Anyone who has traveled to San Francisco has witnessed this curious phenomenon in the many buildings with second-floor windows that are now at street level. This liquefaction on a grand scale would have created a rough separation between animals of various densities.

Massive Super-hurricanes

We would also expect that the superheating of the atmosphere by the impact of the meteors, along with the infusion of hot salt water from the underground aquifers and extreme global volcanism, would have generated immense super-hurricanes. Each of these storms would have further agitated the waters in successive bouts, causing further striations with each passing storm.

It is plain to see that the tremendous heat generated by the meteor strike and the erupting volcanoes would have spawned numerous super-hurricanes that would have stirred up the silt and could have been another global mechanism for striations. Once the ocean waters were high enough to cover most of the land, these hurricanes would have raged unimpeded by the terrain that usually breaks up their rotational motion. These enormous hurricanes would have easily caused successive striations in the strata. Only the freezing of the polar caps and the lowering of the global temperatures would have stopped these massive storms.

The geologic strata evidence reflects massive sedimentation events that catastrophically destroyed complete habitats with animals in all stages of their lives. A gradual scenario, as evolutionists insist, would not contain all the stages of life but would predominantly contain the older specimens coming to their natural death and then being slowly buried in the silt.

Other evidence that the sedimentation layers were essentially the result of the flood is the fact that many petrified trees are found to be crosscutting through several layers of sedimentation, which, according to evolutionists, represent millions of years. This is indisputable evidence that the various layers were deposited at somewhat the same time or the trunks would have decayed long before the gradual deposit could have buried them completely.

The deep layers of sedimentary deposits we find today throughout our planet can more accurately be explained by the catastrophic hydraulic nature of the Great Flood. We are not claiming that all sedimentary deposits were created by the Great Flood but that most of them were.

Gradual deposition did occur prior to the catastrophic flood, but we would expect those layers to contain many fewer fossils, which require water and silt to encase them. These would then be limited to areas where lakes and swamps existed before the Great Flood.

The telltale signs of a mass hydraulic cataclysm are the vast expanse of such evenly thick sedimentary layers throughout the world and the homogeneous nature of the thick layers. Striations made through enormous spans of time could not have even thick layers and should not be composed of such homogeneous layers for two obvious reasons:

1. Had the mechanism that created the strata taken the enormous time periods insisted by gradualists, they would naturally create severe undulations in their thickness, as wind and other factors would have acted upon them in random fashion, eroding some sections more than others. The fact that these layers are so consistently even over enormously large spans speaks of a large-scale singular hydraulic event.

2. Had these deposits been created by the slow rates throughout large periods of time as the evolutionists insist, they would show clear evidence of heterogeneous diffusion. In other

words, if the layers were made slowly, the internal composition of these layers of sedimentary deposits would have been made of much greater variability. The homogeneous nature of the sedimentary layers is direct evidence of a singular event that brought forth in a relatively short time immense and catastrophic sedimentation.

If the content found within these layers were created through millions of years, the enormously thick sedimentary layers visible throughout our planet would neither be homogeneous in nature nor so evenly spaced. The fact that these layers are, for the most part, smooth and uniform throughout the planet speaks of a singular deep-water event and not a long and protracted phenomenon, as the evolutionists wishfully imagine.

Tiny differences in the shape and density of sedimentary particles cause them to sink at different rates through a column of water. The deeper the column, the more pronounced effect it will have on the striation of the sediments sinking.

Strata visible in the Grand Canyon were quite likely caused by the sedimentation of the Great Flood. The erosion of the canyon exposed a thickness of four to five thousand feet of sedimentary rock. The late Dr. Henry Morris contended that the Colorado River does not have enough energy in it to carve out the Grand Canyon and therefore, he postulated that only a catastrophe on the order of the Great Flood could do so.

DATING METHODS: THE THREE PILLARS

Hence, the very fact that these sedimentary layers filled with fossils are found globally, even as much as a mile thick on mountains, point to the following:

1. A time in which even the mountains were covered by deep ocean water
2. Mountain formations that were largely due to the tectonic processes after the Great Flood as the sliding continents ground to a halt and buckled
3. The process of fossil formation indicating hydraulic involvement. No fossils can form without the presence of water to leach the minerals from the ground into the shape of the creature entombed. Moreover, the entombing process must take place before the body decomposes, an event quite rare in normal and gradual circumstances.
4. Rich troves of fossils of creatures from very different ecosystems buried together in massive graveyards all over our planet. How could that happen unless a flood covered the entire Earth?

Can a flood really cover all of Earth?

The Global Near-Extinction Catastrophe

Evolutionists no longer deny that a near-extinction catastrophe struck our planet and caused huge geologic, climactic, and hydrologic changes. There is no doubt that at a single moment in Earth's history, something happened that killed off not only the dinosaurs but also almost 95 percent of all species.

As we have already stated, most modern evolutionists point to the meteor strike in the Yucatan Peninsula as the culprit. It is quite likely that they are right. But we also believe that this enormous strike on the crust of the Earth was not the only one. Together, they could have set in motion the events that broke our single continent of the First

Earth and caused the Global Flood. The existence of multiple mass burial grounds of fossilized organisms seems to point out the high probability that this was caused by a worldwide flood.

We know that the mass extinction process took place in a single incident because animals of prey as well as others were found without evidence of predation. That means that animals, regardless of their species, were killed in a rather short period of time, almost simultaneously worldwide.

Although there are some limited natural processes that could explain the formation of these mass graves, such as the one in Lincoln County, Wyoming, and the fossil beds of Florissant, Colorado, the probability of the factors necessary for this process to occur in so many sites around the planet outside of a worldwide flood are negligible.

Three factors must converge to produce mass fossil graveyards, which include both predator and prey, without signs of predation in the animals fossilized:

1. Some mechanism must produce a mass kill of the organisms.
2. Another mechanism must quickly bury the creatures in quick order before decomposition destroys the corpses of the creatures.
3. Water must be present in order for fossils to be formed.

One of the mechanisms suggested as a possible cause of these mass extinction fossil deposits in the marine ecosphere is the phenomenon known as water bloom. Anyone who has lived in Florida has at some time experienced this phenomenon. Water bloom occurs when an explosive growth in plankton causes the sea water to turn a reddish color, thus the term *red tide*.

This overproduction of plankton depletes all the available oxygen from the water, causing all marine organisms in the vicinity to suffocate. It also creates poisons that, when ingested, will kill most organisms in that water. Depending on the magnitude of the red tide, many marine animals caught within its boundaries die.

But that would not explain how they became interred in silt before the decomposition of their bodies could take place. Nor does it explain the mass burials of terrestrial animals. I have personally witnessed the red-tide phenomenon in Biscayne Bay (Miami) and in the St. Johns River in Jacksonville, Florida. Everywhere this lethal blight strikes, dead fish float on the water, and the waves drive them toward the shores. The smell of rotting fish assaults your nostrils. Within a short period of time, the bodies decompose, and they are gone.

The problem for the evolutionist is that in order for the creatures to become fossilized, they must be interred within a short period of time, before they completely decompose. Certainly, red tides can cause massive kill-offs of organisms, but they provide no method for interment. And the red tides affect only marine organisms. These massive fossil graveyards include giant mammals, reptiles, and other huge land animals that no longer walk the earth. The red tide does not explain how they were interred en masse.

Evolutionists must suppose that either a volcano erupted, emitting a shower of volcanic ash that covered the bodies, or an earthquake created such a stir in the waters that the disturbed silt settled over the bodies and buried them. In such a scenario, all three of the above requirements must be met at the same place and time to reproduce the present evidence found in the strata.

Yes, this may be a theoretical possibility, but when one considers the enormous number of places it has occurred, the chances for all these processes to take place in the specific amount of time necessary before the bodies decomposed is astronomical.

In other words, the red tide must exactly coincide with either a propitiously timed earthquake or a propitiously timed volcanic event in order to create the sedimentation necessary to bury the oganisms in such a short amount of time before they decomposed. But the sediments are not all volcanic. That brings us to evolutionists' biggest problem.

The insurmountable problem they face is that this seems to be a global cataclysm. The extinction did not take place in different areas of our planet at different times. It took place almost simultaneously throughout the entire planet. That is what caused the extinction. Had it not been simultaneous, no extinction would have taken place since the species would have had time to rebound as surviving members in unaffected areas migrated back.

Some have postulated that this mass extinction was caused by some epidemic. Although epidemics can cause extinctions, it is very rare, indeed, that a single epidemic could wipe out all these species. Usually, the pathogens that create extinction potentials for one species offer no danger for another due to their varied immune systems. The odds of multiple epidemics surging simultaneously are quite remote. And that still cannot explain the massive fossil beds that were created by sedimentation in this cataclysmic event.

The far-fetched concept of multiple local catastrophes is inadequate to explain the universal nature evidenced by the fossils. If each of these sites were to be preserved this way and all these events were independent of each other, then the miracle here proclaimed is a feat that requires more faith than I have.

To accept the evolutionary explanation, this coincidence must have taken place simultaneously, numerous times throughout the entire planet, in a carefully choreographed sequence in order to accomplish their imagined cumulative global mechanism. Propitiously timed multiple events would have had to also include hydraulics to create the mass graveyards of land animals found throughout the planet.

In other words, one would have to believe that numerous local floods just happened to occur simultaneously around the entire planet. The law of conservation strongly favors the simpler and more obvious explanation.

The other proposed mechanism promoted by evolutionists is that the single meteor strike in the Yucatan Peninsula created so much dust in the atmosphere that the Earth's vegetation was incapable of surviving. In effect, that would have been the equivalent of a nuclear winter.

That could explain the death of most of the animals, but it does not explain the mass fossil graveyards and the enormous sedimentation that entombed them. Nor does it explain the fossilization of multiple ecosystems in the same fossil graveyards. If their model were true, most of the animals would have died of starvation and would have either decomposed or been eaten by carnivores. That is not what we find in the mass graveyards that contain both vegetarians and carnivores without any sign of predation.

There is another more logical possibility that could provide all the conditions required for mass fossilization of specimens throughout the world: a catastrophic event that was global in nature. As a matter of fact, the very mechanism of the deluge would include volcanic ash activity, as well as massive earthquakes and the hydraulics necessary for fossilization. A global flood provides a much more plausible explanation for the worldwide phenomenon we observe in the fossil record.

Any localized processes or mass starvation events cannot explain the mass extinction of dinosaurs as well as 95 percent of the fauna and their entombment in enormous layers of sedimentation. If the processes were localized and not simultaneous, animals would have migrated back to the previously affected areas, and there would be no extinction. No global starvation event can cause mass fossil graveyards. But at least most evolutionists are now being forced to adopt the global catastrophism model in regard to the near total extinction event that almost ended all life on our planet. It is a step in the right direction.

The fact that sedimentary layers of rock, sometimes tens of thousands of feet thick, are found on mountains also seems to indicate that the processes of sedimentation took place prior to the processes of mountain formation. Sedimentary rock can only be made in the presence of water. These sedimentary layers are contorted in folds, faults, and sometimes overthrusts, indicating the powerful lateral tectonic forces at work after the sediments were laid down as the continents were shifting away from the bulging Mid-Atlantic Ridge. The undulating folds are proof that these tectonic forces were taking place while the sedimentary layers were yet pliable and recently created.

A worldwide flood would better explain these enormous beds of sedimentary rock such as found in the Midwest United States. The universal nature of this catastrophe is clearly evidenced within the rocks. Evolutionists, in order to avoid the biblical narrative, must then suppose that all these mass graveyards were caused by a series of local floods all around the planet in conjunction with a mass starvation event. But the depth of these sedimentary layers says otherwise.

In vast areas of the Midwest (Kansas, Nebraska, Iowa, Illinois, Ohio, etc.), the sedimentary layer is more than a mile thick. Only a deep global flood could account for this enormous sedimentation. No local floods could achieve such depth.

The Coral Reef Argument

The formation of coral reefs is a slow process that gradually builds the reef as organisms die off and the limestone superstructure remains behind. The fact that some large deposits of these reefs are found in extreme northern or extreme southern latitudes, where now there are no warm inland seas, is used as evidence that the Great Flood did not take place due to the continuity of the size of the reef that would have been interrupted by the catastrophe. In other words, because the coral reefs build slowly, because there are no seas there, and because their average temperatures are too cold for coral formation, it must have taken place many years ago when the area was covered under some shallow sea in a milder climate for a long period of time.

DATING METHODS: THE THREE PILLARS

The Silurian rocks of Wisconsin and Illinois are found to be as much as a thousand feet thick and several miles long. Evolutionists contend that the size of these beds could not have been produced within the short time frames that creationists claim our Earth has existed. How could they have grown there so far north?

Two considerations are important. The first is that the continents have shifted. The states of Wisconsin and Illinois are now high in the Northern Hemisphere. But before the cracking of the Earth, New York was touching northern Africa. Alaska was by England and northern Europe.

The North American continent has since then turned counterclockwise and shifted northward and westward. The area where Wisconsin now dwells could hardly grow corals. But before the Earth was cracked, not only was that area further south, but the antediluvian world was warm throughout the entire planet. The greenhouse effect of a small water vapor canopy that existed in the First Earth (similar but nowhere as large as the one on Venus) provided a stable global temperature. There were no polar caps as we have today. The area of the Siberian tundra was then a rich grassland hosting large roaming herds of mammoths, horses, deer, and many other animals.

But there are other possibilities for this seeming anomaly. Our present growth rates are the product of our present temperature and meteorological conditions. If the First Earth had been covered by a small water vapor canopy as our model suggests, the greenhouse effect would have created a much larger area of the First Earth where coral formation was not only possible but more favorable. The increase in oxygen in our prediluvian atmosphere is indicative of a much greener planet that had photosynthesis operating on a much grander scale.

There is no way for us to say with any definitive assurance that the rate of coral formation in the Prediluvian world had to be the same as in our present diminished world. In fact, if we look at the fauna in that period, the opposite would be our conclusion. Everything grew bigger and faster on the First Earth, especially if ocean temperatures were much warmer on a much greater extent of our planet.

It is also possible for corals to have been deposited there by either the enormous hydraulics of the Great Flood or as ejected matter from the area of the meteor strike. The enormous upheaval caused by an event such as the Great Flood could have easily ruptured large chunks of reefs formed in the antediluvian epoch. The hydraulic forces, as well as the ejection of these huge limestone chunks thrust outward upon the impact of the meteor, could have easily deposited them thousands of miles from the impact site.

If our Judeo-Christian model is correct, our First Earth would have had a 35 percent to 37 percent oxygen saturation and a mild climate throughout all four seasons, which would have provided for the more rapid growth of all organisms. For this reason, we have gigantic specimens of all our present fauna fossilized in this period.

Year-round stable ocean temperatures would have allowed such huge coral beds to grow throughout most of the world at accelerated rates, unlike today where corals can grow only within a narrow sector of our tropics where the ocean temperatures are maintained within a small temperature parameter. In our present oceans, the more dramatic seasonal temperature fluctuations of our Second Earth inhibit the growth of corals when the waters are cooler.

While it is true that the hydraulics of a local flood would be hardly enough to account for this specific instance, the mechanism of the Great Flood is more than ample and predicated upon more than one mechanism of force. The impact of seven meteors would have caused enormous earthquakes throughout the entire planet that would have easily cracked large chunks or reefs. The force of the impacts around the immediate area would have instantly vaporized the rock in its immediate vicinity. But nearby reefs could have easily been fractured and ejected by the enormous energy released in these multiple impacts.

Some of the reefs would have traveled up into the stratosphere, returning as molten fiery ejecta. Others would have been easily thrust sideways for many miles by the very energy of the catastrophe. The ring of geysers from the breaking up of the fountains of the deep could have also played a role in expelling large chunks of coral rock to great distances from the sheer force of the ejecting water.

The Hydroplate Theory

The hydroplate theory proposed by Walter Brown, who has a PhD in mechanical engineering from the Massachusetts Institute of Technology, offers a viable explanation for the movement of the tectonic plates, which can rationally account for the global phenomenon of the flood.

If Brown's hydroplate theory is correct, and I suspect that it is, then the First Earth had huge subterranean water chambers that were interconnected throughout the planet. These subterranean chambers were located beneath the granitic substructure of Earth's upper crust. As we have already noted, deep bore wells have shown that salt water still abounds at these subterranean levels.

The mechanism that caused the Great Flood would have had to be capable of releasing this enormous store of subterranean salt water. The creation account specifies that the "fountains of the great deep" were opened first and then the "floodgates of the sky" were opened (Gen. 7:11).

That implies that the mechanism first ripped the crust and allowed for this subterranean water to be released. The weight of the granitic substructure of the continents pushing on the subterranean chambers, along with the violent forces of sudden outgassing produced by this rupturing crack in the crust, would have created a powerful fountain of water gushing out at supersonic speeds throughout the entire Mid-Atlantic Ridge. That crack would have progressed all the way around the world where the crust was severed. As the weight of the rocks were removed by erosion, the basaltic rock below the granitic continent would have been forced upward by the internal pressure in the interior of the Earth, forming what we know today as the Mid-Oceanic Ridges.

The hydroplate theory, from a scientific perspective, more adequately explains the Mid-Oceanic Ridge, the continental drifts, the shape of the continental shelves and slopes, the reason for ocean trenches, the large salt deposits, seamounts and tablemounts, magnetic variations recorded on the ocean floor, the development of the strata, the overabundance of limestone on our planet, the origin of some comets, and many more physical phenomena that are poorly explained by other theories. But we are getting ahead of ourselves. We will cover these aspects in more detail in *The Death of the First Earth*.

The breaking of the "fountains of the great deep" and the resulting supersonic jet of water streaming from the subterranean chambers could have easily thrust enormous chunks of coral from shallow and warm inland seas, which at that time existed over the area of the Mid-Atlantic Ridge, when North America and North Africa were connected to the very point in Central America and the Caribbean where the Chicxulub meteor struck the Yucatan Peninsula. The explosive power of the uncorking of dissolved CO_2 in the water contained within the subterranean chambers was the catalyst that created the outgassing energy that fueled the fountains of the deep. The sudden outgassing could have provided the necessary energy to throw such large pieces of rock great distances.

In addition, the hydroplate theory explains that our planet seems to have more limestone than it could have produced through organic processes. Not all limestone is produced through the organic process of the erosion of marine shells. We will discuss that later in the section on the Great Flood.

The very fact that these corals are found in pieces could point to a violent event such as either giant meteors that could have fractured them and flung them into their present locations or the action of explosive geysers. And in light of the preponderance of evidence of a worldwide volcanic upheaval and the massive craters found in Greenland, Antarctica, South Africa, North America, and the Yucatan Peninsula, this scenario is certainly possible.

The Global Volcanic Upheaval

The geological evidence throughout the world is that there was not only a worldwide deluge but also a worldwide volcanic upheaval. Enormous beds of lava give testimony to this catastrophic event that precipitated a multilayered cataclysm. The lava beds of the Colombian Plateau in the northwestern part of the United States are several thousand feet thick and extend over an area of 200,000 square miles. This gargantuan volcanic upheaval by itself would have had worldwide ramifications. But, like the Colombian Plateau, there are many more examples of enormous volcanic eruptions throughout the entire world.

In India, there was an enormous volcanic eruption. Beds of volcanic rock several thousand feet thick go on for miles. Similar immense lava beds are also found in Russia and South America. More will be said on this subject later as we deal with the issue of the biblical flood and the mechanism that precipitated it.

But for the subject at hand, it can be clearly substantiated that the empirical, physical evidence everywhere on the planet is more consistently explained by a sudden catastrophic event that caused a worldwide flood and the mass extinction of a wide variety of organisms. This single event also caused a marked and radical change in the resulting climate of our planet.

The once stable meteorology of the First Earth gave way to a more volatile and fluctuating climate. The stable crust was fractured. Earthquakes were now part of the ordinary. The water vapor canopy was exhausted, and no longer would the Earth have a stable temperature globally, which led to the formation of the polar ice caps. No longer would the entire Earth be evenly watered by a morning mist. Too much rain in one area now made rocky and eroded terrains bereft of topsoil, and too little rain in other areas left barren desert landscapes. Only a small area of the planet now contains the right amount of rain to be fruitful. Our Second Earth is infinitely inferior to the First Earth.

Once there were no hurricanes or tornadoes. Once there were no snowstorms or pelting hail. Once there were no earthquakes or tsunamis. Once the First Earth flourished with forests that spanned almost the entire surface of the globe. It was a lush green planet vibrant with life. Oxygen saturated our atmosphere. Today, our oxygen concentration in the atmosphere has been reduced by a third as part of the judgment that fell upon our planet.

In the polar regions, instead of ice caps there were fertile plains filled with grasses and roaming wildlife. A wide variety of animals thrived in these northern and southern latitudes. Instead of rocky towering mountains, the earth stretched into gently undulating hills and fertile plains with deep rich loam that allowed a wide variety of organisms to thrive to enormous sizes.

There was but one ocean and one landmass, and the warm ocean was filled with crystal clear fresh water. There was no rain. A mist covered the land every morning, and the morning dew irrigated all the plants. Fresh drinking water abounded, free from pollution. I wonder how many beautiful flowers and delicious fruits were lost in the death of the First Earth.

Both the deep ozone layer and the water vapor canopy surrounding our entire First Earth effectively blocked the cosmic rays, making it an ideal habitat for humankind. Our First Earth was almost a paradise. But our paradise was lost, and our Second Earth was birthed. One day, too, our Second Earth shall die, and the Third Earth shall be birthed by the seven judgments that will come at the end of our age, according to the book of Revelation.

The First Earth died by the Global Flood, but the Second Earth will die by four enormous earthquakes, the last one being a global earthquake that topples mountains and drives islands into the sea. The judgments that will come throughout a seven-year period known in the Hebrew Scriptures as Jacob's Trouble and in the New Testament as the Great Tribulation will consist of a scroll sealed with seven seals. As each seal is broken, the judgments are pronounced. The seventh seal is composed of seven further judgments known as the Seven Trumpets. The seventh trumpet is composed of seven bowls of judgment.

When the Four Horsemen of the Apocalypse come conquering and deceiving people to conquer the world for the Antichrist, they will bring with them war, famine, pestilence, and death. The first earthquake will come in the judgment of the sixth seal and will cause darkness to fall upon the Earth.

> *I looked when He broke the sixth seal, and there was a great earthquake; and the sun became black as sackcloth made of hair, and the whole moon became like blood.*
> —Rev. 6:12

The fact that the sun is darkened and the moon turns red means that this probably also involves a volcanic upheaval that fills our atmosphere with tephra. In those days, Jews and Christians will be persecuted as never before. Their prayers will rise to heaven and arouse the Lion of Judah. The second earthquake will come when the seventh seal is broken, which begins the judgments of the seven trumpets.

> *And the smoke of the incense, with the prayers of the saints, went up before God out of the angel's hand. Then the angel took the censer and filled it with the fire of the altar, and threw it to the earth; and there followed peals of thunder and sounds and flashes of lightning and an earthquake. And the seven angels who had the seven trumpets prepared themselves to sound them.*
> —Rev. 8:4–6

All of this will take place during the first three and a half years of the seven-year tribulation period. During that time, Elijah will bring the hearts of Israel back to God. Heed the warnings of Elijah. Your lives depend upon it. Flee to the Great Succoth prepared for you in the desert where manna and the living water will protect and sustain you from the destroyers.

The third earthquake will strike when the Antichrist attacks Jerusalem and kills Elijah and Enoch. That is the day exactly at the middle of the seven-year period when the Antichrist enters the Holy of Holies in the Jewish Temple and declares himself to be God. It is the abomination that causes desolation spoken of by Daniel (Dan. 9:27) and Jesus (Matt. 24:15).

> *And in that hour there was a great earthquake, and a tenth of the city fell; seven thousand people were killed in the earthquake, and the rest were terrified and gave glory to the God of heaven. The second woe is past; behold, the third woe is coming quickly. Then the seventh angel sounded; and there were loud voices in heaven, saying, "The kingdom of the world has become the kingdom of our Lord and of His Christ; and He will reign forever and ever."*
> —Rev. 11:13–15

The day the Antichrist announces his global conquest is the same day that God announces the beginning of Christ's Kingdom. For the next three and a half years, the seven bowls of judgment shall destroy the kingdoms that had banded together to kill the Jews. But God provides for them a hiding place that Elijah will point them to until the seventh bowl of judgment.

Just when Satan thinks he has finally taken over the world, Elijah and Enoch will resurrect before their very eyes three and a half days later, as the entire world watches, and be taken to heaven. It is a symbol of the resurrection of Israel, now hiding in the Great Succoth for three and a half years waiting for the atonement that will come through the seven bowls of judgment. Later, they will return to Jerusalem next to the Lion of Judah.

> *Then the seventh angel poured out his bowl upon the air, and a loud voice came out of the temple from the throne, saying, "It is done." And there were flashes of lightning and sounds and peals of thunder; and there was a great earthquake, such as there had not been since man came to be upon the earth, so great an earthquake was it, and so mighty. The great city was split into three parts, and the cities of the nations fell. Babylon the great was remembered before God, to give her the cup of the wine of His fierce wrath. And every island fled away, and the mountains were not found. And huge hailstones, about one hundred pounds each, came down from heaven upon men; and men blasphemed God because of the plague of the hail, because its plague was extremely severe.*
>
> —Rev. 16:17–21

In that day, the Second Earth will be destroyed. I believe by the description given here that God will bring the seven continents together once more, and it will begin a third ice age. The tectonic upheavals will cause the mountains to fall and the valleys to rise and the islands to sink into the sea, and Jerusalem will be lifted up so it will no longer be an arid desert but a lush and fertile temperate zone.

The last and fifth earthquake will bring every building in every city around the world to the ground. Not one shall stand. The works of man will crumble into rubble. From the cinders of the Second Earth shall the Third Earth sprout green and tall when the Prince of Peace reclaims the Promised Land and makes the deserts turn to flowers.

Our Second Earth began in darkness and ice, and so shall our Third Earth begin. Soon, the time will come when the ice poles of the Second Earth will melt, and when that first earthquake strikes, darkness will once again cover our planet before the third ice age begins. It is the coming night prophesied by the prophets.

But have no fear, my brothers and sisters. The dawn will come at the time appointed when the Morning Star rises from the east and comes to sit on His throne. From the ashes of our present age will the Kingdom of Heaven, the Davidic Kingdom, be established on our planet. In that day, the Jews hidden beneath the eagle's wings (Rev. 12:1-15) will become the priests of God to the whole world, and peace shall at long last come to Jerusalem. In that glorious day, mourning will turn to gladness, and He will make an everlasting covenant of peace with Israel.

Our rebellion has already brought forth two judgments on our planet. The first was the Great Flood. The second was the confounding of the languages at the Tower of Babel that forcefully created the nations in an attempt to decentralize power and keep the Dragon from too easily grasping global control. The third will be the end of the Second Earth and the complete defeat of the Antichrist and all the destroyers who spilled the blood of innocents and threw truth upon the street to tread upon it. Those who are inclined to disbelieve the first judgment of the Global Flood will also be inclined to disbelieve the coming judgment that will end our Second Earth. They will not be prepared. They will perish.

Those deophobes who defy the will of God are unwitting helpers of the ancient demonic aspirations for global control. Humankind is but a faint shadow of what we once were. And so is our planet but a diminished version of the First Earth. The evidence of the consequence for this rebellion lies beneath our feet for those who have eyes to see and ears to hear. The rocks do not lie. Our planet was once destroyed for our violence by a global flood. That will not be the last global judgment.

The Genesis narrative of Noah's Flood is no fable. It is a historical space-time narrative that is corroborated by the story in the rocks. A single catastrophic flood of a global magnitude over a short space of time could more accurately explain the supposed millions of years that evolutionists insist created these enormous expanses of sediments. Their claim is simply subjectively based on their failed and jaded uniformitarian hypothesis and their increasingly rabid deophobia. It is motivated by the evolutionary need for vast expanses of time to make the impossible seem more probable.

The very mechanism of the Great Flood better explains these gigantic stratified layers preserved for us today. The enormous hydraulics and gigantic hurricanes resulting from such an event, along with the eruption of super-volcanoes, perhaps for several years or even decades after the impact, and the massive earthquakes associated with the sliding of the hydroplates better explains the stratification of the fossils as we find them today.

The eruption of the Mid-Oceanic Ridge, which opened the fountains of the deep, could have easily created in a short period of time the enormous sediment beds we observe today. The jetting water would have eroded the sides of the continents, sending debris into the atmosphere and beyond. Some may have been shot into orbit around the sun as comets and asteroids. Most of the eroded material would have rained back down with precipitation.

In other words, the empirical evidence in the strata does not necessarily imply the millions of years that evolutionists hope for in order for evolution to have a chance. On the contrary, as we shall see, the present empirical evidence seems to point to the conclusion that dinosaurs could not have existed 65 million years ago, as evolutionists claim.

How Old Are the Dinosaurs?

In 2004, Mary Higby Schweitzer, a paleontologist from North Carolina State University, peered through a microscope at a specimen from the fractured thigh bone of a *Tyrannosaurus rex* fossil and found the surprise of her life. According to an April 2006 article in

Discover magazine titled "Schweitzer's Dangerous Discovery," what she discovered was actual dinosaur tissue.

Schweitzer gazed through a microscope in her laboratory at North Carolina State University and saw lifelike tissue that had no business inhabiting a fossilized dinosaur skeleton: fibrous matrix, stretchy like a wet scab on human skin; what appeared to be supple bone cells, their three-dimensional shapes intact; and translucent blood vessels that looked as if they could have come straight from an ostrich at the zoo.

By all the rules in paleontology, such traces of life should have long since drained from the bones (emphasis added) (Yeoman 2006).

The title of the article intrigued me. What is so dangerous about her discovery? The danger is that it contradicts the enormous ages that evolutionists claim separate us from the dinosaurs. Evolutionists were afraid that their cherished long ages required for evolution would be disproved. The danger is that it completely debunks the evolutionary timetable accepted as fact by the evolutionary paradigm of our age.

The soft tissue Schweitzer found could perhaps, in certain extreme cases where it remains frozen, last several thousand years. But to believe the tissue specimen survived 65 million years is absolutely ludicrous and scientifically irrational. No living tissue could survive 65 million years without decomposing.

The fossil specimen taken from the Hell Creek Formation in Montana has sent shockwaves through the corridors of evolutionary-minded paleontologists. The world is flat, and therefore any empirical proof that says otherwise must be faulty. Prominent paleontologists have risen in skepticism over Schweitzer's work, attempting to discredit her meticulous documentation and procedures.

She first ruled out contaminants and mineral structures. Then she analyzed the putative cells using a half-dozen techniques involving chemical analysis and immunology. In one test, a colleague injected rats with the dinosaur fossil extract; the rodents produced antibodies that responded to turkey and rabbit hemoglobins. *All the data supported the conclusion that the T. rex fossil contained fragments of hemoglobin molecules.* "*The most likely source of these proteins is the once living cells of the dinosaur,*" she wrote in a 1997 paper.

The article, published in Proceedings of the National Academy of Sciences, sparked a small fury of headlines. Horner and others regarded Schweitzer's research as carefully performed and credible. Nonetheless, says Horner, "most people were very skeptical. *Frequently in our field people come up with new ideas and opponents say, 'I just don't believe it.' She was having a hard time publishing in journals.*"

Schweitzer was also stymied by her unconventional fusion of paleontology and molecular biology (emphasis added) (Yeoman 2006).

I find Horner's perception of the irrational response of other paleontologists to her research quite illuminating and revealing. Their response is not based on empirical data but upon their inherent bias due to their jaded uniformitarian, gradualist presupposition: "I just don't believe it." Now there is a fine example of scientific and deductive reasoning!

I will tell you what kind of deductive reasoning that is: If the findings don't agree with their preconceived ideas, then they just deduct the facts and continue believing what they want. Is that true science? Is that the unbiased pursuit of knowledge, wherever the facts lead?

What is so unconventional about using the scientific field of molecular biology to determine whether there is, in fact, organic tissue in a fossil? Is paleontology an all-inclusive field that needs no other fields of science to corroborate their findings? What arrogance!

The obvious bias toward any field that would render its cherished presuppositions null and void is quite evident here to the casual observer. But unfortunately, this is the stark reality within the evolutionary paradigm of the modern world of paleontology.

Make no mistake; this is not an isolated case. There is much more empirical evidence that dinosaurs could not have lived 65 million to 70 million years ago; that is, if scientists are willing to see the plain facts staring them in the face. Schweitzer is standing in the middle of the lab room yelling at the top of her voice, "The king is naked!" But the rest of the scientists held under the spell of the evolutionary paradigm are wearing Bose headphones and listening to Darwin's rap with Lyell's lyrics.

> When a group of fossil hunters found a cluster of preserved bird eggs in a city dump in Neuquén, Argentina, they originally believed the shells contained nothing but sand. *Schweitzer placed the remains under scanning electron and atomic force microscopes and concluded that the 70-million-year-old eggs still held embryos containing intact collagen* (emphasis added) (Yeoman 2006).

Here is the story of how it went down. In 2000, at the very turn of the millennium, field crew chief Bob Harmon, involved in excavations in the Hell Creek Formation of Montana, was having lunch when he happened to look up and see a *T. rex* foot bone protruding, from a sandstone cliff.

> Climbing a folding chair balanced on a pile of rocks, Harmon found another bone, then another, then another.
> By the time the team had excavated all the bones and encased them in plaster, the collection weighed 3,000 pounds, heavier than the helicopter could lift. With no

other way to transport it, scientists reluctantly split the plaster jacket and broke the T. rex's 3.5-foot-long femur. In the process, the fossil bone shed some fragments. Workers wrapped them in aluminum foil and shipped them to North Carolina State University, where Schweitzer had just started teaching. "Jack just gave me the chunks and said, 'See what you can do with them,' she recalls. . . . Her lab was still stacked with unpacked cartons when she opened the cardboard box from the T. rex dig and pulled out the biggest fragment. Looking at it with the eyes of a biologist, she immediately saw it was more than a fossil. Time and history began to unwind. "Oh, my gosh," she said to her laboratory assistant, Jennifer Wittmeyer. "It's a girl. And it's pregnant."

What Schweitzer saw was medullary bone, a type of tissue that grows inside the long bones of female birds. Medullary bone is produced during ovulation as a way of storing the calcium needed for egg production; then it disappears. "I looked at it under the dissecting scope," Schweitzer says. "There was nothing else it could be." *The medullary bone even contained gaps and mazelike fiber patterns resembling those of modern birds.*

Until that moment no one had ever identified that tissue in a dinosaur, making it impossible to definitively sex such an animal. . . . Wittmeyer had been pulling the late shift, analyzing pieces from the T. rex limb. She had just soaked fragments of medullary bone in dilute acid to remove some calcium phosphate. This was an unusual procedure to carry out in a dinosaur lab. Scientists typically assume that a fossilized dinosaur consists of rock that would entirely dissolve in acid, but Schweitzer wanted to get a closer look at the fossil's fine structure and compare it with that of modern birds. That night Wittmeyer marveled at a small section of decalcified thighbone: "When you wiggled it, it kind of floated in the breeze."

Schweitzer and Wittmeyer pondered the meaning of the stretchy sample, feeling mystified and ecstatic. The remains seemed like soft tissue—specifically matrix, the organic part of bone, which consists primarily of collagen. Yet this seemed impossible, according to the prevailing understanding. "Everyone knows how soft tissues degrade," Schweitzer says. "If you take a blood sample and you stick it on a shelf, you have nothing recognizable in about a week. So why would there be anything left in dinosaurs?"

Next Schweitzer examined a piece of the dinosaur's cortical bone. "We stuck the bone in the same kind of solution," she says. "The bone mineral dissolved away, and it left these transparent blood vessels. I took one look and I said: 'Uh-uh. This isn't happening. This is just not happening.'" She started applying the same treatment to bone fragments from another dinosaur that she had acquired for her dissertation. "Sure enough," she says, "vessels all over the place."

Less than a month later, while Schweitzer was still collecting data on the soft tissue, came a third score. Wittmeyer walked into the lab looking anxious. "I think maybe some of our stuff's gotten contaminated, because I see these things floating around, and they look like bugs," she said. Worried that she would lose her dinosaur blood vessels before she could publish an article about them, Schweitzer rushed to rescue the sample. *What she found startled her. Through the microscope she could see what looked like perfectly formed osteocytes, the cells inside bone* (emphasis added) (Yeoman 2006).

It is important to note that Schweitzer is not a creationist, and although she professes to be a Christian, she holds to the evolutionary presupposition. She has no axe to grind; on the contrary, her findings have made it quite difficult for her to receive funding from a field that is radically antipathetic to evidence that could disprove their cherished evolutionary ideals. Few scientific journals are willing to publish findings that would debunk the evolutionary timetable.

To this date, there has not been an attempt to ascertain whether or not the DNA of these samples is still intact. My suspicion is that no one will move in that direction because it would create such incontrovertible evidence against evolutionists' presupposed bias toward their insistence on long ages. That is absolutely indispensable to them in order to give evolution a chance to be even remotely plausible. So much for the altruistic principle of the scientific methodology!

The idea that organic tissue could remain intact for 65 million years in a natural environment is hardly believable to any credible scientists. It cannot even be argued that this material has been kept frozen for all this time since, according to their evolutionary timetable, we have gone through several ice ages since. And several times, the area of Montana has been free of the glaciers that could have preserved it.

Even if it had been encased in ice continually, it would be almost impossible to believe that it could preserve the tissue for 65 million years. If you don't believe me, leave a steak outside, buried in the dirt, and see what happens within a few days. But under the evolutionary timetable, Montana has been free of glaciers several times over many thousands, if not millions, of years, according to the evolutionary geologic column.

As it turns out, Schweitzer's accidental finding is no fluke. Repeated attempts to subject dinosaur fossils to the acid mixture have consistently produced soft tissue matter. It would be quite disturbing for evolutionists if someone had the testicular fortitude to do a carbon-14 dating on the soft tissue. Since carbon-14 is better equipped to date organic tissue, I would be willing to bet that the tissue is no more than several thousand years old. Such a finding would turn the evolutionary timetable upside down. Alas, I will not hold my breath.

Obviously, the mineralization process in the formation of fossils was not complete, and organic material is still present in these samples. That itself is evidence that they could not have existed 65 million years ago. Even allowing for a 500,000-year interval for complete mineralization of the fossil, which far exceeds reality by leaps and bounds, the mineralization process would have been complete, at the very least, 64 and a half million years ago. How is it possible that tissue still exists in dinosaur bones 65 million years after the creature died?

The television program *60 Minutes* did an interview with both the archaeologist and the biologist involved in this case. It covered the accidental findings and gave many wonderful slides of the vessels and tissue samples under the microscope, which proved that they were, in fact, tissue. I waited with bated breath for the crucial question to be raised and wondered how it would be answered. But not once did they ask the question, "How could living tissue survive intact 65 million years?" It was as if someone had found a picture of the king naked, and all they did was talk about his shiny crown.

To date, the evolutionary scientific paradigm has effectively squelched any news on this matter. But no wonder. It is a ticking nuclear bomb that threatens to destroy the evolutionary house of cards. If you do not believe me, then Google it.

Nevertheless, in light of the discovery that perhaps most of the dinosaur fossils may have tissue yet preserved in them, continued insistence in the evolutionary assumption of long ages can only be classified as subjective bias and regressive dogma, bordering on self-deceit. That is hardly the stuff of true science. The square peg just does not fit in the round hole.

What the evidence suggests is simply that *Tyrannosaurus rex* ranged our planet not so long ago. It proves that dinosaurs were not extinct 65 million years ago. It may very well be that these terrible creatures that brought such violence on Earth may have been selected for extinction by the judgment of the Great Flood. What we can say for certain is that the ecological conditions in the beginning of our Second Earth were such that creatures of great size were certainly at a great disadvantage to survive due to the scarce resources left in the wake of the global cataclysm.

At any rate, it is clear that the phylogenetic tree and the geologic column are simply products of an evolutionary assumption created through circular reasoning. The empirical fact is that the theory of evolution has failed to produce a viable mechanism to adequately support its foundational premise that species evolve into other species. And it has failed to prove that life has existed for the long ages that evolutionists propose.

The geological column has simply been artificially created to fit into their preconceived idea of how it should be ordered on the basis of their comparative structures and consequent placement within the phylogenetic tree. I ask the reader, just who are the real history-deniers?

Radiometric Dating Methods (the Third Pillar)

This brings us to the last pillar that evolutionists dogmatically claim to support their evolutionary edifice. That, of course, is their claim that accurate dates into great antiquity can be obtained through radiometric dating. We have already discussed that the so-called geologic column is never found with more than four of their layers together in the supposed order described by the column, and that it is simply devised artificially through so-called index fossils from their supposed order within the phylogenetic tree.

We have also seen that the so-called overwhelming fossil evidence in the strata is, at best, spurious and completely subjective, and the differences within the strata can be best explained by a worldwide deluge. Now we will look into the reliability of radiometric dating.

Radiometric dating is the supposed mechanism through which evolutionists "prove" the enormous ages they postulate in order for evolution to take place. That is, the imagined ages of the geologic column are supposedly vindicated by radiometric dating methods.

Carbon-14 Dating Method

In 1946, Willard F. Libby (1908–1980) discovered the carbon-14 dating method while working at the University of Chicago. The method depends on the fact that organisms contain a constant amount of radioactive carbon while they are living. When the organism dies, the carbon-14 isotope begins to break down and decay.

The cosmic radiation from the sun causes the production of the C^{14} atom. Within a few minutes from the time the cosmic ray strikes our upper atmosphere and creates the carbon isotope, it combines with oxygen to form a carbon dioxide molecule. Today, this molecule is quickly diffused within our atmosphere by the strong jet streams that circle our planet.

These high-speed, upper-level winds are the result of uneven heating at the surface of the Earth. The hotter equatorial region causes the air to expand and rise, while the colder polar regions cause the air to contract and sink. These massive rivers of air in the sky are the primary cause of our modern weather patterns. The diffusion of this carbon dioxide with the carbon-14 isotope is certain in our postdiluvian system, but not so prior to the Great Flood.

An Earth with a thick ozone layer and a water vapor canopy would tend to keep those C^{14} isotopes in the upper atmosphere. A more evenly warmed surface of the Earth would not create the glaring disparities that cause today's energy-filled, upper-level winds.

Since the precipitation of the water vapor canopy and the destruction of the global forests that covered our First Earth, our climate and oxygen and carbon atmospheric levels have changed radically. Our present Earth contains radically less oxygen and radically more carbon due to the processes that brought forth the Global Flood and the destruction of our First Earth.

This dating method is based entirely on the amount of C^{14} found in organic matter. As long as the organism is alive and exchanging with the atmosphere, the ratio in the living organism maintains the ratio that is found in the lower atmosphere where the organisms live. Once the creature dies and no longer exchanges with the atmosphere, that ratio begins to diminish as the isotope decays.

Since all living organisms are exposed to the supposedly constant rate of this isotope during their lifetime, and since the half-life of the isotope is 5,730 years, then by measuring the amount present after an organism's demise, scientists can theoretically extrapolate backward and calculate their time of death.

There are, however, some problematic assumptions that cannot be scientifically corroborated. The first assumption is that our atmosphere has always been as it is now. This is a critical mistake because the ionization rate could most assuredly vary radically if our model of the First Earth is correct. Here is an example:

- Our Van Allen Belts were stronger, thus impeding much more cosmic radiation and preventing the carbon isotope from forming. Our atmosphere once had a water-vapor canopy around it to also further shield it from radiation from the sun. So there is no way to accurately predict the exact amount of the carbon isotope that was created in the First Earth. The book of Genesis tells us that a water vapor canopy shrouded the Predilluvian world. The First Earth was rather like our sister planet Venus, except that the water vapor canopy on Earth was significantly much lighter. This thin water vapor canopy acted as a greenhouse, allowing the good radiation in and warming the planet almost uniformly throughout its entire surface, while reducing the cosmic radiation that causes the C^{14} isotope. That alone would have significantly

reduced the amount of C^{14} produced on the atmosphere during that period.
- Moreover, in such an environment, the C^{14} isotope would tend to remain isolated in the upper atmosphere because the First Earth did not have the ferocious upper-level winds we now have in the Second Earth to diffuse it evenly throughout all levels of the atmosphere.
- If the rays of the sun are either enhanced or shielded, then obviously the result would be that the ratio between the C^{12} molecules and the C^{14} isotopes would vary accordingly. A thicker, more protective layer of ionosphere such as what would be predicted if our oxygen concentration was (as agreed by evolutionists) 35 percent to 37 percent during the First Earth. That would greatly inhibit cosmic radiation from producing the C^{14} isotope on the surface of the planet. This lower fraction of C^{14} in the lower atmosphere would make all organic samples from that period seem much older than they really are.

*

The second assumption is that the geologic processes that exist in our Second Earth were the same in the First Earth. If, as our Judeo-Christian model stipulates, seven striking meteors actually cracked the continental plates into seven major continental plates, then here is what we would expect:

- The initial impact as well as the re-entering ejecta would have created a global conflagration that burned the enormous forests that thrived in the idyllic conditions of the First Earth. That alone would have caused an enormous amount of carbon to enter our atmosphere and change the carbon ratios dramatically.
- In addition, the volcanic upheaval initiated by these catastrophic strikes would have caused an infusion of volcanic gases on a global scale that would have also dramatically changed the carbon levels in our atmosphere.

DATING METHODS: THE THREE PILLARS

Evolutionists concede that it was a meteor that destroyed the dinosaurs of the world and practically wiped out all life on Earth. The proof, they claim, is in the KT boundary containing levels of iridium that are found only in asteroids. We do not dispute that. Beyond that, the analysis of the KT boundary in more than 140 places around the world shows four common traits that are indicative of a catastrophic meteor apocalypse. The science here is pretty straightforward:

- Scientists find shocked quartz; that is, quartz grains with deformations produced by the enormous power of high-energy impacts (Bohor, Modreski, and Foord 1987, 705–9).
- Scientists have also found spherules, which are droplets of impact that created melts (Smit 1999, 75–113).
- Most important to our discussion, scientists have also found a layer of carbon soot, which represents a global conflagration where the forests of the entire Earth were burned by re-entering ejecta from the meteor collisions (Wolbach et al., 1998).
- The study of the pollen after that catastrophic event shows a spike in the pollen of ferns and an enormous reduction of the pollen of angio-sperms that previously dominated all areas of Earth.

What evolutionists fail to realize is that the single meteor that formed the Chicxulub crater would have created an enormous introduction of carbon monoxide into the atmosphere and carbon soot into the soil in its aftermath. It would have dramatically changed the carbon levels absorbed by any living things for a long period after that catastrophic event.

Their error is created by calculating the C^{12} to C^{14} rates the same during the First Earth and the Second Earth. The cataclysm that brought forth the Global Flood would have been six times as dramatic given the impact of seven meteors. That day changed dramatically the carbon rates for years to come. So not only do we have an enormous change in the carbon contents in the Second Earth, but we have a reduced rate of cosmic radiation reaching our atmosphere during the First Earth, reducing the carbon isotope production.

The larger ionosphere and the water vapor canopy had an enormous beneficial impact on our First Earth. They formed a very effective blanket to keep radiation out and trap heat in on the entire surface of the planet. That greenhouse effect provided the conditions that propagated a rich and lush fauna that could support the giant specimens so common at that time and as our fossil record clearly indicates.

We will refer to this topic in more detail in our discussion of the Great Flood in the fifth book of this series, *The Death of the First Earth*. But for now, suffice it to say that there is no way evolutionists can claim dogmatically that this ionization rate has always been constant throughout the entire history of the Earth. This is just another uniformitarian speculation created by their desperate need for long ages.

*

The third false assumption is that the rate of cosmic rays is globally constant on the surface of our planet. As a matter of fact, cosmic radiation is not even constant on our planet today. We know that there are some areas closer to the poles where the protecting ozone layer around our planet has completely decayed, leaving huge holes in which a much greater concentration of radiation leaks through to Earth's surface.

Furthermore, this dating method also assumes that the cosmic radiation coming from the sun is a constant. No such assumption can be made. We also know that the sun goes through an 11-year cycle in which cosmic radiation fluctuates. But the severity of these fluctuations may increase or decrease in other broader cycles we do not yet know about because of the short time we have been monitoring our sun with modern scientific equipment that can measure such changes.

Seasons of intense sun spot activity result in enormous spikes of cosmic radiation. Those spikes would result in skewed C^{14} isotope formation rates. Scientists cannot dogmatically stipulate that our sun has always been exactly as it is in our modern era. Such an extrapolation cannot be dogmatically accepted as anything but speculation.

*

The fourth false assumption is that our magnetosphere has remained constant. It is the magnetosphere that provides our greatest protection from cosmic rays. The fluctuation of the Earth's magnetic field could greatly influence the amount or rate of cosmic rays that enter our atmosphere. In fact, our Earth's magnetic field is the primary protector against cosmic rays.

It is because Mars solidified and cooled that it lost its magnetic field and subsequently its atmosphere. Once the magnetic field was gone, the cosmic rays simply blasted Mars's atmosphere into outer space and sterilized the planet. That is the very real danger we face should we lose our magnetic field.

However, if the magnetic field were considerably stronger in the past, that would directly affect the amount of radioisotopes produced by severely limiting the action of cosmic rays on our atmosphere. And that would cause us to think that specimens dated from earlier time periods were much older than they would be in reality. The lower rate of the production of the isotope C^{14} would deceive us into thinking that the specimen had been decaying much longer than it actually had.

It is quite probable that the meteor strikes that precipitated the Great Flood and forever changed our orbit around the sun by 5 million miles may have caused a disruption in the flow of our Earth's metal core. That would have surely resulted in magnetic fluctuations. In addition, the resulting two ice ages that followed the Great Flood may have even cooled the Earth's core just enough to diminish our magnetic field.

Recent studies of the magnetic field have revealed that it is, in fact, diminishing at an alarming rate. In a NASA article titled "Earth's Inconstant Magnetic Field," researchers declared in a recent meeting of the American Geophysical Union that the Earth's magnetosphere has weakened 10 percent since the nineteenth century (NASA 2003). It is not clear whether this weakening is a periodical cycle that may be associated with the shift in poles, which has already happened many times in Earth's history.

More cosmic rays mean there are more isotopes today than existed before, and our modern ratio is completely off kilter from that of the First Earth.

*

The fifth false assumption is the fabricated propaganda that these radiocarbon tests are always consistently accurate. If testing for a given specimen results in varying dates, then we can obviously conclude that it is not an absolutely reliable technique that can be paraded as unassailable proof. "It may come as a shock to some, but fewer than 50 percent of the radiocarbon dates from geological and archaeological samples in northeastern North America have been adopted as 'acceptable' by investigators" (Ogden 1977, 167–173).

*

The accuracy of this dating method is greatly exaggerated to the public, which is deceived into thinking that the radiometric results are uniform and trustworthy. The technical difficulty of measuring quantities consistently when the age is greater than the half-life renders the procedure unreliable past that point.

Evolutionists claim they can push the envelope to some 40,000 years. The actual reliable figures are closer to about 4,000 to 5,000 years because that is as long as we have written records to verify the accuracy of the dates.

The next level is a bit more tenuous. It is the time before the Great Flood and before a written record in which our present meteorological conditions are radically different from the conditions before the destruction of the First Earth. There is no written record

DATING METHODS: THE THREE PILLARS

from which to verify the different dates. It is then purely speculative as to which of the discordant dates are right or wrong.

So I think we have made it abundantly clear that from the Great Flood back, it is simply a guessing game because we have no way to verify the many components that could seriously impact the rate of the isotope production. To extrapolate from our present condition is simply irrational.

But we must understand that even dates that are after the Great Flood sometimes vary wildly. Evolutionists use circular reasoning to verify which dates are acceptable and which are not. All discordant dates from their presupposed evolutionary timetable are simply trashed. Again, we find the same circular reasoning. The ages adopted by investigators are ages that simply agree with evolutionary dating. Those that do not are discarded or ignored. Some of you may be surprised at this statement:

> C-14 dating was being discussed at a symposium on the prehistory of the Nile Valley. A famous American colleague, Professor Brew, briefly summarized a common attitude among archaeologists towards it, as follows: "If a C-14 date supports our theories, we put it in the main text. If it does not entirely contradict them, we put it in a footnote. And if it is completely out of date we just drop it" (Save-Soderbergh and Olsson 1970, 35).

*

The sixth false assumption is that dating organic substances in the vicinity of the fossil will give you the date of the fossil. Jared Diamond, author of *The Third Chimpanzee*, has spent 30 years studying evolution and is a committed evolutionist. In his book *Guns, Germs, and Steel*, he attempts to weave all of history in an evolutionary panoramic sweep. To his credit, he objectively discusses some of radiocarbon's technological problems in dating.

Once the plant or animal dies, though, half of its carbon 14 content decays into carbon 12 every 5,700 years, until after about 40,000 years the carbon 14 content is very low and difficult to measure or to distinguish from contamination with small amounts of modern materials containing carbon 14....

Radiocarbon is plagued by numerous technical problems, of which two deserve mention here. One is that radiocarbon dating until the 1980s required relatively large amounts of carbon (a few grams), much more than the amounts in small seeds or bones. Hence scientists instead often had to resort to dating material recovered nearby at the same site and believed to be "associated with" the food remains—that is, to have been deposited simultaneously by the people who left the food. A typical choice of "associated" material is charcoal from fires.

But archaeological sites are not always neatly sealed time capsules of materials all deposited on the same day. Materials deposited at different times can get mixed together, as worms and rodents and other agents churn up the ground. Charcoal residues from a fire can thereby end up close to the remains of a plant or animal that died and was eaten thousands of years earlier or later (Diamond 1999, 95-96).

A new technique called accelerator mass spectrometry, which requires smaller amounts of material for testing, is being used. However, that technology is plagued with its own particular problems. But let us put aside all these reservations in regard to accuracy. Even if we were to grant evolutionists their proposed 40,000 to 50,000 years, the technique is incapable of dating anything other than organic material from once living things. True

DATING METHODS: THE THREE PILLARS

fossils are made of minerals and cannot therefore be dated with this method.

The collagen in the *T. rex* fossils found in Montana, however, could be analyzed with carbon-14 because the fossils contained organic tissue. Here is what those fossils revealed:

> Researchers have found a reason for the puzzling survival of soft tissue and collagen in dinosaur bones—the bones are younger than anyone ever guessed. Carbon-14 (C-14) dating of multiple samples of bone from 8 dinosaurs found in Texas, Alaska, Colorado, and Montana revealed that they are only 22,000 to 39,000 years old. Members of the Paleochronology group presented their findings at the 2012 Western Pacific Geophysics Meeting in Singapore, August 13–17, a conference of the American Geophysical Union (AGU) and the Asia Oceania Geosciences Society (AOGS) (Fisher 2012).

The response to the researchers was a predictable denial of the facts and an attack on the credibility of their work.

Since dinosaurs are thought to be over 65 million years old, the news is stunning—and more than some can tolerate. After the AOGS-AGU conference in Singapore, the abstract was removed from the conference website by two chairmen because they could not accept the findings. Unwilling to challenge the data openly, they erased the report from public view without a word to the authors. When the authors inquired, they received the following letter from the program chairpersons.

They did not look at the data, and they never spoke with the researchers. They did not like the test results, so they censored them (Fisher 2012).

AOGS Society T03550141H
AOGS Secretariat Office
C/o Meeting Matters International
Tel: (65) 6472 3108 Fax: (65) 6472 3208
Add: #06-23, ONE COMMONWEALTH
1 Commonwealth Lane, Singapore 149544
Email: info@asiaoceania.org

Hugh Miller, Consulting Chemist
Paleo Group, USA
Email: hugoc14@aol.com

Dear Mr. Miller,

Presentation: BG02-D3-PM2-Leo2-005: A Comparison of δ13C & pMC Values for Ten Cretaceous-jurassic Dinosaur Bones from Texas to Alaska, USA, China and Europe

As a result of comments from attendees at the recent AOGS-AGU (WPGM) meeting in Singapore we have examined your abstract which was delivered in session BG-02.

The interpretation which you present in your abstract is that the age of various dinosaurs, previously interpreted as being Mesozoic in age, are less than ~50,000 years. Your report that these ages were calculated using C-14 methods. There is obviously an error in these data. The abstract was apparently not reviewed properly and was accepted in error. For this reason we have exercised our authority as program chairs and rescinded the abstract. The abstract will no longer appear on the AOGS web site.

Program Chairs,
Minhan Dai, Xiamen University
Peter Swart, University of Miami

The response of the AOGS program chairs, Minhan Dai of Xiamen University and Peter Swart of the University of Miami, was simply this:

> There is obviously an error in these data. The abstract was apparently not reviewed properly and was accepted in error. For this reason we have exercised our authority as program chairs and rescinded the abstract. The abstract will no longer appear on the AOGS web site (Fisher 2012).

Now those are some real history-deniers, Mr. Dawkins, and it is the entrenched and dogmatic evolutionary mindset that consistently ignores the data to continue to believe in their evolutionary illusion.

DATING METHODS: THE THREE PILLARS

Now I do not believe that dinosaurs actually lived 22,000 to 39,000 years ago. That error in the carbon-14 method is quite likely due to the difference in the carbon isotope ratios prior to the Great Flood. But beyond that, there are scientific studies that concluded that DNA should not remain intact after 10,000 years, so even those figures have been stretched beyond the real capability of the DNA to exist intact.

The real truth is that laboratory experiments done by evolutionists have shown that complex molecules, like the DNA, have been observed to hydrolyze at rates that are incompatible with the vast evolutionary gradualist dating claims. Brian Sykes, a Fellow of Wolfson College and Emeritus Professor of Human Genetics at the University of Oxford, wrote in the prestigious journal *Nature*, "No DNA would remain intact much beyond 10,000 years" (Sykes 1991, 381).

*

Extremely complex molecules like DNA have a tendency to rapidly break down in the absence of the magnificently designed repair mechanism that keeps them whole while the specimen is alive. Therefore, if laboratory studies conducted by evolutionists clearly show a measurable and quantifiable rate of deterioration, then we can safely conclude that no DNA should be found older than 10,000 years. But that round peg just does not fit in the preconceived evolutionary square hole. So they simply ignore it.

The C-14 test measures the carbon content in a specimen. It must therefore be a carbon compound such as tissue, bone, or a tree. A true fossil is neither a bone nor a tree. It is composed of minerals that through time leached into the bone or tree and replaced the organic compound with the surrounding minerals, thus preserving its shape.

Old bones often look like fossils. But if we place our tongue on bone, it will stick due to the many fibrous holes. If you place your tongue on a true mineralized fossil, it will not stick. The fossil will be slick because it is made of stone and does not have all those tiny little air sacs.

This mineralization process consequently turned what was once living matter into a rock, or fossil, which carries the imprint of the specimen. Therefore, a true fossil is incapable of providing any useful information through carbon-14 dating, not just because there is no carbon in the fossil to measure but also because the C-14 dating method does not have the ability to date that far back with any accuracy.

*

The seventh and final false assumption made by evolutionists is that the oceanic level of carbon and the plant absorption ratio have always been the same as they are today. Of all the carbon dioxide that is emitted into the atmosphere, it is estimated that plants absorb one quarter of it, and another quarter is dissolved into the ocean. In the oceans, direct air-to-sea exchange is helped by wave action and storms. The extent of the forests that existed in the First Earth dwarf the measly few forests that now are strictly limited by the drastic temperature changes globally created by the polar ice caps. Thus, the absorption of carbon from the atmosphere would have been much greater during the First Earth.

In addition to the direct air-to-sea absorption of carbon in oceans, the availability of carbonate also determines the rate of CO_2 absorption. These carbonate deposits are made by calcite from shells being dissolved into the water. The acidity of the ocean controls the rate at which the shells dissolve. In turn, the addition of CO_2 in the ocean increases this acidity and promotes the dissolution of the shells. But imagine the hydraulics of the Global Flood and the radical impact it would have had on the carbon absorption in the ocean for the Second Earth.

It is then logical that if the available carbon in the atmosphere and the oceans have changed radically, it is impossible for any realistic and consistent ratio to be established that could give us precise dates beyond that point in time.

DATING METHODS: THE THREE PILLARS

There are seven reasons to believe that the oceanic carbon levels today are radically different from those of the once pristine ocean water of the First Earth.

a. The uncorking of the subterranean aquifers by the meteor strike released enormous amounts of trapped CO_2 gas that had been dissolved into the water by the great pressure of the granitic substructure above them. The jetting plumes of water saturated with carbon dioxide poured out onto the surface of the planet, changing forever the chemical constitution of our atmosphere as well as our ocean waters.

b. This radical increase of CO_2 shifted the pH of ocean water to a much more acidic state, creating massive beds of carbonate on the ocean floors in a rather short period of time as the shells of marine organisms were dissolved in the churning waters.

c. The massive hydraulics involved in tsunamis from entering ejecta and from shifting continents also added to the spike in the process of dissolving minerals into the ocean water. The churning motion of the hydraulics greatly increased the absorption rates in the resulting aftermath of the Great Flood.

d. The enormous waves and churning ocean precipitated by superhurricanes also greatly increased the air-to-sea absorption rates.

e. The two following ice ages also caused a marked decrease in ocean temperatures that helped absorb even more CO_2. Cold water far exceeds the capacity of warm water to hold CO_2.

f. The release of methane and CO_2 by decomposing life after the Great Flood added more carbon into the ocean and into the atmosphere in a concentrated level during a relatively short period of time.

g. Massive volcanic eruptions (both underwater and above land) would have spewed more CO_2 into the atmosphere, and for the volcanoes underwater, the CO_2 would have been directly injected into the ocean as the continents ripped apart.

Extrapolating backward from our Second Earth to the First Earth is therefore impossible. The jaded uniformitarian hypothesis is the blind spot in the radiometric clocks, which falsely assumes that our present ecosystem has not undergone radical changes in short periods of time in the past. In fact, evolutionists ought to remove their blinders before the warming of our oceans causes a sudden release of CO_2 into our atmosphere that may quickly drive us back into a third ice age.

Uranium Thorium Dating Method

Since mineralized fossils cannot be dated with the C-14 method, anthropologists are left with the option of several other available tests. The first is the uranium-thorium-lead method of the surrounding material.

Uranium is a radioactive element that eventually disintegrates or decays into lead. Scientists therefore label uranium as a parent element and lead as a daughter element. That process may involve a series of steps in which one daughter element gradually decays into another daughter element until at last an inert element remains that has no radioactivity. Subatomic particles called alpha and beta particles, as well as gamma rays, are emitted through this process of radioactive decay. The loss of these components causes the parent element to change into the daughter element, sometimes through a long chain of intermediates.

For example, the parent uranium 238 decays into the inert daughter element lead 206 in this fashion:

> U-238—alpha—Th-234—beta—Pa-234—beta—U-234—alpha—Th-230—alpha—Ra-226—alpha—Rn-222—alpha—Po-218—alpha—Pb-214—beta—Bi-214—beta—Po-214—alpha—Pb-210—beta—Bi-210—beta—Po-210—alpha—Pb-206, which is a stable element.

Bi = bismuth
Pa = protactinium
Pb = lead
Po = polonium
Ra = radium
Rn = radon
Th = thorium
U = uranium

This decay is extremely slow. It is so slow that it is almost imperceptible. Presently, it takes a million grams of uranium an entire year to disintegrate 1/7,600 of a gram.

The half-life of uranium is estimated at 4,500 million years. In other words, that is how long it would take 1 gram of uranium to decay into half a gram of lead. By measuring the difference between the daughter element and the parent element, one could theoretically establish a dating method.

But accomplishing this is not as straightforward as evolutionists insist. Because the half-life is so long, any specimens that do not contain large amounts of materials are quite likely to produce great variations in the dates due to the difficult calculations. In any given case, the dates that are wildly incongruent are simply tossed aside, and an average date of those that are similar is calculated. More than 51 percent of the dates are usually tossed out.

Decay through the emission of alpha and beta particles, as well as gamma rays, allows the energy of the atom to become more stable. In other words, the electromagnetic property of the subatomic particles is one aspect of the forces that govern the emission of this radioactive decay. The other aspect is the weak nuclear force, which holds the particles intact.

For instance, when the nucleus of an atom has too many protons (positively charged particles), it causes excessive repulsion within that nucleus (like particles repel). That causes a particle composed of two protons and two neutrons to tunnel out of the nucleus as an alpha particle.

When, on the other hand, the nucleus has too high a ratio of neutrons to protons, a neutron turns into a proton and electron (as we shall later see, it also emits an antineutrino in the process). The electron is emitted as a beta particle. But there are two other types of beta decay. When the neutron-to-proton ratio is too small, a proton turns into a neutron and a positron (positive electron). The positron is emitted as a beta particle. And when the neutron-to-proton ratio is too small, another option is to capture an electron and turn a proton into a neutron. Thus, both the electromagnetic force and the weak nuclear force have interplay in this decay process.

In addition, gamma rays are emitted when the nucleus is at too high an energy. The nucleus emits a high-energy photon called a gamma particle and falls into a state of lower and more stable energy.

If the electromagnetic forces within the atoms as well as the weak nuclear force could be externally influenced through fluctuations in our magnetic field, and either a resulting increase or decrease of cosmic radiation, then the decay rate would fluctuate accordingly. Another geophysical process such as an increase in extreme pressure and heat due to tectonic shifting would also result in elevated energy levels of the atoms and would therefore also alter the decay rate.

Evolutionists will insist that the decay rates are fully trustworthy. They dogmatically claim that they are a true constant that can be relied on completely. But in 2010, researchers at Stanford University and Purdue University found otherwise. Their research was not on radiometric dating but random numbering. Scientists use long strings of random numbers for various calculations. However, since the process utilized in making the sequences influences the outcome, these long strings are difficult to produce.

DATING METHODS: THE THREE PILLARS

Ephraim Fischbach, a physics professor at Purdue University, was analyzing decay rates of isotopes as potential sources of random numbers, without human interference. The accepted wisdom maintained that radioactive materials decay at an overall constant rate, but the individual atoms decay randomly and unpredictably. Fischbach thought that by timing the random clicks of the Geiger counter, which registers when a molecule decays, he could come up with the desired random strings.

Sifting through the mountains of published data on specific isotopes, the researchers found many disagreements for the measured decay rates. This startling information seemed in direct contradiction to the dogmatic declarations in college classes everywhere that insist these decay rates are absolute constants.

Researchers' data, sifted from such places as the Brookhaven National Laboratory on Long Island and the Federal Physical and Technical Institute in Germany, showed that there was actually a seasonal variation in the decay rate. That struck researchers as very odd, indeed. How could seasonal changes affect decay rates within atoms? But the numbers did not lie. Decay rates were faster in winter than in summer.

"Everyone thought it must be due to experimental mistakes, because we're all brought up to believe that decay rates are constant," said Peter Sturrock, professor emeritus of applied physics at Stanford University and an expert in the inner workings of the sun (Stober 2010).

Then a fortunate solar flare on December 13, 2006, provided a crucial clue to the mystery. Nuclear engineer Jerry Jenkins, while measuring the decay rate of manganese-54 (an isotope used for medical purposes, which has a short decay life) noticed that the decay rate dropped during the solar flare. In fact, the drop in rate began a day and a half before the flare was observed. As a side note, this correlation could potentially serve to predict coming solar flares.

Since the decay aberrations were measured during the middle of the night, Jenkins and Fischbach reasoned that whatever particle was responsible for the change in the decay rate must have traveled through the Earth since the sun was hidden behind the Earth during the anomaly. The only known particle with such capability is the mysterious neutrino. The culprit could not have been the cosmic rays since they cannot penetrate through the entire Earth.

Skeptics everywhere were angered at the implications to their holy mantra of radioactive dating necessary for their evolutionist propaganda. Many insinuated that the aberrations were created by seasonal environmental influences on their instrument's detection systems.

Fischbach, Jenkins, and their colleagues published in response a series of papers for the First International Conference on Astroparticle Physics titled "Nuclear Instruments and Methods in Physics Research, Space Science Reviews," which convincingly silenced the opposition.

While visiting the National Solar Observatory in Arizona, Sturrock was given a copy of the findings. He noticed that the swings seemed in sync with the Earth's elliptical orbit around the sun, thus oscillating when the distance between the Earth and sun was closest, therefore exposed to more neutrinos.

Sturrock knew that the continuous barrage of neutrinos bombarded by the sun also regularly fluctuates as the sun rotates and shows a new face. He suggested that they sift through the data again and look for a correlation between the sun's rotation and the decay rates.

The researchers were astounded to find a recurring pattern every 33 days. However, that was odd because the sun revolves every 28 days. But the riddle is no riddle. It seems that the core of the sun, where the nuclear fusion takes place that produces these neutrinos, spins more slowly than the surface.

Thus far, researchers have found three separate events connected to the sun that alter the decay rates. First, proximity to the sun during the Earth's elliptical orbit around it decreases the radiation rate. When the Earth is in the part of the ecliptic that was extended by the forces that created the Great Flood, the Earth is less affected by the neutrinos due to their greater distance from the sun, and radiation increases. Second, solar flares emitting massive neutrino surges decrease the radiation rate. We know that our sun goes through an 11-year cycle when these storms greatly increase, but we have no record of the long cycles that may show wide divergences in these magnetic solar storms. Third, the spin of the sun's core every 33 days seems to show an uptick of the emission of neutrinos, which also alters the radiation rates.

But the mystery regarding the culprit that causes this fluctuation in decay has not yet been adequately answered. No one knows how these ghost-like particles we call neutrinos, which are supposed to not interact with matter, accomplish this. Perhaps the neutrinos impact matter more than previously believed, and the fluctuation only shows in the unstable radioactive elements. Or perhaps the fluctuation is caused by a particle that we do not yet know.

What is a neutrino? When a neutron decays (breaks up into smaller particles), physicists notice that it forms a proton and an electron. But the total energy of the neutron is not conserved. That is, the energy of the proton and the electron added together was less than that of the neutron. The law of conservation tells us that the total energy of any reaction should remain the same. Hence, Wolfgang Pauli in 1930 suggested that this extra energy was carried away by a tiny neutral particle that was hard to detect. He named the particle *neutron* before the name had been attached to the heavy particle in the nucleus we now recognize as the neutron. Later on, Enrico Fermi, in order to stave off confusion, dubbed the tiny particle a neutrino (Italian: little neutral one).

Since then, we have discovered that neutron decay actually produces an antineutrino besides the proton and the electron. The forces of gravity, strong nuclear force, or the electromagnetic force did not cause this decay of the neutron. It was the weak nuclear force that was responsible for this phenomenon.

The strong nuclear force holds the nucleons, protons, and neutrons bound in the nucleus. It is what compensates for the repulsive force of positively charged protons tightly packed in the nucleus. But the weak nuclear force is what holds these particles intact.

Remember that protons, electrons, and neutrons are made up of distinct combinations of the three families of quarks. What holds these quarks together to form either a proton or a neutron is the weak nuclear force.

The small particles, like the electron and neutrinos, were then dubbed *leptons*, from the ancient Greek word for small. The two heavy particles in the nucleus, the proton and the neutron, were then dubbed *hadrons*, from the ancient Greek word for large. That is why the particle accelerator in Switzerland is called the Large Hadron Collider.

Since then, we have discovered several kinds of neutrinos. There is an electron neutrino, a muon neutrino, and a tau neutrino. They have different sizes and energies. Here again, we have another example of symmetry in the particles. It seems that leptons come in three families, like quarks.

Although the decay rate changes are minimal, the importance of this research is that it overturns the old dogma that decay rates are unchangeable by exterior forces. Whether or not the neutrino is the culprit, the fact is that the decay rates are susceptible to exterior influences.

The evolutionist has historically assumed that our present observations of these decay rates had been unaltered throughout Earth's history by any exterior forces. Furthermore, there are several more false assumptions that are necessary in order for the enormous ages of radiometric dating to be accurate.

First, the evolutionist falsely assumes that the sample of the parent isotope taken initially did not contain any daughter element when the Earth was formed. There is no empirical evidence that proves that assumption since we were not there at the beginning to know whether there was any daughter element present at the moment of creation.

In addition, we do not find in our geologic surveys an evenly distributed topography of the basic elements. Any given sample may contain an uneven contribution of these elements, altered by exterior forces of nature. Therefore, no ratio between the parent and daughter element can be measured as a standard for any period. The evolutionist simply measures in a given specimen the amount of uranium and the amount of lead and then assumes that the lead was the result of radioactive decay of the uranium. That is, however, a very large assumption. I would like to borrow their magic crystal ball that allows them to look into the past and affirm their dogmatic assumption with such conviction.

It is impossible for us to dogmatically insist that all daughter elements were strictly the product of radioactive decay. Since we were not there at the beginning, no absolute ratio can be dogmatically established. Without this starting ratio, it is impossible to come up with any dogmatic dates. Several hypothetical equations have been set forth to try to compute the amount of primordial lead Pb204 and ratios of isotopic compositions of lead such as Pb206, Pb207, and Pb208, but all of them are dependent on guesswork and evolutionary presuppositions, which, in effect, render the argument circular.

The second false assumption is that the decay rates of radioactive minerals are constant. In fact, rates can be more accurately labeled statistical averages and not deterministic constants because that statistical average depends entirely on which samples are accepted and which are summarily cast out because they differ from the researchers' subjective preliminary presupposition. We have already documented that decay rates can be altered by several environmental factors. Let us look at some of them.

- If the mineral is bombarded by an increase of cosmic rays, the decay rates may increase. Hence, in the First Earth, with a much more robust barrier system for stopping cosmic rays, the decay rates may have been much lower. On the other hand, if the mineral is bombarded by neutrinos from outer space, it can also alter the decay rate and decrease it. Since the First Earth traveled in a nearly circular orbit before being thrust out 5 million miles further at one end in the ecliptic around the sun by the seven meteor strikes, it stands to reason that it was experiencing a much heavier dosage of neutrinos year-round, unlike the Second Earth, which has an elliptical orbit that carries it further from the sun for half a year.
- In addition, if by chance other radioactive materials were ever nearby the specimen being considered, they could also have altered the decay rates.
- There are physical processes that may have rapidly accelerated the decay rates for a period of time. If great physical pressure is brought upon any sample of radioactive mineral, it would also radically alter the decay rate by increasing it. In the ignition of an atomic bomb, for example, radioactive material is placed under enormous pressure from a primary, nonnuclear explosion. That radically changes the radioactive emission of alpha particles, beta particles, and gamma particles in such rapid succession that it leads to a chain reaction. It is the almost simultaneous release of all this energy within the atom that causes the atomic blast, the release of the enormous power of the strong nuclear force being unleashed.
- Cosmic radiation is basically the nuclei of atoms traveling at a very high speed. Most of them are hydrogen nuclei or helium nuclei. "It is now known that most cosmic rays are atomic nuclei. Most are hydrogen nuclei, some are helium

nuclei, and the rest heavier elements. The relative abundance changes with cosmic ray energy—the highest energy cosmic rays tend to be heavier nuclei. Although many of the low energy cosmic rays come from our Sun, the origins of the highest energy cosmic rays remains unknown and a topic of much research" (Davies 2016). It is impossible for us to determine whether the rate of high energy cosmic rays has been constant throughout Earth's history when we do not really know where they come from.
- The amount of cosmic radiation absorbed is dependent not only on our position in the Earth relative to the strength of our magnetosphere (higher radiation at the poles than at the equator), but it is also sensitive to altitude. The higher the altitude of the specimen, the higher the dosage of cosmic radiation it will experience. Consideration of any sample must, therefore, take this into account.

We have already discussed the shifting tectonic (hydraulic) plates during the splitting of the continents within a short period of time and the enormous increase in pressure associated with the shifting of huge and enormously heavy continental landmasses made of at least 10 miles of granitic rock in depth. That monumental increase in pressure must have wildly increased the radiation rates during that process.

There were also powerful impacts of these enormous meteors and their resulting pressure waves bouncing back and forth through the interior of the Earth. Such enormous pressure could have radically sped up the radioactive decay in ways we have no way to measure. Deep-water columns of the Global Flood would have also added pressure on the bedrocks below.

I highly suspect that the trauma that brought forth the Great Flood and the separation of the continents radically increased the radiation rates and produced daughter elements in copious numbers that now have dramatically slowed down. That could fool us into believing that the creation of these daughter elements took a much longer time than it did.

In short, many of the elements of this global catastrophe would have created drastic variations in pressures that wildly fluctuated within a relatively short period of time. Furthermore, the two ice ages, which twice covered most of our planet under ice a mile thick, would have added further stress to minerals below the giant weight of the glaciers above them, which could also have increased the radiation rate.

To have an accurate statistical average of the radioactive rates of any mineral sample in order to use it as a reliable chronometer, all these factors must be computed into the equation. But there is no way to know the extent of these factors and the exact timing involved to adequately compute their impact on the decay of radioactive material. For all practical purposes, the radioactive rate is an unknowable variable for the entire history of the Earth.

The third false assumption is that this specimen of radioactive material was hermetically sealed and free from contamination. For the accuracy of this statistical average to be correct, it must be within a closed system. However, materials in the natural environment are almost never within a closed system. Unless that sample were encased in a waterproof lead container for its entire duration, it could not be accurately dated. To do so, we would need to factor in all the outside forces that acted upon it during that interval.

- Our atmosphere is being continually bombarded by cosmic rays, neutrinos, high energy mesons, gamma rays, X-rays, and many other high-energy particles traveling close to the speed of light. Some of them penetrate several hundred feet deep into the ground. They penetrate even deeper into ocean water, reaching depths of 4,590 feet below the surface. This ambient radiation may vary from time to time and cause dramatic fluctuations in decay rates. Harold S. Slusher in his *Critique of Radiometric Dating* states:

> At any temperature or pressure, collisions with stray cosmic rays or the emanations of other atoms may cause changes other than those of normal disintegration. *It seems very possible that what is called "spontaneous disintegration" of radioactive elements is related in some way to the action of cosmic rays, and, if so, the rate of disintegration may vary from century to century according to the intensity of the rays.* The evidence for a strongly increasing change in the cosmic ray influx is most favorable in the light of Dr. T. G. Barnes' investigation of the decay of the Earth's magnetic field (emphasis added) (Slusher 1973, 18).

As we have already seen, our magnetic shield buffers most of these cosmic rays, but in spite of that, in our diminished Second Earth, much more radiation breaks through and causes damage to atoms and molecules. There is a second layer of protection called the Van Allen radiation belt. High-energy cosmic rays collide with atoms and molecules within the Earth's atmosphere to create that belt that surrounds the Earth. The zones were named after James Van Allen who discovered them in 1958. Data transmitted by the *Explorer 1* satellite provided startling information.

There are two zones for the Van Allen belt. The inner zone is the most energetic and centered about 1,860 miles above the surface of the Earth. The outer region is centered between 9,300 and 12,400 miles from the surface. It seems that the Van Allen belts are most intense around the equator and notably absent around the poles.

Apparently, the cosmic rays strike neutrons and split them into protons and electrons (and antineutrinos). Some neutrons are ejected back from the atmosphere, but a percentage of them are broken into protons and electrons. These protons are highly energetic, with energy exceeding 30 million electron volts.

These particles bounce back and forth in spiral paths from one pole to the other, controlled by the Earth's magnetic field through a mechanism called the magnetic mirror effect. The outer, less energetic belt consists of helium ions ejected from the sun as well as the protons and electrons. In this outer belt, the protons are less energetic than those of the inner belt. The electrons there are the most energetic particles with energies upward of several hundred million electron volts.

The ability of cosmic rays to cause the decay of atoms is incontrovertible. Any changes in cosmic radiation through either unusually large magnetic solar flares or the reduction of our magnetic field may therefore cause wide variations in the decay rates of radioactive elements on the surface of the Earth. Therefore, no absolute rates can be established with any certainty for the entire history of the Earth.

- Other environmental factors such as leaching can alter the ratios of parent-to-daughter elements. In other words, the presence of water can leach out some of the material and alter the ratio from parent-to-daughter material. For instance, we know that lead (Pb) is susceptible to leaching with mild acids. Global mechanisms such as the Great Flood would have radically changed those concentrations in differing circumstances throughout the planet to create an untraceable original ratio.
- When samples of uranium and lead are taken to determine their ratios, scientists should carefully test the lead isotope content in order to remove from the equation Pb 204, which, being non-radiogenic, has no radioactive parent. It is time-consuming and expensive but essential for an accurate analysis of the real ratio between the parent and daughter element. That is not always done.

The fourth misconception is that all isotopes in a specimen have been created strictly by radioactive decay. Not all lead isotopes are created by radioactive decay. For example, Pb 207 is generally believed by evolutionists to have been created by the decay of uranium 235. However, it could have also been created from Pb206 through a neutron capture from nearby material.

In his book *Prehistory and Earth Models*, Melvin Cook estimates that most elements that evolutionists assume developed only through radiogenic decay could have been formed through similar reactions. If only a certain percentage of that is true, then the ages described by radiometric dating are absolutely useless.

The fifth misconception involves yet another unknown variable when dating objects through radiometric dating of the soil that surrounds the object in question. How can we assume that the date of the soil surrounding the fossil we are examining is the same as the age of the fossil? If I walk outside my house and step on the soil, it may or may not be contemporary to me. If the soil was formed by the decay of plants in my lifetime, then that soil is my contemporary. But if for some reason wind or water or even humans have excavated the area, it may be that I am standing on layers that are thousands of years my antecedent. Thus, the conclusion that radiometric dating is a knowable and reliable constant to date fossils is merely an illusion.

Potassium Argon Dating Method

The half-life of potassium is about 1,300 million years. Consider the fact that the dates evolutionists need for fossil confirmations are in the range of 65 million years for dinosaurs, 14 million years for *Ramapithecus*, and 3 to 4 million years for *Australopithecines*. If it takes 1,300 million years for potassium to reach its half-life, then 3 to 4 million years (the dates of the *Australopithecine*) represent a miniscule percentage of that huge number. The difficulty in measuring the ratio accurately presents a considerable challenge when there is no credible way to ensure that the ratio of parent and daughter elements in the specimen has not been compromised in the past 1,300 million years. That is a pretty long time to assume that the specimen has remained intact from exterior influences.

Unlike uranium, potassium is more readily present in most geological materials, rendering it a more practical method for evolutionists. Several false assumptions, however, form the basis of this radiometric clock.

1. The method is dependent on the observation that presently all naturally occurring potassium contains 0.01 percent of a radioactive isotope, which upon decay forms calcium and argon. There must be accurate knowledge of the abundance of K40 and its decay constant for the past 1,300 million years in order for the computations to be reliable. The assumption is that this 0.01 percent has been constant throughout all time. That, of course, is unverifiable and must be taken by blind faith. The release of the subterranean aquifers during the Great Flood may have wildly changed potassium isotope levels by bringing material deep below the continental blocks to the surface.
2. The second assumption is that decay constants are consistent throughout all ages. Even today's decay constants are not consistent. The research from Purdue University and Stanford University clearly shows otherwise. Henry Faul, speaking on decay constants, states, "Most of the common decay constants have assigned errors of 2%, but the uncertainty in the decay constant of rubidium 87 is much greater. The two values now in use differ by 6%" (Faul 1966, 3).
3. The third assumption is that the specimen has been hermetically sealed and kept from any cosmic radiation throughout its history. As we have already documented, there is no way to determine what the cosmic radiation has been during the last 7,000 years, much less for 1,300 million years.

4. The fourth assumption is that the specimen's decay rate has not been accelerated by tectonic pressures. In response to this, Dr. Slusher writes, "In areas where tremendous tectonic activity has taken place, highly discordant values for the ages are obtained. The difficulties associated with these criteria are numerous" (Slusher 1973, 18).
5. At the time the mineral was crystallized, it must have remained free of any ambient argon-40. Any contamination from the exterior would throw the ratios off.
6. Then, after crystallization, there must be an assurance that no argon-40 should leak from the specimen in question. Spikes in temperature caused by either volcanic activity or friction from sliding landmasses would cause gas to expand and escape.
7. After the crystallization process, there must also be an assurance that the potassium has not leached out. That is especially so in the presence of water. A global flood event would render this assumption obsolete.
8. Finally, there must be accurate knowledge of the relationship of the data from the specimen that is obtained and the specific event that is being dated. That is, the surrounding material containing the potassium must be directly linked to the fossil that is being dated.

Holes in the Cosmic Umbrella

Almost universally, scientists have been warning us of the detrimental effects that our carelessness has caused to our protective ozone layer and the Van Allen belt. Large holes have been detected in certain areas, and movements to remove from the public consumer such products as freon gas have helped stem the tide. But other products such as styrofoam are still considered by environmentalists a very real danger.

Many environmentalists have given us dire warnings of skin cancer and the like if we as a culture continue to be careless in this regard. If, in fact, these protective layers have deteriorated as dramatically as they suggest, it stands to reason that the radioactivity associated with this deterioration has also increased. The present evidence makes clear that the level of cosmic radiation is not a reliable constant. If cosmic radiation impacts decay rates, then it is impossible to insist that for 1.3 million years, that has been a reliable constant.

In addition to these protective belts that buffer us from cosmic rays, we are also fortunate to have a magnetic shield that encompasses our planet. The magnetosphere is our primary cosmic umbrella. Without it, we would not survive.

One of the most spectacular moons of Jupiter is Io, whose constant volcanic eruptions are spewing gases into the surface of the planet. The size of Io does not allow it to hold onto an atmosphere, and its lack of magnetic shield provides no protection from these cosmic rays.

Although gravity is not strong enough to keep these gases on the surface of Io as they erupt, the interaction between the solar radiation striking these gases forms a kaleidoscope of colors in magnificent arching plumes like multicolored fountains that are fascinating to the eye. Unfortunately, those very same rays that create these spectacular shows of color would be utterly lethal to humans.

The luminescent show of the northern lights (aurora borealis) is similar in this impressive visual effect. But as beautiful as they may be, if these cosmic rays from our sun were to reach the surface of our planet unhindered, humanity would soon die from their lethal radiation.

Since 1880, scientists have been aware of the fact that the magnetic shield is deteriorating. Horace Lamb's work compared to Karl Friedrich Gauss's original measurements bore this out. There is evidence that the magnetic field has changed polarities more than once, and with that change, there might have been fluctuations in the intensity of the field.

Scientists believe that this magnetic field is caused by the currents of the molten iron in the outer core of the Earth, which is believed to be composed of four layers:

- The outer hardened crust consisting of a thickness varying from 5 kilometers to 30 kilometers thick
- The mantle consisting of molten magma about 2,900 kilometers thick
- The outer core of molten iron estimated at about 5,100 kilometers
- A solid inner core of iron at the very center of the planet

Scientists believe that the complex patterns of turbulent convection within the outer core are responsible for generating the geomagnetic field (similar to the magnetic field produced with a flow of charged particles in a coil of wire). Thus, this geodynamo creates the magnetic field around our planet that protects us from the harmful radiation of the sun.

It is this magnetic field that gives us a much safer environment on the surface of our planet. But that is not a static situation, and scientists have learned that, since the 1830s when the magnetic field was first measured, the intensity of the field has already lessened 10 percent. But there is new evidence that seems to indicate that it is weakening at a much faster pace than previously believed. In Fiona MacDonald's May 11, 2016, article "New Study Shows How Rapidly Earth's Magnetic Field Is Changing," she said:

> This isn't the first research to show that Earth's magnetic field is changing. Our magnetic field has always been in flux, and over the past few years it's become clear that the invisible bubble that protects our planet from the harsh conditions of outer space has been getting weaker and weaker.
>
> According to scientists' best estimates, the field is now weakening around 10 times faster than initially thought,

losing approximately 5 percent of its strength every decade. But they don't really know why, or what that means for our planet (MacDonald 2016).

These circulating currents of molten iron, six times the volume of the moon, constitute the so-called geodynamo that creates the magnetic field. Understanding the inner workings of this geodynamo has been quite elusive to us until just recently. In 1960, Stanislav Braginsky, now at the University of California, Los Angeles, proposed that heat escaping the inner core has caused it to grow larger, producing two extra sources of buoyancy that drive convection.

As liquid iron cools and solidifies into crystals in the outside of the solid inner core, latent heat is released as a by-product, and the process contributes to thermal buoyancy. The process is also exacerbated by the fact that less dense chemical compounds such as iron sulfide and iron oxide are excluded from the inner core crystals, which then rise through the outer core and create further buoyancy. That expansion of the outer core, caused by the buoyancy, may be at the heart of the interference in the convection patterns that creates the observed shifts in the magnetic field.

Concurrently, this expansion of the outer core may also have some significant influence on the change in pressure of the crust/magma boundary. In turn, that may be responsible for the increase in volcanism and earthquakes prophesied to occur in the latter days in the Holy Scriptures. A marked increase in this activity is well documented within the last 200 years.

No one listening to the news can deny that high magnitude earthquakes such as in Chile (2010) and Japan (2011) are increasingly more numerous and powerful.

Earthquake Frequency Rates by Decade

Within the last 20 years, through the measurements and mapping of the magnetic field made possible by the satellite *Magsat* (1980) and a second satellite Ørsted (1999), scientists have been able to compare the magnetic field at the mantle/core boundary through mathematical projections. All the computations seem to point to the possibility that we are headed for another polar reversal. The expansion of the outer core may be the cause of the resulting weaker field, which translates for us as less protection from these harmful cosmic rays.

I suspect that the once ideal and stable environment of the First Earth was completely disrupted by the meteor strikes, with many wide-ranging repercussions whose ramifications are at play even today. The force of that impact may have completely disrupted the convection patterns below the Earth's crust, causing our magnetic field to begin this process of deterioration. That decrease in our magnetosphere means that we will be experiencing an increase in cosmic radiation.

There are several other radiometric tools used by evolutionists, but all of them suffer from the same subjective assumptions that have already been enumerated, and I would just be repeating myself. In short, the variability in these unknown constants renders these radiometric chronologies more wishful thinking than true science and makes evolutionists the real believers in miracles.

There is, however, one useful radiometric dating method that allows us to compare the ages of different fossils to determine whether they belong to the same time period.

Fluoride Dating Method

The fluoride test measures the amount of fluoride present in any number of given objects. The comparative study then can differentiate whether any two objects belong to the same time period. The test cannot tell us how old the object is. It can only tell us whether two or more objects are contemporary. This, of course, is useful if two fossils are found in close vicinity; then the test can at least verify if they are of the same time period.

The *Pithecanthropus* find by Eugène Dubois in Java, as we shall see later, could have profited from this technique. This form of testing can only give us a comparative analysis, which can be useful to determine whether two items are of the same date, but does nothing to inform us of their actual antiquity.

Now, let us examine the data proposed by evolutionists for the evolution of man. Let us objectively scrutinize the fossil record offered for the evolutionary lineage of man and rationally consider whether, in fact, the theory of evolution remains true to the empirical data.

CHAPTER 5

THE ORIGIN OF MAN

On March 1, 1972, my firstborn son was born. I was barely 20 at the time and plenty scared about being able to care for this new responsibility. His mother had labored long because my son had decided he wanted to come into this world butt first. "Yup, that's my son all right," I said to the doctor when she informed me of the problem.

"Why are you always doing things backward?" my wife said.

"Kind of, but I prefer to think of it as going against the stream."

"You're just a rebel," she said, tilting her head slightly to the right, giving me a side-glance as she disappeared into the operating room.

The doctor performed a C-section, and for the first eight hours of my son's life, he lived inside a hyper-oxygenated incubator. My wife was recovering from surgery, and they would not let me into the recovery room. But they told me I could see my baby boy.

I watched through the window at that tiny little baby wiggling his arms and legs inside the incubator, and fear gripped my heart. The doctor had told me that the nurses had mistakenly overdosed my wife and that the baby took longer than normal to respond. They feared he had been without oxygen too long and may have sustained some mental injuries as a result.

Tears rolled down my cheeks as the words rattled in my brain. I stared transfixed for 15 minutes at that little frail body with such tiny delicate fingers until the head nurse told me my time was up and they needed me to wait in the lobby. The hospital in which my son was born overlooks Biscayne Bay in Miami. I walked outside and sat on the seawall, looking up at the stars over the ocean, and wept.

When my tears ran out, I lay back on the grass and stared up at the starlit sky. I was amazed at how deeply I could love a baby I had just met and not even touched. My heart exploded from both love and fear. "How can such a stupid rebel like me care for such a precious little thing?" I asked God. I closed my eyes, and then an unexplainable peace filled me. I don't really know how to describe it. It just came over me like a warm blanket in the cold. I felt a supernatural presence that took my fear away. I knew that I would be making mistakes, but I also knew that God would have my back.

Eight hours later, my wife was sound asleep and recovering when the nurse came in and said, "Your baby is stable, and we can get him out of the incubator." She saw the tears in my eyes as I tried to hide my emotions and asked me if I wanted to feed my baby. I nodded, afraid to speak, with a lump in my throat.

The nurse dressed me in a blue hospital gown with mask, cap, and booties and led me into a room with a rocking chair. She placed my baby in my hands and gave me a bottle to feed him. I cradled him in my left arm and watched his tiny little lips desperately grip the nipple. "This is your first meal," I said to my son. "Your name is Henry. Well, it is Michael Henry, but I will call you Henry." I didn't know that a father could love his son so much. I was utterly amazed. He is now more than 40 years old, and I love him even more. There was no damage to his brain. In fact, his IQ is way above normal, and he is much more intelligent than I am.

I will never forget that day. There are days that become seared into our memories—some good and some bad. I was seven years old when my father was taken as a political prisoner in Cuba. I sat on his lap in a rocking chair in our living room and watched through the window behind us as a Jeep and a truck pulled up in front of our house. Militiamen scurried from the truck and surrounded the house. The young lieutenant came through the door holding a pistol and handcuffed my father. They put him in the back seat of the Jeep and drove away as the militiamen ransacked the house looking for guns.

I ran outside the front door with my little brother Frank and watched them drive away. Mom was crying hysterically, and I ran back inside the house and went to her side. She told me to go to my uncle's house and let him know what was going on. I burst through the screen door at the back of the house and ran toward my uncle's house, but I was immediately grabbed by one of the militiamen and thrown to the ground. He pointed a rifle at me. I froze, not knowing exactly what was happening as I looked into the muzzle of his rifle.

Fortunately, another militiaman came to his side and pushed the rifle away, saying, "What are you doing? He is just a boy." He was Ricardo, the father of some of my play friends from school. He picked me up and pointed me toward my uncle's house, and I took off like a bat out of hell.

That day, too, is seared in my mind. I did not know whether I would ever see my dad alive again. He was sentenced to a 10-year prison term, but it was later reduced to five. My dad had made my maternal grandfather promise that if anything happened to him, he would take the family to America. At first, my mother refused to leave my father in a communist prison, but eventually she realized our future there was in grave peril.

And so my grandparents and my mom took us to America, the land of the free. That day is also seared in my mind—June 30, 1961. I had four brothers and a sister then. My dad's mom (Mema) and his sister (Tati) were already living in Miami when we came. They lived in a small two-bedroom apartment in Calle Ocho, the now famed Cuban district of Miami. My grandmother's apartment was just across from a restaurant called the Pizza Palace. I watched through the screened window as beautiful, long-legged blond girls in tight shorts skated to the windows of the cars and placed a tray with their food on the windows. "What a country!" I thought.

How different everything was from my rural home. I was nine years old and living in a different nation where I did not know the language. That night, lying on a blanket on the floor with my brothers, I watched the lights of the cars reflected off the bedroom wall glide by time and time again. It was a typical sweltering Miami summer day, and the apartment had no air conditioning.

But the heat was not the worst of it. For a boy raised on a farm where all he heard at night were crickets and dogs barking in the distance, the noise was overwhelming. The boom boom of the jukebox across the street seemed even louder at night. Sirens and horns and cars whooshing by brought a cacophony of sounds that reverberated in my skull. It would take me some time to acquire the ability to ignore those sounds. Needless to say, I did not sleep a wink that night.

What is the common thread of transcendent days so etched into our minds? I have long thought about that. It seems to me that they reflect our intrinsic knowledge of the transcendence of human life. Whether it is gaining or losing a life, we inherently know that human life has great significance beyond the material things we possess. I would have traded all the treasures of this world to know my newborn son was healthy and whole. I would have traded all the treasures in the world to get my father back. When everything is taken from you, there is hopefully family to strengthen you.

Why have humans developed such a high view of human life if we are nothing more than impersonal matter randomly produced without any purpose or higher significance?

That is the heart of the matter. Who is man? Where did he come from? Do we have any higher value or transcendental meaning than an organic machine? The battle between the evolutionary worldview and the Judeo-Christian worldview rages most fiercely on this crucial fork in the road.

All that we have discussed so far leads to the overriding question of the transcendental significance of man. Is man simply an organic machine composed of stardust? Or is man more than the sum of his parts? Is he an accident in the cosmos with no designed purpose or higher significance? Or did a loving Creator design him with previsioned purpose and infinite transcendental value?

In *Machine or Man?* the first book of this series, we explored these two possible alternatives from a philosophical perspective. There are only two rational alternative answers to this question, and they will impact not only the personal choices that we make but also, and just as important, the culture that rises from them. Each of us reaches that fork in the road of life whether we like it or not. What choice we make has tremendous consequences. Let us look at those two roads.

1. On the first road, the Creator, who wished to imbue man with infinite worth and value that transcends the rest of material existence, made man in His image. This is the Judeo-Christian worldview.
2. The second road is the naturalist/Darwinist/materialist, or atheistic worldview. Man is nothing more than the fortuitous consequence of an impersonal evolutionary biochemical accident in the cosmos. On this road, man is but an organic machine without purpose or any transcendental significance.

You might object to the first answer, claiming that this viewpoint is the result of subjective faith and not grounded on scientific evidence and reason. Yes, it is based on faith, but so is the second worldview. And no, the first answer is based on reason since it actually meshes more accurately with the empirical data.

Facts are not a worldview. A worldview is a way of interpreting the facts. All worldviews require faith in the interpretive power of their system. But true faith is not opposed to reason. It is reason that brings forth the light of truth, and it is truth that we must believe in. Truth is that which does not contradict reality. I invite you to reason with me.

One worldview leads to the position that man, created in the image of a transcendent God, has a basis for meaning and transcendent value. It provides a basis for understanding the humanness of man. It provides a basis for understanding the true value of personhood. It provides a basis for individual rights that cannot be abrogated by any human government because they were given to us by God. Man is man, a material and spiritual being with a purpose other than just surviving.

The other road leads to a social structure in which the survival of the fittest is the matrix of reality. There is no transcendent value to man and no basis for truth, morals, or meaning in life. Man is man, simply a chemical machine. And there is therefore no basis for individual rights. In the survival of the fittest, the only right is the right of the powerful to prey upon the weak. But no matter how hard our brain wants to believe it, when we reject God, our hearts reject this sterile view of man. The atheistic worldview simply flies against the reality of our humanness.

Why is it that every person in this world, no matter what he or she has convinced their mind to believe, knows intrinsically that their life has transcendental value? Every person in this world mourns for the loss of loved ones. We hate death because it separates us from those we love. We instinctively know that we ought to have individual rights. We instinctively know that evil is real. We instinctively hate injustice. We instinctively know that the abuse or slavery of another human being is evil.

We do not mourn for cockroaches when we step on them. We do not mourn for mosquitoes when we spray them with insecticide. Every person breathing on this planet, regardless of the religion they have been taught, knows that human life is sacrosanct. Why? Because we have been created in the image of God. Life, human life, is special beyond all others. God breathed life into man, and he became a living soul. Man, the being, descended from the father of all. We were hardwired by God to know that instinctively.

Why is it that every human knows intuitively that evil is real? Why do we hate injustice? The Darwinist/atheist has a problem here. He cannot call anything evil if all truths are relative and there is no ultimate paragon (i.e., God) to declare what is good and what is evil. All choices are sameness in an accidentally and randomly guided universe. In this atheistic state, there is no meaning to love or art or music and no basis for individual freedom. Everything is simply the brute action of electrochemical signals in the three pounds of gray matter inside our skulls, which will flicker for a moment and then fade away forever. On such a road, the drinking of a glass of water and genocide has no moral difference. All choices are amoral in a universe where there is no God. Personhood is an electrochemical illusion in our brains. Love is just a survival instinct with no deeper significance. When there is no God, man is his own god, and evil is just a personal choice. No one has the right to condemn another human's choice of good or evil. All is sameness. Power becomes the matrix of reality.

It is because we have been made in the image of God that we are hardwired to know that evil is real and that human life has infinite transcendental value, which becomes the foundational premise for our God-given individual rights. On this road, we are not an accident in the cosmos. We are the persons, the beings, whose works of art or music are a legitimate and unique expression of our individual souls that have transcendental meaning. No state has the authority to infringe on our God-given individual rights because they were not granted to us by the state.

And so we see that the atheist cannot really live consistently with his mechanistic and sterile worldview. It flies against his inner being. It flies against reality. It fails the litmus test of reality. So the atheist says in his head that there is no God, but he must live in a dichotomy, for he cannot accept fully the dire and sterile implications of his worldview, and thus he lives largely under the premise of the Judeo-Christian worldview except for those specific areas that he rebels against.

Yes, faith is part of the process of accepting any worldview. But Judeo-Christian faith is based on reason. We have at this point seen that the design of living things exhibits specified complexity that cannot be randomly created through natural processes. If we are true to reality and remain rational, we can only conclude that life was designed by an intelligent being.

We have discussed the improbability of abiogenic synthesis of the basic building blocks of cells, such as the highly complex proteins that are filled with specified information written in codes. No random forces can create codes. Codes are the product of a mind. That is also true for DNA and the even more improbable abiogenic development of a single living cell with its multifaceted and interconnected metabolic processes each of which would have had to evolve simultaneously by random chemical reactions. I simply do not have enough blind faith to be an evolutionist.

We have discussed the failure of the major evolutionary assumptions that originally gave evolution a mechanism to garner scientific credibility. There is no valid mechanism to turn one species into another. All their mechanisms have failed to show any empirical evidence that one species has evolved into another.

We have discussed the circular reasoning used in dating methods to prop up their enormous ages to give gradualism a chance to be plausible. We have detailed the evidence in the rocks that show that sedimentation was not the product of gradual deposition but of a global catastrophic nature that buried all ecosystems equally, interring marine, terrestrial, and flying creatures.

Now we come to the inquiry of the origin of man. Is man an evolving ape that earlier evolved from monkeys? Man, says the evolutionist, ascended from the apes. That, they claim, is evidenced by the fossil record of our human ancestry and especially by the fancy paintings in our biology books that surely prove this.

The final project in the construction of the imaginary house of evolution is the roof. Undeterred by the fact that the rest of the house has so far been nothing more than a fragile edifice fabricated with smoke and mirrors, the evolutionists cap their edifice with their crowning achievement: the fossil evidence for the evolution of man from apes.

The Fossil Evidence Proposed as Man's Evolution (the Roof of the House of Cards)

This crowning achievement is no concrete empirical evidence as they suggest. In considering the fossil evidence for the evolution of man, evolutionists are faced with their most daunting obstacle. The appalling lack of intermediate fossils that can link species together in a uniform and smooth progression is even more pronounced in the supposed ascent of man from apes than in most other species. Here and there, evolutionists propose candidates that they artificially shove between two species, attempting to bolster their supposed chain of succession.

But if evolution is the gradual, almost imperceptible change they tell us it is, then we should have just as many intermediates as we have samples of the resulting species. No such thing exists, and this is especially so in regard to the supposed evolution of man.

Soon after Darwin's theory was popularized by Huxley, anthropologists began the search for man's ancestry in the fossils. The search to find the link to our supposed ancestral apes became the search for the so-called missing link.

Fueled by the zeal to find the corroborating evidence for this new theory, anthropologists went searching with undaunted optimism for the fossils that would prove evolution. Soon, they imagined, the evidence would be so overwhelming that it would forever shatter the scientific plausibility of special creation.

Within a few years, a fossil lineage was formed that showed man's gradual ascent from apes. It was the icing on the cake. But as we study this lineage, we will find that this supposedly concrete evidence has been continuously discarded and changed, so the only thing that has truly evolved is the supposed lineage of our ascension from apes. In fact, this ancestral lineage has more in common with the shell game I saw in Washington Square Park in New York where a young and an adept magician fooled all incomers, as we shall now see.

After 200 years of searching, evolutionists are still hard-pressed to create a sequential lineage that shows a continuous chain of beings evolving from apes to humans. At best, the lineage is quite sporadic with huge gaps. But more importantly, as we explore these fossils, we will see that they have absolutely no interconnection. It is simply more smoke and mirrors.

To be sure, the biology books are replete with artists' renditions of apes that slowly walk more upright and whose features appear more and more humanlike. But the fossils simply do not warrant the optimistic and spurious artistic renditions found in these textbooks. As a matter of fact, the skull features of man appear suddenly and fully formed without any precursors. And some evolutionists are finally admitting this truth. "Out of nowhere, our sharp chin, weak brow, and high forehead appear in the fossil record. These particular features are utterly unpredictable on the basis of what preceded them" (Stanley 1981, 151).

Man appears abruptly in the fossil record, and all attempts to create a lineage have been eventually discredited and overturned as new fossil evidence has risen to the surface. The dogmatic claims of one anthropologist after the other have been discredited and shown not to be what they so ardently believed. We will now recount the sham history of the evolutionary connect-the-dots ancestral line from apes to humans. By the way, I am not alone in this claim. Even some evolutionists, including Dr. Steven M. Stanley, a paleobiologist at Johns Hopkins University, are beginning to admit this reality.

THE ORIGIN OF MAN

Looking back over the various members of the human family just described, we see that the old connect-the-dot approach to human evolution simply will no longer work. The dots were bits and pieces of humanoid remains that, in blissful ignorance, we could once align according to gradualistic preconceptions. The dots have now become lines of descent that in many cases depict little change over long stretches of time and that sometimes even overlap. The more fossil evidence we accumulate the longer becomes the duration of the little-changing entities we call species (Stanley 1981, 154).

I quite agree with Dr. Stanley, but I would probably change the phrase from "blissful ignorance" to "wishful ignorance."

The fossil record has shown that the supposed lineage of man was simply an artificially contrived grouping of several species of apes that never show any evolutionary transformation into another species. The more fossils we accumulate, the longer the period of each of these species is shown to exist, without any really significant change in their morphology.

To add injury to embarrassment, most of these species have in time been shown to overlap one another in the strata, proving that they were living at the same time and one therefore could not have been the evolutionary predecessor of the other. Instead, what evolutionists are gradually realizing is that these rare specimens of apes are simply extinct species that were wiped out by the Great Flood, and not only do they exhibit the gigantism prominent within the First Earth, but they also exhibit a much greater variety in the character complex than the modern species of apes.

Of course, Stanley has not abandoned the theory of evolution. He has just simply admitted the obvious truth, plainly depicted by the fossil evidence. Honest people must face the truth that the fossils just do not provide this imagined gradual development from apes into *Homo sapiens*.

For this reason, many scientists are now adopting the theory of punctuated equilibrium. After several hundred years of excavations, it has become painfully obvious that there is no gradual, step-by-step evolution from apes to humans. "The dots were bits and pieces of humanoid remains that, in blissful ignorance, we could once align according to gradualistic preconceptions" (Stanley 1981, 154). Hence, evolutionists are adopting a view of evolution in which changes from one species to another are done by sudden giant leaps. To their credit, at least this theory is more reflective of the true evidence found in the fossils.

I remember the first time I saw a movie projector when I was a child growing up in a rural community in Cuba. My mother had a film reel of a circus show, and all my friends would come to watch the elephants and the lion trainers. I was fascinated by this machine that could show the moving scene on a screen as if I were there watching it live. I asked my mother how the reel could produce the moving pictures.

After the show, she took the reel and held the strip up to the light. As I peered intently, I was able to see the individual pictures, each almost identical to the previous. But as she moved the film slowly, I was able to discern the minute changes. She then explained to me that as the reel sped through the light projector, it blended them together and created the illusion that the animals were, in fact, moving.

Much later, in America, when I was taught the theory of evolution, I imagined animals changing in this same almost imperceptible way through time. If evolution were true, then each species would have hundreds of in-between intermediates that would gradually and almost imperceptibly change from one form to the other, just as the pictures did in that movie reel. I had become an atheist in those days and believed wholeheartedly in the Darwinian model.

It was not until later that I came to realize that evolution did not adequately answer the origin of the universe, the origin of life, the origin of man, or the origin of the species. Instead of thousands

THE ORIGIN OF MAN

of pictures for a movie that should be 11 million to 14 million years long, what we find in the artificially created lineage of man are five or six still pictures and nothing in between. Not quite convincing!

It is as if the movie reel were composed of only five or six pictures with thousands of blank pictures in between. Moreover, the five or six pictures are of completely different species that are each found fully formed and unchanged throughout the entire fossil record of their existence.

The plain fact is that each picture is either fully human or fully ape. The evolutionist adamantly states that these five or six pictures are, in fact, our ancestors. Any creationist who dares to deny that is considered ignorant of the science of paleontology. The fact is that it is only their dogma that has evolved. In reality, these pictures of the "proof" have been changed continuously from the beginning like the shell game I referred to in Washington Square Park.

Some evolutionists cannot even agree which pictures ought to be displayed in the reel. How can they insist dogmatically that man has evolved from apes when the pictures in the reel have changed continuously from the very start? The evidence in that reel has never been constant; only the imaginary reel has been constant.

The exterior image portrayed to the public is one of utter assurance in the absolute credibility of the supposed fossil evidence, assuring us of an undisputable unbroken continuity from ape to man. All of us have seen the marvelous drawings of apes hunched over and slowly becoming more erect, and finally, their faces have become more like man. How can we deny it? It is right there drawn for all eyes to see the gradual change from ape to man.

But in reality, this portrayal in drawings is far from the truth. Their absolute dogma of the individual skeletons that are supposed to comprise our evolutionary heritage has changed and changed again over and over as new fossils come to light and disclose the error in their preconceived gradualist bias. Species after species that were once dogmatically acclaimed as our ancient ancestors have now been clearly shown to be simply extinct forms of apes or fully human specimens. That is a historical fact.

Neanderthal Man and Cro-Magnon Man

In 1856, a skeleton was found in a cave in southern Germany's Neander Valley when two quarrymen shoveling debris struck a bone. The workmen showed the bones to their foreman, who thought the remains were those of a cave bear. Fortunately, the foreman had the foresight to show the bones to a local schoolteacher who happened to be an amateur historian. The surprised teacher immediately recognized that these bones were human but yet different from common human skeletons. The skeleton was then named after the valley in which it was found. In the nineteenth century, the German word for valley was *thal*, and hence the name Neanderthal.

The skull of this new human specimen deviated from ours since it had a markedly heavier eyebrow and a more massive skeletal frame. The skeleton was immediately heralded as the missing link and named *Homo sapiens Neanderthalensis*. Artists subsequently portrayed the skull with a heavy brow, a thick hairy hide, ape-like nostrils, and a U-shaped jaw, which gave it a very pronounced ape-like appearance.

Anthropologists immediately assumed that Neanderthal man was an ancient ancestor of the Cro-Magnon species. The artists depicted him stooped over in typical gorilla fashion and covered him from head to toe in thick, coarse hair, as is customary in apes.

It just so happened that the first of the Neanderthal men found had been stricken with severe arthritis, and that misled anthropologists to assume that his shape was more ape-like than the subsequent skeletons found. Subsequent finds showed clearly by the connection of the spinal cord to the skull that Neanderthal man stood completely upright, just as humans. Nevertheless, the public appearance of the renditions of Neanderthal changed very slowly afterward. Although this particular individual was unusually more robust than modern men, the exaggerated skeletal aberrations of this first find were simply caused by arthritis.

> Neanderthals, as most people know, were stocky creatures compared to us. They were not however, stooped at the shoulder and bent at the knee, as sometimes reconstructed. Part of the problem here is that the La Chapelle-aux-Saints Neanderthal, a middle aged male whose skeleton attracted much attention early in this century, misled his chief interpreter. As it turns out, this particular Neanderthal was slightly deformed by arthritis! The limb bones of Neanderthals were heavier than ours, and it is inferred that their grip was more powerful. Apparently, they were in general considerably stronger for their height. *Both males and females had pelvises somewhat different in form from ours, and the Neanderthal shoulder blade was also distinctive. In comparison to Homo sapiens, Neanderthals were built for strength rather than swiftness* (emphasis added) (Stanley 1981, 152–53).

For close to a century after the discovery, evolutionists were adamant that Neanderthal was our ancestor. Time and time again, discoveries were made of completely human remains being found antecedent to Neanderthals, but the evolutionary blinded establishment set aside these discoveries as inconclusive. Finally, in 1947, this evolutionary assumption was proved dead wrong with incontrovertible evidence.

> At last in the summer of 1947, Mlle. Germaine Henri-Martin from a cave at Fontechevade near the village of Montbrun, in France, brought to light a modern-type fossil from a level well below that at which Neanderthal Man was customarily found. All the circumstances of this find were such as to guarantee its acceptance by

anthropologists everywhere. In fact, the bones came from an undisturbed level sealed below a thick layer of stalagmite that in turn underlay the Neanderthal level in this area. There could never be any argument as to the validity of this find. Modern man here preceded his one-time supposed predecessors.

G. Heberer has given a short and instructive summary of the present state of our knowledge of Homo sapiens. First, we know that modern types were contemporary with Neanderthal Man; secondly, the two types sometimes appear intermingled in a single deposit; and, finally, before the appearance of Neanderthal Man there existed individuals, more like modern man than Neanderthals were themselves (Custance 1975, 196–97).

Not only does the Adamic race precede the Neanderthals in the geologic strata, but the latter disappears inexplicably along with all hybrid forms. Since that time, numerous finds have verified conclusively that Neanderthal man came into existence after Cro-Magnon man and then existed alongside Cro-Magnon man for some time before becoming extinct. Yet during that entire time period, both Neanderthals and Cro-Magnon existed without any apparent evolutionary change in their morphology (Stanley 1981, 153).

The empirical fact that examples of both races were found in single deposits shows that they intermingled socially. Moreover, obvious hybrid forms have been found. That is a point little addressed by evolutionists, as we shall later see.

Today, even evolutionists have conceded that Neanderthal man, although more massive in structure, is 100 percent *Homo sapien* and displays many of the same variety of skeletal features found in the character complex of Europeans today. The fact that modern man has been found in strata older than their supposed evolutionary ancestors made him older than his evolutionary forbears. Therefore, they could not have been our ancestors. Evolutionists have now conceded them to an evolutionary dead end.

In other words, Neanderthals were completely human in every respect with the important differences that they possessed an even greater cranial capacity than the average modern man and a decidedly superior physical form. They were not a more primitive specimen but instead a more robust and advanced specimen. The evolutionary biased renditions of Neanderthal as brutish and ape-like with thick coarse hair covering its body were nothing more than fanciful biased projections based on no scientific data. It was simply based on their evolutionary presupposition.

If anything, Neanderthal man was evolutionarily a superior specimen to man. He was more heavily muscled through the chest with proportionally broader shoulders. He had a 60 percent greater lung capacity, which gave him a pronounced edge in endurance. The generally massive features of his skeletal system such as thicker limbs, skull, and jaw were initially used as evidence of a more primitive form of man when, in fact, it gave him an unquestioned advantage in a world presumably guided by the evolutionary mantra of the survival of the fittest.

Modern anthropologists still insist that Neanderthal is an inferior race to the human species, although perhaps not chronologically more primitive. If anything, their increased cranial capacity made them more advanced than we are today. At least from an intellectual capacity, since their brain was markedly larger than modern man, it can be said that they were, indeed, superior to our form in intelligence.

Moreover, strictly from an evolutionary point of view, since they were distinctly more powerful and able to out-compete Cro-Magnon man both in battle and in hunting, with a marked superiority in brute force and endurance, then it can be said that they were more capable of surviving in a physically competitive environment. If the underlying matrix of reality were truly the survival of the fittest, then Neanderthal man should have completely taken over the human population.

All the physical evidence points to a much superior form that should have been able to overpower Cro-Magnon man, yet modern anthropologists, ignoring these basic facts, painted a picture of Neanderthal man as intellectually inferior to us because, from an evolutionary standpoint, they cannot otherwise explain their extinction. Here, their evolutionary mantra has been neutered.

Initially, they had eagerly hoped to make Neanderthal man an evolutionary precursor to Cro-Magnon man in order to fill the void of intermediates between ape and man. Once their supposed evolutionary link was completely discredited, they still had to explain why they became extinct through their evolutionary grid. Hence, against all physical evidence, they continue to paint Neanderthal man as an inferior species to us.

Why? Because Neanderthal man became extinct, and Cro-Magnon man survived. So in order to remain consistent with their underlying evolutionary hypothesis of the survival of the fittest, they must conclude that Cro-Magnon must have been superior. And so, in spite of Neanderthal man's superior cranial capacity and physical prowess, evolutionists conclude that he must have been inferior from an evolutionary perspective. The idea that the Noahic Flood could have wiped out their entire race as well as all forms of hybrids between Cro-Magnon and Neanderthals is completely unacceptable to Darwinists.

Initially, evolutionists insisted that Neanderthals were intellectually inferior to us and tried to make a case of it by the nature of the sophistication of the tools found with the skeletons. But the differences evolutionists expected in their tools are not exactly uniform among the finds.

> In a cluster of limestone caves southeast of Paris, archaeologists have found a distinctive assembly of modern looking tools, beads, and ornamental objects dated to about 36,000 years ago. Initially scientists assumed that these artifacts,

which belong to a culture known as Chatelperronian, were the work of early modern humans in Europe. But then fossils were found with a Chatelperronian deposit, and they were clearly Neandertals (Olson 2002, 89).

The variation among the many archaeological finds has shown that there is no technological superiority held by Cro-Magnon man over Neanderthal man. The theory of the Cro-Magnon technological superiority has been nothing more than speculation based on their evolutionary hypothesis. But it is their evolutionary hypothesis that should have alerted them to this Tartufery.

Let us look at it from an evolutionary perspective. What possible evolutionary selective pressure could have produced a much larger brain yet an inferior intellect? For what purpose would it exist? Why would evolution create a larger brain with a much greater need for sustenance, with no selective advantage? It is a complete paradox from an evolutionary standpoint.

Our brain is an extremely sensitive organ that requires a continuous and steady supply of blood sugar to function. It is the most energy-demanding organ in our bodies and is responsible for more than half the obligatory energy requirements of our system. The typical modern man requires approximately 2,200 calories per day to live, while the Neanderthal, with a much larger brain and more massive body structure, required a minimum 4,030 calories per day.

Moreover, studies of the structure of the Neanderthal cranium show that the area of cognitive thinking in his brain was equally developed with modern man. Thus, his ability to think in abstract forms was equal or greater to ours due to his greater size.

Some have suggested that perhaps Neanderthal's inferiority resulted from not having a language, but that is nothing more than speculation and grasping at straws. As a matter of fact, the very idea that language could have evolved and that the vocal cords and the intricate neural cortex and circuitry needed for language to be possible could evolve in sequential steps is sheer nonsense. What possible selective advantage would a partial vocal cord serve?

The complex neurocircuitry that governs the tongue, the lips, and the mouth, as well as the muscles that control the vocal cords to stretch them and contract them in the right proportions to create the desired sounds, must work in complete synchrony or there can be no language. Moreover, without hearing, language is inaudible. Thus, the entire hardware of the hearing system must also evolve in synchrony to allow speech the opportunity to be heard and understood. Both mechanisms are irreducible to simpler components that evolve in stages.

Nevertheless, the assertion that their greater brain capacity would have produced an inferior capability to evolve language is preposterous, to say the least. There is simply no clear empirical evidence that can suggest why Neanderthals became extinct and modern man did not. As a matter of fact, the opposite is the case. Recent DNA samples from Neanderthals found in El Sidron, Spain, have revealed that they contained a version of a gene found in modern humans called FOXP2 that controls speech and language ability and facial muscles.

In other words, Neanderthals had the same capacity for language as we do. That finding throws the inferiority theory out of consideration, for it evidences that Neanderthals did have the capacity to speak. There simply is no clear evidence that can suggest, from an evolutionary standpoint, why Neanderthals became extinct and modern man did not.

Much to my amusement, El Sidrón, Lalueza-Fox, and Holger Römpler of the University of Leipzig announced that they had isolated a pigmentation gene from another Neanderthal specimen, which I thought to be quite illuminating in light of their previous dogma regarding the Neanderthal's appearance. The gene, called MC1R, indicates that this individual had red hair and pale skin, perhaps even freckles.

THE ORIGIN OF MAN

The old depictions of Neanderthal as a swarthy, dark-skinned, hairy, and hunched over ape-like creature have been shown to be nothing more than wishful projections from evolutionists who desperately wished to make of him a missing link between man and ape. Their evolutionary spectacles were knocked off their faces by the raw empirical data, and yet they stooped to pick them up again and donned them undisturbed without missing a beat.

Contrary to the empirical evidence, which in the overwhelming majority of the cases where a human specimen is found to have that fair-skinned, red-haired pigmentation gene, individuals possess a pointed nose. Yet they continued to show Neanderthal in their depictions with a flattened Negroid nose. They do that simply because they must create a segue between the flat-nosed ape and modern man to remain within their evolutionary gradualist presupposition.

It would be comical if it were not so sad. The beautiful flat nose of our black brothers is no less of an evolved nose than the aquiline nose. It is not an evolutionary segue between ape and man. It is simply one of the genetic variations that were contained in the DNA of Adam, which evidences the marvelous creativity of our God. That is nothing more than a faint or veiled allusion to the old evolutionary claims popular in the nineteenth and twentieth centuries that black men were less evolved and inferior to white men.

Since we cannot really say much of anything about the shape of the nose from a skull because the soft tissue or cartilage is not preserved, it is in every respect unscientific to assume that Neanderthal had a flat nose. The base of the nose may have been larger because the skull itself was larger, but their noses could well have been prominent aquiline noses for all we know.

And if our present-day examples are to be considered—that is, if we use the uniformitarian hypothesis accurately by extrapolating into the past our present observations—and if at least some of them had red hair and freckled light skin, it would make more sense to say that these at least would have had a pointed nose.

I would venture to say that Neanderthals represented every type of colored skin existing in the genetic pool of the Adamic race prior to the Great Flood. In fact, if we use the uniformity of natural causes correctly, we can stipulate that this variability in the original genetic pool was much greater than the limited variations that were preserved in the family of Noah. We see in every kind of living thing this phenomenon of diminution in the variety of the character complexes of organisms. It is the indirect evidence of the historicity of the catastrophic effect of Noah's Flood on all fauna.

Moreover, during the First Earth, this variation was made greater as the Nephilim bred with the daughters of Eve. Evidence from recent digs in Spain clearly shows that Neanderthal man and Cro-Magnon man did, in fact, interbreed, as fossils have been found that exhibit the hybridization of the two species.

We can point to *Homo heidelbergensis* and *Homo ergaster* as two examples of this hybridization. Since evolutionists have not been able to demonstrate our superiority over Neanderthal man, they have now hit upon a new idea. They have now theorized that the genetic peculiarities of Neanderthal man were swallowed up by Cro-Magnon man because of our greater numbers. In other words, they were assimilated into our species, and we bear their genes in us today.

Recent morphological studies have shown clear distinctions between Neanderthals and humans. Some Australians carry similarly shaped skulls, but none have the enormous and massive corporal size exhibited by Neanderthals. In the author's view, these skull similarities are superficial. The real distinctions are genetic distinctions.

There is a clear genetic difference between the children of Adam and Eve and the Neanderthals. Of the thousands of DNA samples taken of humans throughout the world from every possible race, every sequence produced by the samples collected shows an undeniable trace to the mitochondrial Eve and not to the specific markers that were intrinsic to Neanderthal man. Clear divergence and monophyly of the HN mitochondrial DNA (mtDNA) control region suggest a long separation of the HN and HS female lineages. There may have been interbreeding between Neanderthal and Cro-Magnon man, but there is no trace today of those Neanderthal genes in man. More than 4,000 recorded sequences in the current European gene pool show a complete absence of mtDNA from Neanderthals. How can that be?

In other words, through modern advancements in technology, scientists have been able to study the DNA of Neanderthal man and have concluded that our present DNA is completely void of the peculiar DNA markers found in them. But this is a mystery to them, for the human historical evidence shows that man has always, without exception, tended to breed with all possible suitors. And in fact, the evidence unearthed in Spain supports the very fact that they did interbreed. Yet today, there are no traces of the Neanderthal genes found in modern man.

But if you were to speak to an evolutionist, he or she would tell you that we have Neanderthal genes by pointing to those genes they had in common with Cro-Magnon and avoiding the obvious DNA markers that made them distinct from Cro-Magnon man, as we shall now document.

Similar studies have concluded that Cro-Magnon man's gene pool was very similar to modern man's. Now we know that Cro-Magnon and Neanderthals lived concurrently and were found in single deposits. How could it be that if they interbred we would not have retained the distinct Neanderthal DNA markers in modern man?

Initially, attempts to mark the DNA of Neanderthal man were unsuccessful, but in 1996, two young German archaeologists armed with the latest technology succeeded.

> In the early 1990s the prospects of obtaining DNA from Neandertal bones seemed little better than that. But, as laboratory techniques continued to improve, two young

German researchers, archaeologist Ralf Schmitz and geneticist Svante Paabo, became increasingly confident that they could obtain mitochondrial DNA from Neanderthal fossils. Furthermore, they didn't want just any old Neanderthal. They wanted to sample the very bones found by the quarrymen in 1856. Needless to say, the curators of the bones were not eager to sacrifice parts of their irreplaceable fossils to an unproven technique. "It was like getting permission to cut into the Mona Lisa," recalls Schmitz. But, he and Paabo persisted. Schmitz cajoled the museum curators, emphasizing the publicity that a positive find would generate. Paabo demonstrated techniques he had developed in his university of Munich laboratory that offered at least some prospect for success.

Finally the museum agreed. In 1996 a professional bone preparer carefully sawed a half-inch wide, eighth-of- an- ounce chunk from Neandertal man's right upper arm bone. Paabo took the plastic vial containing the bone sample back to his lab and handed it to graduate student Matthias Krings, who had just spent nearly three years trying unsuccessfully to extract DNA samples from Egyptian mummies. "At the beginning I didn't have much hope that it would work," says Krings, who is now employed by a biotechnical-consulting firm in Munich. "I was having trouble getting DNA from samples that were 5,000 years old. Now I had a sample that was at least 35,000 years old, and maybe more than 100,000 years old."

Krings ground up a small section of the bone, mixed the powder with a liquid solution, and removed the DNA-containing portion using a centrifuge. He then mixed the DNA with what are called molecular primers. These primers latch onto specific regions of DNA—in this case, two twenty-base-pair segments known to exist in the

THE ORIGIN OF MAN

Mitochondrial DNA of modern humans and thought likely to exist in Neandertals. By adding the proper compounds, one can copy all of the DNA between a pair of primers, yielding twice as much DNA as in the original sample. The cycle is then repeated. After two cycles, the DNA has increased four times; after three cycles, eight times; and so on. In this way, even very tiny fragments of DNA can be copied many times, yielding enough DNA for sequencing.

My description makes the process sound easy. In fact, it's devilishly hard. Coaxing DNA that is tens of thousands of years old from tiny fragments of bones requires endless care and hundreds of separate laboratory manipulations. Krings put in one-hundred-hour weeks for months on end.

But, then he began to find fragments of DNA that were clearly different from the DNA of today's humans. At position 16,223 in the mitochondrial sequence, where most humans have a cytosine, the sample from the bone had thiamine. At 16,254, instead of the usual guanine, the sample had adenine. "I can still remember the feeling I had," Krings says. "By this time I was able to spot a difference if I saw one, and when I saw differences in the extraction, I knew we had something." Using different primers, Krings was able to piece together a mitochondrial DNA sequence of 379 nucleotides from the fossil. This sequence differed from the standard modern human sequence at twenty-seven locations—far too many for the DNA to have come from mitochondrial Eve.

Krings couldn't celebrate yet. He needed an independent confirmation of the results. He sent a separate sample of the bone to Mark Stoneking, then at Pennsylvania State University, and Stoneking passed it on to graduate student Anne Stone. Now an assistant professor at the University of New Mexico, Stone had just finished her

Ph.D. and still had a few months before graduation, so she agreed to do the project. But it was much more difficult than she had expected. "Even grinding the bone into powder was hard," she says. "I had to drill it full of holes, like Swiss cheese." Not until the day of graduation did the results finally begin to emerge from the sequencer. While her parents waited in her apartment, Stone ran back and forth to the lab. "I called Germany and began to read the differences to Matthias," she recalls. "I'd say, I got this base pair at this position, and he would cheer. Then I'd say, I got this base pair at this position, and he would cheer again." "I can tell you," says Krings, "we had a party that night." When the paper describing the sequence was published a few months later, one paleoanthropolgist called it "as exciting as the Mars landing" (Olson 2002, 82).

Outside of divine intervention, it is inconceivable that these DNA markers of the Neanderthals would not have been contained in modern man if they had interbred. Even Olson admits that the propensity of man to have sexual encounters with anything possible leaves little doubt that they would not have interbred somewhere along the line. Yet he is dumbfounded to find that there is no DNA evidence of these distinct DNA markers of Neanderthals present in modern man.

The lack of evidence for interbreeding between modern humans and Neandertal is a mystery. Modern humans— well, males at least—will copulate with almost anything. According to data gathered by Alfred Kinsey and his colleagues in the 1940s, 8 percent of American men reported having sexual experiences with animals. Among men who grew up on farms, the percentage was much higher—approaching 50 percent. As modern human males began encountering Neandertal women in the Middle East and Europe, it seems inconceivable that they would not have mated with them, no matter how different they looked (Olson 2002, 83).

Just because we do not have these 27 Neanderthal genetic markers does not mean they did not interbreed. "This sequence differed from the standard modern human sequence at twenty-seven locations—far too many for the DNA to have come from mitochondrial Eve" (Olson 2002, 83). But that is precisely the conundrum; here we find indisputable evidence that they did interbreed with Cro-Magnon in Spain, yet there are no traces of their DNA in modern man. The evidence simply points to the total annihilation of this race of beings from the planet and of any of the individuals who would have carried their genes. Both *Homo heidelbergensis* and *Homo ergaster* are hybrid breeds of Neanderthals and Cro-Magnon. Their similarities will be discussed later in the section on *Homo erectus*.

Could it be that Neanderthal man was, in fact, the Nephilim of Genesis 6? Could it be that they were not the legitimate seed of Adam and Eve and God destroyed them during the judgment of the First Earth? Could it be that they were bred for the single purpose of profaning the seed of Eve to prevent the coming of the Son of God that would fulfill the prophecy of Genesis 3:15? How else can we explain not only their extinction but also the fact that all humans who contained their genes perished with them? Whatever was the cause of their extinction, it could not have been anything other than a global extinction event, considering the wide range of their habitat throughout an enormous area of our world.

Today, most evolutionists see the Neanderthal as an extinct sister race of the same *Homo sapiens* species, which, for some unknown reason, became extinct. Instead of mentioning the indisputable fact that none of us today could have come from them because we lack these peculiar genetic markers in our genome, they have deliberately chosen to speak of the many genes that we do have in common in order to deceive the public into thinking that we have somehow evolved from them.

In fact, many are now saying that we carry Neanderthal genes within us. The opposite is the case. Man came first, and man's genes were used to create the tyrannical Neanderthals. They carry our genes, but they also carry some very highly specialized genes that made them superior to man in every way but spiritual. Those demonically engendered genetic markers have been eradicated by God through the judgment of the Great Flood. Again, the historicity of the Genesis narrative is supported by the empirical data.

This kind of evolutionary propaganda through half-truths is unconscionable. But deception is the art of propaganda, and evolutionists are masters at this craft. Nevertheless, the strata indisputably show that Cro-Magnon preceded Neanderthal. Hence, in reality, it was the Neanderthals who carried a portion of our genes, except that some were mysteriously altered to create their monstrous size and superior capabilities. Yet in the end, their demonic plan to profane Eve's bloodline was foiled by the Great Flood.

The Art of Selling Evolution

There is another curious observation I would like to make. Although the evolutionists have verbally abandoned their ape-like representation of the Neanderthal man, the renditions in the biology books continue to be drawn as if he were somewhat ape-like. Now there is a great divergence between different artistic renditions of the same species in either representing Neanderthal as more ape-like or more man-like. In the final analysis, it is fair to say that the end product resembles basically what the initial bias or prejudice of the artist is to begin with.

Untrained individuals who see these artists' renditions immediately assume that the artists' conception is completely accurate in depicting the way they really looked. The fact is that these fossil bones do not tell us anything about the soft flesh or cartilage or of the texture and color of the skin or the hair patterns of the creature. These are the things that give us our facial characteristics.

In an article titled "Anthro-Art" in *Science Digest*, the bias of this interpretive art was discussed:

> The closest we will ever come to seeing our earliest ancestors is through paintings and sculptures created by artists who work with anthropologists.
>
> Unfortunately the vast majority of artist's conceptions are based more on imagination than on evidence. But, a handful of expert natural history artists begin with the fossil bones of a hominid and work from there. Such a procedure calls for a detailed understanding of anatomy. Most bones have tiny ridges and grooves called muscle scars, each corresponding to a particular muscle. From these scars good artists can estimate the size of muscles that have long since vanished.
>
> Once the artists have identified various bony landmarks, they shape strands of clay into simulations of muscle fibers and press them against a plastic cast of the fossil. One by one they build up the muscle layers, add fat pads where they might be expected and, finally, cover the muscle with a sheet of clay to represent the skin.
>
> *Much of the reconstruction however is guesswork. Bones say nothing about the fleshy part of the nose, lips or ears. Artists must create something between an ape and a human being; the older the specimen is said to be, the more ape-like they make it.*
>
> Although skin color is also largely conjecture, most anthropologists assume that tropical specimens were dark and Temperate Zone specimens were light, since each color is advantageous in its latitudes. Hairiness is a matter of pure conjecture.

> *The guesswork approach often leads to errors. Recently the discovery of preserved hominid footprints showed how wrong some artists had been in giving Neanderthals divergent big toes that resembled those of apes. The ancient footprints revealed that millions of years before the Neanderthals the hominid foot was completely modern* (emphasis added) ("Anthro-Art" 1981, 41).

The subjective bias is here gingerly and subtly alluded to but candy-coated with words like *expert* in order to feign some measure of scientific credibility: "Much of the reconstruction however is guesswork. Bones say nothing about the fleshy part of the nose, lips, or ears. Artists must create something between an ape and a human being; the older the specimen is said to be, the more ape-like they make it" ("Anthro-Art" 1981, 41).

The fact is simply that the artist represents the skull in the fashion that it fits within their imagined evolutionary ladder. And that is the whole of it. Beginning with the presupposition that evolution is a fact, they then extrapolate what our ancestors might look like as they allegedly transitioned from ape to man.

The older the supposed fossil, the more ape-like the rendition will be. And the younger the fossil is supposed to be, the more human-like the rendition will be. The skulls cannot by themselves provide enough evidence to warrant an absolute or accurate representation. So they must rely on conjecture and dress their conjecture with pseudo-scientific jargon to convince the masses.

The wide nose and full lips of the Neanderthal rendition is nothing but pure conjecture. That Neanderthal could just as well have had an aquiline nose and thin lips. And this choice in the rendition of the underlying skull would not contradict one single thing about the shape or features of his skull. As a matter of fact, if we are to consider the hard data—the genes that show they had red hair and fair skin—then an aquiline nose would be indicated.

THE ORIGIN OF MAN

The plain fact is that with some exceptions, anthropologists cannot generally differentiate between a Negroid, Aboriginal, Eskimo, or European skull today. If such incredibly diverse features cannot be discerned from the skulls, how can evolutionists with good conscience claim to know the soft tissue and facial features of Neanderthal man? How could honest scientists allow the obvious deception perpetrated on the populace with these subjective renditions? They not only condone it but also promote it because it is designed to convince the gullible public of their evolutionary hypothesis.

These are not accurate representations. At best, they are subjective and speculative interpretations, the product of mere conjecture and wish projection. Scientists should not resort to such smoke-and-mirror tactics if they hope to gain the trust of the general public.

Most of us are familiar with the illustration found in most evolutionary biology books, the supposed scientific drawing that starts on the left side with an ape humped over. To the right, in increasingly more upright fashion, the drawings become ever more human-like until all the way to the right, there is a completely human specimen. Seeing is believing, and the unsuspecting public is convinced by the spurious propaganda. We have been led to believe that these artistic renditions are absolutely accurate. But nothing could be further from the truth.

Their evolutionary hypothesis simply subjectively determines the physical characteristics of the specimens drawn. But this is quite an impossible feat to substantiate scientifically when the skull features of our extant human species are so similar, in contrast to these divergent images, that there is no real way to correlate the two. W. E. Le Gross Clark, the late professor of anatomy at Oxford University and an ardent evolutionist, writes:

> It may indeed be possible to identify a skull of a modern Negro, an Australian Aboriginal, or a European, in individual cases where the racial characteristics are exception-

ally well marked; but the variations within each group is so great that skulls of each type may be found that are impossible of racial diagnosis. This difficulty may be illustrated by reference to the well-known skulls from the late Paleolithic sites of Grimaldi near Mentone and Chancelade in the Pordogne Valley, on the significance of which there has in the past been considerable controversy.

The Grimaldi skulls had been held by many anthropologists to be definitely Negroid in type, and they were commonly accepted as good evidence of the existence of a Negroid race in Europe during Aurignacian times. Yet others, also from a study of the actual remains have pronounced categorically that they show no real evidence of Negroid affinities but are simply variants of the "Mediterranean Race" somewhat distorted perhaps, that now inhabit southern Europe.

The Chancelade skull of Magdalenean Age, has been compared by the famous anatomist Testut, with that of an Eskimo, and this diagnosis was accepted by many reputable anthropologists. The conclusion again, has been vigorously denied by equally distinguished anthropologists who maintain that it is only a variant of the Cro Magnon type of Homo Sapiens.

Now it is probable that there are no racial types in which the skull characters are more distinctive than Negroes and Eskimos; yet, experts fail to agree when faced with single skulls whose claims to these types are in question. If a decision proves so difficult in such cases, it will be realized how much more difficult or even impossible, it will be to identify by reference to limited skeletal remains minor racial groups with less distinctive characters (emphasis added) (Clark 1955, 55–56).

Who were these people whom paleontologists refer to as the Grimaldi skulls? In 1872, M. E. Riviere took advantage of a road being built from Marseilles to Genoa, which skirted the foot of the cliff near Baousse Rousse (Red Rocks) to study the ancient deposits. He undertook the work of excavating nine caves called the Grimaldi Caves.

On March 26, 1872, below a stalagmite floor in what is known as the Cavillon Cave, Riviere discovered a human skeleton. This now famous skeleton is known as the Menetone Man and is exhibited at the Anthropological Gallery of the Paris Museum.

In 1873, three more skeletons were unearthed in what is known as the Cave of Baousse da Torre (Rock Tower). In 1874, Riviere excavated the Grottes de Enfants, so named because he extracted two skeletons of children there. In 1901, two skeletons were found at a much lower level. They were labeled the Grimaldi race because there were some obvious differences in their anatomical structure to the others skeletons that were considered Cro-Magnon man.

> All these human spoils were found in conditions resembling those already observed in Dordogne. Here as there, the skeletons were accompanied by a whole series of objects, particularly by a quantity of shells which had been used for the purposes of decoration or of dress....
>
> The new skeletons exhumed from the Grottes de Enfants had been the object of true burial. The articles deposited with them resembling those accompanying the skeletons previously discovered perforated with shells, objects of decoration, bones colored red, and so on. *Dr, Vernau recognized the fact that the two skeletons from the lowest levels represented a special race, which he called Grimaldi race.* The skeletons from the upper layers, like those discovered by Riviere, Julien, and Abbo, entirely agree with the Cro Magnon type....
>
> With regards to the skeletons, which we shall consider first of all, the opinions of anthropologists are somewhat

at variance. In all these Men of the Reindeer Age, some anthropologists distinguish varieties of only one race of Homo sapiens. Others are inclined to distinguish as many as there are specimens. I think that the truth lies between these two views. . . .

The two skeletons of the Grimaldi race lay at a lower level. Discovered on 3d June 1901, they were carefully exhumed and conveyed to the Monaco Museum. . . . the negroids are, therefore, Aurignacian, like all the Cro Magnon men. . . . Here we have one chief reason for regarding these fossils as Negroid, if not actually negro. The negroid affinities are likewise indicated by the characters of the skull. The heads are large. The skulls are very elongated, hyper-dolichocephalic and seen from above they represent a regular elliptically shaped contour, with flattened parietal bosses. The skulls are also very high so that their capacity is at least equal to that of the average Parisian of our day: 1580 cc in the case of the young man and 1375 cc in the case of the old woman. The mastoid apophyses are small, the face is large but not high, *whilst the skull is excessively elongated from the front backwards; so that the head might be called unbalanced or disharmonic. The forehead is well developed and straight; the orbital ridges project only slightly, the orbits are large deep and subrectangular; their lower border is reverted towards the front* (emphasis added) (Boule 2010, 152–56).

The fascinating thing is that the description of their skulls is consistent with the expectations of a Neanderthal–Cro-Magnon hybrid, but the elitist mentality of the Eurocentric evolutionists of that day led them to consider these skulls, which had some Cro-Magnon qualities as well as some Neanderthal qualities, as Negroid.

Men like Boule regularly referred to blacks and Japanese as men of the lower races or sometimes the savage or inferior races, thinking that the European whites were the most evolutionary advanced humans on the planet. They could not bring themselves to believe that Cro-Magnon, the ancestors of the Europeans, could have intermingled with such bestial men as Neanderthals to produce hybrids. Their "pure" bloodlines could not contain such bestial blood. For that reason, all the early reconstructions of Neanderthals were dark-skinned and swarthy. Obvious hybrids such as *Homo heidelbergensis* were allocated to superficial extinct sidelines that lived alongside but not in contact with their ancestors. Speaking of *Homo heidelbergensis*, Boule commented, "In the Mousterian period it represented a belated type existing side by side with the direct ancestors of Homo sapiens; its relation to the latter was similar to that which exists at the present day between the races we call inferior and superior races. Perhaps one might go so far as to say that it was a degenerate species" (Boule 2010, 144).

Contrary to their horse-blinded prejudice, the hyper-dolichocephalic skull is not a Negroid characteristic; it is predominantly a Neanderthal characteristic, but in a less dramatic fashion, it is also the predominant shape of the white European skull. Projecting orbital ridges are not a Negroid characteristic; they are a Neanderthal characteristic. These individuals were hybrids of Neanderthals and Cro-Magnon man.

But what can we say about these god-aspiring men who arrogantly divine the whole shape of a creature from the evidence of a single tooth? Is that really science, or is it wizardry? Is it really empirical fact, or is it clairvoyance?

Suffice it to say that the marvelous drawings shading a gradual humanization of some supposed ancestral ape and culminating in modern man is the product of pure conjecture, with only their evolutionary bias as a base. They are nicely done and convincing to the uninitiated. I have often wondered whether they hired a consulting firm from Madison and 5th Avenues in advertising or public relations.

Ape-Like Features: Hominid and Hominoid Classifications

There is some confusion in the ranks of evolutionists as to the labeling of categories that refer to man's ancestry. The following categories are probably the most widely accepted by evolutionists:

- Hominoid: all classes of apes
- Hominid: the three subgroups that form the supposed ancestral line of man
    - *Homo habilis*—supposedly the earliest ancestors of man, referred to as men-like apes.
    Under this category, they list the following species: *Australopithecus afarensis*, the oldest; *Australopithecus Africanus*; *Australopithecus robustus* (*Zinjanthropus*).
    - *Homo erectus*—intermediary category that evolutionists are hard put to fill. In this category, they place the *Pithecanthropus* and *Sinanthropus*, which they refer to as ape-like men.
    - *Homo sapiens*—the human species that they artificially divide into three categories: Neanderthal, Cro-Magnon, and *Homo sapiens* (modern man)

There are, however, several features that can differentiate to some degree the skulls of humans from the skulls of apes. The form of the ape's jaw is more U-shaped, while the human jaw is more parabolic; that is, the side profile of the human shows a flatter face and the distinctive human chin, while the Neanderthal's shows a receding chin.

In addition, there is a more pronounced and thicker brow ridge in apes. However, we can also find in human samples such as *Neanderthalensis* a thicker brow ridge. There is also a slight difference in the dentition. The problem is that evolutionists often draw hard lines using measurements of individual skulls, which do not account for the wide differentiation that exists within a given kind called the character complex.

The eminent W. E. Le Gros Clark warns specifically of this tendency in anthropologists. Since most of them are not vertebrate taxonomists, they have a tendency to jump to conclusions in comparison studies when they do not possess a large number of samples of the species in question. That is essential in order to establish a character complex that takes into account the wide variability that exists within all species or kinds.

> Vertebrate taxonomists are of course, well accustomed to taking account of groups of characters in their assessment of the zoological status of an animal, and they are quite conversant with the phrase "character complex." But, anthropologists and human anatomists, (perhaps from lack of experience in the practice and principles of taxonomy) often tend to focus their attention on single characters in their discussions of relationships; or if they take into account a list of several characters, they tend to treat them as an assemblage of separate individual units without recognizing that in combination they constitute a functional pattern that must be treated as a whole (Clark 1955, 16).

When scant fossil evidence is all that exists, it is rather dubious to conclude absolute and concrete criteria without having access to the data necessary to map the extremes of the variability within the species in question. That is the "character complex" that Le Gross Clark refers to. And there can be no definitive conclusions without this data to create a complete range of the variables within a particular kind.

Another measurement used to differentiate between apes and humans is the cranial capacity. Modern man on average has a cranial capacity of approximately 1100 cc. to 1200 cc. (the size of a woman's cranium is slightly smaller). The cranial capacity gives us an idea of the size of the brain, but caution must be taken.

Although size is relatively important, it is not a directly proportionate measurement of intelligence. Otherwise, we could conclude that the average man would be more intelligent than the average woman. That is not so. But there is somewhat of an indirect relationship between the size of the brain and the general intelligence of the creature. So we could say that the cranial capacity of man being greater than apes gives man an intellectual superiority.

There is, however, such a wide difference in the parameters within a species that it is difficult to make much on the basis of this single measurement when the discrepancy is not significant. If I were to find the skull of a Pygmy in Africa and compare it to a Masai tribesman, there would be a distinct and radical difference in size. That difference would not, however, directly correlate with the intellectual potential of a Pygmy or a Masai tribesman.

If I were to compare the skull of a Great Dane and a Chihuahua, I might conclude from an evolutionary perspective that the larger sample was more advanced. That is, of course, ridiculous. They are both contemporaries of the same kind.

Therefore, when anthropologists find only a few remains and dogmatically classify their findings in their imagined evolutionary scale without the benefit of establishing a character complex, they inevitably push the envelope toward their predisposed bias. Without question, there is a large measure of conjecture involved, which is based on their initial presupposition. I am sure that there are a great many sincere anthropologists who attempt to be objective in their work, but unfortunately, the very nature of their hypothesis subliminally intervenes.

As a matter of fact, in some cases, the bias has been so strong that some have reverted to fraud. However, I would like to interject that these few examples of fraudulent cases do not represent most anthropologists. I may not agree with their evolutionary presupposition and the coloring it gives their findings, but they are not charlatans. For the most part, they are sincere scientists, and they must be respected as such by Christians and Jews who hold to another worldview. And I would hope that the respect one day will be mutual.

But what these examples do show is the immense pressure that evolutionists face to come up with substantiations of their imagined sequential lineage from apes to man. No doubt, the frustration they face in obtaining this chain of ancestors is reflected in the attempts of some less honest to shore up the evidence with contrived data.

I am careful here to again assert that there are many honest people who simply have made erroneous assumptions without any malintentions. However, evolutionists must also admit that some attempts to fabricate an ancestral lineage of apes to man have been less than honest.

One example I consider an honest mistake is that of the Nebraska Man (*Hesperopithecus haroldcooki*).

Nebraska Man

In 1922, a tooth was discovered in Western Nebraska, which, according to the eminent paleontologist of that day Henry Fairfield Osborn, displayed the combined characteristics of ape and man. From the evidence of a single tooth, lo and behold, the eminent paleontologists were able to create an entire human/ape-like being through the wizardry of the evolutionary imagination wand. Paleontologists argued whether to designate this "missing link" an ape-like man or a man-like ape. He was named *Hesperopithecus haroldcooki*.

Hesperopithecus haroldcooki

The *Illustrated London News* carried a drawing of this creature, now popularly referred to as the Nebraska Man. For five years, articles about the Nebraska Man heralded it as the missing link. Proof that man had evolved from apes was now hard evidence. Or was it?

Oops! In 1927, it was discovered that this tooth belonged not to man, but to an extinct peccary (pig).

Perhaps they should have been a little more humble and a little less arrogant in their interpretive prowess. So much for establishing a character complex! Nevertheless, this was not a perpetrated hoax. It was an honest mistake, precipitated by their zeal and total faith in the evolutionary presupposition. Well, anyone can make a mistake. However, sometimes it is not a mistake but rather a deliberate fraud such as *Eanthropus dawsoni*.

Piltdown Man: *Eanthropus dawsoni*

In 1912, specimens from a gravel pit near Piltdown, England, were also declared to be the so-called missing link. Arthur Smith Woodward, the director of the Natural History Museum in London, and Dr. Charles Dawson, announced the discovery of part of a skull and mandible that was later named *Eanthropus dawsoni*, or the Dawn Man. The jawbone had ape characteristics, except for the teeth that showed the type of wear associated with humans. The skull appeared to be quite human.

For 40 years, the Piltdown Man, as it became popularly known, was accepted by the world's greatest authorities as an authentic link in our ancestry. Evolutionists universally heralded *Eanthropus dawsoni* as the much-touted missing link, and for almost half a century, it enjoyed all the prestige of a full scientific classification, falsely sustaining the evolutionary presupposition of the sequential human evolution from apes.

With the development of fluoride testing by Kenneth Page Oakley in the 1950s, science obtained a useful tool in its investigative arsenal. The fluoride test is a comparable age determinant that is able to compare the relative age of a variety of bones in a given find. In other words, the test can determine whether they are of the same period, and therefore, it can verify whether the bones belong together or are from separate times.

When the remains of the Piltdown Man were tested, scientists discovered that the jawbone was not even a fossil and was, in fact, the jawbone of an orangutan. The fluoride test showed conclusively that the skull and jawbone did not belong together. Oops!

Further scrutiny revealed that the bones had been subjected to iron salts in order to give them the appearance of age. The teeth had been filed down to resemble man's dentition. In short, for 40 years, "experts" in the field of paleontology believed in a deliberately fabricated hoax, until the truth dawned upon them and the Dawn Man saw his sunset.

Well, you might say, anyone can make two mistakes.

Java Man: *Pithecanthropus erectus*

The story of *Pithecanthropus* begins in the late 1800s when Dr. Eugene Dubois, a Dutch paleontologist, became convinced that the missing link would be found in the East Indies. Dubois, on an assignment for the Dutch army, was stationed in Java. In 1891 near the village of Trinil, he unearthed a skullcap along the banks of the Solo River.

The skullcap had a low-sloping forehead with heavy low ridges. Dubois estimated the cranial capacity to be about 900 cc., although such an estimate with only a partial skull is veritably impossible and, at best, dubious.

Approximately one year later and 50 feet from the skullcap, Dubois unearthed a human femur and subsequently assigned it without any scientific justification to the same individual of his previous find. Sometime later, he found two molars and named his find *Pithecanthropus erectus*, popularly referred to as Java Man.

His discovery was dated at approximately 500,000 years old. There was considerable controversy again in the categorizing of this creature. The British wanted it to be a man-ape, and the Germans wanted it to be an ape-man. The French paleontologist Boule doubted that the finds were consistent with a single individual.

> Such are the facts. If we possessed only the skull and the interpretation of the teeth, we should say that we were dealing with the face of a large Ape; if we had only the femur, we should declare we were dealing with only a Man.... A first and important question arises: Did the skull cap, the teeth, an the femur found separately and at more or less considerable intervals of time and distance belong to the same being? (Boule 2010, 72).

In addition to his earlier finds, Dubois also found at nearby Wadjak in the same approximate strata the fossils of two human skulls, subsequently known as the Wadjak skulls. These had the cranial capacity of 1550 cc. and 1650 cc., making them considerably larger than the ape skulls and more in line with human skulls.

Unfortunately, Dubois concealed his Wadjak find because he knew that it would discredit his *Pithecanthropus*. The obvious inference is that *Pithecanthropus* could not be our ancestor if it was found within the same strata where humans existed.

THE ORIGIN OF MAN

For 30 years, he kept his secret until in 1922, when a similar find was about to be announced and he was prompted to let the cat out of the bag. When faced with the discovery of humans in the same strata some 30 years before, the experts concluded that the skulls of *Pithecanthropus* were those of an extinct giant gibbon.

Following Dubois, several naturalists have laid stress on the resemblance between the Pithecanthropus remains and the corresponding portions of a Gibbon's skeleton. In that case, why not assume that Pithecanthropus represents a large form, a giant Ape, related to the Gibbon group?

This hypothesis is not new; it was clearly stated by several naturalists, particularly by Volz. The bone fragments that are in it favour; the most recent geological studies tending to post-date the layer also support it. The new argument, which I think I can bring forward in its favour, is that we know several examples of comparative cases.

In all countries during Pliocene and Quartenary times, there were giant forms of animals whose living representatives are now gradually reduced in size. In addition to the great edentates of South America, Megatherium and Giyptodon, which Cuvier named Giant Sloths and Armadillos, to the enormous Australian marsupial, Diprotodon, to a giant Pangolin found in Java in the same layer to Pithecanthropus, to the Trogon theriuim of European Pleistocene deposits, which is really a sort of giant beaver, in addition also, to the whole series of large running birds of Madagascar and of New Zealand recently extinct, examples amongst primates themselves are not awanting.

Pilgrim found in the Siwalik Hills was the remains of a monkey, which he named Dryopithecus giganteus. Megaladapis of the recent geological formations in Madagascar is none other than a giant Lemur. Archeolemur and Hadropithecus, from the same layers, are also Lemurs of larger size than the living forms; but they show morphological characters of a higher order, denoting tendencies towards the higher ape type for the tendency towards greater perfection is not exclusively confined to the human branch.

We may therefore consider that Pithecanthropus, discovered in the same zoological region as the modern Gibbons, may have been a large species either of the genus Gibbon, or rather of a closely allied genus related to the same group (emphasis added) (Boule 2010, 74–75).

Oops, again! The femur that Dubois found 50 feet from the skull was found to be fully human, and the skull was recognized as simply that of a giant gibbon and should not have been associated with the human femur at all.

Dubois deliberately lied to the world for 30 years, and scientists accepted his claim that the gibbon skull and human femur represented a new missing link he called *Pithecanthropus*. That was nothing less than a hoax. But in all fairness, the clairvoyant arrogance of some anthropologists who can describe a whole specimen from a few tidbits of bone is also a hoax. Many anthropologists have been swept away by this fever, and even the great Marcellin Boule documented this:

> These attempts coming from medical men and being based principally on human anatomy, are far too hypothetical, since we possess no data for the reconstruction of the base of the skull, the whole face, and all the apparatus of the lower jaw. It is astonishing to find a great paleontologist like Osborn also publishing attempts of this kind. Dubois ventured still further in the realm of imagination when he exhibited at the International Exhibition of 1900, in the Dutch Indies pavilion, a painted model of Pithecanthropus as he appeared in life! . . .

> But it must be distinctly stated, and in this case repeated, that resemblance does not always imply descent. Even if the sum of his known characters (poor at best), Pithecanthropus actually forms a structural link between that large ape and man, it does not necessarily follow that he must be regarded as a genealogical link, and this distinction is not, as has been asserted, merely a question of words. . . .
>
> In the present state of our knowledge, I do not think that we are yet in a position to believe that there was any direct descent between Pithecanthropus and Man, such as the genealogical tree prepared by Dubois would indicate (Boule 2010, 73).

This was not an unintentional and honest mistake, but another example of a deliberate misrepresentation of the empirical data to prop up the evolutionary illusion. G. K. Chesterton writes poignantly about this scientific ruse.

> He produces his little bone, a little collection of bones, and deduces the most marvelous things from it. He found in Java a piece of a skull, seeming from its contour to be smaller than the human. Somewhere near it he found an upright thigh-bone and in the same scattered fashion some teeth that were not human. If they all form part of one creature, which is doubtful, our conception of the creature would be almost equally doubtful. But the effect on popular science was to produce a complete and even complex figure, finished down to the last details of hair and habits. He was given a name as if he were an ordinary historical character. People talked of Pithecanthropus as of Pitt or Fox or Napoleon. Popular histories published portraits of him like the portraits of Charles the First or George the Fourth. A detailed drawing was reproduced, carefully shaded, to

show that the very hairs of his head were all numbered. No uninformed person looking at its carefully lined face and wistful eyes would imagine for a moment that this was the portrait of a thigh-bone; or of a few teeth and a fragment of a cranium (Chesterton 1925, 40–41).

Now, interestingly, after Dubois's Java find and before revealing the Wadjak skulls, another discovery was made in another excavation by Gustav Heinrich Ralph von Koenigswald (1902–1982) in 1906, about 40 miles away in Sangiran.

Von Koenigswald was born in Berlin, Germany. Due to his contact with Dutch geologist K. Martin, he was able to take part of a geologic survey in Java, financed in part by the Carnegie Foundation. During the survey, he unearthed fragments of a jawbone with some teeth and several fragments of a skull with one full skullcap. The findings were heralded as proof of the legitimacy of Dubois's *Pithecanthropus* and labeled *Pithecanthropus II, III, and IV*. Ironically, Dubois criticized this classification, but von Koenigswald did not budge.

What was the exact evidence that von Koenigswald found?

1. A juvenile calvarium from Mojokerto, 1931
2. A piece of a skull brought to him by a native assistant (when offered money, the natives broke up other pieces and brought him many splinter pieces)
3. One skullcap from Sangiran, which was an exact duplicate of Dubois's *Pithecanthropus*
4. One mandible from Sangiran
5. One maxilla with diastema, 1939
6. Jaws assigned by him to *Meganthropus paleojavanicus*
(The Java fossils are housed in the Senckenburg Museum.)

Here is the real kicker. Although all the experts had been forced to concede that this first *Pithecanthropus* found by Dubois was nothing more than a skull of a giant gibbon, and although the Sangiran skullcap found by von Koenigswald was exactly the same as that of Dubois, von Koenigswald's skull was considered by evolutionary paleontologists as a legitimate ancestor to man. Hence, his classification of *Pithecanthropus* remained viable in their imaginary ladder of evolution to man.

Why? Because they desperately need it to shore up their empty chain of intermediates from the presupposed evolution of apes to man.

Further discoveries of this giant gibbon would continue to be placed in the *Pithecanthropus* lineage in order to fill this embarrassing gap. The reader must understand that across our planet in times past, animals grew much larger than their counterparts today. That is what Boule meant when he referred to Dubois's *Pithecanthropus* as a giant gibbon. In Australia, there were giant kangaroos, rhino-like marsupials that were as large as a cow (*diprotodonts*).

There was also a much wider differentiation in the fauna than the meager character complex of the few species presently extant after the catastrophe of the Great Flood. The variety of life on our planet today is but a miniscule fraction of what the planet exhibited before the Global Flood. In Australia, there was a marsupial "leopard," a 400-pound flightless bird that made the ostrich look like a canary. Eagles once soared through the skies with a wingspan of 10 feet. Paleontologists refer to that universal phenomenon as the megafauna.

The apes were no different. There were giant gibbons and a wide variety of robust apes similar to modern-day gorillas, chimpanzees, and orangutans, which are now all extinct. These giant apes often had a considerably larger skull capacity than their modern counterparts, indicative of the gigantism phenomenon of the First Earth.

The increase in their cranial capacity may seem to make them an ideal transitional form between modern apes and modern man, while all along they are simply giant forms of extinct varieties of apes. This miscalculation has been at the root of a lot of the misinformation regarding our supposed ancestors.

The biblical record gives us a description of the antediluvian world that is much closer to God's original intent for Earth. And the physical record found in the fossils supports this view. Everything grew bigger, stronger, and more robust, from the insects to the reptiles to the mammoths.

The vegetation was so rich and dense that it could support an incredibly more diverse variety of organisms. What few and meager forms remain represented in our present ecosystem are but a mere fraction in number and in size of the variants that once roamed our luscious antediluvian planet. And we can see this trend even in man, for Cro-Magnon man also had a greater cranial capacity than modern man. All the ancient civilizations record the vastly superior longevity of early man compared to modern man.

Evolutionists immediately dismiss this information as mythological, simply because it does not match their preconception of the evolution of man toward a more refined and perfect specimen. Instead, it seems to point toward the Judeo-Christian consensus that recognizes the downward deterioration of our planet and man, which leads to the inevitable decline of civilizations as we continue on our path of rebellion toward God.

When considering our present fauna, we are but a shadow of what we once were. Man's longevity had been declining all the way up to our modern times. It has been only in the last century that, through the advancements of industrialization in food production and the miracles of modern medicine, we have been able to somewhat reverse that course. These technical advancements have raised the standard of living for humans and improved their general diet, causing us to grow almost a foot taller than the average size of a man in the past two centuries..

The average height of a man during the Civil War was around five feet four inches. I will never forget when I saw for the first time the uniform of a Confederate soldier displayed in the Smithsonian Institute. It was so small that I thought it was a child's uniform. And the low doors and narrow stairs in some of the 800-year-old German pubs I have visited attest to the same phenomenon. The average height of Western man in the third millennium is now approaching six feet.

The forward vector of time does not support evolution but rather devolution in all species. In fact, this recent upswing in our size is only possible because of the direct impact of the quality of our diet. Advancements in modern farming have provided a better diet during our time than in the past.

Similarly, those species who lived on the First Earth with a more abundant variety of foods were, for the most part, more robust and larger. As a result, there were significant differences within each of the species. In other words, a much wider character complex existed within the species. Some were larger, and others were smaller. The variability within each kind was definitely much greater.

The evolutionary idea that a successive lineage from apes to man can be made by sticking these giant ape skulls between modern apes and man is an absolute joke. Using the same evolutionary logic, if we were to compare the size of the skull of an ancient eagle, which had a 10-foot wingspan, to our modern eagles, we could easily say that our modern eagles were the ancestors of the ancient eagles that lived during the time of the megafauna. Nevertheless, evolutionists, using this skewed logic, place the skulls of giant extinct apes artificially into our lineage because they desperately need some transitional forms.

The choice to do so is more than deceptive when one considers the case of *Pithecanthropus*. As a matter of fact, today, most evolutionists now speak of the *Pithecanthropus* as belonging to the category of *Homo erectus*. It must be noted that when *Pithecanthropus* was first "invented," they were considered to be men-like apes (*Homo habilis*). But due to the scarcity of fossils in the *Homo erectus* category, they have, out of necessity, been artificially elevated to the ape-like men category.

In the face of this kind of fabrication and fraudulent science, the absolute certainty and confidence in the interpretive powers Darwinists exude to the public is astonishing to me. It seems absolutely deplorable to me that scientists would dogmatically and tenaciously hold onto their conclusions, even when the evidence they produced for *Pithecanthropus* had been shown to be the remains of giant gibbons.

Both Boule and Vallois confirmed that von Koenigwald's finds were simply those of the same giant gibbon Dubois had found. The late Marcellin Boule was the director of the French Institute of Human Paleontology and an evolutionist.

In spite of the fact that these fossils were clearly shown to be those of a giant extinct gibbon, evolutionists continue to speak of *Pithecanthropus* as if he really were an ancestor of man. Why?

The reason is plain and simple. Because, without *Pithecanthropus* and *Sinanthropus* as fillers, evolutionists would have a gap of 3 million years between *Australopithecine* and modern man and nothing to show the sequential evolution they imagine. They just can't afford a 3-million-year gap and maintain that there is some continuity in their imagined sequential lineage. In other words, there are two groups of still photographs at each end of a 3-million-year movie filmstrip.

Evolutionists claim that 1.5 million to 1.9 million years ago, the *Australopithecine* evolved, increasing his cranial capacity from about 400 cc. to 800–900 cc., becoming *Homo erectus*. The *Australopithecine* is in the lower category of *Homo habilis* (men-like apes). Without the *Pithecanthropus* and *Sinanthropus*, they would have had nothing in the middle category of *Homo erectus* (ape-like men).

According to the out-of-Africa scenario, which is perhaps the most popular, evolutionists believe that *Pithecanthropus* migrated out of Africa and populated India and Eurasia and then moved as far east as China and down into Java. Others believe that they evolved separately in these continents. However, most evolutionists agree that the likelihood of man having evolved twice is quite unlikely.

The next example brought forth to fill this newly created *Homo erectus* category is *Sinanthropus*. The story of *Sinanthropus* begins with a curious find shortly before World War II in Peking, China.

Peking Man: *Sinanthropus*

Dr. Davidson Black, professor of anatomy at Union Medical College in Peking, found a single tooth, a lower molar. Apparently, having learned nothing from the peccary tooth of *Hesperopithecus haroldcooki*, Dr. Black confidently made an astounding prognosis. From this fragmentary evidence, before anything else was excavated, he announced to the world that he had discovered the remains of an ancient hominid and named this creature *Sinanthropus pekinsis*, which later became popularly known as Peking Man.

Did Mr. Black forget the embarrassment of Henry Fairfield Osborn for his *Hesperopithecus haroldcooki*? His categorical declaration based on a single tooth was met with great skepticism by all except the zealous evolutionists hankering for the substantiation of their cherished theory. The pressure to substantiate his claim must have been tremendous.

Later on, some 25 miles outside of Peking, China, at Chakoutien, Black claimed that he found fragments of some 30 skulls, 11 mandibles, 47 teeth, and a few small fragments of limb bones. These fossils came from a cave in some limestone cliffs. The initial cave was later referred to as the lower cave since a second cave was later excavated above it. In the upper cave, they found fragments of some 10 men.

The entire story is shrouded with mystery since all the material excavated has disappeared, leaving only two teeth for scientists to study. Sometime between 1941 and 1945, the "real" fossils disappeared, and all we have left are plaster copies and descriptions made by Franz Weidenreich.

It was Weidenreich, in an office at the American Museum of Natural History, who later merged *Sinanthropus* and *Pithecanthropus* into a new category called *Homo erectus*. At that time, he presumed that von Koenigswald had been killed by the invading Japanese. After the war, von Koenigswald was released from a prisoner of war camp and joined Weidenreich at the American Museum of Natural History.

Numerous stories have been offered, attempting to account for the mysterious disappearance of the skulls in China, the most common of which is that the Japanese seized them in World War II. Why the Japanese would be particularly averse to proving man's descent from apes is not quite clear, especially when their elitist mentality quite nicely correlated with the evolutionary mantra of the survival of the fittest. What possible national interest the Japanese would have in absconding anthropological evidence has never been addressed.

As a matter of fact, von Koenigswald was imprisoned by the Japanese when they invaded Java, and although he had managed to hide most of his fossils, they did confiscate a skullcap. What history does show is that the Japanese did not destroy it but rather presented it to Emperor Hirohito. It was returned after the war.

Prior to that, in 1937, von Koenigswald had invited Weidenreich to visit Java in order to examine his recent excavations. Weidenreich went on to China to study the fossils of *Sinanthropus*. In 1939, von Koenigswald took several of his fossils and traveled to Peking in order to compare the two species with Weidenreich's. The similarities were so acute that both scientists determined they were of the same species and thus abandoned the genus *Sinanthropus* in favor of the earlier genus *Pithecanthropus*. Sometime after that, Weidenreich instead placed both under the new classification of *Home erectus* (upright man), which brought the fossils of *Pithecanthropus* and *Sinanthropus* to a higher level in the evolutionary ascent toward man and further away from *Homo habilis* with the simple swish of their evolutionary wands.

So what have we learned thus far? We have the skullcaps of giant gibbons in Java and a few unverifiable plaster molds of God knows what from Peking, which now form the lynchpin between man and *Homo habilis*. Sounds like a real solid case of scientific nonsense the likes of which would not have been admitted at a high school science exhibit.

On the basis of the evidence at hand, in a court of law, the judge would soundly boot them out of the courtroom. The evidence of plaster casts is legally nothing more than hearsay and would be totally inadmissible as evidence of anything but wishful thinking and smoke and mirrors in a court of law. Oh, but they do have two teeth.

Notwithstanding, evolutionists have since determined that both *Sinanthropus* and *Pithecanthropus* are really one and the same creature. That really means that they are both fossils of the same extinct giant gibbon. That is to say, according to Boule and Vallois, there is less difference between *Pithecanthropus* and *Sinanthropus* than within the variety that is usually found within one species, such as Neanderthal Man.

Le Gros Clark says:

> The genus Sinanthropus (Peking Man) was at first based on a single tooth and the name was retained and employed for many years, even by those who felt dubious about its validity.
>
> *With further discoveries in China and Java, it became clear that Sinanthropus was really not distinguishable from Pithecanthropus (Java Man)* and it was included in the genus of early hominids. Now, however, even the generic term Pithecanthropus, has been discarded for most anthropologists have agreed that the type to which it was applied comes more properly within the genus Homo, with the specific distinction of *Homo erectus* (emphasis added) (Clark 1955, 22).

The further discoveries in China to which Clark is referring are the plaster casts, and the further discoveries in Java are those of von Koenigswald. So in essence, what we have is nothing more than an extinct, giant gibbon that lived in Java and China, which was initially regarded by all as man-like ape in form and now has been reclassified as ape-like man.

The name *Pithecanthropus* associated with the dubious Dubois has therefore been dropped for obvious propaganda reasons, and the name *Homo erectus* has been given to the giant gibbon. Even if we were to unearth 6,000 *Pithecanthropus* or *Sinanthropus* skulls, all we would have is 6,000 skulls of an extinct giant gibbon.

Lacking any other in-betweens to prop up their imagined evolutionary ladder, this extinct gibbon has been ceremoniously elevated artificially to the *Homo erectus* (upright men) category lest the emptiness of that category cause much anxiety among evolutionists. Since that time, other fossils have been added to the *Homo erectus* category, which is distinctly different in morphology. We will address this later.

Returning to the curious case of *Sinanthropus*, glaring and conspicuous by its absence is any record of long bones associated with these 30 plaster casts of skulls. What are the chances that 30 skulls would become fossilized while the corresponding long bones would disappear? Could it be that the long bones so clearly pointed to simian origin that they were conveniently overlooked?

To me, it smacks a little of the dubious Dubois's Wadjak skulls. The pressure created by his premature declaration of the existence of a link between apes and man (*Sinanthropus*) with only one tooth as evidence may have played a part in this scenario. The sheer audacity displayed by evolutionists that imagine they can declare dogmatically such extravagant claims with such scarce evidence as a single tooth is without question unscientific and can only be accredited to subjective extrapolations made solely on their preconceived bias of an evolutionary ascent from ape to man. Even Boule, a committed evolutionist, comments on this audacious tendency in paleontologists he found in Cuvier.

> This poverty of material is not only regrettable in itself; there is a danger that it may lead us to serious error. It may be said that practically every day we learn, often at the

expense of our pride as paleontologists, that incomplete evidences must be interpreted with great caution; that *the famous law of correlation of characters, formulated by Cuvier, of which it has been so often said that it enabled him to reconstruct an entire fossil by means of a single bone of its skeleton, is very often at fault; that nature takes a kind of pleasure in varying combinations in the most unforeseen manner, and that she produces associations of characters expressly made to lead astray such naturalists and still retain absolute faith in the attractive Cuverian legend.*

In reality, in order fully to appreciate the nature of a fossil animal, and to assign to its true place in the group to which it belongs, mere fragments of bones are in most cases insufficient (emphasis added) (Boule 2010, 65).

Yet the evolutionary hypothesis is based entirely on the Cuverian legend, the famous law of correlation of characters formulated by Cuvier. It is that presupposition that associations in character stipulate genealogical connections. By assuming that animals evolve, they choose character similarities that provide for them the illusion of genealogical continuity.

They can then assume the supposed stage of the animal's development and extrapolate from that assumption how the animal would have been, using only fragmentary fossils as their base. But in the case of *Sinanthropus*, this is especially poignant when the basis for Black's audacious conclusion came from only one tooth. Indeed, Black must have been a master clairvoyant. It is strange, indeed, that none of the skulls are now available for scientific inquiry. All we have left are plaster molds.

Moreover, almost every skull cast showed signs of having been broken as if the creatures had been hunted and taken to the cave to be eaten by another hunter. The question then becomes, "Who is that hunter?" And if the creature had been hunted for food, where are the long bones?

Weidenreich, who is supposedly responsible for having made the plaster casts, thinks they were brought into the caves by hunters, but as trophies. In essence, the skulls were trophies of the hunt. Of course, Weidenreich's explanation is that the creature hunted his own kind. But, I ask you, is it really conceivable that a creature such as this would have such a highly developed intelligence so as to require trophies?

Boule and Vallois expressed serious doubts about this claim. Comparing all the evidence surrounding the site and its stratigraphic level, it was obvious that the inhabitants of that region had a stone industry, as evidenced by the kilns unearthed. Gibbons do not build stone kilns, even if they were giant gibbons.

It is more in conformity to the whole body of archaeological evidence unearthed that the skulls were gibbons that were hunted by men. These, no doubt, are the same men who were found in the upper cave. Since the intellectual development of this supposed *Sinanthropus* with a cranial capacity of only about 800 cc. could not account for the building of the sophisticated stone industry found in these premises, it is the more logical conclusion.

On the very site where these skulls were supposedly unearthed, thousands of quartz stones with large cut limestone were brought from a considerable distance. The quarrying of the limestone had dug a gash of about 200 yards wide and 50 yards deep into the hill.

A layer of soot on one side and enormous heaps of ash all about are testimony to a once thriving stone industry, a feat that is impossible for these supposed human ancestors possessing a limited intelligence. Moreover, the custom of eating monkeys is an ancient tradition in China, and monkey brains are considered a delicacy, even today.

Clearly, to the objective student, there can be no doubt that the lime kilns were created for a stone industry. The tools found were of fine workmanship and undoubtedly of human origin. Gravers and scrapers are not primitive tools and bespeak a higher level of civilization than could conceivably be ascribed to a creature like *Sinanthropus*.

The megafauna of the antediluvian time is evidenced here in these giant gibbons that they are so desperately trying to jam like a square peg into a round hole in our ancestry. Both the Predilluvian men we call Neanderthal and Cro-Magnon possessed a greater skull capacity than Postdiluvian or modern man.

Why should it be any surprise that Antediluvian apes were, as all the other animals, much larger in those days? Certainly, the existence of giant gibbons with a cranial capacity that far exceeded their modern counterparts would be in line with all the observable data of that time period for every other species.

Since that time, several new fossil finds have been added to the *Homo erectus* classification to bolster its depth. In 1961, a highly eroded (by wind and sand) skull was found in Chad by Yves Coppens. It was called *Tchadanthropus uxoris*, which highly mimicked the *Australopithecines*. It was therefore initially labeled a specimen of *Homo habilis* to which all the *Australopiths* belong but later ceremoniously elevated to *Homo erectus* like the *Pithecanthropus*.

Moreover, these remains, now classified as *Homo erectus*, show absolutely no evolution within their species. The fact is that in the comparative analysis of all the *Homo erectus* fossils found, there is no appreciable change in morphology within that species that evolutionists can point to as a progression toward *Homo sapiens*. In other words, those that were apes remained apes, and those who were men remained men.

> More importantly, there was no approach toward Homo sapiens in forehead development or, we may infer, in intellect. G. P. Rightmire has in fact, measured several features of the skull and teeth of Homo erectus. He has found no evidence that any of the features, including cranial capacity, underwent statistically significant change during more than

> *a million years of biological time. This does not rule out a small amount of change, but as far as we can tell, throughout his existence Homo erectus did not vary greatly in form.* He was a distinctive long-lived species. Certainly he varied somewhat in form from time to time and place to place, but less variability is displayed among all known specimens of Homo erectus than among the living populations of our own species (emphasis added) (Stanley 1981, 148).

The real truth in regard to this supposedly solid sequential ladder from ape to man is that from the very beginning, every attempt to make a solid sequence has failed miserably as new evidence was unearthed. The theory of evolution has been pawned off as scientific fact, using the supposed sequence of the fossil record as empirical evidence of the evolution of man. But in reality, this sequential lineage has been simply a fabrication in their minds, which time and time again has been discredited and often purposefully rearranged by their instinctual bias.

It seems that the necessity of creating an evolutionary ladder from ape to man plays a crucial role in the imaginations of paleontologists. Boule, in the first quarter of the previous century, makes mention of that fact already rearing its head.

> Although fossil monkeys are absolutely unknown in North America, Ameghino nevertheless announced the existence of higher monkeys in South America, on account of anatomical remains which have been subject of much discussion. The late paleontologist has described an atlas vertebrae and a femur from Monte Hermoso, which he considers a Miocene locality. . . . He sought to prove that these bones belonged to a creature which united his Homunculus to the genus Homo, and which he named Tetraprothomo. . . . He was thus led to conceive a completely new human phylogeny: Tetraprothomo was said to have been followed by Tri-

prothovw, this by Diprothomo, which was supposed to have given rise to Prothonio, from which in its turn would have arisen the genus Homo. We shall see later that these stages were purely figments of the imagination. . . .

It must be confessed, however, that paleontology has not yet revealed any indisputable transition form, any material proof of hereditary connection between the ape form and the human form, for we cannot attribute any conclusive value to the Homunculus of Ameghino, or the Antluopdiis of Schlosser. The significance that the later scientists attribute to Propliopithecus is quite hypothetical. Sivapithecus is still only a monkey, although it shows very interesting tendencies towards the human structure (emphasis added) (Boule 2010, 59–60, 65).

Homunculus patagonicus is an extinct monkey that lived in the area of Argentina, whose fossil was discovered by Ameghino in 1891. His imagined lineage of man from this South American monkey was, however, rejected by European paleontologists. But Boule clearly felt that the European choice of *Sivapithecus* from Northern Italy is not much better.

At that point, *Ramapithecus* became the accepted specimen that modern paleontologists believed to be in our ancestry. As we will later discuss, *Ramapithecus* may be the female of *Sivapithecus*. Modern evolutionists attribute *Ramapithecus* as our ancient ancestor occupying the unique place after *Dryopithecus* and before the 11-million-year gap to the *Australopithecines,* which first formed their category of men-like apes.

Without question, most evolutionists today regard Ameghino's lineage to *Homo* from *Homunculus patagonicus* as nothing more than fanciful imagination. But so was Dubois's representation of *Pithecanthropus*, and yet they did not discard his figment of imagination. What's more, they have sought to expand it.

To begin with the imagined sequence is more like a disjointed wish list that changes with the wind as new evidence discredits the previous claims. More strikingly, there are unexplainable giant gaps between the links that should be clearly substantiated by fossil evidence, were evolution true. Again, the evolution of the theory of evolution is the only real evolution that is taking place.

As we will see, this supposedly concrete evidence for man's evolution from apes is anything but concrete. Specimens that were once dogmatically shown as definitive proof of our ancestral lineage from apes are time and again found to be only an extinct ape species.

In several cases such as the Wadjak skulls, the finding of fully human skulls in the same strata or even in previous strata showed conclusively that humans lived either at the same time or prior to them. That should have thoroughly discredited their place as our ancestors, and yet they somehow mysteriously remain enshrined in their imagined lineages.

As we will now see, the lineage from *Hominoid* to *Hominid* is as ever-shifting as the desert sands. According to classical Darwinists, the lineage of the old-World monkeys *Cercopithedae* evolved some time before the modern gibbon from a common ancestral *Anthropoidea*. Further up the family tree lived a monkey known as *Proconsul*, which initially was thought to be the common ancestor for apes and humans.

From *Proconsul* evolved the *Dryopithecus*, which is now believed to be the common ancestor of both apes and man. Following *Dryopithecus*, we find in this ladder toward the ascent of man the creature known as *Ramapithecus*, which, according to their first fossil reconstruction, exhibited a more human-like jaw. Both *Dryopithecus* and *Ramapithecus* are considered *Hominoid*, or fully ape-like creatures, but they are so closely related that they could easily be variants of the same species.

Moving up the evolutionary ladder from *Ramapithecus*, the *Hominid* classes began to evolve. Hence, the order in the old classical lineage was as follows:

1. *Dryopithecus* (*Hominoid*)
2. *Ramapithecus* (*Hominoid*)
3. The first to evolve as hominids were the *Australopithecine* (*Homo habilis*).
4. Then came *Pithecanthropus*, *Sinanthropus*, and *Rhodensis Soloensis* (*Homo erectus*)
5. Then evolved Cro-Magnon and Neanderthals. The Neanderthals were initially thought to be our ancestors but are now recognized as fully human and an extinct form of man that appeared after Cro-Magnon. Paleontologists would now include Neanderthals alongside Cro-Magnon under *Homo sapiens*.

In other words, from *Ramapithecus* to Cro-Magnon, there are four still photographs or four separate species in the evolutionary movie reel that should contain thousands of pictures or species ever changing in almost imperceptible steps through 14 million years. Each of those photographs may have several different representations of the same creature, but these are the normal variants within any given kind.

In the *Homo erectus* category, which initially contained only *Pithecanthropus* and *Sinanthropus* (considered a single species and which are, in fact, just very big gibbons), new fossil finds are being added to beef up the sagging credibility of the first two candidates. Some are apes and others are human hybrid variations with Neanderthals, which ought not to be included in any category that contains apes.

Homo georgicus

In 1991, a Georgian scientist named David Lordkipanidze, assisted by an international team, unearthed fossilized skulls and jaws in

THE DESCENT OF MAN

Diagram 11. The Classical Human Evolutionary Lineage

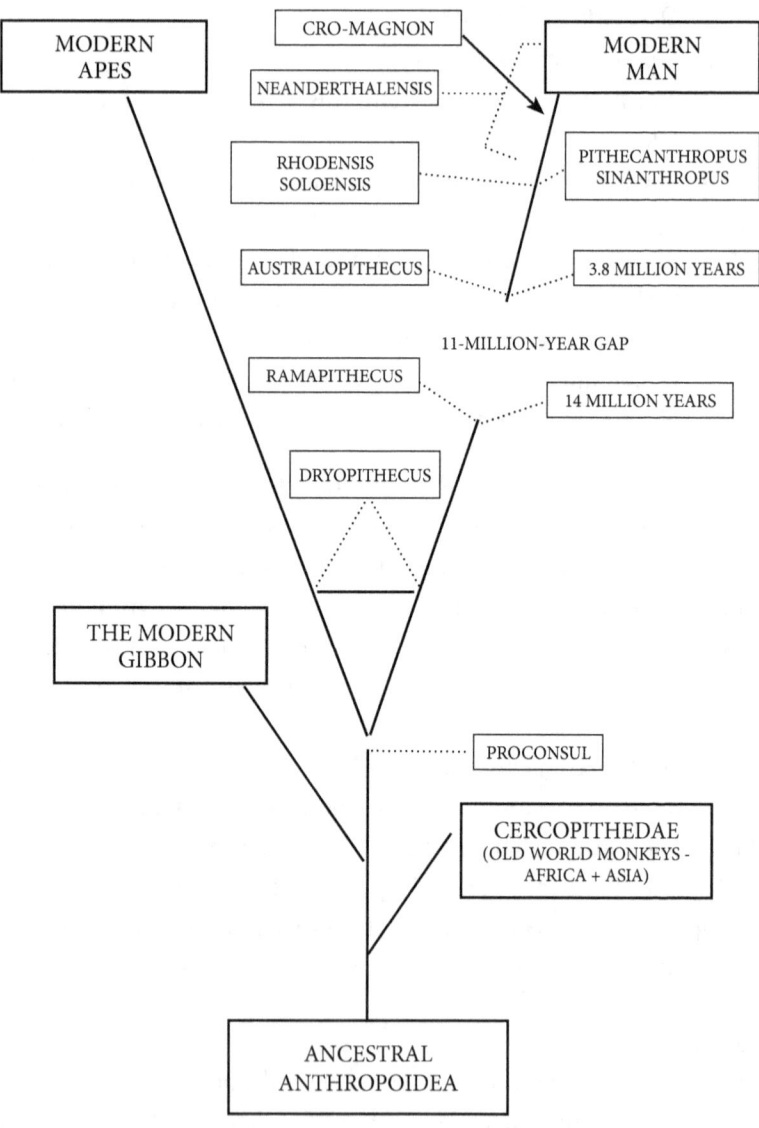

Dmanisi, Georgia. Initially, they thought these remains belonged to *Homo ergaster*, but the size difference finally convinced them to classify it as a separate species, *Homo georgicus*. The skull was around 600 cc., much smaller than the *Pithecanthropus* at 900 cc.

In spite of its much smaller cranium, the Dmanisi creature was placed by paleontologists in the *Homo erectus* category as a divergent subgroup, calling it *Homo erectus georgicus*. This creature with a much smaller cranium had a slightly flatter face, which prompted paleontologists to classify it in the *Homo erectus* category.

When the fossil skull D2700 was unearthed, it was at that time the smallest *Hominin* cranium ever discovered outside Africa. In 2003, however, a much smaller cranium was found in the Iles of Flores and named *Homo erectus floresiensis*.

These apes had primitive skulls and upper bodies that were consistent with all apes but were said to have a more advanced spinal column and lower legs, which allowed them greater mobility. They did not have the distinctly human foot with unopposable toes aligned straight for fast locomotion. They were fully simian animals that happened to have a slightly flatter face. Again, the Cuverian legend, the famous law of correlation of characters formulated by Cuvier, works its magic to link species in an imagined genealogical sequence based on certain anatomical similarities.

If we begin with the presupposition that evolution is a fact, then any anomalies observed in variations of apes that might be closer to the human form can be categorized in an arbitrarily created ladder of progression. In other words, by comparing whatever characteristics the different variants have that better match human beings, the assumption is automatically made that they are closer to us genealogically. That artificial construct is no more proof of evolution than if I were to form such a ladder with existing variants of any given kind.

An equally valid case can be made that these apes, prior to the Great Flood, had a much richer variation within their kinds than we can observe in our more limited biosphere today. *Homo georgicus* was just an ape with a slightly larger cranium than modern apes and a slightly flatter face than most apes, but it was fully simian in all respects.

Homo ergaster

The case of *Homo ergaster* is, however, quite distinctly different, although there is still great disagreement among paleontologists on its classification. The name published by Colin Groves and Vratislav Mazak in 1975 comes from the Greek word for *workman*. Some view *Homo ergaster* as belonging to *Homo erectus* and consider it distinctly the African variant of *Pithecanthropus* and *Sinanthropus* in Asia. But there is a great gulf between the simian Asiatic candidates and the fossils of the Turkana Boy, which are distinctly human.

The original find was a mandible (KNM-ER 992) unearthed near Lake Turkana in Kenya (then Lake Rudolf). In 1984, a more complete skeleton was unearthed by paleontologists Kamoya Kimeu and Ann Walker, also near Lake Turkana, Kenya. The juvenile skeleton was nicknamed the Turkana Boy. It was later discovered that the Turkana Boy suffered from a disease that malformed his spinal column, causing narrower cervical vertebrae, which led the discoverers to think it was a more ancient creature since his column was much narrower than man's.

But outside of this anomaly, the almost complete skeleton (KNM-WT 15000), missing only the hands and feet, showed some remarkable similarities to man. There is a wide gulf between the ape-like features of *Pithecanthropus* and *Sinanthropus* and the human-like morphology of the Turkana Boy.

There is also a significant difference in the dimorphism (difference between males and females of a species) observed in *H. ergaster* and the *australopithecine*. That is, around 20 percent less dimorphism is observed in *H. ergaster* than documented in the *Australopithecines*.

Paleontologists view this difference as an evolutionary advancement toward the human species from their more primitive counterparts since humans show less dimorphism as well.

It must be noted that the morphological difference between the Turkana Boy and modern man is less than the difference between modern man and Neanderthals. In fact, the Turkana Boy may be a hybrid of Cro-Magnon and Neanderthals, as we shall see.

Another feature often mentioned as evidence of *H. ergaster's* advanced evolutionary state compared to the *Australopithecines* is the less sloping forehead and less prominent zygomata (cheekbones), which would make it a step closer to the shape of the human skull from that of typical apes. There is no doubt that the difference between them is great. In fact, they exhibit the same features found in Neanderthals—heavy eyebrows, thicker bones, more massive bodies, and sloping hyper-dolichocephalic skulls.

Let us take a closer look at Turkana Boy (KNM-WT 15000). There is no denying that this skeleton has features that are human-like. His much larger body and cranium are indicative of that. Although the Turkana Boy has been found to have a disease that created a much thinner spinal column, his size (five feet three inches tall) indicates that as an adult, he may have reached well over six feet in height. His cranium (880 cc.) has a volume that is consistent with the juvenile variability found in *Homo sapiens*.

It is almost impossible to guess what his cranial capacity would be at adulthood since it is impossible to guess how tall he would be with any precision. Some archaeologists speculate that his skull size at maturity would be around 1100 cc. But this is sheer speculation. It could well have been 1900 cc. In either case, it is well within the character complex of modern man, which ranges from 900 cc. to 1800 cc.

Evolutionists would be inclined to make his cranial capacity lower than that of man in order to make him a less developed ancestor. But the already 880 cc. capacity at the age of eight would undoubtedly make his skull size predictably much greater than evolutionists wish.

Estimates of the ages in juveniles are made from both tooth eruption and epiphyses, which separate the centers of bone formation at one or both ends of the bones in juveniles. Therefore, the joining or fusing of the epiphyses with the mid-section of long bones is a criterion for estimating the age of juveniles.

The tooth eruption of the Turkana Boy, if compared to modern humans, would equate to a juvenile of about 11 to 12 years old. If it were compared to apes, it would be about six to nine years old. If it were compared to Neanderthals, it would be about seven to nine years old because they reached puberty by eight or nine years old, maturing much faster than Cro-Magnon or modern man.

In the Turkana Boy, most of the centers of bone formation had appeared but had not fused, particularly in the hip bones; hence, it would indicate a juvenile who, compared to Neanderthals, would be between seven and nine years old.

The cranium of the Turkana Boy as well as KNM-ER 3733, another skull that shows many of the same features, is also dolichocephalic, a distinct feature they have in common with Neanderthal men.

It is rather doubtful that enough fossils have been found to truly establish a character complex for them; thus, predictions based on a few partial skeletons are speculative at best, especially when we know that the Turkana Boy suffered from a skeletal disease. What we can say is that although a bit more slender, they more closely match the morphology of the Neanderthals than anything else.

If I were a betting man, I would wager that DNA samples would show that the Turkana Boy has a genetic interconnection between Neanderthals and man but that none of his Neanderthal DNA markers will be found in our modern species. Evolutionists will no doubt claim that these hybrids are rather ancestors of both lineages, but in fact, it is more probable that they are simply hybrids that, like the Neanderthals, did not make it across the bottleneck of the Great Flood.

Nevertheless, they were radically different from the distinctly simian aspects of *Pithecanthropus* and *Sinanthropus* in the size of their crania as well as their morphology and should therefore not be categorized in the same *Homo erectus* group. Instead, these hybrids should be recognized as another distinct race of humans, like Neanderthals. Their ability to form specialized weapons such as spears and their ability to harness the use of fire and other tools separate them from the apes, which only use rocks or sticks not modified in any way through intelligence. The similarity between the Turkana Boy, Neanderthals, and Cro-Magnon is simply the evidence of interbreeding between the two distinct races of the humankind prior to the Great Flood. This evidence is not limited to Africa.

Homo heidelbergensis

In 1907, several workmen digging in a commercial sandpit near the German village of Mauer found a massive human-like jaw. The following year, Otto Schoetensack wrote a formal description of that jaw. Since it was near the city of Heidelberg, Germany, he named it *Homo heidelbergensis*.

The similarities between Neanderthal and *Homo heidelbergensis* have been downplayed lately in order to avoid the idea that it may have been a hybrid. Evolutionists would much rather make *heidelbergensis* an ancient descendant than a hybrid to prop up their imagined lineage of Neanderthal. Nevertheless, Boule, who also proposed that it was a more ancient descendant, candidly spoke of the amazing similarities.

> The lower jaws of Homo Neanderthalensis resemble the jaw of Homo heidelbergensis (i.e. the Mauer Jaw) in their general form, strength, and dimensions, so much so that if the Mauer jaw is articulated with the La Chapelle skull, the general aspect of the whole skull is little altered. It is true that certain differences do exist, but the points of resemblance are so great that they lead us to believe in a close, if not direct, relationship between the ancient owners of these jaws (Boule 2010, 144).

Most evolutionists now divide *Homo erectus* by geographical notation. *Homo ergaster* is considered the African variation. *Homo heidelbergensis* is considered the European variation, while *Homo erectus* is considered the Asiatic variation. But neither the *H. ergaster* nor the *H. heidelbergensis* variants is related to either *Pithecanthropus* or *Sinanthropus* as they contend. Unlike the morphology of the creatures that were first labeled as *Homo erectus*, the anatomical aspects of the legs and arms of both the Turkana Boy and *heidelbergensis* are exactly the same as humans.

Their skeletal morphology and cranial capacity are within our range and not that of the giant gibbons. In fact, the specimens of *heidelbergensis* found in the Sima de los Huesos (pit of bones) inside a cave at Atapuerca Spain are quite clearly the fossils of a hybrid between Cro-Magnon and Neanderthal that exhibited a larger cranial capacity than our average human beings today. Those could hardly be considered in the same category as the *Pithecanthropus*.

The remains of some 30 individuals were found; all of them were either teenagers or very young adults. That seems to indicate that they might have been killed sacrificially by throwing them into the abyss of the pit. Pits in occult symbolism universally represented entrances into the underworld.

From the earliest days of our planet, humankind has sacrificed other humans inside caves and into pits during their occult rituals. That would be quite in line with the Neanderthals who, according to Hebrew tradition, were nearly all cannibals whose worship of the Mother Goddess introduced to our world human sacrifices, eating human flesh, and drinking blood in occult rituals.

The archaeological evidence corroborates their penchant for cannibalism. At nearly all the sites, evidence of cannibalism abounds, showing that there was, indeed, a distinct difference in their spiritual leanings. They were bred for a single purpose, and their physical traits were designed to overpower and conquer the Adamic race—to conquer Cro-Magnon man and profane the lineage of the promised

Messiah announced in Genesis 3:15 by the very voice of God. That was the very first prophecy given to humans after their expulsion from the Garden.

In 2008, the tooth of a young Neanderthal child was discovered in the Scladina cave in Belgium. It was subjected to X-rays with a machine called a synchrotron, which provides an image with high resolution that enables us to see growth lines and stress lines in an individual. The three-dimensional hatch of daily and longer periodic growth lines in the teeth are like tree rings that provide a code. Stress lines enable scientists to analyze the life of the individual. To scientists' great surprise, this child, who was determined to be eight years old, was reaching puberty some four years earlier than modern humans. That means that Neanderthals were capable of reproducing at a much earlier age, a decided advantage over the children of Adam and Eve.

It seems they were genetically engineered to be an awesome force to reckon with for the Adamic or Cro-Magnon race. They were structured more massively with larger flaring lungs and most likely even possessed a superior intellect due to their larger brains. Add to this their knowledge of the craft of sorcery, and the Neanderthal was a formidable foe, indeed. Their larger brains created a greater need for nutrition, which eventually led them to use humans as part of their diets and become a threat to the Adamic race.

A comparison of the skulls of *H. ergaster, H. heidelbergensis,* and Neanderthals shows their distinct similarities and their dissimilarity to Cro-Magnon man. Notice that the shape of the skulls in *ergaster, heidelbergensis,* and *Neanderthalensis* is more elongated than the more rounded skull of Cro-Magnon. They have the distinct hyperdolichocephalic and larger skulls that are elliptical in shape rather than the more rounded and smaller skull of modern man.

All three have the characteristically heavy eyebrow ridges and more massive jaws. They have a sloping forehead and more pronounced cheekbones. Their bones are denser, and their frames are stockier than Cro-Magnon and modern man. Their mouths project

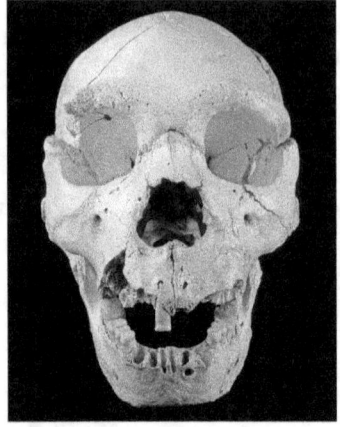

Homo heidelbergensis
Skull # 5 from Sima de los Huesos in Atapuerca, Spain

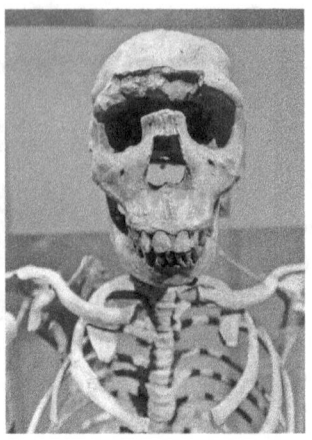

Homo ergaster
Skull of Turkana Boy

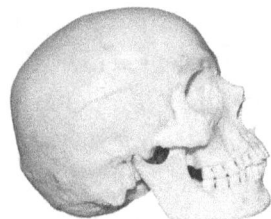
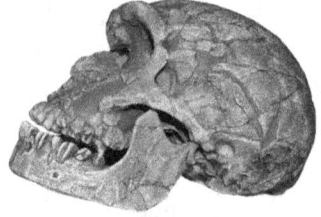

Cro-Magnon man and Homo Neanderthalensis

forward, while their chins recede. Their teeth are larger and more massive, and yet they are in every way quite similar to our own species. In fact, if we compare them to our character complex and not to a single cranium, we would see that they are simply variants of our kind prior to the Great Flood.

It might surprise you to know that human skulls in Australia have been found to exhibit some of these unambiguous common traits among the fossils, which paleontologists consider evolutionary stages. They include the supraorbital tori, the flattish receding foreheads, prognathic faces, and the large jaws found in Neanderthals and the two hybrid forms (*ergaster* and *heidelbergensis*).

In opposition to the evolutionary time frame, the remains from Kow Swamp in Victoria, Australia, have slightly more pronounced features than those found in New South Wales. But the intriguing thing is that the remains in Willander Lakes, Mungo, in South Wales (35,000 years) are, in fact, older than those of Kow Swamp (15,000 years). Hence, the more recent remains display the most pronounced features, which are supposed to be more ancient in the evolutionary ladder. And even more impressive, the Australian Cossack skull, which is supposedly only 13,000 years old, has even more robust features than the Kow Swamp skulls, making them appear almost gracile.

These modern aboriginal remains feature the same supraorbital tori, flattish receding foreheads, prognathic faces, and large jaws typical of the three aforementioned variations of the humankind. These features found in Australian aboriginals are simply variants of the human genome of our day. These genetic factors found in man were much more exaggerated prior to the Great Flood in the human variant Neanderthal and its hybrid breeds. They are in no way more ancient throwbacks to apes.

Evolutionists such as Boule, seeing these remarkable traits in aboriginal Australians, initially falsely concluded that they were a more primitive race and more closely related to Neanderthals.

> All that can be admitted in this respect is that the Australian group of men, certainly one of the least developed groups of modern mankind, is less far removed than other races from the primitive forms, and that, in consequence, it ought to have certain common characteristics in common with the Neanderthal type (Boule 2010, 141).

Nothing can be further from the truth. In fact, DNA studies have shown conclusively that Australian aboriginals are a more recent people than most of humankind. Moreover, none of the genetic markers in Neanderthals have been found in the Australian aboriginal people. There are no descendants of Neanderthals or of their hybrids left in the Second Earth. They were all wiped out during the death of the First Earth.

Now, most evolutionists readily admit that the diversity in modern man has been quite limited by some bottleneck in history where our genetic pool was severely curtailed. What we have represented in these three archaic variants (*ergaster*, *heidelbergensis*, and *Neanderthalensis*) are simply the variations of the human genome that existed prior to the Great Flood due to interbreeding between Neanderthal and Cro-Magnon. But the differences among these variants do not warrant separate classifications. They form the spectrum of the character complex of predilluvian humans. There is no evolution depicted by these fossils. There is only the devolution of the Adamic race created by the Nephilim.

In fact, the variation in the size of Predilluvian men was also great. Some hybrids were even taller than the typical Nephilim, such as the Turkana Boy, and perhaps less Neanderthal in appearance. Such are the specimens referred to as the Chancelade race and the Predmost race:

> Hardy excavated a rock shelter at Raymonden, a commune in Chancelade, near Perigueux, and found a human skeleton under the lower Magdalenian floors of occupation, that is to say, in the upper stages of the Reindeer Age. The doubled-up unnatural posture of the skeleton pointed to a deliberate burial. As at Mentone, the corpse must have been sprinkled with red ochre. The skeleton exhumed with great care, was examined by Dr. Testut, who established it as the type specimen of a new race called the Chancelade race. It is now at the Museum at Periofueux. . . . In 1891 they yielded a human skeleton, lying 4 meters below the surface of the soil rich in Mammoth and Rhinoceros remains. This skeleton

partly destroyed at the time of its discovery, is said by Obermaier to have been richly decked with ornaments; round about it there were collected more than six hundred pieces of the Tusk Shell (Dentaliuiit) once strung into a necklace or a breast ornament, several discs of stone pierced or decorated, and a tiny human figure wrought in ivory. Some bones preserved traces of deep red coloration. This again was also the case of true burial. *The skull badly preserved, is dolichocephalic; certain anthropologists refer it to the Cro-Magnon type, others regard it distinct from that type.*

The locality of Predmost near Prerau, which also lies in Moravia, possesses an important Paleolithic settlement enclosed in a covering of gravels and clays surrounding the "Hradisko" rock. Excavations carried out from time to time since the year 1880 have revealed a cold climate Pleistocene fauna, so rich that the Mammoth is represented by remains of 800 to 900 individuals. In addition this settlement has yielded a collection of flint instruments comprising more than 30,000 specimens, a whole series of products of an industry in ivory, in bone and in Reindeer horn, and works of art, in particular a curious statuette in ivory representing a Mammoth.

Some human remains have also been found at different times. In 1894 Maschka discovered a large burial ground containing forty complete skeletons, as well as the remains of six other individuals. The bodies were protected by a sort of stone rampart. The skeleton of a child bore a necklace formed of forty small oval beads of ivory. This burial must have been prior to the main archaeological layer, which belonged to the Solutrean period. *The skulls are dolichocephalic; the male skulls have marked orbital ridges; the long bones point to a great height (1.80 meters 5 feet 10.8 inches)* (emphasis added) (Boule 2010, 153–54).

All the skeletons above were considered Cro-Magnon but were recognized as having distinct peculiarities not commonly found among our modern human skeletons. These similarities with Neanderthals seem to point to hybridization and to a character complex prior to the Great Flood that was much greater in scope than presently evidenced among the descendants of those who survived the Great Flood.

The similarities have not escaped the notice of some evolutionists. Milford Wolpoff of the University of Michigan and Alan Thorne of the Australian National University have proposed the abolition of *Homo erectus* altogether on the grounds that the species is insufficiently distinct from *Homo sapiens*. They have concluded that these archaic *Homo sapiens*, including Neanderthals, should be reclassified into a single species that is subsequently subdivided into races. They contend that *Homo habilis* and *Homo erectus* are too far apart morphologically to both be called *Homo*.

Although the variability of this extreme dolichocephalic expression, as well as the supraorbital ridge and the pronounced cheeks (zygomatic arches) in humans, existed more commonly prior to this bottleneck, there is some evidence that certain environmental pressures may exacerbate their expressions. Arthur Custance has argued that these supposedly primitive features may be accentuated by their eating habits. Custance believed that the variations may be attributed entirely to the functioning of the jaw mechanism, which may affect the size and shape of the brow ridges, the forehead, and the zygomatic arch.

These supposed primitive features, he claims, are due to the eating of uncooked foods in childhood. He theorized that the chewing of raw meat and the act of tearing it from the bones (also chewing hides to soften them) would create a much more massive jaw. The process would deform the skull, depressing the skull, making the brow ridges more prominent, and forcing outward the zygomatic arch. Juveniles lacking bone-hardening substances such as calcium would be particularly prone to this deformation. He cites as known examples Hooten, Howells, and Hrdlicka (Custance 1975, 183–84, 208–211).

Boule, in describing the skull of Neanderthals, says:

> The maxillaries stand out as a continuation of their zygomatic arches, and accentuate the muzzle like form of the face. . . . In its dimensions the face exceeds the largest known human faces. . . . An immense development of the orbital arches characterizes all known skulls of Neanderthal Man. They unite in a projecting unbroken line. . . . Turner suggests that perhaps they heightened an appearance of ferocity which was of some value in the struggle for life. *In the opinion of many anatomists their development is directly related with that of the jaws and the apparatus concerned in mastication* (emphasis added) (Boule 2010, 123).

I may be more inclined to accept that this genetic trait may have been favored by cultures like Neanderthals (and their hybrids) who were inclined to eat raw meat, who needed a much higher daily caloric intake to maintain their more massive bodies. The genetic variability was not created by eating raw meats but selected favorably by the genetic pool of those who did. That is microevolution and not Lamarckian evolution or macroevolution at work.

Nevertheless, the point is that many of these fossil remains considered by evolutionists as ancestors to our race within the category of *Home erectus* and even some categorized as Cro-Magnon subsets are, in fact, nothing more than hybrids of Neanderthals and Cro-Magnon man, which display a gradation of traits, some more common to Neanderthals and others to Cro-Magnon.

We now continue in our examination of this fossil evidence to a more primitive level, following the evolutionary lineage from

Homo erectus to their supposed ancestors, *Homo habilis*. It must be noted that there is a greater similarity between *Pithecanthropus* or *Sinanthropus* and the *Australopithecines* than with the hybrids of Neanderthal, which evolutionists insist are supposed to also be in the *Homo erectus* category.

Australopithecus africanus and robustus

The next groups of fossils evolutionists claim to be our ancestors before *Homo erectus* are the *Australopithecines*. Two distinct varieties were initially classified. The more robust in form was *Zinjanthropus* or *Australopithecus robustus*. The more gracile variant was named *Australopithecus africanus*.

The story of *Australopithecus* began in 1924, when Raymond Dart found the remains of a hominoid and named it *Australopithecus africanus* (Southern Ape of Africa). He had originally labeled him simply an extinct ape, but after noticing some distinct features in the skull and teeth, which he interpreted as human-like, he then reclassified his find in the hominid category. The most celebrated of his fossils was found in a lime mine at Taung near the town of Kimberly, South Africa. The juvenile fossil remains were named the Taung Child.

Most of his working associates at the time, including Sir Arthur Keith, a renowned anatomist and fellow anthropologist, disagreed with Dart's conclusions. They asserted that this was nothing more than an ape with some interesting but irrelevant parallel features with man. Again, the Cuverian legend waves its magical wand and creates an imagined lineage of man.

> [B]ut after Dart examined the teeth further, he decided that *A. africanus* was a hominid. This claim created considerable controversy, most workers at that time claiming that *A. africanus* was an ape with some interesting but irrelevant parallel features with man (Gish 1979, 115).

On July 17, 1959, Dr. Louis Leakey and his wife found in the Olduvai Gorge of Tanzania another similar specimen that they named *Zinjanthropus* (East Africa Man). The name Zinj was taken from the medieval East African region of Zanj. Sponsored by the National Geographic Society, Leakey's findings were immediately popularized with the extravagant claims that he had made a unique and momentous scientific discovery of another of our ancestors. Only after the din subsided did Leakey admit that his discovery was nothing more than a variety of the same creature Dart had previously discovered.

Today, it is generally accepted that *Zinjanthropus* is simply a variant of *Australopithecus robustus* and related to *Australopithecus africanus*. Some minor differences between the two variants were noted. *A. africanus* measured on average about four feet high, while *A. robustus* averaged between four feet six inches and five feet, with more massive teeth and jaws. His cranial capacity was a bit larger than *A. africanus*, about 500 to 550 cc.

In addition, *A. robustus* possessed a more pronounced saggital and supramastoid crest, a bony ridge also found in gorillas and orangutans. These apes were obviously vegetarians with large molars approximately an inch across for processing coarse food. Initially, both were placed in our lineage, but after some time, *A. robustus* was removed, and *A. africanus*, which was more gracile and therefore more human-like, became the accepted ancestral link.

Their cranial capacity averaged 450 cc., which is slightly larger than a chimpanzee and about a third of man's cranial capacity. In time, the more gracile *Australopithecus africanus* became our accepted ancestor. *A. robustus* was seen as an evolutionary dead end and thrown out of the bus.

Drawings of *Australopithecine* were illustrated in all the textbooks of universities, and it was a foregone conclusion that the Darwinian model was yet again confirmed by the fossils—well, for a little while anyway.

On November 24, 1974, Donald Johansen discovered fossil remains of an even more slender variant of *Australopithecus* and labeled it *Australopithecus afarensis*. The fossil remains were of a female, who was named Lucy. It seems that the Beatles's song "Lucy in the Sky with Diamonds" had been played all through the night of the discovery (Johanson and Edey).

The more petite variant stood about three feet six inches tall and was considered even more ancient than *A. africanus*. However, today, the idea that the *Australopithecine* eventually evolved into *Homo erectus* has fallen from grace. As a matter of fact, the fossil evidence now shows that those populations categorized as *Homo habilis* (the *Australopithecines*) were living at the same time as *Homo erectus (Pithecanthropus* and *Sinanthropus*) and could therefore not be their ancestors.

> By approximately 1.6 million years ago, *when the youngest Homo habilis populations now recognized lived at Olduvai, Homo erectus was already in existence near Lake Turkana!* Even the slender Australopithecines lived on until perhaps two million years ago, and they may have co-occurred with *Homo erectus*, also near Lake Turkana, about 1.6 million years ago (the evidence is under debate). *In light of these facts, the old idea of Australopithecus africanus being gradually transformed into Homo erectus by way of Homo habilis is now difficult to defend* (emphasis added) (Stanley 1981, 149).

Cherfas and Gribbin have stated that the gracile forms of the *Australopithecines* are nothing more than extinct variants of pygmy chimpanzees, while the more robust fossils represent an extinct form of gorillas (Gribbin and Cherfas 1981, 592–95).

*

THE ORIGIN OF MAN

"Oops! Wait a minute. Hold the bus. Our ancestral lineage changed again," said Rocksy holding up his arm.

"Really?" replied Bullshingle, slamming on the brakes.

"Yup! Throw *africanus* under the bus with *robustus*."

"Not the gracile *africanus*?"

"Yup! Both of them. We found them living in the same strata as *Homo erectus*."

"Really? You mean the really old apes that were supposed to be our ancestors lived at the same time as *Homo erectus*?"

"Yup! It's a bit embarrassing, but don't tell anybody."

"You don't say!"

"Well, you have to understand, this paleontology stuff is not so easy."

"You can say that again. It's making my head spin."

"That's not all."

"What else?"

"Well, it seems that when this guy Bromage came up with the science behind the growing of bones."

"You mean that guy that studies them through bone scans?"

"Yeah, the same. He studied the face of the famous Taung Child thinking it would show evidence of bone surface patterns like humans, but instead, he found the patterns that were exactly typical of monkeys and apes."

"Oops!"

*

Two years before Johanson unearthed Lucy, Leakey made another astounding discovery that also sent the lineage of the *Australopithecine* out of our ancestry. In 1972, Bernard Ngeneo found a skull in Lake Rudolf, Africa, which was declared to be fully human and older than the *Australopithecines*. Ngeneo was part of Leakey's and his zoologist wife Mary Leakey's team. The skull was named Skull KNM-ER 1470. Now the problem is that the skull was dated at almost 3 million years old, making it older than the *Pithecanthropus* as well as the *Australopithecine* fossils. How then could these *Australopithecines* and the *Pithecanthropus* and *Sinanthropus* be our ancestors if we have a human skull older than their fossils?

His new skull KNM-ER 1470 (found in Lake Turkana, Kenya, in 1972) was said to have thin walls and be devoid of the heavy eyebrow ridge, as well as the supra mastoid crest that is common to apes. The skull was fully human in shape except that it had an estimated cranial capacity of only 810 cc. Although an aboriginal female was reported as having 900 cc., the average human skull is larger. Again, we must return to the establishment of a character complex to make any sense out of the conclusions we can infer from single samples of cranial volumes.

To begin with, it is not true that our cranial volume alone accounts for our intelligence. We have many examples of human beings with small crania who were geniuses. According to Boule, the skull of La Chapelle-aux-Saints had a volume of 2000 cc., which is much larger than the average human skull. He claimed that Bismarck's skull had an estimated volume of 1965 cc. But other Neanderthal skulls have been measured at about 1400 cc. The Gibraltar skull was 1300 cc. The skull of the Man from La Chapelle was 1600 cc.

> What do these figures signify? Do they give us the measure of the intellectual or psychic faculties of our fossil Man? Nothing could be more uncertain. We know of course that the brain capacity may vary enormously in a series of recent men selected for their eminence, from 1320 cc (the anatomist Meckel) or 1420 cc (Raphael) to 1950 cc (La Fontaine), that is to say.... Considered by itself, then this capacity cannot be taken as a criterion of the intellectual standard of a human being (Boule 2010, 136–37).

In other words, single measurements mean little without a character complex to place it in the proper perspective. Attempts to build evolutionary lineages with skull sizes can therefore be quite deceptive.

Nevertheless, having found skulls that were obviously more human-like than the *Australopithecines* and older, Leakey then sat down and reassembled our supposed ancestral lineage in yet another new order.

Leakey believed that his Skull 1470 was more advanced in morphology and yet older than the *Australopithecines* and therefore removed the more ape-like *Australopithecines* from our lineage. The idea that gradual changes in the morphology of apes led to the development of man was considered a foregone conclusion. All they needed was to fill in the blank spots. Evolutionists believed that the strata would be the key to finding these gradual transitions from ape to man. But connecting the dots was proving to be quite vexing.

The fossils in the strata have created great frustration for evolutionists. They showed that *Homo habilis* has been found in the

Diagram 12. Leakey's New Lineage

EXTINCT APE AGE	*EXTINCT APE*	*EXTINCT APE*	*EXTINCT APE*
(1 M.Y.)			Homo Erectus (skull)
(2 M.Y.)	Zinjanthropus (skull) Olduvai Gorge 1969	1969 (skull) Olduvai Gorge	1960 O. Gorge (skull)
(3 M.Y.)	Lake Rudolf (mandible) 1972 (skull) Lake Rudolf 1969	Homo Habilis (skull) Lake Rudolf 1978	1968 (Skull 1470)
(4 M.Y.)			L. Rudolf 1972
(5 M.Y.)	Robustus	Africanus	Homo Line

11 Million Years of No Evidence
Ramapithecus (14 Million Years Ago)
Dryopithecus

same layers as *Homo erectus*. More problematic yet, some classified as *Homo erectus* have also been found in the same layers as *Homo sapiens* and could therefore not have been our ancestors. Hence, there has been no gradual evolution from *Homo habilis* to *Homo erectus* culminating in *Homo sapiens*. They were all three contemporaries of one another, living in the First Earth. But don't take my word for it; listen to an evolutionist.

> For decades the availability of only scattered fossil remains of the human family permitted a gradualistic orientation to dominate within physical anthropology, a field which has itself generated rather little basic evolutionary theory. In recent years, the factual picture has changed.
>
> With enthusiasm for the single species hypothesis already flagging, Richard Leakey and Alan Walker in 1976 described remains of Homo erectus, a species of our own genus, found with a species of robust australopithecine within a thin stratigraphic interval in East Africa. The two species clearly coexisted. . . . Leakey believed that our species, Homo sapiens, overlapped in time with the extinct species Homo erectus, but he remained a staunch gradualist. As a result, he claimed that we could not have evolved from Homo erectus, and he looked to another lineage for our ancestry (Stanley 1981, 139).

That sent evolutionists into a tailspin. The alleged large endocranial volume of Skull 1470, along with the flat-face feature shown in the reconstruction undertaken by Leakey's wife Mary (a qualified zoologist and paleontologist) and the anatomist Bernard Wood made this skull appear more human-like than the rest of the supposed evolutionary line that came after it. The lack of pronounced supraorbital tori (heavy brow ridges) and a high-domed forehead as opposed to a flatter forehead in apes made this find quite unpopular with many of

THE ORIGIN OF MAN

the evolutionists who had grown to like the previous lineage, which, although scant, had at least provided a basic skeleton for their theory.

It must be noted that the skull was pieced together from 150 small fragments of bone. A great controversy brewed as anthropologists saw their entire *Homo erectus* and *Homo habilis* fossils thrown out.

Not surprisingly, from 1977 to 1992, various reconstructions of Skull 1470, which emphasized its ape-like features more than its human-like features, began to appear in the literature. The cranial capacity was then changed to 752 cm^3. The initial ancient date of 3 million years old was soon revised to 1.9 million years old. I suppose that 1.9 million looks a little better than 2 million years; it's a psychological thing. Now, they categorized him as a member of *Homo erectus,* naming him *Homo rudolfensis.*

*

"Uh Oh," said Rocksy. "Stop the bus again."

"Why?" asked Bullshingle.

"Well, uh, it looks like Leakey's Skull 1470 was incorrectly constructed. It is now clear that it is another *Autralopithecine*. And it is now only 1.9 million years old."

"Wait a minute. You mean the reconstruction of the skull may have been guided by their evolutionary bias?" asked Bullshingle crossing his arms across his chest.

"Shhh! You can't say that," Rocksy said, holding a finger to his lips.

"Why?"

"Those pesky intelligent design guys might hear you."

"Oh! And what about their dating change?"

"Oh, no, that is an exact science."

"Then how come they changed it by .1 million years?"

"I know, I know. Look, we know it cannot be 3 million years old because it wouldn't fit in our line, you see?"

"Oh."

*

Skull 1470, which was supposed to be *Homo erectus*, was, in fact, an *Australopithecine*. Christopher Hummer, a creationist researcher, brought attention to a number of *Australopithecine* traits in the newly reconstructed skull.

- The skirt-like occipital flaring typical in *Australopithecines*
- The long, ape-like upper lip
- The ape-like cranio-facial index of the newly reconstructed skull now was 59.0, which places it well within the normal *Australopithecine* range (51.0–64.5). The typical human range is 30.0 to 45.0.

Beyond that, the researchers now found that the teeth sockets were as large as those of the *Australopithecines*. The forehead was now flatter with noticeable *supraorbital tori* (heavy eyebrow ridge). Well, anyone can make four mistakes. Hmmm!

In 1995, Leakey quietly produced another reconstruction of the skull, which was quite similar to that of Pellegrino, consigning Skull 1470 back to *Homo habilis*.

In March 2007, a team led by Timothy Bromage, an anthropologist at New York University, reconstructed the skull yet again. The new reconstruction looked very ape-like, and the cranial capacity was changed to 526 cm^3. That poor skull went from being human in the attic to being *Homo erectus* on the first floor and was finally thrown in the basement as *Homo habilis*.

*

"Oops! Hold the bus again," screamed Rocksy.
"What now?" asked Bullshingle, slamming on the brakes.
"You have to let *africanus* and *robustus* back on the bus."
"Why?"
"Well, they found out 1470 is an *Australopithecine* after all. They are back on the line again."

"They are our ancestors again?"

"At least for now, anyway. Modern bone-scanning techniques have proved that KNM-ER 1470 is an *Australopithecine* beyond any reasonable doubt."

"You don't say!"

Yeah, by that same guy, Bromage, that studied the Taung Child."

"You mean the bone-scanning guy?"

"Yup. He studies the way bones grow and found that in reality, Skull 1470 bears a strong resemblance to a hyper-robust and extremely gorilla-looking fossil of another *Australopithecine* called the Black Skull."

"Wow! What a nightmare! Is the Black Skull from Darth Vader?"

"No, silly. The Black Skull is *Australopithecine* KNW-WT 17000, referred to as *A. ethiopicus.*"

"That's not the same skull. It looks much smaller to me."

"Yeah, it's the same skull. It turns out the ape had a small brain all along. Bromage thinks it is only 526 cm^3."

"You mean the skull went from 900 cm^3 to 526 cm^3? Did the bones shrink?"

"No, it turns out Leakey and his wife forgot to put their reading glasses on when they pieced the bones together."

"Oh. But how did the reconstruction change the size of the teeth sockets?"

"It didn't."

"You mean they were the same size in both reconstructions?"

"Yup! They just didn't notice. That's why I wear my glasses around my neck."

"Where did the heavy eyebrow ridges come from?"

"They were there. They just put the puzzle pieces together in the wrong sequence."

"But I thought they really studied those bones."

"Well, yeah, but they don't have the colored picture outside the box to go by, so they have to invent one in their minds, you see?"

"Oh. But what if they invent the wrong one?"

"It doesn't matter. Who's gonna know? They are the experts."

"Okay, let me get this straight. He is not human and he is not a *Homo erectus*. Now he is an *Australopithecine* from the *Homo habilis* category, right?"

"Right, but that is better for us."

"Why?"

"Well, we can use the *Australopithecines* and the *Homo erectus* to fill our lines again. That stupid skull made them quite embarrassingly small."

"Oh, I see."

*

Australopithecus afarensis (Lucy)

In 1978, Dr. Donald C. Johanson of the Cleveland Museum of Natural History turned the tables on Leakey by announcing his discovery of a fossil in Ethiopia that was supposedly older than Skull 1470 and supposedly more human-like in its skeletal features. The dating of this fossil is reported to be about 3.8 million years old.

The name given to this newly discovered creature was *Australopithecus afarensis*. Sometime later, Mary Leakey also found samples of this creature in Tanzania. Dr. Johanson claims that even at this early age, *A. afarensis* had fully developed bipedal locomotion.

The cranial capacity of this creature is about the same as a chimpanzee, averaging about 400 cc. The remarkable claim is that the skeleton suggests this creature was able to have upright bipedal locomotion like a human.

This is the fossil *Australopithecine* named Lucy that we previously spoke of. It is about three and a half feet tall, weighing approximately 60 pounds. Johanson believes that approximately 2.5 million years ago, *A. afarensis* split into two divergent lineages, one leading to man and the other to *A. africanus* and *A. robustus*. Johanson agrees with Leakey that *Australopithecus africanus* could therefore not be part

THE ORIGIN OF MAN

of our lineage and as a result, he placed the *africanus* species as a divergent lineage that became an extinct ape.

Australopithecus afarensis now became the official ancestor of man. From this creature, evolutionists then claimed *Australopithecines* and *Homo erectus* evolved.

Johanson then created another new lineage, sending our two imaginary friends, Rocksy and Bullshingle into conniptions.

*

"Woah! Hold the bus again," Rocksy screamed, holding out his hands.

"Now what?" complained Bullshingle as he slammed on the brakes.

"Throw Skull 1470, *africanus* and *robustus*, back out of the bus."

"I just let them in, man. Why?"

"Lucy kicked them out. Now she is on the line."

Diagram 13. Johanson's New Lineage

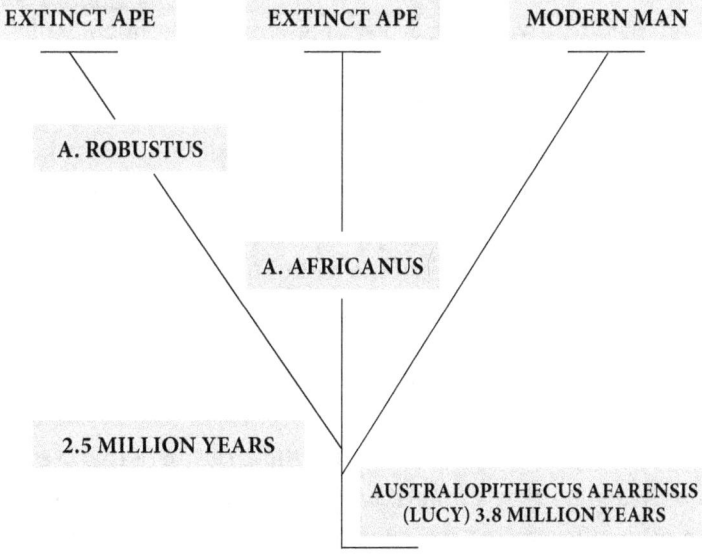

"Dude, you're wearing out my brakes, man."

"Never mind your brakes. Look at my chart. I need an erasable marker."

*

There are several false evolutionary assumptions that must be addressed. The primary false assumption commonly made by Darwinists is that bipedal locomotion must exclusively be the trait of human beings. Their assumption is predicated upon the notion that if there are no animals extant today that have bipedal locomotion other than man, then any ape exhibiting that characteristic must be related. That, however, is pure conjecture on their behalf. That assumption is not based on empirical evidence; it is merely assumption.

Second, the assertion that Lucy walked completely upright is not an absolute certainty, and there is quite a bit of debate in that regard. Studies of Lucy's entire anatomy, and not just her knee joint, show that bipedal motion would have been quite unlikely for Lucy (Spoor 1994, 645–48).

> Lucy's species—A. afarensis—for all its bipedal ability, retained relatively long arms, suggesting that it might still have occasionally ascended into the trees. A recent analysis of fossils from a young A. afarensis found in 200 in Dikika, Ethiopia, indicates that the species had rather apelike shoulders, which presumably rendered it a proficient climber. So perhaps, Lucy like Ardi and other species that came before and after had the best of both possible worlds (Jungers, quoted in Harmon 2013, 48).

And even if Lucy did walk upright, all it proves is that there was an ape that walked upright. It only serves to reiterate that a common designer was responsible for the creation of this creature. It is only logical that similarities would exist in the vast array of locomotion alternatives exhibited by the living creatures that God has designed. Just because we have no apes that walk upright today in the same manner that humans do does not mean they could not have existed in the much richer variation of the genetic pool in apes that existed prior to the Great Flood.

Locomotion similarities do not prove evolutionary lineage nor do they prove familial ties. Could we say that an ostrich with two legs is more closely related to us than a horse with four legs? That is a purely arbitrary designation.

It is, however, more likely due to the anatomical structure of her limbs that Lucy simply swung from tree limbs in the same manner as pygmy chimpanzees or orangutans today (Jungers 1982, 676-78).

Speaking of the rather scant and over-interpreted evidence for the *Australopithecine*, Dr. Duane Gish writes:

> In more recent years, however, this view has been challenged by Sally Lord Zuckerman, famous British anatomist, and by Dr. Charles Oxnard professor of anatomy and anthropology at the University of Chicago.
>
> For over fifteen years a research team headed by Lord Zuckerman studied the anatomical features of man, monkeys, apes, and the Australopithecine fossils. Practically all the available important fossil fragments of Australopithecine, along with anatomical specimens from hundreds of monkeys, apes, and humans were compared. No one has done a more thorough and careful study on the status of Australopithecus then Lord Zuckerman. Concerning the claims by Le Gros Clark and others that Australopithecus should be classified as a genus of the Hominidae (family of man) rather than as a genus of the anthropoid apes, Lord Zuckerman said:
>
>> But I myself remain totally unpersuaded. Almost always when I have tried to check the anatomical claims, on which the status of Australopithecus is based, I have ended in failure.

Lord Zuckerman's conclusion is that Australopithecus was an ape, in no way related to the origin of man.

Oxnard's research has led him to say:

> Although most studies emphasize the similarity of the Australopithecine to modern man, and suggest therefore, that these creatures were bipedal tool makers, at least one form of which (*Australopithecus africanus* – "*Homo habilis,*" "*Homo Africanus*") was almost directly ancestral to man, a series of multivariate statistical studies of various post cranial fragments suggest other conclusions.

From his results, Oxnard concluded that Australopithecus did not walk upright in human manner but probably had a mode of locomotion similar to that of the orangutan.

He states:

> Multivariate studies of several anatomical regions, shoulder, pelvis, ankle, foot, elbow, and hand are now available for the Australopithecines.
>
> These suggest that the common view, that these fossils are similar to modern man or that on occasion when they depart from a similarity to man they resemble the African great apes, may be incorrect. Most of the fossil fragments are in fact uniquely different from both man and man's nearest living genetic relatives, the chimpanzee and gorillas.
>
> To the extent that resemblance exists with living forms they tend to be with the Orangutan.

Oxnard's conclusions are then, that Australopithecus is not related to anything living today, man or ape, but was uniquely different (emphasis added) (Gish 1979, 121–22).

It seems quite probable that this creature was nothing more than an extinct type of orangutan that perished in the Great Flood.

Although they do not recognize the extinction mechanism of the Great Flood, Dubois and Vallois came to the very same conclusion for the *Pithecanthropus* (Java Man) and *Sinanthropus* (Peking Man) and concluded that they were simply an extinct species of gibbons.

Man's attempt to join together animals that possess similar traits, as if they belong to a common stock, is artificial and scientifically unestablishable as absolute proof of anything other than proof that they possess similarities in traits.

God is infinitely creative and has provided us with creatures that possess incredibly diverse and sometimes unique and unexpected features, such as the previously mentioned duck-billed platypus. But the platypus is not the evolutionary link between birds, reptiles, and mammals. Why should an ape that has the unusual and aberrant ability to walk upright be an evolutionary link between ape and man?

If there was an ape before the Great Flood that happened to walk upright, then all it would prove is that there was an ape before the Flood that walked upright. What is so startling about an ape having bipedal locomotion? I think it is more startling that there are carnivorous plants, fire-breathing insects, and animals that can produce their own light. There are lizards that walk on water on two legs. There is a certain creosote bush that grows in Arizona and New Mexico that is reported to be 11,000 years old. Now that is really amazing!

There is a grave tendency by evolutionists to not take into account the wide variations within a given species—the complete character complex of a given kind. This variation was especially pronounced in the species that lived before the Great Flood. Only 4 percent or 5 percent of the variations in species that existed before the Great Flood have survived to our present time. The magnificent variety within given kinds would have been absolutely astounding to us today. To dogmatically make assertions on a specific individual find is at best tenuous and quite precarious from a scientific perspective.

The real fact is that *Australopithecus afarensis* is simply a slight variation of *Australopithecus africanus*, and the variability is quite insignificant. However, if we accept Johanson's lineage, it leaves us with an even greater gap with absolutely no intermediate fossils between *A. afarensis* and modern man.

> *Australopithecus afarensis* is the name recently suggested for some ancient slender australopithecines. The oldest of these, which exceeded three million years in age, were unearthed by Mary Leakey and her colleagues at a site in Tanzania known as Laetoli. Here the slender australopithecine apparently left the remarkable sets of footprints (tracks much like our own) that have been discovered in volcanic ash. The Laetoli fossils and Ethiopia remains younger than three million years have been united under the name *Australopithecus afarensis*. Those who have proposed this name regard the populations to which they apply it the true ancestors of the genus Homo. The idea is that these forms gradually formed to Homo habilis. It is claimed that they resemble Homo slightly more closely than do the slender australopithecines traditionally assigned to *Australopithecus africanus*. The latter is asserted to exhibit specializations diverging from the condition of Homo and its true ancestors—specializations such as strengthened jaws and slightly enlarged molars and premolars.
>
> *In truth what has been called Australopithecus afarensis is a slender form that differs little from the populations known as Australopithecus africanus. Some would unite them as a single species* (emphasis added) (Stanley 1981, 149).

The truth of the matter is that both *A. afarensis* and *A. africanus* simply exhibit slight variations within the character complex of this species of apes. But by placing *A. afarensis* in this new evolutionary lineage, we now not only have an immense gap between *Ramapithecus* and *A. afarensis* of some 11 million years, but we also have a much wider 3-million-year gap between *A. afarensis* and modern man than existed in the previous lineage between *A. africanus* and modern man. In reality, the sequence, offered as supposedly proof positive of our ape ancestry, is the only thing that is really evolving. Nevertheless, in spite of all the shifting of the shells and sleight of hand, the gaps that remain are enormous and inconceivable to reconcile if evolution had really taken place through gradual, almost imperceptible changes, as evolutionists so ardently believe.

Ardipithecus ramidus (Ardi)

In 2009, the discovery of a remarkably complete skeleton, supposedly dated 4.4 million years ago, was announced as also having bipedal locomotion. This slender creature was uncovered in the Afar region of Ethiopia.

> Many paleontologists anticipated that a hominin dating to that era would have many traits seen in chimps and other modern apes, including large canine teeth for aggression based social systems, very long arms and fingers for climbing in trees, and wrist adaptations for knuckle walking, among other features.
>
> Instead, the slight *A. ramidus* is what Tim D. White of the University of California, Berkeley, who led the team that discovered Ardi, has described as a "mosaic organism" that possesses characteristics of later hominins and ancient apes—but not so much of chimpanzees. Like humans, Ardi has reduced canine teeth, which researchers think might signify a transition away from a male dominated social system toward a more cooperative system revolving among pairs who form long-term bonds. Also among modern African apes, Ardi's high degree of wrist extension suggests that when she walked on all fours, she supported her weight on her palms rather than her knuckles. Meanwhile

Ardi's fingers were relatively long and curved—helpful for climbing trees—but her wrist and hands might have prevented her from swinging between branches as capably as chimpanzees do. . . .

Whereas her relatively flat feet and divergent big toe (or hallux) would have aided arboreal locomotion, the stiffness of her foot and her minor toes ability to flex backward would have facilitated bipedal walking. Her pelvis was badly crushed, leaving some details about her leg motion unknown. But, William Jungers of Stony Brook University says that from what he can tell, the short distance from Ardi's hip bone and sacrum (the triangular bone at the base of the spine) is similar to that found in modern humans and other hominins known to have walked upright. Additionally the foramen magnum, the opening at the base of the skull through which the spinal cord exits, is located quite far forward in Ardi—a trait that many scientists read as an indication of a vertical stance (and possible bipedalism) when she was on the ground. Some researchers however, wonder whether she was instead only able to stand upright intermittently, for example, if she needed to hold something in her hands (Harmon 2013, 42–49).

Whether Ardi truly had bipedal locomotion cannot be absolutely ascertained, especially with the pelvis so fractured. It is more likely that Ardi walked upright for sporadic periods, as other apes do today. Her arboreal capabilities are clearly represented by her divergent big toe used for grasping branches.

Nevertheless, the supposedly more evolutionarily advanced characteristics shown in her anatomical structure in a creature that is clearly older than Lucy (4.4 million years) more credibly obviates that these design characteristics constitute a variety of models the Creator engineered to illustrate His genius and creativity.

As a matter of fact, at a site called Burtele in Ethiopia's Afar region, another find consisting of only eight small foot bones shows great similarity to Ardi's foot and is dated at supposedly 3.4 million years old. That would make it a contemporary of Lucy.

Not only did it live at the same time as Lucy, but the sites of their finds were about 48 kilometers apart. So there is no doubt that they cohabitated in the same area. That means that these unique features were nothing more than variations in God's designs who lived alongside one another prior to the mass extinction cataclysm of the Great Flood.

> Like Ardi, the Burtele animal probably walked on the outer edge of its foot when it was upright (avoiding the big toe because it would not propel the walker forward as ours does).... Without a medial cuneiform bone (a large bone in the middle of the foot) from Burtele, it is difficult to know how far akimbo its toe was, notes Jeremy De Silva of Boston University (Harmon 2013, 565–69).

These functional similarities in different kinds cannot be used as proof of familial connections, as evolutionists are prone to do. Their dogmatic conclusions are simply a direct product of their fundamental evolutionary assumption. The only scientific conclusion that can be drawn is that their ancestral lineages have been utterly shattered consistently by new finds. In other words, there is no clear ancestral lineage from apes to man supported by the fossil evidence.

Homo rudolfensis

In August 2012, a team led by Meave Leakey published a new report on *Homo rudolfensis* in *Nature* magazine. She found three new fossils—two jawbones with teeth and a face—in northern Kenya. The face fossil was obviously from a juvenile of the species, which resembled the KNM-ER 1470. Meave argued that KNMER should therefore not be classified as a large member of *Homo habilis* but of a separate species of *Homo rudolfensis*.

The face was described as flat from the eye sockets to the incisor teeth. The shorter and more rectangular jawbones were, according to Meave, quite distinct from the typical *Homo habilis*. These fossils were dated at about 2 million years ago, thus making the *Homo rudolfensis* find a contemporary of the *Australopithecines* and *Homo erectus* in the early Pleistocene of Eastern Africa (Leakey et al. 2012, 201–204). That would once again throw the *Australopithecines* out of the lineage.

*

"Hold the bus again," Rocksy screamed, holding his hand out again.

"What now?" asked Bullshingle, frustrated as he stepped on the brakes.

"Hey, don't kill the messenger."

"What happened now?"

"Well, it seems that Meave Leakey found another fossil that she claims is a different species from the *Australopithecine*, called *Homo rudolfensis*."

"So?"

"Well, they are in the same early Pleistocene age of eastern Africa as *Homo erectus*."

"And?"

"Well, silly, if they lived at the same time as *Homo erectus*, they cannot be their ancestors."

"Then who is left in the bus?"

"Uh, I'm not really sure now." Rocksy responded scratching his head. "This is very confusing."

Bullshingle nodded in agreement and responded, "I hope she had her glasses on this time."

*

Of course, Leakey's argument sent many Darwinists into another tailspin of angst. Once again, their lineage was decimated. Tim D. White of the University of California reportedly complained, "How can practitioners in this field possibly expect to be able to accurately identify fossil species based upon a few teeth, jaws and lower faces in light of what we know about the great variation found among different individuals in a single living species?" (Kaplan 2012).

Truth be told, White is obviously right! His critique, based on the character complex of species, should be kept in mind as the following two sections on *Ramapithecus* unfold.

From Dryopithecus to Ramapithecus and the 11-Million-Year Gap

If we evolved from apes in a gradual step-by-step evolutionary process, there should be ample evidence of this continual ancestry, as Dawkins described with his illustration of shrews to rabbits. Instead, what we find is that between the earliest *Australopithecines* find (Lucy) and the next supposed ancestor, *Ramapithecus*, there is an immense gap of 10 million to 11 million years with absolutely no fossil evidence to corroborate the supposed ancestral lineage from apes. In other words, evolutionists do not have a missing link. They have, according to their own dating methods (even if we were to accept their dating claims as legitimate), more than 63 percent of the chain missing.

Even with *Ramapithecus* in the lineage, there is a 10-million to 11-million-year gap with zilch—not one single intermediate fossil to substantiate the evolutionary claim that apes evolved into man. We have discovered that the *Australopithecines* were contemporary to *Homo erectus*; hence, they could not have been their ancestors. We have also discovered that *Homo sapiens* were also contemporary to the *Homo erectus*; hence, they could not have been their ancestors, either. That means we are left with nothing from the evolutionary lineage that can connect man with apes.

I know that Dawkins claims men did not evolve from monkeys, but actually monkeys are in their supposed evolutionary lineage. Let us turn our attention to the very first monkeys that were supposed to be our ancestors. Moving down from the *Australopithecine* apes for a span of 11 million years of no connecting fossils, we find *Ramapithecus*, which is supposedly preceded by the earlier *Oreopithecus*. And finally, several million years earlier, at the fork in the road, *Dryopithecus* is touted as the supposed lynchpin ancestor from which our lineage, as well as that of modern apes, bifurcated and developed into different lines. That is to say, *Dryopithecus* is thought to be the common ancestor from which both *Homo sapiens* and modern ape lineages differentiated (see Diagram 11).

But are these monkeys really part of our heritage? Truth be told, I actually agree with Dawkins; I do not think that man evolved from monkeys either because the empirical data just do not support it. What are the scientific criteria used by evolutionists to support this claim? Starting at the beginning of our supposed evolutionary lineage, from the point of bifurcation between the apes and man, we have their proposed candidate *Dryopithecus*—the lynchpin that supposedly connects us to modern apes.

In 1856, Édouard Lartet found a jawbone of a large monkey in Saint Gudens of southern France. He named the monkey *Dryopithecus fontani*. It caused a great sensation when Lartet and Jean Albert Gaudry declared that *Dryopithecus* was more closely akin to man than any other known monkey. In 1890, the discovery of a better preserved lower jawbone fueled that speculation even further. Later discoveries in the Siwalik Hills in Italy showed that there were actually three variations of this species of monkeys, varying in sizes.

> First of all there is the European genus Dryopithecus, rediscovered by Pilgrim in the Siwalik Hills, where it is represented by three species, one of them a giant of its kind (Z. giganteiis). If to these three species be added the European forms, the genus Dryopithecus seems to embrace

a group of Anthropoid Apes having manifold variations and forming a special branch now extinct. Certain of its smaller branches more closely related, judging at least from the character of their dentition, to the human stock, as Lartet and Gaudry first believed. A similar opinion has been expressed during the last few years. Dryopithecus would seem then to have been an ancestral and synthetic form (Boule 2010, 63).

Because the dentition of *Dryopithecus* seemed to be a little more like man than monkey, the conclusion was made that they are our ancestors. Lacking any other alternative, evolutionists proposed that *Dryopithecus* is the common ancestor of both modern man and ape. David Pilbeam, one of the eminent evolutionists with a rare genuine sense of objectivity, expressed his doubts about that conclusion, admitting the lack of scientific data to justify such a choice. "It has come to be rather generally assumed, albeit in a rather vague fashion that the pre-Pleistocene hominid ancestry was rooted somewhere in the Dryopithecinae" (Pilbeam 1968, 1335).

*

Pilbeam is convinced that the *Dryopithecines* were too specialized as apes to have produced hominids. Most evolutionists capitulate to the *Dryopithecinae,* only because there is nothing else on the horizon from which to choose. The problem is that the variations between *Ramapithecus, Oreopithecus,* and *Dryopithecus* are quite minimal and could be nothing more than variations within the character complex of a single species. Taking into account that this variability within a single species is found much more pronounced prior to the Great Flood than we have in extant animal species today after the genetic bottleneck created by the cataclysm, it is rather doubtful that all three of these specimens represented several species.

For example, Dr. Robert Eckhardt, a paleontologist at Pennsylvania State University, made 24 measurements comparing the fossil teeth of *Dryopithecus* and *Ramapithecus*. His findings after comparing the range of variations between these two species and the range of variations within modern chimpanzees (character complex) in a research center and in wild chimpanzees in Liberia were very revealing. The range of variation in the chimpanzee population was greater than the variations between the *Dryopithecus* and *Ramapithecus* for 14 of the 24 measurements. It was the same for one and less for nine of them.

How, then, can *Ramapithecus* be separated from *Dryopithecus* and declared a distinct hominid race on the basis of such fragmentary evidence as the slight differences in dentition that can be found within a single species? Again, the character complex is neglected in order to stipulate or magnify the importance of singular characteristics of individual creatures that serve to artificially prop up evolutionists' failed evolutionary link to man. That is not objective science.

Eckhardt concluded simply that there was no compelling evidence for the existence of any distinct hominid species during this epoch unless the definition of hominid was to be applied to any ape that just happens to have small teeth and a corresponding small face. His conclusions were published in *Scientific American* (Eckhardt 1972, 94–103).

Several million years after *Dryopithecus*, *Ramapithecus* supposedly appears within our ancestral lineage, providing the only link between the *Dryopithecinae* and *Homo sapiens*. The fact is that evolutionists desperately needed to have *Ramapithecus* there because otherwise the gap would be some 14 million years from *Dryopithecus* to the *Australopithecine*, and another 3.8 million years to *Homo sapiens*. Since the *Australopithecines* have been found in the same level as *Homo erectus*, they cannot be part of the lineage. Thus, the gap is 17.8 million years, according to their time reckoning.

The problem is further complicated by the fact that there are no real identifying characteristics that would cause either *Ramapithecus* or *Dryopithecus* to be considered our ancestors. *Ramapithecus* was placed in this spot in our ancestry based solely on the erroneous assumption that it possessed a parabolic-like jaw that was deemed more human-like. *Oreopithecus*, which is accepted by some and not by others as an intermediate between *Dryopithecus* and *Ramapithecus*, was chosen because it may have walked uprightly in the shuffling motion of orangutans.

What these animals have in common is a much smaller face than most monkeys and reduced canine sizes, coupled with some form of bipedal motion. But none of these things prove in any way that they are related to human beings. There are monkeys with big heads, and there are monkeys with small heads. There are monkeys with big canines, and there are monkeys with small canines. There are monkeys with big tails, and there are monkeys with small tails or almost no tail at all. There are monkeys with huge red butts, and there are monkeys with smaller plain butts. There are monkeys that walk on their hind legs, and there are monkeys that swing from limbs. The arbitrary alignment of these characteristics, following the Cuverian legend for magical clairvoyance, is used to confidently place the specimens in some imaginary evolutionary scale where they are ceremoniously and artificially associated with humans as our genetic ancestors.

Did *Oreopithecus* have bipedal motion? Yes, but it was nothing like the bipedal motion of man. *Oreopithecus* walked in the same shuffling and swaggering fashion as orangutans. The hallux formed a 100° angle with the other toes enabling the foot to act as a sort of tripod when the animal was in the erect position. But this arrangement was not in any way suitable for fast bipedal locomotion. Instead, the development of arms and hands showed that he was extremely well adapted to arboreal habitats. The creature weighed about 66 to 77 pounds and could have also survived in swampy environments, as many of our modern monkeys have adapted.

Ramapithecus' teeth have marks that indicate that the ape may have had a coarse diet, unlike the soft fruits and shoots of the wet forests that are the common diet of modern apes. They lack the large canine teeth common to most Old World monkeys. But there may be a very good explanation for this. *Ramapithecus* is now thought to be the female of *Sivapithecus*. Females generally have much smaller canines than their male counterparts.

Sivapithecus was discovered by Pilgrim, also in the Siwalik Hills, and was initially placed in our evolutionary tree. But Boule was not impressed with the evidence used by Pilgrim to do so.

> There is finally the curious genus of Sivapithecus, recently discovered and described by Pilgrim, who has hesitated to place this new fossil Primate among the Hominians. It is only known from some isolated teeth and two jaw fragments, by means of which Pilgrim has attempted the restoration of the lower jaw. The general form of the latter more resembles the human form than the jaws of any other anthropoid ape, living or fossil. It has indeed the canine of an anthropoid ape, but the true molars in their general appearance are more human in type than those of any known ape.
>
> Pilgrim has no doubt that the character of the lower jawbone of Sivapithecus justify the conclusion that this fossil belonged to the direct progenitors of the human race, *a conclusion the importance of which contrasts with the slightness of the evidences on which it is based* (emphasis added) (Boule 2010, 63).

Boule admits the "slightness of the evidences on which it is based." Nevertheless, he does not refute Pilgrim's proposal. However, he notes that others did.

> More recently, Gregory has keenly criticized the restoration made by his English colleague and has opposed his

conclusions. He does not admit that Sivapithecus should be classified with the Humans, and considers it rather to be closely allied to Dryopithecus and to the Orangutan. In his turn he also has attempted a restoration of the fossil jaw, and has succeeded in creating a form much more like the jaw of a female orangutan than that of the most primitive human being (Boule 2010, 63).

In other words, the reconstruction of the *Sivapithecus* jaw did not resemble man but rather an orangutan. It just so happens that the initial configuration of *Ramapithecus* was also leaning toward the human and was later shown to be quite the opposite. The connection between *Sivapithecus* and *Ramapithecus* was not made earlier because of the great difference perceived in the shape of the jaws of the two specimens prior to the discovery of the true shape of *Ramapithecus*'s jaw. Now that the cat is out of the bag, there is basically no difference between the jaws of *Ramapithecus* and *Sivapithecus* except for the size of the canine, which is typically greater in males.

Ramapithecus was first found in India, where the ape has been given the name of the Hindu god Rama. All that initially existed as evidence, for this creature was a handful of jaws, along with some teeth, found in Africa, India, and Eurasia. There are no skulls or hipbones that can tell us anything about the shape of the creature and his gait, much less about the species's character complex.

But if you listen to the evolutionists speak of *Ramapithecus*, you would think that the physical evidence is absolutely overwhelming. Richard Leakey, even in 1977, optimistically considered these few specimens, to be considerable evidence, at least compared to the pioneering primate.

> What, then, do these observations have to tell us about the behavior of our ancient ancestor *Ramapithecus*? *Compared with the fossil remains from Montana of the pioneering primate, the evidence concerning Ramapithe-*

> *cus is considerable—though in absolute terms it remains tantalizingly small: fragments of upper and lower jaws, plus a collection of teeth, representing perhaps thirty or more individuals, are all we have from which to piece together a picture of the gradual transition from ape to hominid.* We do know at any rate that the fossil remains have been discovered as far apart as India, Kenya, Hungary, Pakistan, and Turkey (emphasis added) (Leakey and Lewin 1977, 67).

What he really means is not "tantalizingly small" but frustratingly small. He optimistically says that "the evidence concerning *Ramapithecus* is considerable." Considerable? "Fragments of upper and lower jaws, plus a collection of teeth, representing perhaps thirty or more individuals." That is considerable? What planet is he from? That sounds like a used car salesman trying to sell me a Corvette. (I guess that dates me.) The fact is that the scant evidence is not even capable of establishing a character complex that would give us some real parameters to ascertain the variations within the species of the creature. Tim D. White's criticism of Meave Leakey should also be considered here.

What Richard Leakey did not mention is that digs made between 1975 and 1977 found a complete jaw of *Ramapithecus*. The entire evolutionary premise for placing *Ramapithecus* in this spot, because it had a parabolic jaw that resembles a human jaw, was shown to be nothing more than a deceptive reconstruction of the bone fragments. Well, perhaps deceptive is too strong a word. Self-deceptive is more likely. They wished so much to see it that they saw it.

In other words, the complete U-shaped jaw (ape-like jaw) of this creature was found, and that makes it an open-and-shut-case—*Ramapithecus* is just an ape, an extinct form of the orangutan. And yet, even after their initial embarrassment, they still cling to the illusion that *Ramapithecus* is in our lineage because they have nothing else to replace it with.

*

"Bullshingle, hold the bus," said Rocksy as he held his hand high and blew his whistle.

"No, not again!" replied Bullshingle as he slammed on the brakes, leaving a cloud of dust billowing in the air.

"Yup," said Rocksy as he stuck his head in the door and wiped his brow with his hand.

"What now?"

"Throw *Javapithecus* out of the bus."

"Why?"

"Well, it's a bit embarrassing."

"Just whisper it to me."

"Ok, come closer."

Cupping his hand to Bullshingle's ear, Rocksy whispered, "They reassembled the fragments of his jaw and found out he was an orangutan after all."

"No, not again!" said Bullshingle, nodding his head. "Hey, maybe they should ask my grandson K. C. to help. He is really good with those puzzles."

"Well, it's even more complicated than you think."

"What do you mean?"

"Well, this is also a bit embarrassing."

"What now?"

"They kind of goofed up the jaw bone of *Ramapithecus*, too."

"No way!"

"Yes way! They found a complete one, and it was not anything like the human jaw. Their reconstruction was also flawed."

"Did you tell them about keeping their glasses around their necks?"

"Yeah, but they say they get in the dirt when they're digging."

"Should I throw *Ramapithecus* out of the bus?"

"No."

"What do you mean, no?"

"Just keep smiling. Maybe no one will notice. Heh heh!"
"But why?"
"Shh!" said Rocksy, motioning with his hands. "Not so loud."
"Sorry, but why?" whispered Bullshingle.
"We have nothing else between *Dryopithecus* and man, so we are just going to quietly keep it in the lineage and hope no one notices."
"Good plan!"

*

Lo and behold, a complete jaw was found that absolutely disproved their wishful thinking and showed that *Ramapithecus* possessed a U-shaped jaw, which was predictably ape-like. There was no similarity to the parabolic jaw of man in the jaw of *Ramapithecus*, like the *Pithecanthropus* reconstruction done before it. Yet the specimen was kept in the lineage even though the original reasons for placing it there were completely disproved.

Well, anyone can make five mistakes. Hmm! I think there is a discernible pattern here.

So, we have the *Australopithecines* and then 11 million years of silence, with *Ramapithecus* on the other end (with only a couple of jaws and teeth for evidence, which we now know are completely ape-like), and finally, the very dubious *Dryopithecus*. I'd say that it's not the link that is missing. It's the whole chain.

In an article in *Science Digest* in 1981, Dr. Pilbeam, with his usual frankness, expressed his doubts that *Ramapithecus* was in our lineage at all.

> Nevertheless, a reinterpretation of Ramapithecus' human like jaw by David Pilbeam of Yale, one of the experts on the species, now suggests that *Ramapithecus was an ancestor of neither modern humans nor modern apes. Instead, Pilbeam thinks it represents a third lineage that has no living descendants* (emphasis added) (Pilbeam 1981, 36).

The main impetus for first assigning *Ramapithecus* to our lineage in 1932 was the singular characteristic of a parabolic jaw. The evolutionary assumption is that apes with a parabolic jaw are automatically more man-like. Unfortunately, the complete jaw found blew that notion out of the water. But there is a greater problem with that type of thinking; it discounts the possibility that within the ape kingdom, a species may possess this anomaly as simply an aberrant variant. Does that aberrant variation exist today?

There is actually a modern-day baboon found in the high altitudes of Ethiopia that possesses the very same characteristic parabolic jaw and the small face that *Ramapithecus* was supposed to have. Moreover, this species, known as *Theropithecus galada*, also has the same dentition, while still remaining in every sense of the word an ape.

Apparently, *Theropithecus,* having the very same characteristics that were supposed to be a segue between apes and man, forgot to evolve. This variant with a parabolic jaw is simply an anomaly in the ape kingdom. However, it is not our ancestor. *Theropithecus* is alive and well in Ethiopia today.

To repeat the words of Boule, "It must be distinctly stated, and in this case repeated, that resemblance does not always imply descent" (Boule 2010, 73).

The plain fact is that they have no real scientific reason to place these apes in our ancestry, except that they have nothing else to replace them with. Again, the "missing link" is really a "missing chain." As a matter of fact, the evidence for evolution is so sparse that any evolutionist who is truly honest must admit that this is true. Even Richard Leakey admits it. "If we are honest we have to admit that we will never fully know what happened to our ancestors in their journey towards modern humanity: the evidence is simply too sparse" (Leakey 1977, 10).

So much for the smoking gun evidence predicted by evolutionists during the heady days of the Darwinian revolution. But the evidence is really only sparse for the *evolution* of man and the *evolution* of animals. There are plenty of fossils that show the species fully formed and abruptly appearing in the strata. What is not available is the evidence for intermediates, the very "stuff" of the evolutionary hypothesis.

What is truly sparse is the chain that evolution should have created if, in fact, it was responsible for the ascent of man from apes in intermediate, minute, and accruing steps. There are plenty of fossils, just not the kind they want to find to build their imaginary chain.

Not only are the few ancestral fossils claimed by evolutionists spurious, but there ought to be thousands if not millions more intermediate forms between them that should be amply recorded in the strata if evolution had taken place. After all these many years of concerted effort by thousands of evolutionists, financed by universities and museums and private foundations throughout the entire planet, the absence of transitional fossils can no longer be ignored. How long will they allow the king to strut his stuff in the buff?

However, the evolutionary shuffle game continues unabated. Now, Leakey places *Ramapithecus*, instead of 14 million years ago, around 11 or 12 million years ago. In this way, the gap is reduced somewhat, at least in his mind. But regardless, the gap of 11 million years is equally daunting and inexplicable for evolutionists.

> *If it seems remarkable that evidence concerning the earliest hominids is so sparse, still more remarkable is that there exists virtually no trace of their descendents, over a period lasting from about ten million years to five million years ago. And after that five-million–year gap, the first glimpse consists of a single jaw fragment of uncertain provenance.* Not until the period beginning three million years ago does any real, *solid evidence* appear. By then it seems, there was not just one hominid type, but several (emphasis added) (Leakey 1977, 67).

What he calls "solid evidence" is nothing more than smoke and mirrors. By moving *Ramapithecus* up a little on the line, Leakey reduces the huge gap between *Ramapithecus* and the *Australopithecines*. But the fact still remains that in his new line between *Dryopithecus* and *Australopithecus*, there are still more than 14 million years, with only "a single jaw fragment of uncertain provenance" and a few teeth "from which to piece together a picture of the gradual transition from ape to hominid," which has now been shown to have a fully ape-like jaw. All of this shuffling amounts to nothing because the complete jaw of *Ramapithecus* found in 1977 shows that it was not even parabolic. Today, most paleontologists have removed *Ramapithecus* from our lineage. They pin their hopes on Ardi, who, in fact, is simply Lucy. With their magical dating methods, they insist that Ardi was several million years older than Lucy, although Ardi's bones were found in the same layer as Lucy's, indicating that Ardi was not an ancestor of Lucy.

Not Homo erectus but Homo sapiens

As we have already seen, *Pithecanthropus* and *Sinanthropus* were the first candidates to be placed in the *Homo erectus* category. They were simply simian specimens, but they are not the only ones there today. Other fossils have been placed in this lagging midsection to prop it up.

These fossils, which the evolutionists have artificially tried to pry by force into our ancestry, are either fully simian giant specimens that have simply become extinct or members of the human race such as the Neanderthals and their hybrids with Cro-Magnon man. What we are really left with is either the fossils of unusually large primates that became extinct during the radical change in climate produced by the Great Flood or hybrids created by the interbreeding of Neanderthals with Cro-Magnons.

In every case, the fossils of men were found abruptly and fully formed from the very beginning. The fossils of simians are found fully simian in every respect. Some may have had a greater cranial capacity than modern apes, but that is hardly proof of evolution since we find this phenomenon of gigantism throughout the entire planet for that time period.

It is really not that there was a tendency for gigantism back then; it's that we are a diminutive form of the world that was. That is, the Antediluvian world was the way we were meant to be. And we are not the way we were meant to be today, for our world continues to degenerate from the pristine and ideal world it was created to be. We are not evolving. We are devolving. We are not ascending. We are descending.

We have literally devolved into inferior specimens of our ancestral progenitors. We are presently dwarfs compared to the robust creatures who once roamed our planet. We truly are but a shadow of what we once were.

Only through the development of antibiotics and modern farming methods have we been able to turn the tide of devolution, which has steadily marched downward throughout all of human history. Today, contrary to the norm in history, each successive generation seems to be progressing in stature and moving back to the specimens we once were. But only time will tell whether this brief pause in devolution will be derailed by the outworking of human greed—war, famine, and pestilence.

Modern man is not an evolved improvement of Cro-Magnon man. On the contrary, Cro-Magnon was a much healthier specimen of humanity both physically and intellectually. Since their cranial capacity and life spans were greater than ours, there can be no other conclusion. We have devolved!

In fact, due to our technology today, we have just begun to reverse the natural course of diminution due to our inferior habitat. Dr. Lee Meadows Jantz of the University of Tennessee's Forensic Anthropology Center has done some research on comparative skull sizes between the 1800s and our modern times. It turns out that the average skull size in white males has increased 200 cubic centimeters within the last 200 years. Women's skull size has increased 180 cubic centimeters. That translates to a 6.8 percent increase in the overall size of the skulls. In that same period, we have had a 5.6 percent increase in weight and a 2 percent increase in femur length.

According to the research, those changes are directly due to our superior nutrition. What evolution failed to do over several thousand years, nutrition has easily accomplished in two centuries.

We can readily see that the larger skull sizes in simians during the First Earth has nothing to do with evolution toward the human species and everything to do with the greater nutrition available in the more fertile habitat. Were it not for irrigation pumps, fertilizers, and modern farming techniques, we would have continued down the path of diminution.

The whole evolutionary house of cards has been shown to be nothing more than smoke and mirrors propped up by circular reasoning, which can be toppled by the simple breath of knowledge and true reason.

There is great disparity between the newer specimens placed in the *Homo erectus* category, which are really human beings, and the simian skulls of the original specimens in this category. These hybrid specimens between Neanderthal and Cro-Magnon could still not have been our ancestors because we have also discovered that those fossils exist within the same strata as Neanderthals and Cro-Magnon. They have been found to be living side-by-side with humans as contemporaries. Even Leakey admits that.

> With enthusiasm for the single species hypothesis already flagging, Richard Leakey and Alan Walker in 1976 described remains of Homo erectus, a species of our own genus, found with a species of robust australopithecine within a thin stratigraphic interval in East Africa. The two species clearly coexisted.... Leakey believed that our species, Homo sapiens, overlapped in time with the extinct

species Homo erectus, but he remained a staunch gradualist. As a result, he claimed that we could not have evolved from Homo erectus, and he looked to another lineage for our ancestry (Stanley 1981, 139).

The simple fact is that these more recent additions have been artificially placed in the *Homo erectus* category, and they are quite distinct from the simian forms of *Pithecanthropus* and *Sinanthropus*. As a matter of fact, these fossil remains that have been categorized as *Homo erectus* are so far removed from *Pithecanthropus* and *Sinanthropus* that we must conclude that they are deceptively mislabeled. They are only variants of the *Homo sapiens* kind and are simply placed as *Homo erectus* only to build the category, which is to begin with a fabrication of their evolutionary presuppositional grid.

But if man did not evolve from apes, then where did he come from? In the late 1980s, Allan Wilson, a geneticist at the University of California, Berkeley, along with another research group at Emory University in Atlanta, Georgia, were involved in the study of the DNA of the mitochondria. The mitochondrion is an organelle of the cell that produces energy necessary for the cell to accomplish the many and varied biochemical processes of life. It is called the cell's power plant.

The uniqueness of the mitochondrion is that the DNA in it is exclusively passed down from the mother. Mitochondria, as it turns out, pass from generation to generation only through the female. Since the male DNA does not mix with the mother's in this specific organelle, the DNA remains largely unchanged, allowing us to trace the maternal line back through time.

At times, rare mutations in the mtDNA change one of the "letters" the mother passes on to her progeny. That change, which allows scientists to analyze the relatedness of people throughout our planet, is then traceable throughout her family tree from that moment forward.

That, of course, is not the normal DNA in our cells. The DNA in the nuclei of our cells is the by-product of both parents and the deciding factor in all our physical characteristics. Samples of placenta from women representing all racial groups were souped in a blender, spun in a centrifuge, mixed with a detergent that breaks up cells, dyed fluorescent, and spun once more in the centrifuge.

The results of the analysis of the mitochondrial DNA were astounding. The actual difference between the races was so small and insignificant that it was completely unexpected. The actual physical differences that separate Australian Aborigines from Europeans and Eskimos and Negroid are totally irrelevant compared to our genetic compatibility. It turns out that we are much more closely related than anthropologists had ever previously imagined. We have all come from a single matriarch.

Darwinists have long postulated that apes from different parts of the world have evolved through eons into many varied species of which man has developed into the different races. These races have been categorized principally by the color of their skin, hair, and eyes, and even from the shape of their skulls and the sizes of their bodies. These superficial distinctions have little to do with our genetic heritage. Richard Leakey, voicing the popular idea that most anthropologists have traditionally exclaimed, asserts that there was never a single place or center where modern man originated. It is the belief of the vast majority of evolutionists that humans slowly but inexorably evolved from ancestral apes in different parts of the world simultaneously.

Many use the words *race, people, nation, language, culture*, or even *civilization* indiscriminately and often interchangeably without really understanding what they mean. Even scientists are under the illusion that our physical appearance, including stature, skin color, and shape of the skull, is what determines a race.

> We must really impress on our minds the fact that the race, by which we mean the continuity of a physical type

transmitting blood relationships, represents an essentially natural group, possibly having and as a rule actually having nothing in common with the people, the nationality, the language, and the customs, which corresponds to purely artificial groupings of no anthropological significance and connected only with those historical events of which they are the products. Thus there is no Breton race, but a Breton people; no French race, but a French people; no Aryan race, but Aryan languages; no Latin race, but a Latin civilization. De Quatrefages wrote: *"A people changes its language, its customs, its crafts, sometimes in a relatively short period; it cannot with the same rapidity lose its stature, its colour, and the form of its skull"* (emphasis added) (Boule 2010, 179).

Boule clearly distinguishes that nationalities do not comprise a race but erroneously states that the stature, color, or shape of the skull can differentiate races. These superficial physical traits such as the color of our skin, our hair and eyes, or the shape of our noses or skulls are nothing more than variations within the human genome that existed in the genetics of Adam and Eve. These physical attributes are superficial window dressings and do not determine our genealogy. In fact, the genetic differences among us are absolutely minute compared to the differences between the variants of any other species. We are all children of this mitochondrial Eve. All humans are one race.

Although the old guard continues to hang on for dear life to the failing gradualistic concept of evolution and is still bucking against the goads of empirical data, some are beginning to accept the data at its face value. Stephen Jay Gould, a committed evolutionist speaking on this matter, said:

> *If it's correct, and I'd put money on it, this idea is tremendously important.* . . . *It makes us realize that all human beings, despite the differences in external appearances are*

really members of a single entity that's had a very recent origin in one place. There is a kind of biological brotherhood that's much more profound than we ever realized (emphasis added) (Gould 1988, 47).

The genetic evidence does not match the evolutionary gradualist lineage of humankind. Instead, it corroborates the Judeo-Christian worldview that sees all of humankind as descendants of our Firstfather and Firstmother. All human beings breathing on this planet since the birth of the Second Earth have the same set of archaic parents at least ten times over, beginning with Firstmother, Eve, and Firstfather, Adam: (1) Adam, (2) Seth, (3) Enosh, (4) Kenan, (5) Mahalalel, (6) Jared, (7) Enoch, (8) Methuselah, (9) Lamech, and (10) Noah.

If we were to invent a subclassification for humanity called a subrace in our Second Earth, it could only be the natural lineage of Shem, Ham, and Japheth, the three sons of Noah. But you will find that neither the color of our skin, eyes, or hair or the shape of our skulls or noses, or even our stature have anything to do with this subclassification. It is purely genetic, and we find examples of all the superficial, physical traits in all three lineages from Noah.

Let us take, for example, some of the descendants of Ham, who had four sons: (1) Cush, (2) Mizraim, (3) Put, and (4) Canaan. From the Persian Gulf, the descendents of Cush and Put traveled west and then south into the areas we now know as Ethiopia, Sudan, and Somalia. So the descendants of Cush and Put who settled further south into Africa became the darker-skinned ancestors of the many varied African people of today. The name Cush means black. It seems that Moses's wife was a Cushite, which apparently did not set well with his brother and sister, Aaron and Miriam, according to Numbers 12:1. But our dark-skinned brothers emanated also from the line of Shem through the children of Abraham and his wife Keturah.

The Cushites probably traveled from the western side of the Red Sea and up the Nile River toward its southern source in Ethiopia (Abyssinia), settling in that region around the headwaters of the Nile River and around Lake Victoria.

Those who ventured south into Central Africa, following the Nile River, eventually became isolated from the inhabitants of North Africa and the Middle East by the inhospitable desert that continuously expanded as the planet warmed. Therefore, the isolation was created not only by the differences in the languages but because of their remote geographical location, allowing for a dramatic genetic differentiation that brought forth the darker-skinned features of the beautiful African people.

The name Ham seems to mean swarthy or dark, and therefore, some of his descendents may have carried a more pronounced representation of these genes from Ham. As a direct result of the geographical isolation created by the Sahara Desert, those who traveled below it were not watered down later by genetic mixing with the descendants of the other two brothers.

And yet it is also from Ham that the blond, blue-eyed Aryan people descended. Canaan, as previously stated, was the youngest son of Ham. It seems that Canaan settled initially in the area we now call Palestine, and they were perhaps the early people called Natufians by modern archaeologists. Others ascending from Canaan established the Hittite civilization, which extended from the upper Euphrates in modern-day Iraq and Turkey to Palestine.

Canaan, therefore, fathered the Hittites, Jebusites, Girgashites, Hivites, Arkites, Sinites, Arvadites, Zemarites, and Hamathites. Sidon, the firstborn of Canaan and the grandson of Ham, settled in the area of ancient Phoenicia, and there he established the city named after him, perhaps around 2750 BC.

It was about that time that Tyre was founded, but perhaps not only from the descendents of Ham but also Japheth, the ancestor to the great seafarers who lived in Greece, Italy, Carthage, all the islands

THE ORIGIN OF MAN

of the Mediterranean, Spain, and eventually Ireland. The two people then freely mixed, along with some of the descendents of Eber (who came through Shem), creating the unique blend of the Phoenician people of that day.

From the Hittite civilization, some traveled eastward from the upper Euphrates into the area of ancient Persia, conquering the Elamites who descended from Shem. Eventually, they also became interspersed throughout the area of the southern steppes of Russia. In Persia, their resulting civilization competed with the Semitic Elamite people for control of much of that area.

Now, these Aryan people, who eventually took over the land of the Elamites, became the Indo-European people (Aryan). From that region of Iran (Persia), the ancient Aryans expanded in two directions. A group of them eventually traveled south into India from Persia, conquering the darker-skinned initial inhabitants of the Indus-Sarasvati civilization.

Two more migratory waves of Aryans traveled north from Persia and the steppes of southern Russia. One group traveled west, eventually trekking through the entire breadth of Europe. The other traveled north and east through central China, eventually reaching the Pacific Ocean.

The languages in central China all the way to the China Sea bear the marked influence of the Indo-European language. Countless graves have given us skeletons of these Indo-European people with fair hair and skin all through central China. In the opposite direction, another Aryan migratory wave traveled west across Europe. They are the people we know as the ancient Celtic tribes and the Nordic people.

We do not know what motivated the Aryans to migrate in these three specific patterns. Perhaps they perceived that global warming was creating a more arid condition in their ancient homes, and they set out in search of a more suitable environment. Or perhaps it was just plain greed for pirated booty.

What we do know is that some 2,000 years after the Great Flood, the Aryan people migrating westward through Europe became known as the Celtic tribes. By that time, they had already migrated all the way west into the northern area of the Iberian Peninsula. They were then called Celtiberians. From that area of modern-day northern Spain (Galicia), they finally navigated north through the Atlantic into Ireland and England, mixing with the original natives descended from Japeth who had already occupied that region for at least a thousand years. Those native inhabitants of Ireland and England descended from Japheth and arrived there by boat from the Mediterranean region long before the Celtic migration reached the Atlantic.

Sometime during their western trek through central Europe, a branch of the Indo-European people split and traveled into the northern parts of Europe, populating the area we now know as Scandinavia.

There, those ancient descendants of the Aryans remained fairly isolated from the other inhabitants, thus retaining their fair complexions and light eyes, which were characteristic of the ancient Aryans. From that area in Scandinavia they swooped down into England, meeting the branch that had previously bifurcated and migrated up into the islands from the south (see *The Secret of the Lost Knowledge*). Later, they invaded the area of France that we know as Normandy. The Gallic tribes in France had by that time interbred with the Italian conquerors who had originally descended from Japheth.

As you can now see, from the lineage of Ham, we have both our African brothers and our blond, blue-eyed Aryan brothers. Within his genes existed these expressions, which seem to create radically different appearances. The biblical model predicts that those superficial characteristics are insignificant from a genetic point of view and, more importantly, insignificant from God's point of view.

Not only does the DNA evidence that these geneticists discovered totally contradict their multi-genesis evolutionary claim, it unequivocally shows that the traditional evolutionary guided divisions of races are completely artificial. The evidence points to a common origin in a singular matriarch, which they have ironically and reluctantly named Mitochondrial Eve. We are but one race of human beings, in spite of our outward appearances.

The great movements of people throughout our history, and especially so in our modern era where travel is so quick and easy, have aided in the comingling of humanity, and ironically, it is leading us back toward the path of our beginnings. Instead of greater differentiation due to geographical isolation, we are seeing a trend toward the intermixing of our genes to resemble the genetic phenotype of perhaps Noah, our tenth forefather after Adam. What has become abundantly clear is that the only way to test our true heritage is through DNA haplotype comparisons, which could map the lineage of Shem, Ham, or Japheth. Geneticists may not acknowledge that lineage as described in the scriptures, but the continuity of the mitochondrial DNA does not lie.

Of course, the geneticists who performed these tests and came up with this astounding enigma for the evolutionists are also coming from an evolutionary presupposition. And for that reason, they are quick to point out that this idea of a single matriarch may not necessarily point to a single woman as the matriarch of the human species. In other words, it would mean that if there were other matriarchs at the beginning of our human race, then all their genes became dead-ends. That is to say, the progeny of all the other females who "evolved" in other parts of the world became extinct. That means that only the genes from the Mitochondrial Eve were successfully passed on to modern man.

That this convoluted disclaimer is even considered is clear testimony of their deophobic subjective bias in considering any evidence that smacks of the Bible narrative. What are the chances that of the entire competing hominid, only one female will successfully pass on her genes to the entire world? Maybe in a small-sequestered environment that could be plausible. But when we are considering multiple and diverse groups that are geographically separated by thousands of miles, it is very hard to swallow.

To assert this when the grand scale of the entire population of the world is being considered is pure fantasy, unless there was a global mechanism that could have brought these other lineages to extinction—the Great Flood. That is the conundrum they face.

Those of us who believe the scriptural narrative understand that Neanderthals were partly human, but they were not the children of God. They were engendered by the Enemy of Man to destroy the lineage of Adam and Eve. They were bred for a single purpose: to destroy the world of men. The fact that they bred with the children of Adam is proved by the hybrid forms of *Homo heidelbergensis* and *Homo ergaster*, as well as many others that wait to be announced should DNA testing be successful in their remains. We also know from the archaeological evidence that their breed spanned the entire geographical area occupied by Cro-Magnon in Europe, Africa, the Middle East, and even Siberia, and yet today, after more than 4,000 recorded sequences in the current European gene pool, there is a complete absence of the 27 DNA markers from Neanderthals in modern man.

How could a cataclysm that spanned that geographical area exclusively wipe out Neanderthals and their hybrids and allow only the pure Adamic genes to survive? What evolutionary tale could be spun to explain that? The empirical fact is that every human on this Earth descends from Adam and Eve. How can evolution explain that?

In addition to pulling the rug out from under the anthropologists with this pronouncement of our singular matriarch Eve, they have raised another very sensitive issue for the evolutionist—the issue of the age of humanity. Humankind has not existed for the millions of years that evolution requires.

The geneticists began to calculate the age of Eve by computing the number of mutations that have occurred in the mitochondrial DNA. The assumption is that the more mutations observed in a given group, the more ancient the group ought to be. In addition, if the rates of mutations can be calculated, then one could conceivably extrapolate backward to the time of this Mitochondrial Eve.

However, their initial estimates were made using faulty evolutionary assumptions and circular reasoning. For example, evolutionists assumed that chimpanzees and humans had a common ancestor some 5 million years ago. Since the mtDNA between chimps and humans differs in 1,000 places, they erroneously concluded that one mutation occurs every 10,000 years.

They also assumed that these mutation rates are a constant. Since the mutation rates are the result of cosmic radiation and, as we have already seen, the rate of mutations has increased since the Great Flood due to the decreased protection caused by the reduction of the ozone layer and the weakening of our magnetosphere. So it can hardly be maintained that we can with any certainty know the rate of mutations in the past.

In another study, using Australian aborigines, similar false assumptions were featured. They began with the premise that Aborigines first populated Australia some 40,000 years ago. By computing the very low difference in the mutations in their mtDNA and dividing it through 40,000 years, evolutionists come up with a very low number of mutations that allows them to date the Mitochondrial Eve as far back as they could justifiably stretch.

But in spite of jumping through all these hoops and much to the chagrin of the evolutionists, the age they computed was still way too young for the likes of Leakey. The study came up with a calculation of 100,000 to 200,000 years for the age of humankind.

Of course, those of us who claim that the rate of mutations is not a constant dispute that figure. Evolutionists indeed need a time frame that is extremely large in order to provide enough time for the changes that must take place in a gradualist evolutionary timetable. But the findings have categorically contradicted the 14-million-year dates supposedly determined through the fossils in the strata and have thrown them completely out the window.

The supposedly iron-clad radiometric dates of our ancestral lineage have been completely wiped out by the genetic study, which itself was riddled with evolutionary extrapolations to extend that age.

Evolution needs at minimum (discounting the Hominid) 3 million to 4 million years to create a modicum of credibility so the extremely improbable has a chance to appear plausible. Even if we take their top number, a mere 200,000 years is quite a discrepancy and completely irreconcilable with the gradualist evolutionary processes. There simply is just not enough time for the evolution of the species to take place in such a short period of time through the Darwinian mechanism of the survival of the fittest.

But that was not the end of it. The bad news got even worse. In 1997, a study announced an even more shocking surprise for die-hard evolutionists. It kicked up a dust cloud of invective tirades and subjective disbelief. The news was that the mutation rates of mtDNA were 20 times more rapid than previously assumed.

> If molecular evolution is really neutral at these sites [occurs at a constant rate], such a high mutation rate would indicate that Eve lived about 6,500 years ago, a figure clearly incompatible with current theories on human origins (Loewe and Scherer 1997, 422).

Perhaps it is the evolutionary "current theories on human origins" that are the ones that are "incompatible" with reality. The actual date of Eve would probably be a few thousand years. Since the water vapor canopy of the First Earth offered significant protection against the cosmic radiation that produces mutations, the vast number of these mutations took place after the Great Flood. Moreover, the higher percentage of oxygen in the atmosphere meant that the First Earth had a proportionately larger ozone layer as well. Therefore, the mutation rate during the time of the First Earth would have been much less than in our present inferior environment.

THE ORIGIN OF MAN

Regardless of the cause, evolutionists are most concerned about the effect of a faster mutation rate. For example, researchers have calculated [previously] that mitochondrial Eve—the woman whose mtDNA was ancestral to that in all living people—lived 100,000 to 200,000 years ago in Africa. *Using the new clock, she would be a mere 6,000 years old* (emphasis added) (Gibbons 1998, 29).

As a result of the destruction of the human race prior to the Great Flood, the wife of Noah became, in essence, the second Eve of the Second Earth some 6,000 years ago. Perhaps this "new clock" is pointing to the time of the bottleneck in human history that separated our First Earth from our Second Earth.

*

"Snap! Six thousand years old! What do we do now?" asked Bullshingle, flailing his arms in exasperation.

"Just keep smiling. Maybe no one will pay attention to it," whispered Rocksy.

*

The result of the initial study had produced two possible initial sources where this Eve could have lived. Some geneticists feel that the most likely place of origin is Africa, but there was also strong evidence for China.

However, more recent studies have shown that Europe may have also been where she originally lived (Baringa 1992, 686–87). However, this may be better explained by the fact that these are the three places where the descendants of Noah migrated when they left the ark's landing place.

Let's see what have we discovered so far in regard to Leakey's claim of the "solid evidence" for the origins of man. A recent origin, a singular place of origin, a singular person of origin, and the brotherhood of all races—it sure sounds to me like the story of Adam and Eve in the scriptures. What a coincidence!

Geneticists are now attempting to go a step further in their search for our primordial progenitors. Researchers in England, France, and the United States are extending the search for Adam. Their research is presently focused on the Y chromosome, which is exclusively in the male gender. The search for Adam is considerably more complex since that part of the DNA in the cell's nucleus has considerably more genes than in the mitochondria.

Stephen Gould once said he would put his money on it that the empirical data of the genetic Adam corroborates the genetic evidence of Eve. In 1995, a study of 38 men from around the world showed no changes in the segment of the Y chromosome that is always inherited from the father.

If man had evolved from apes through one man (Adam) during the last three and a half million years, we should expect to find 133 mutations in our present population. Had this Adam lived 500,000 years ago, we would expect to find 19 mutations. Had he lived only 150,000 years ago, we should expect to find 5.5 mutations. But, to their complete surprise, no changes were found (Dorit, Akashi, and Gilbert 1995, 1183–85).

Oops! The genetic evidence for our primordial patriarch and matriarch clearly substantiate an age of only several thousand years for the human family. The evolutionary rationalization used to explain this contradiction to their claims states that the genetic components of all other women in the last three and a half million years of evolutionary human history have become extinct. Subsequently, only one woman, who lived just a few thousand years ago, survived to bear the more than six-billion-member family of the singular human race.

How many women would have lived throughout these three and a half million years? Of all the women living in separate parts of the world throughout all generations, only one was able to pass her genes down to modern man. How is that possible in an evolutionary reality?

In essence, what they are insinuating is that many unforeseen local catastrophes must have caused all other women and their progeny in all parts of the world to die off, allowing only one Eve to survive and pass on her genes to us. Moreover, the probability of this happening through local causes in every part of the world becomes even more improbable when we compute into these odds the genetic evidence of Adam. Then it becomes exponentially more improbable that this would happen to Adam as well as Eve.

What shall we say now of Richard Dawkins's comment regarding our ignorance?

> If the history-deniers who doubt the fact of evolution are ignorant of biology, those who think the world began less than ten thousand years ago are worse than ignorant, they are deluded to the point of perversity (Dawkins 2009, 85).

Modern genetics proves that Mr. Dawkins and his fellow evolutionists are the real history-deniers. The empirical data simply show that we had only one set of parents who lived only a few thousand years ago. Period. End of story. The entire evolutionary speculation of multiple geneses from various apes and millions of years of gradual evolution is in contradiction to reality. God designed the miracle of life and specially created man to inhabit His incredibly complex and elaborate universe for His glory.

Adam and Eve were space-time historical human beings who walked the Earth. Noah and his wife were also space-time historical human beings who parented the Second Earth. Every human being walking on this planet is related at least ten times over by the ten patriarchs between Adam and Noah. The stranger is but a family member we have yet to get to know.

Regardless of the color of our skin, the shape of our nose, the texture of our hair, the color of our eyes, or any other external variation, our genetic brotherhood is so tight that we are practically indistinguishable from one another. That is evidence that favors special creation and not the ascent of man from apes in varied regions of our planet.

Our Firstfather was Adam, and our Firstmother was Eve. That should not be a surprise to anyone who is a student of antiquities. Cultures throughout the entire world have given us the same basic creation story, with only slight variations. Elements such as the creation of man from clay and the creation of dry land from a watery chaos are common to most major cultures. These things are simply ignored by evolutionists and dismissed as mythology. Unfortunately for them, they cannot dismiss the genes.

What Then?

In the final analysis, we are left with only one verifiable contribution to science from Darwin's evolutionary theory. Selective pressures can cause adaptive changes to those within a species, allowing one trait or another to gain preeminence in the genetic pool. That may result in an apparent evolution, but it is restricted to finite limits that are predetermined by the genetic variability built in from the moment of creation within the genome of each kind.

We, therefore, can safely conclude that there is such a thing as microevolution within a species, but there is absolutely no evidence of macroevolution; that is, evolution from one species into another. No living kind has ever changed into another kind.

And yet, in spite of the scientific evidence I have just outlined, most US public school systems have explicitly censored any worldview outside of naturalism. I think it is scientifically revolting that some, in the name of science, refuse to allow the opposing views to be considered and compared in the public education arena. It has always been a clear sign of inferiority to fear free and unfettered open dialog in the public square.

Those who have reason on their side have no fear of an open debate. But those who, through indoctrination, have created a paradigm built on a foundation of straw have a great deal to fear from open dialog. There is no intellectually defensible or adequate reason to prevent the open discussion of scientific data regarding the origin of our universe and the origin of life in the taxpayer-supported free marketplace of ideas.

Those who claim that teaching the science of intelligent design is promoting religion by the country or state fail to see that just because a religion happens to agree with science does not mean that science is the same as religion. In fact, they have made their naturalistic science into the religion of atheists.

What has been instituted in these supposed centers of education is nothing less than indoctrination and censorship. Only when all opposing schools of thought are objectively considered and the student is encouraged, through reason, to select which view he or she deems worthy does true education take place. Today, there is sadly less freedom to truly educate in our public schools than has existed in some Marxist totalitarian states.

It appears that we have reached a new apex in the institutionalization of societal coercion and the indoctrination of our children for the purpose of social engineering. And in my mind, their motives are, at the very least, highly suspect. Such monolithic censorship has historically been the enemy of free thinkers everywhere and the death of true science.

The appalling censorship of scientists who have, through their rational capacity, accepted intelligent design rather than the evolutionary paradigm is wholly inexcusable in a society that purports to value freedom of thought. In the name of pluralism, our modern colleges have courses in pornography, but intelligent design is taboo.

In summary, the naturalist by priory dismissal of the possibility of a Creator is left with no choice but to blindly believe that the universe evolved from nothing. Through some nebulous "quantum fluctuation," the Big Bang occurred, producing enormous amounts of hydrogen that eventually formed into stars.

These stars then created the higher elements within them (a process not disputed by the proponents of intelligent design). But then these higher elements eventually evolved into complex molecules through purely random reactions that eventually evolved into life. This life eventually evolved into human beings.

In other words, hydrogen (a tasteless, colorless, odorless element) through chance chemical processes and copious amounts of time became a human being. To be more precise, if we begin from the beginning, nothing evolved into a human being. Now that is real faith!

The evidence of an arbitrary choice made in the many processes that comprise the functions of the living cell is completely ignored by evolutionary biologists. If it does not fit into their square hole, the round stick is just simply hidden under the table and forbidden from the public square.

I am not asking the reader to make a blind leap of faith. I am simply asking you to examine the evidence. The evolutionary concept is simply at odds with the reality observed. True empirical data and rational reasons have been presented here to support the fact that this masterfully engineered and highly ordered universe could not have evolved from random chemical processes. The evidence presented has not been speculative or mystical in nature. I now leave it up to the reader to consider the implications that should naturally follow.

In considering the origin of the universe, the origin of life, and the origin of humans, the biblical narrative stands as the most scientifically verifiable postulate. The evidence overwhelmingly points to the existence of an intelligent, all-powerful, master designer. To believe anything less is to take a blind leap of faith.

Faith is not the antithesis of reason. It is the consequence of reason. Without reason, there can be no substantial foundation for true faith. Truth is unified. True science is in harmony with true spiritual truth.

I have often been asked by evolutionists, "How can you believe in a God you have not seen? How can you trust a God you cannot see?"

Christians must be careful when speaking with evolutionists. Too often, I have seen debates in which Christians are more concerned about winning the debate than caring about the individual who may have honest questions about the reality of God.

To this legitimate question I answer, "The question behind your question is, 'If I told you that looking through a special telescope or microscope you could see Him, would you want to see Him?'"

Most people simply shrug my question away and say, "That is impossible."

But some will say yes.

To those I say, "This is the first prerequisite of a true scientist. A true scientist must be willing to accept the direction in which the data point. We cannot see a tiny quark inside a subatomic particle with our naked eye. But we can deduce its existence through deductive and inductive reasoning by the energy and traces of the path created when we split a neutron or an electron.

My eyes have not seen the physical face of God, but I have seen the manifold evidence of His intellect in the marvelous design of every aspect of our universe. I have seen the symmetry that permeates our universe at every level, and it is impossible for me to rationally conclude that this was a random accident. The code of DNA cannot be produced by serendipity. Our humanish soul is inescapable. We cannot crush a coconut and with the same callousness crush a human skull. Even humans bear the fingerprint of God. And when I came to the intellectual decision that a master designer must have designed and engineered our space-time continuum, I decided that I wanted to know who He was.

It is only then that I began to experience the reality of God in a much deeper way than can be described through simple human senses or words. You will not be able to see Him without first coming to either the telescope or the microscope of faith.

But the path to true faith is not blind. It is based on reason. It is not that there is not enough evidence that points to His reality. It is that humans do not wish to bow to the authority of a God who will hold them morally accountable.

For this subversive, underlying reason, naturalists throughout the last few centuries have ridiculed and labored to discredit the biblical account of the Great Flood as a mythological fairy tale. They have seized upon the Darwinian theory of evolution and the jaded uniformitarian hypothesis to discredit the worldwide deluge account, insisting on the slow, gradual, almost imperceptible process of ongoing evolution over the concept of catastrophism exemplified by the Great Flood.

Belief in the Great Flood was considered by many from the seventeenth through the twentieth centuries as superstitious ignorance. And ever since, they have molded a universally adopted paradigm of absolute uniformitarianism in order to establish enormous ages for the process of gradualism in evolution to have a chance at being plausible. But as we have seen, it is the jaded uniformitarian hypothesis and the Darwinian hypothesis that have become discredited and are found wanting by the illumination of true science.

In spite of the overwhelming evidence amassed in the last decades that has scientifically shown that meteor strikes did take place on Earth and that they caused a global catastrophe unparalleled in Earth's history, many scientists still hold onto the failed jaded uniformitarian hypothesis. This meteor strike, which most evolutionists now credit with the extinction of dinosaurs, produced undeniable global consequences of an unprecedented nature, causing countless species to become extinct. But that was only one of seven such meteors. We will look at those in the next book of this series, *The Death of the First Earth*.

And yet evolutionists still refuse to admit that there could have been a global flood. In their naturalistic bias, they have continued to insist that the numerous flood accounts found in all cultures are simply referring to local floods, even though the accounts almost unanimously specifically claim otherwise.

If the biblical model is correct, then there should be empirical supporting evidence to prove its historicity. In the final book of this series, we will explore the overwhelming scientific, anthropological, and historical evidence to support the biblical model regarding the death of the First Earth.

REFERENCES

Adler, Jerry, and John Carey. "Enigmas of Evolution." *Stephen Jay Gould Archive.* https://dbpedia.org/page/Punctuated_equilibrium.

"Anthro-Art." 1981. *Science Digest* 89 (April): 41.

Aristotle. *History of Animals* I.6.

Barinaga, M. 1992. "'African Eve' Backers Beat a Retreat." *Science* 255, no. 5045 (February): 686–87.

Barrow, John D., and Frank J. Tipler. 1996. *The Anthropic Cosmological Principle.* New York: Oxford University Press.

Belmonte, Juan Carlos Izpisua. 2016. "Human-Animal Embryos: A Potential New Source of Transplant Organs." *Scientific American* (November): 34.

Bendewald, Jim, and Frank Sherwin. 2004. *Evolution Shot Full of Holes.* Madison, WI: Evidence Press.

Blankley, Tony. 2003. "Cloning and the Chinese." *Townhall*, September 24, 2003. https://townhall.com/columnists/tonyblankley/2003/09/24/cloning-and-the-chinese-n1127333.

Blavatsky, H. P. 1877. *Isis Unveiled.* Wheaton, IL: Theosophical Publishing House.

Bohor, Bruce F., Peter J. Modreski, and Eugene E. Foord. 1987. "Shocked Quartz in the Cretaceous-Tertiary Boundary Clays: Evidence for a Global Distribution." *Science* 236, no. 4802 (May): 705–09.

Bottum, J. 2000. "The Pig-Man Cometh." *The Weekly Standard*, October 23, 2000. https://www.weeklystandard.com/j-bottum/the-pig-man-cometh.

Boule, Marcellin. 2010. *Fossil Men: Elements of Human Paleontology.* Memphis, TN: reprinted by General Books, original publication by Oliver and Boyd, Edinburgh.

Chain, Ernst. 1982. "Was Darwin Wrong?" *Life Magazine,* April 1982.

Chesterton, G. K. 1925. *The Everlasting Man.* New York: Image Books.

Clark, W. E. Le Gros. 1955. *The Fossil Evidence for Human Evolution: An Introduction to the Study of Paleoanthropology.* Chicago: The University of Chicago Press.

Clay, Albert T. 1922. *Hebrew Deluge Story in Cuneiform.* New Haven: Yale University Press. http://etana.org/sites/default/files/coretexts/20411.pdf.

Coppedge, James F. 1973. *Evolution: Possible or Impossible? Genes, Proteins, and the Laws of Chance.* Grand Rapids, MI: Zondervan.

Custance, Arthur C. 1975. *Genesis and Early Man, Vol. II.* Grand Rapids, MI: Zondervan.

Darwin, Charles. 1845. *The Voyage of the Beagle.* Charles Darwin Classic Literature. https://charles-darwin.classic-literature.co.uk/the-voyage-of-the-beagle/ebook-page-185.asp.

———. 1979. *The Origin of Species.* New York: Random House.

Davies, Bethan. 2016. "Cosmic Rays." *AntarcticGlaciers.org.* May 6, 2016. http://www.antarcticglaciers.org/glacial-geology/dating-glacial-sediments-2/cosmic-rays/.

Dawkins, Richard. 2009. *The Greatest Show on Earth.* New York: Free Press.

Diamond, Jared. 1999. *Guns, Germs, and Steel.* New York: W. W. Norton and Co.

Dorit, R. L., H. Akashi, and W. Gilbert. 1995. "Absence of Polymorphism at the ZFY Locus on the Human Y Chromosome." *Science* 268, no. 5214 (May): 1183–85.

REFERENCES

Eberlin, Marcos. *Foresight*. 2019. Seattle: Discovery Institute Press. In Mansey, Sheref S., Jason P. Schrum, Mathangi Krishnamurthy, Sylvia Tobe, Douglas A. Treco, and Jack W. Szostak. "Template-Directed Synthesis of a Genetic Polymer in a Model Protocell." *Nature* 454 (July): 122–25.

Eckhardt, Robert. 1972. "Population Genetics and Human Origins." *Scientific American* 226 no. 1 (January): 94–103.

Faul, Henry. 1966. *Ages of Rocks, Planets, and Stars*. New York: McGraw Hill.

Feduccia, Alan. 1985. "On Why Dinosaurs Lacked Feathers." In *The Beginning of Birds: Proceedings of the International Archaeopteryx Conference, 1984*. Eichstatt, Germany: Jura Museum (January 1, 1985): 76.

Fisher, John Michael. 2012. "Carbon-14-Dated Dinosaur Bones Are Less Than 40,000 Years Old." *New Geology*. newgeology.us/presentation48.html.

Gibbons, Ann. 1998. "Calibrating the Mitochondrial Clock." *Science* 279 (January): 28–29.

Gilbert, Scott, John Opitz, and Rudolf Raff. 1996. "Resynthesizing Evolutionary and Developmental Biology." *Developmental Biology* 173, no. 0032 (1996): 357–72.

Gish, Duane T. 1979. *Evolution: The Fossils Still Say No!* San Diego: Creation Life Publishers.

Gleiser, Marcelo. 2001. *The Prophet and the Astronomer*. New York: W. W. Norton and Company. Google Books.

Goldschmidt, Richard. 1940. *The Material Basis of Evolution*. New Haven, CT: Yale University Press.

Gould, Stephen Jay. 1988. "The Search for Adam and Eve." *Newsweek*, January 11, 1988.

Gran, Rani. 2008. "Solar Variability Striking a Balance with Climate Change." *NASA*. (May 7, 2008). https://www.nasa.gov/topics/solarsystem/features/solar_variability.html.

Gribbin, John, and Jeremy Cherfas. 1981. "Descent of Man – or Ascent of Ape?" *New Scientist* 91, no. 1269 (September): 592–95.

Grocholski, Brent. 2014. "Unraveling Ringwoodite Hydration in Mantle." *Science* 346, no. 6207. (October): 311–12. https://science.sciencemag.org/content/346/6207/311.3.

Gronstal, Aaron L. 2014. "Under the Bright Lights of an Aging Sun." *Astrobiology Magazine*. July 4, 2014. https://www.astrobio.net/news-exclusive/bright-lights-aging-sun/.

Haile-Selassie, Yohannes, Beverly Z. Saylor, Alan Deino, Naomi E. Levin, Mulugeta Alene, and Bruce M. Latimer. 2012. "A New Hominin Foot from Ethiopia Shows Multiple Pliocene Bipedal Adaptations." *Nature* 483 (March): 565–69.

Harmon, Katherine. 2013. "Shattered Ancestry." *Scientific American* 308, no. 2 (February): 42–49.

Heidel, Alexander. 1949. *Gilgamesh Epic and Old Testament Parallels*. Chicago: University of Chicago Press.

Hume, David. 1772. "An Enquiry Concerning Human Understanding." https://www.marxists.org/reference/subject/philosophy/works/en/hume.htm.

Hutton, James. 2004. *Theory of the Earth*, Volume 1. Project Gutenberg. http://www.gutenberg.org/files/12861/12861-h/12861-h.htm.

Johanson, Donald C., and Maitland A. Edey. 1981. *Lucy: The Beginnings of Humankind*. New York: Simon and Schuster.

Jungers, William 1982. "Lucy's Limbs: Skeletal Allometry and Locomotion in Australopithecus Afarensis." *Nature* 297 (June): 676–78.

———. 2013. Quoted in Katherine Harmon. "Shattered Ancestry." *Scientific American* 308, no. 2 (February): 48.

Kaplan, Matt. 2012. "Fossils Point to a Big Family for Human Ancestors." *Nature* (August). https://www.nature.com/news/fossils-point-to-a-big-family-for-human-ancestors-1.11144.

Leakey, Meave, Fred Spoor, M. Christopher Dean, Craig S. Feibel, Susan C. Antón, Christopher Kairie, and Louise N. Leakey. 2012. "New Fossils from Koobi in Northern Kenya Confirm Taxonomic Diversity in Early Homo." *Nature* 288 (August): 201–04.

Leakey, Richard E., and Roger Lewin. 1977. *Origins: The Emergence and Evolution of Our Species and Its Possible Future.* New York: E. P. Dutton.

Lewin, R. 1980. "Evolutionary Theory under Fire," *Science* 210, no. 21 (November): 883–87.

Lewontin, R. C. 1974. *The Genetic Basis of Evolutionary Change.* New York: Columbia University Press.

Loewe, Lawrence, and Siegfried Scherer. 1997. "Mitochondrial Eve: The Plot Thickens." *Trends in Ecology and Evolution* 12, no. 11 (November): 422.

MacDonald, Fiona. 2016. "New Study Shows How Rapidly Earth's Magnetic Field Is Changing." *Science Alert.* May 11, 2016. https://sciencealert.com/new-study-shows-that-earth-s-magnetic-field-is-weakening-more-rapidly-than-we-thought.

NASA. "Earth's Inconstant Magnetic Field." 2003. *NASA Science*, December 29, 2003. https://science.nasa.gov/science-news/science-at-nasa/2003/29dec_magnetic field.

Ogden III, J. Gordon. 1997. "The Use and Abuse of Radiocarbon." *Annals of the New York Academy of Science* 288 (February): 167–173.

Olson, Steve. 2002. *Mapping Human History: Genes, Race, and Our Common Origins*. New York: Mariner Books.

Pearcey, Nancy. 2004. *Total Truth: Liberating Christianity from Its Cultural Captivity*. Wheaton, IL: Crossway Books.

Pilbeam, David. 1968. "The Earliest Hominids." *Nature* 219 (September): 1335–38.

———. 1981. "Ramapithecus' Humanlike Jaw." *Science Digest* (April): 36.

Popol Vuh: Part One. LitChart. https://www.litcharts.com/lit/popol-vuh/part-one.

Save-Soderbergh, T., and Ingrid U. Olsson, eds. 1970. "C-14 Dating and Egyptian Chronology." *Radiocarbon Variations and Absolute Chronology*.

Schaeffer, Francis A. 1982. *The God Who Is There*, Volume 1 Westchester, IL: Crossway Books.

Silvers, Lee M. 1997. *Remaking Eden: Cloning and Beyond in a Brave New World*. New York: Avon Books.

Simon, Eric, Jane Reece, and Jean Dickey. 2012. *Campbell Essential Biology with Physiology*, 4th ed. Upper Saddle River, NJ: Pearson Education.

Slusher, Harold. 1973. *Critique of Radiometric Dating*. San Diego: CA: Creation Life Publishers.

Smit, J. 1999. "The Global Stratigraphy of the Cretaceous-Tertiary Boundary Impact Ejecta." *Annual Review of Earth and Planetary Sciences* 27 (May): 75–113.

Smith, Wesley J. 2004. *Consumer's Guide to a Brave New World*. San Francisco: Encounter Books.

Snelling, Andrew. 2009. A. *Earth's Catastrophic Past, Vol. 2*. Dallas, TX: Institute for Creation Research.

REFERENCES

Spoor, Fred. 1994. "Implications of Early Hominid Labyrinthine Morphology for Evolution of Human Bipedal Locomotion." *Nature* 369 (June): 645-48.

Stanley, Steven M. 1981. *The New Evolutionary Timetable: Fossils, Genes, and the Origin of Species.* New York: Basic Books.

Stober, Dan. 2010. "The Strange Case of Solar Flares and Radioactive Elements." *Stanford Report* (August). https://news.stanford.edu/news/2010/august/sun-082310.html.

Stove, David. 1995. *Darwinian Fairytales: Selfish Genes, Errors of Heredity, and Other Fables of Evolution.* New York: Encounter Books.

Stürzenbaum, S.R., J. Andre, P. Kille, and A.J. Morgan. 2009. "Earthworms, Genomes, Genes and Proteins: The (Re)Discovery of Darwin's Worms." *Proc. Biol. Sciences* 276, no. 1658 (March): 789–797.

Sykes, Bryan. 1991. "The Past Comes Alive." *Nature* 352 (August): 381–82.

Thatcher, Oliver J., ed. 1915. *The Library of Original Sources, Vol. II.* Milwaukee, WI: University Research Extension.

Tolkien, J. R. R. *The Fellowship of the Ring.* Deviant Art. https://www.deviantart.com/hahaiseeurmind/art/Galadriel-Monologue-7745546.

The Utah Statesman. 2003. "To Clone a Mule: History Offers Mixed Messages." June 2, 2003. https://usustatesman.com/to-clone-a-mule-history-offers-mixed-messages/.

White, Tim D., Berhane Asfaw, Yonas Beyene, Yohannes Haile-Selassie, C. Owen Lovejoy, Gen Suwa, and Giday WoldeGabriel. 2009. "Ardipithecus Ramidus and the Paleontology of Early Hominids." *Science* 326 (October): 75-86.

Wolbach, Wendy S., Dieter Heymann, Thomas E. Yancey, M. H. Thiemens, E. A. Johnson, D. Roach, and S. Moecker. 1998. "Geochemical Markers of the Cretaceous-Tertiary Boundary Event at Brazos River, Texas, USA." *Geochimica et Cosmochimica Acta* 62, no. 1 (January): 173–181.

Yeoman, Barry. 2006. "Schweitzer's Dangerous Discovery." *Discover*, April 26, 2006. https://www.discovermagazine.com/the-sciences/schweitzers-dangerous-discovery.

INDEX

A

accelerator mass spectrometry 276
age of gigantism 182
alpha particles 290
Alpha Point 138–139
Ameghino 360–361
American Geophysical Union 274, 277
ampullae of Lorenzini 157
angio-sperms 271
Antarctica 195–196, 201–202, 204, 210, 253
anthropic cosmological theory 59
Anthropoidea 362
antineutrino 284, 287
Antluopdiis 361
Apollo asteroids 19, 171–172, 211
Apophis 172
Archaeopteryx 36, 54–55
Archaeoraptor 51–53
Archeozoic Era 176
Ardipithecus ramidus (Ardi) 395
ATP 33
aurora borealis 298
Australopithecus afarensis 338, 380, 388–389, 393–394
Australopithecus africanus 378–380, 388, 392–394
Australopithecus robustus 378–379

B

Barnes, T. G. 293
basalt rock 199, 201, 204–205
Belayev, Dimitry 80
beta particles 282–283
biodomes 179–180, 195
Biotransplant 115
bipedal locomotion 388, 390, 393, 395–396, 403
Biston betularia 71
Black, Davidson 353
blastocyst 117
Blavatsky, H. P. 2
Boule, Marcellin 346, 352
Braginsky, Stanislav 300
Bromage, Timothy 381, 386–387
Brookhaven National Laboratory 285
Brown, Walter 251

C

Cambrian Burgess Shale 227
cancer 102, 111, 297
cannibalism 140, 211, 214, 223, 370
carbon 14 dating method 268
Carboniferous Montceau Shale 229
catastrophic sedimentary deposits 184–185
catastrophism 14–15, 17–18, 22, 41, 163, 166, 247, 432
catatonic state 159
cause-and-effect 61
Cedarberg Formation 228

Cenozoic Era 51, 107, 177
Cercopithedae 362
Chancelade race 374
character complex 52, 63–64, 76, 78–79, 82, 84–85, 87, 98, 146, 313, 318, 338–340, 342, 349, 351, 367–368, 372, 374, 376, 382, 393–394, 399, 401–402, 405–406
Chesterton, G.K. 347
Chicxulub crater 173, 193, 271
Chilcotin Group 203
chimera human-animal hybrids 120
circular reasoning 140, 143, 147, 152, 154–155, 176, 183, 267, 275, 310, 413, 423
Clark, W.E. Le Gross 333, 339
Coleman, William 123
Colombian Plateau 253
Columbia River Basalt Group 203
cones 158, 203
continental drift 20, 252
convergent evolution 56–59, 158
Cook, Melvin 295
Coppens, Yves 359
coral reefs 248
coronal mass ejections 112
cosmic radiation 92–93, 111–112, 114, 181, 268–270, 272, 284, 290–291, 294, 296, 298, 301, 423–424
cosmic rays 92, 110, 112–114, 254, 272–274, 286, 290–294, 298, 301
cranial capacity 319–320, 339–340, 344, 349–350, 352, 358–359, 367, 370, 379, 382, 385–386, 388, 412
Cretaceous Djadokhta Formation 234

Cretaceous Santana Formation 231
Cretaceous Tepexi Limestone 233
CRISPR/Cas9 116
Cro-Magnon man 214, 318–321, 324–325, 335, 337, 350, 370–371, 377, 411–412
Cro-Magnon species 316
Custance, Arthur 376
Cuverian legend 357, 365, 378, 403
Cuvier 345, 356–357, 365

D

Dart, Raymond 378
Darwin, Charles 14, 164
Darwin's Fantasyland 106
Darwin's finches 81
daughter element 282–283, 288–289, 291–292, 294
Dawkins, Richard 427
Deccan Traps 202–203
deophobes 39–40, 71, 258
De Silva, Jeremy 397
Devonian Thunder Bay Limestone 229
Diamond, Jared 275
Diprothomo 361
diprotodonts 349
Dmitry Belayev 80
DNA 3–4, 9, 11, 33, 36, 47, 70, 87, 94, 131, 141, 153, 156, 161, 265, 279, 310, 322–329, 368, 373, 414–415, 420–422, 426, 431
Drosophilidae 91
Dryopithecinae 401–402
Dryopithecus 345, 361–363, 383, 399, 400–403, 405, 408, 411
Dryopithecus fontani 400
Dubois, Eugene 301, 343
dysteleological 61, 68–69, 94

INDEX

E

Eanthropus dawsoni 342–343
earthworm 37, 151–155
Eckhardt, Robert 402
E. coli 96, 98
Einstein, Albert 134
Eldredge, Niles 29, 41
Elijah 256
endolymphatic pores 158
Enoch 256, 417
Eohippus 48
Epic of Gilgamesh 205
Equus asinus 67
Equus burchelli 67
Equus caballus 67
Equus grevyi 67
Equus zebra 67
eugenics 35
evolutionary conservation 154

F

First Earth 6, 23, 26, 56, 64, 92–93, 113–114, 170, 180, 182, 192–193, 199–200, 205–208, 211, 213–215, 218–221, 223, 243, 249–254, 258, 268–272, 274, 280–282, 290, 301, 313, 324, 329, 349, 351, 374, 384, 413, 424–425, 432–433
First International Conference on Astroparticle Physics 286
FitzRoy, Robert 164
floodgates of the sky 180, 207, 216–217, 251
fluoride dating method 301, 343
forty-percenters 32
fossil graveyards 180, 187, 225–226, 244–245, 247
FOXP2 322
fruitfly 154

G

Galapagos Island 81–82
Galileo 167
gamma rays 282–284, 292
gaps 24–26, 28, 30, 46, 263, 312, 362, 395
Gaudry, Jean Albert 400
Gauss, Karl Friedrich 298
Gemini 214–215
gemmules 87–88
Genesis singularity 136–138
genetic devolution 100
genetic pool 66, 73, 82–83, 85–86, 90, 93, 103–105, 324, 374, 377, 391, 428
genetics arms race 119
genetic splicing 115
genetic variability 66, 79, 82, 178, 377, 428
genotype 72–73, 79, 85, 90–91, 103, 105, 124
geodynamo 299–300
geologic column 106, 140–141, 156, 175–178, 184, 237, 265, 267–268
germline mutations 111
Gibraltar skull 382
Gish, Duane T. 391
glycolysis 33, 57
Gobi Desert 234
Goldschmidt, Richard 121
Gould, Stephen Jay 28–29, 41, 43, 60, 416, 426
gradualism 15, 17, 22–23, 28, 41–42, 44–45, 51, 55, 123, 129, 131, 166, 177, 180, 184, 186, 310, 432

Grand Canyon 56, 187, 242
granitic rock 181, 197, 199, 205, 211–212, 291
Great Chain of Beings 36
Grimaldi skulls 334–335
Grottes de Enfants 335
Groves, Colin 366

H

hadrons 288
hairpin bend 144, 146
Harmon, Bob 262
Hell Creek Formation 260, 262
Heshvan 208, 215
Hesiod 216, 221
Hesperopithecus haroldcooki 341, 353
Hikurangi 203
history deniers 30, 40, 92, 147, 223, 267, 278, 427
HLA gene 109
hominid 331–332, 338, 353, 362–363, 378, 401–402, 406, 410–411, 421, 424
Hominoid 338, 362–363, 378
Homo erectus 97, 329, 338, 351–353, 355–356, 359–360, 363, 365–366, 369–370, 376, 378, 380–381, 384–386, 388–389, 398–399, 402, 411, 413–414
Homo erectus floresiensis 365
Homo ergaster 324, 329, 365–366, 370, 372, 422
Homo georgicus 363, 365–366
Homo habilis 338, 351–352, 354, 359, 363, 376, 378, 380, 383–386, 388, 392, 394, 398
Homo heidelbergensis 324, 329, 337, 369–370, 372, 422
Homo rudolfensis 385, 397–398

Homunculus patagonicus 361
hopeful monster theory 123
Hubble Space Telescope 167
Hume, David 163
Hummer, Christopher 386
Huxley 50, 71, 106–107, 311
Hydroplate Theory 251–252
hyper-dolichocephalic 336–337, 367, 371
Hyracotherium 48–49

I

Iguazu Falls 200–201, 204, 220
Indus-Sarasvati 419
inheritance of acquired characteristics 85, 89
intermediates 23–24, 26, 28, 30, 36, 40, 45, 49, 53, 64, 70, 122, 145–148, 161, 282, 311, 314, 320, 349, 410
iridium 210, 271

J

Jacobsen, Steven 212
jaded uniformitarian 18, 20, 22, 25, 165–167, 174, 176–177, 179, 237, 259, 261, 282, 432
Java Man 343–344, 355, 393
Johansen, Donald 380
Judeo-Christian Cosmological Model 17, 61, 92, 133, 137
Jupiter 44, 165, 167–168, 171, 298

K

Keith, Sir Arthur 378
KT boundary 209–210, 271
Kuiper cloud 169
Kuiper, Gerard 169
Kurte'n, Bjorn 49

INDEX

L

La Brea tar pits 193
La Chapelle skull 369
Lalueza-Fox 322
Lamarck, Jean-Baptiste 164
Lamb, Horace 298
Large Hadron Collider 288
Lartet, Édouard 400
leaching 31, 294
Leakey, Louis 379
Leakey, Mary 381, 388, 394
Leakey, Meave 399
Lenski, Richard 96
Leo 214
Libby, Willard F. 268
Linnaeus 159
liquefaction 239–240
lithification 228
Lucy 380–381, 388–391, 396–397, 399, 411
Lyell, Charles 14, 162

M

macroevolution 27, 30, 40, 65, 78, 80, 94–96, 101, 106, 109, 122, 178, 377, 428
macromutations 90–91, 98, 105–106, 121–123
magnetic mirror effect 294
magnetosphere 92, 113–114, 273–274, 291, 298, 301, 423
Magsat 300
mammoths 249, 350
Manihiki 203
Maniitsoq, Greenland 196
Mars 273, 328
Mauer jaw 369
Mayr 69
Mazak, Vratislav 366
MC1R 322
McDonald, Fiona 299
megafauna 349, 351, 359
Meganthropus paleojavanicus 348
Mendel 87
Mercury 171, 200
Mesozoic Era 177
microevolution 27, 40, 65, 78, 98, 121, 122, 377, 428
micromutations 106, 122
Mid-Atlantic Ridge 197, 199, 201–202, 204–205, 213, 217, 248, 251–252
Mid-Oceanic Ridge 199, 201, 252, 259
Mitochondrial Eve 421, 423
modern synthesis 27, 40
Modern Synthesis 28, 40
Monod, Jacques 68
Mount Currie Conglomerate 188
mtDNA 325, 414, 423–425
Mt. Olga 189
mutations 43, 66, 89, 90–96, 98–99, 101–105, 108–111, 113–114, 122, 149, 178, 414, 422–424, 426

N

Namibia 201, 204
National Academy of Sciences 83, 261
National Solar Observatory 286
natural selection 2, 13, 27, 65–66, 68, 71, 73–74, 80–81, 85, 124–127
Neanderthal genetic markers 329
Neanderthal man 120, 316, 318–321, 324–325, 329–330, 333
Neanderthals 6, 36, 214, 223, 317–320, 322, 324–325, 328–329, 330, 332, 337, 363, 367–374, 376–377, 411, 413, 422

near-Earth-orbit (NEO) 168
near extinction bottleneck 110
Nebraska Man 341–342
Nematoda 152
Nemget Basin, Ukhaa Tolgod Area 234
neo-Darwinism 89–91
Neoplatonists 34
Nephilim 6, 214, 223–324, 329, 374
neuromasts 158
neutrino 286–288
Newton 133
Ngeneo, Bernard 381
Nippur 216
nuclear winter scenario 195

O

Oakley, Kenneth Page 343
olivine 212–213
Ontong Java Plateau 203
Opisthocomus hoatzin 55
Ordovician Soom Shale 228
Oreopithecus 400–401, 403
Oxnard, Charles 391
ozone layer 92, 113–114, 254, 268, 272, 297, 423–424

P

Paleozoic Era 177
panspermia 58–59
parabolic jaw 406, 408–409
parent element 282–283
Pauli, Wolfgang 287
Pdx1 gene 116–117
Pellegrino 386
peppered moth 71–72, 74–75
Perseid meteor shower 172
phenotype 65–66, 72–74, 76, 82, 85–86, 90–91, 101–102, 421

pheromones 65–66, 72–74, 76, 82, 85–86, 90–91, 101–102, 421
Phylogenetic Tree 140, 143
Pilbeam, David 401, 408
Pilgrim 345, 400, 404
Piltdown Man 342–343
Pithecanthropus 301, 338, 343–349, 351–356, 359, 361, 363, 365–366, 368, 370, 378, 380–382, 393, 408, 411, 414
Plato 34
Platyhelminthes 30–31, 152
Pluto 169
Potassium Argon Dating Method 295
Precession of the Equinoxes 214
Principles of Geology 162, 164
prognathic faces 372–373
Propliopithecus 361
Proterozoic Era 176
punctuated equilibrium theory 41, 53–54
Purdue University 284–285, 296

Q

Quantum Genes 84

R

Radiometric Dating 113, 141, 143, 267–268, 284, 288, 293, 295, 301
Ramapithecus 295, 361–363, 383, 394, 399–411
receding chin 338
receding foreheads 372–373
reentering ejecta 198–199
Rhodensis Soloensis 363
Rightmire, G.P. 359
Ring of Fire 213

INDEX

ringwoodite 212
Riviere, M.E. 335
Rods 158
Römpler, Holger 322

S

saggital and supramastoid crest 379
Salk Institute 116
Sangiran skull cap 348
Schankler, David M. 48
Schmitz, Ralf 326
Schoetensack, Otto 369
Schweitzer, Mary Higby 259
Second Earth 93, 172, 182, 207–208, 213–214, 250, 254, 257–258, 267, 270–271, 280, 282, 290, 293, 374, 417, 425, 427
sheet flooding 183, 186, 188, 190, 195, 226
Shinarump Conglomerate 187–188
shocked quartz 271
Shoemaker, Gene 173
Shoemaker-Levy 9 167, 171
Siberian Traps 202–203
Silvers, Lee M. 4
Sinanthropus pekinsis 353
Sivapithecus 361, 404–405
Skull KNM-ER 1470 381
Slusher, Harold S. 293
Smith, William 162
Snelling, Andrew 187
solar constant 112
Solar Radiation and Climate Experiment (SORCE) 113
space trash theory 56, 107, 122
speciation 43, 93, 95
specified complexity 10, 33, 60, 62, 70, 94, 107, 130–131, 177–178, 310

specified integration 70
spherules 271
Stanford University 284–285, 296
steady state theory 17–18, 22, 41, 44, 178
stem cells 116–118
Stone, Anne 327
Stoneking, Mark 327
strong nuclear force 288, 290
subterranean ocean 212
Sumerian 216
sunspots 112
super hurricanes 183
super volcanoes 224
supraorbital tori 372–373, 384, 386
Swift-Tuttle comet 172
Sykes, Brian 279

T

tablemounts 252
tapetum lucidum 158
Taung Child 378, 381, 387
Tauraco corythaix 55
Taurus 214–215
Tchadanthropus uxoris 359
teleological 68
teleonomic 69
Tetraprothomo 360
T. G. Barnes 293
The Island of Dr. Moreau 115
The New Evolutionary Timetable 42
"The Pig-Man Cometh" 115
Theropithecus galada 409
The Third Chimpanzee 275
third ice age 257–258, 282
Thorne, Alan 376
time dilation 134–135
Tjuta, Kata 189–190
Tower of Babel 111, 258
transhumanism 1, 9

transitional forms 28–29, 351
Triassic Cow Branch Formation 231
Triassic Mont Giorgio Basin 230
Tunguska River asteroid 166
Turkana Boy 366–370, 372, 374
Tyrannosaurus rex 259, 266

U

Uluru Arkose 188–190
underground aquifers 192, 202, 205, 213, 219, 240
uniformitarianism 14–18, 22, 41, 44, 174, 178, 432
University of Oxford 279
Uranium Thorium Dating Method 282
U-shaped jaw 316, 406, 408

V

Vallois 352, 355, 358, 393
Venturi effect 182, 213, 217, 220
Vernal Equinox 214–215
vestigial organs 69, 100
Virgo 214
von Koeningswald, Gustav Heinrich Ralph 348
Vulpes 80

W

Wadjak skulls 344, 348, 356, 362
Walker, Alan 384, 413
Wallace, Anthony F. C. 2
water vapor canopy 92, 114, 181–182, 249, 253–254, 268–269, 272, 424
Watson, James D. 4
Weidenreich, Franz 353
White, Tim D. 395, 399, 406
Wilkes Land meteor 201
Willis, J. C. 121
Wilson, Allan 414
Wolfson College 279
Wolpoff, Milford 376
Wood, Bernard 384

Z

zeedonk 68
Zinjanthropus 338, 378–379, 383
Zuckerman, Sally Lord 391–392
zygomatic arches 376–377

www.ingramcontent.com/pod-product-compliance
Lightning Source LLC
Chambersburg PA
CBHW071940220426
43662CB00009B/923